Gilchrist's
Guide To Golf
Collectibles

Roger E. Gilchrist

ALEXANDER Books

Founded 332 B.C.

a division of Creativity, Inc.

65 Macedonia Road
Alexander, NC 28701 USA
(704) 255-8719

TM

Publisher: Ralph Roberts

Vice-President/Operations: Pat Roberts

Senior Editor: Barbara Blood

Editors: Susan Parker

Cover Design: Gayle Graham

Interior Design & Electronic Page Assembly: **WorldComm®**

Copyright ©1998 Roger E. Gilchrist

10 9 8 7 6 5 4 3 2 1

Library of Congress Cataloging-in-Publication Data

Gilchrist, Roger E.,   1949-
    Gilchrist's guide to golf collectibles / Roger E. Gilchrist.
       p.   cm.
    Includes index.
    ISBN 1-57090-075-2   (alk. paper)
     1. Golf--Collectibles--Prices.   2. Golf--Collectibles--Catalogs.
 I. Title.
    GV965.G45   1997
    796.352'075--dc21   97-33582
                                    CIP

Alexander Books™ —a division of **Creativity, Inc.**—is a full–service publisher located at 65 Macedonia Road, Alexander NC 28701. Phone (828) 252–9515, Fax (828) 255–8719. For orders only: 1-800-472-0438. Visa and MasterCard accepted.

Alexander Books™ is distributed to the trade by Midpoint Trade Books, Inc., 27 West 20th Street, New York NY 10011, (212) 727-0190, (212) 727-0195 fax.

This book is also available on the internet in the **Publishers CyberMall**™. Set your browser to http://www.abooks.com and enjoy the many fine values available there.

CONTENTS

Dedication

This book is dedicated to my father, Stanley Vincent Gilchrist, who has always led by example; and to my wife, Cathy, who pushed and pulled me far outside my comfort level.

Acknowledgments:

This book could not have been completed without the help of:

Larry Hancher	Ronnie Watts
Andrew Duckett	Sherwood & Faye Pinkston
Bobby Grace	Spanky Mcie
Erin Wadopian	Missy Cook
Joan Wadopian	David Rice
Gabe Whitmire	Holly Mathews
Scott Walsh	Rick Rodgers
Charles Searle	John Lanshe
Louis Bartoletti	George & Helen Sanders

Foreword

W hat's it worth?"
This book answers that question. For two and a half years I have collected information, facsimiles, and examples. I've insisted on the accuracy of prices and in the fields where my expertise was less than others I enlisted the help of five, very knowledgeable, recognized authorities. This book would not be the accurate reference it is without the help of Jim Butler, Byron Eder, Mark Emerson, Eldon Steeves, and Timothy Thorn.

A collectable is only worth what someone else is prepared to pay for it. The prices enclosed are representative of prices realized at auction, dealer sales, or private treaty. One always hears of the high prices realized for items such as $25,000 for a George Low Sportsman Melrose Park ILL Wizard 600 or $40,000 for a Ping Trainer Putter. These are rare instances and the price is often justified because of outstanding condition or in some cases two or three people whose ego got the better of them at auction. This guide is reality based.

The prices listed are all based on dealer retail sales. Should you wish to sell to a dealer, expect to receive approximately one half of the listed prices. Dealers must make a living, they have contacts you do not, and the price a dealer will pay is probably as good, if not better, than selling privately because often the "collector" is reluctant to purchase something at a fair value.

This book is a guide only. The prices are an accurate representation of the market as I see it. There may be some errors and for those I apologize. I seek your input; I always seek items for illustration in future editions. If you have any comments please feel free to contact the author.

Roger E. Gilchrist
PO Box 969
Freeport, FL 32439

PUTTERS
by Jim Butler

J im Butler and his wife, Kathy, are the owners of Table Rock Golf Club in Centerburg, Ohio. A collector and dealer in classic clubs for many years, his expertise in the values of putters, woods, irons and wedges is recognized throughout the world. His impressive inventory is constantly changing. He can be contacted at:

Jim Butler
Table Rock Golf Club
3005 Wilson Road
Centerburg, OH 43011
www.tablerock.com
800-688-6859, Fax:740-625-7851

The putter is probably the most personal of all the clubs in the golf bag. This means putters are the most popular of all the clubs collected. Almost all golfers have more than one putter. Arnold Palmer openly admits to having thousands of putters and has used most of them at one time or another. Ben Crenshaw on the other hand primarily uses his trusty blade putter, changing the shaft and grip as the mood strikes him. Everyone seeks that one putter that gives twenty-five putts a round.

There are thousands of putters made. It is impossible to list them all. The most currently collected putters are included here. Many putters mentioned are limited editions or private issues and not readily available. Some putters are issued strictly as collectibles and the prices reflected are for as new condition. A putter's value sometimes depends on who is using it on the PGA Tour and so prices widely fluctuate depending upon its popularity.

For putters not issued as collectibles, the prices reflect clubs in good and original condition only and the prices depend on many variables. The band on the shaft, shaft condition, head condition, and grip condition all play a role in deciding on the value of a putter. Subtle differences in putters can make a difference in the price. Bobby Grace, for example, has a red shaft label for those putters issued in the United States, while the shaft band is green for those issued in Japan or Europe. Many putters are first seen as prototypes before being fine-tuned and issued through retail outlets. The abbreviation BeCu is for Copper Beryllium, a metal chosen for its softer feel. The abbreviation BeNi is for Beryllium Nickel. The digits after Ping putters are the last three digits of the postal zip code where the clubs were manufactured. The digits can be found on the back of the face at the end of the address.

Putters are sold under a numerical system. For example an eight or nine out of ten. Ten means as new condition.

COMPANY PUTTER	VALUE
Acushnet:	
102 Semi Mallet	$40
8M Mallet	$40
Bullseye 1987 PGA Championships Logo	$65
Bullseye 36A	$40
Bullseye 3A Flange	$30
Bullseye 5A Heel Shafted Flange	$75
Bullseye Double	$100
Bullseye FL5S	$40
Bullseye Heel Shafted Flange	$50
Bullseye LFL5F	$40
Bullseye L-XM6S	$50
Bullseye M5C Offset	$50
Bullseye M5P Offset Paddle Grip	$40
Bullseye ML-XF55	$75
Bullseye OSUP4P Paddle Grip	$45
Bullseye OSUP4S Pat. Pending Paddle	$45
Bullseye OSUP5S Pat. Pending	$45
Bullseye Standard Flange	$40
Bullseye Wide Flange	$75
Bullseye Wide Flange Offset	$75
Dyno Paddle Grip	$30
El Rio Combo Mallet	$50
ER50 Brass Aluminum Mallet	$75
Goldboy Paddle Grip	$30
HBH5S	$25
LaFemme 34A	$35
LFLI6S	$45
Straight In Paddle Grip	$25
Tartan	$35
Tartan Paddle Grip	$400
American:	
Mallo-Matic	$30
Tommy Armour:	
550SL T Line	$45
Collector	$60
Ironmasters Model A-5	$125
Silver Scot 708	$45
Silver Scot 709	$45
Silver Scot Collector	$95
TDA-40 3852 Center Shaft	$150
ZAAP	$30
Auld Golf:	
Spin-In	$20
Tom Bass:	
Model 1	$125
Bridgestone:	
E-4	$45

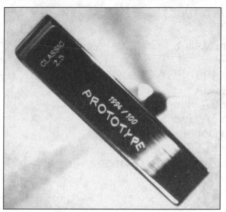

Cameron Classic 2.5 Putter

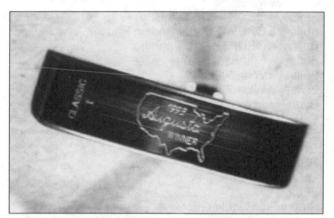

Cameron Classic 1 Augusta Winner Putter

Cameron Classic X Putter

COMPANY PUTTER	VALUE
Bridgestone(cont.):	
Floyd Mallet	$45
Bristol:	
Colonial Mallet	$60
Competitor	$30
Copper Mallet	$75
Dandy	$65
GL600 Tour Model	$200
Melrose Park ILL. Wizard 600	$300
Oakmont	$90
Sea Island Brass Black Shaft	$100
Sea Island Copper	$150
Tropicana	$150
Victura Sixty	$50
Winged Foot	$60
Wizard 600	$550
Browning:	
Automatic	$20
Bullet:	
Hi Caliber IV	$20
Hollow Point Tour	$35
Burke:	
7-11	$20
Contender	$10
Ding-A-Ling	$300
Chick Harbert Personal	$5
Overspin Magician	$30
Overspin Marksman	$30
Overspin Medallist	$30
PGA	$40
PGA Ace	$60
PGA Brass	$40
PGA Texan Mallet	$60
Pro Burke Mallet Brown Shaft	$75
Sav-A Shot 21 Blade	$30
Sav-A-Shot	$25
Sav-A-Shot 143 Mallet	$65
Sav-A-Shot 163 Brass	$40
Burton:	
Avenger	$20
Butchart-Nicholls:	
Brass Head	$25
John Byron:	
Dale Head	$175
MO1 Milled Putter	$100
Model 1	$55
OMG5	$195
Frank Sinatra 1993 Invitational	$75

Cameron-Tiger Woods
U.S. Amateur Champion Putter

Cameron-Tiger Woods Masters
Champion 1/270

Cameron-Tiger Woods Masters
Champion-Stainless Steel-1/21

COMPANY PUTTER	VALUE
Callaway:	
Billet Series Brass	$50
Billet Series Black	$50
Bobby Jones Hickory	$100
Bobby Jones BJ1	$75
Bobby Jones BJ2	$75
Bobby Jones BJ3	$75
Lil Poison I Hickory	$50
Lil Poison II Hickory	$50
Lil Poison III Hickory	$50
The Purist Hickory	$75
The Purist Mallet	$50
S2H2 Blade	$60
S2H2 Brass CM-1	$75
S2H2 Brass CM-2	$75
Tuttle	$60
Tuttle II	$75
Scotty Cameron:	
1995 Black Set Of 7 Pieces (500 Made)	$4,000
1996 Copper Set Of 8 Pieces (500 Made)	$3,500
1997 Platinum Set Of 8 Pieces (100 Made)	$7,500
Classic 1	$1,200
Classic 1 AMF Black Shaft	$2,500
Classic 1 Augusta Winner	$500
Classic 1 Augusta Winner Loomis Graphite Shaft	$3,500
Classic 1 Augusta Winner Stainless Steel	$2,600
Classic 1 Copper	$2,000
Classic 1 Masters Choice Stainless	$4,000
Classic 1 Mini Model	$4,000
Classic 1.5	$800
Classic 1.5 Augusta Winner	$7,000
Classic 1.5 Prototype	$1,600
Classic 2	$800
Classic 2.5	$800
Classic 2.5 Prototype	$1,600
Classic 3	$800
Classic 5	$1,000
Classic 6	$800
Classic 6 Black Prototype	$1,600
Classic 6 Copper Plate Prototype	$2,400
Classic 6 Experimental Prototype	$1,600
Classic 6 X94	$1,200
Classic X AMF	$1,200
Classic X Copper	$2,500
Classic X Prototype	$2,000
Classic X Unstamped	$1,500
Catalina	$160

Cameron Mallet Putter

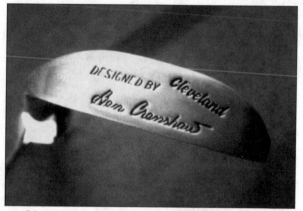

Cleveland Designed by Ben Crenshaw
Putter

Dunlop Mustang Putter

COMPANY	PUTTER	VALUE

Scotty Cameron(cont.)**:**

Coronado	$160
Del Mar	$275
Laguna	$160
Mallet Prototype Billy Andrade	$1,600
Napa	$160
Newport	$160
Private 4 Reserve	$750
Sante Fe	$160
Scottsdale Anser	$4,000
Scottsdale 946	$1,000
Scottsman	$1,600
Scottsman 942	$1,600
Scottsman 945 Prototype	$1,200
Scotty Dale 029	$2,500
Sonoma	$160
Tiger Woods Stainless Masters Winner (21 Made)	$20,000
Tiger Woods Black Masters Winner (270 Made)	$8,000
Tiger Woods Tournament Of Champions (7 Made)	$5,000
Tiger Woods U.S. Amateur Satin Silver (960 Made)	$4,000
Tiger Woods U.S. Amateur Stainless Steel (20 Made)	$6,000

Cera Sports:

Coors TZ Premier 1	$50
Coors TZ QC2	$65

Cleveland:

Classic Copper	$300
Classic Small Letters	$75
Designed By	$60
Designed By BeCu	$500
Designed By Ben Crenshaw	$225
Designed By Ben Crenshaw Chrome	$250
Designed By Ben Crenshaw Milled Black	$450
Designed By Black	$225
Designed By Classic	$175
Designed By Large Letters	$250
K.G. 1 Milled	$50
K.G. 10 Milled	$75
K.G. 9 Milled	$50
Nelson	$75
OJM Tour Action Classic Collection	$85
Corey Pavin	$250
Corey Pavin Low #	$750

Cobra:

King Cobra Mallet	$40
Milled Series	$35
Springfield Mallet	$40

Ray Cook:

American Open Model 1	$25

COMPANY	PUTTER	VALUE
Ray Cook(cont.):		
	American Open Model 2	$25
	American Open Model 2 Brass	$45
	American Open Model 3	$25
	American Open Model 4	$25
	Billy Baroo BB1	$50
	Billy Baroo III	$65
	Billy Baroo IV	$50
	Blue Goose	$25
	Blue Goose II	$30
	Classic Plus II	$15
	Peter Kostis	$50
	Lil Poison	$85
	M-1	$50
	M-1-X Mallet	$30
	M-1-3G Mallet	$50
	M-1-S Mallet	$30
	MBA	$65
	M8 Aluminum Mallet	$30
	Nugget 21	$75
	Nugget 22	$20
	The Original	$35
	P-3 Offset	$40
	San Antonio Texas	$65
	Silver Ray	$30
	X15	$50
	X15 Mallet	$70
	X100	$15
Cougar:		
	Instinct II Bi-Metal	$30
Otey Crisman:		
	164HB Selma	$50
	164HM	$30
	16HBW Mallet	$35
	18H Mallet	$50
	215 Selma	$45
	340H	$30
	35H Brass Blade Square Hickory Shaft	$100
	38H	$75
	3HW	$45
	700H Selma	$35
	70HB Selma	$65
	720H Selma	$60
	74HB Mallet Brass Aluminum	$75
	7H Offset	$25
	GTH	$40
	Klik 2	$75
	NN1 Brass Head	$120

COMPANY PUTTER	VALUE
Diawa:	
8711B Pro Balance	$45
Advisor I Pro Milled	$75
Advisor II Pro Milled	$75
John F. Drake:	
Pendulum Putter	$45
Dunlop:	
Black Max Plus	$20
Dow Finsterwald	$35
Mustang	$20
Pulsar	$20
Epperson:	
Mallet	$20
Fernquest & Johnson:	
Californian	$60
Tony Lema Westerner Black Chrome	$600
Ken Venturi	$200
Westerner Large Stamp 600 Style	$650
Westerner Small Stamp 600 Style	$350
First Flight:	
9 Blade	$45
C Aluminum Mallet Head	$35
Pong	$150
Jim Flood:	
Basakward	$35
Ken Giannini:	
92 Tour Special	$75
Handmade	$75
Golfcraft:	
EJ Brass Flange	$25
El Rio	$30
Ralph Guldhal Blade Yellow Sheath Shaft	$50
Frank Johnston Escondido Continental	$50
Lloyd Mangrum Combo F. Johnson Fiberglass Shaft	$75
Pro Zone Stainless	$25
Rose City	$60
X-Heavy A2 Mallet	$45
Bobby Grace:	
2200 BeCu	$75
2200 Brass Flange	$100
2200 Handmade Long Hosel (200 Made)	$900
2200 Handmade Short Hosel (50 Made)	$1,350
AN-7 Mallet Headed Putter	$45
AN-7 Masters Limited Edition Of 100	$2,750
Custom Tour Handmade Mallet Fat Kid	$1,800
Custom Tour Handmade Mallet Fat Lady Swings	$1,800
Custom Tour Handmade Mallet Fat Man	$1,800
Custom Tour Handmade Mallet Hawk 5M	$1,800

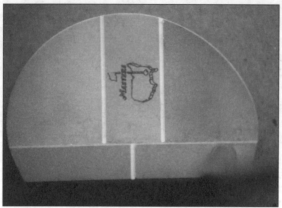

Bobby Grace AN7 Masters Putter 1/100

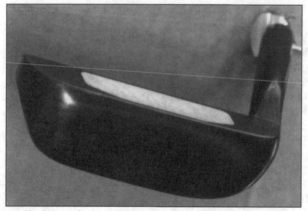

Bobby Grace Tour Forged 2200 Putter
H.S.M. Insert

MacGregor Chieftain Putter

COMPANY PUTTER	VALUE
Bobby Grace (cont.):	
Custom Tour Handmade Mallet Little Lady	$1,800
Cute Kid	$50
Fat Lady	$50
Fat Man Handmade Prototypes (10 Made)	$4,500
T.S. Grace Cavity Back Milled	
One Piece Blade (100 Made)	$1,150
T.S. Grace Handmade	$500
T.S. Grace Handmade Club	
Model Blade (150 Made)	$1,250
T.S. Grace Handmade Diamond	
Model Blade (15 Made)	$2,500
T.S. Grace Handmade Heart	
Model Blade (80 Made)	$1,150
T.S. Grace Handmade Spade	
Model Blade (30 Made)	$1,950
T.S. Grace Stainless Steel Cavity Back	
No Hosel Face Balanced (100 Made)	$950
Numbered In The Cavity	$1,250
Little Lady	$50
Little Man	$50
Scottsdale KBI	$150
Scottsdale KBI BeCu	$225
Scottsdale KBI Set Of Three Different Metals	
Cavity Blades (50 Made)	$1,750
Freddie Haas:	
Ben-Nek Model 102 Mallet	$75
Hot Rod	$125
Walter Hagen:	
Black Jack	$75
Cascade	$150
Cascade 350	$225
Gentle Ben	$150
The Haig	$35
The Haig 350	$35
Intruder	$75
Lucky Lefty	$60
Performer	$100
Silver Star	$30
Tom Boy	$60
Triangle Sta-Brite	$35
J. C. Higgins:	
#3-885-0	$10
Ben Hogan:	
1400	$85
Apex HB-1	$40
Exact Balance	$35
His Own	$35

COMPANY PUTTER	VALUE
Ben Hogan (cont.):	
HT-1 Apex	$30
Immortal	$20
Mentor P 300	$20
P 148	$20
P112	$20
P155 Mallet	$70
Radar	$40
Radial P 02	$20
Sinker	$75
Sovereign	$225
Square Line Brass	$45
Sunburst Medallion	$25
Texan 1410 Brass	$60
Ben Hogan MacDougall Carnoustie Series:	
P101	$75
P103	$75
P105	$75
P107	$75
P109	$75
P111	$75
P200	$75
P202	$75
P204	$75
P206	$75
P208	$75
P210	$75
The Hustler:	
Brass	$20
Jock Hutchison:	
Blade	$10
Frank Johnson:	
Original 107	$75
Kroydon:	
S 10 Blade Copper Insert	$120
Spider	$30
Thunderbolt Mallet	$30
George Low:	
600N	$300
Bristol Melrose Park ILL. Wizard 600	$4,500
Sportsman Melrose Park ILL. Wizard 600	$7,500
Wizard 200	$200
Wizard 250	$400
Wizard 300	$400
Wizard 500	$400
Wizard 800	$400
Lynx:	
Bengal	$125

COMPANY	PUTTER	VALUE

Lynx(cont.):
| | Bobcat | $50 |
| | M-20 Mallet | $25 |

Elmer Lyons:
| | Persimmon Mallet | $50 |

MacGregor:
	#11 Aluminum Block	$75
	Tommy Armour IM With XXX's	$150
	Tommy Armour IM5 With XXX's	$150
	Tommy Armour IM6 With XXX's	$150
	Tommy Armour IMG	$125
	Tommy Armour IMG Head Like IMG5 With XXX's	$1,000
	Tommy Armour IMG5 Satin Finish	$1,200
	Tommy Armour IMG5 With XXX's	$2,500
	Tommy Armour IMG6 With XXX's	$1,500
	Tommy Armour IMGL	$750
	Tommy Armour IMGL A Siteline	$600
	Tommy Armour IMGL With XXX's	$1,400
	Tommy Armour IMGN	$450
	Tommy Armour IMGT	$800
	Tommy Armour Ironmaster Green Shaft	$140
	Tommy Armour Silver Scot 3801	$400
	Tommy Armour Silver Scot 3852	$400
	Tommy Armour Silver Scot 3852S	$400
	Tommy Armour Silver Scot 3903	$400
	Tommy Armour Silver Scot Lassie	$200
	Herman Barron Ironmaster	$125
	C5B Chrome Head And Black Shaft	$250
	CB106 Black Shaft And Head	$100
	CB5 Black Head And Shaft	$225
	CBG5 Black Head And Shaft	$400
	CBGL Black Head And Shaft	$400
	CBN	$65
	CBR Black Mellonite	$75
	Challenger 606 #10	$10
	Chieftain	$20
	Perry Como 148	$275
	Perry Como Mallet 144	$225
	CNGL	$25
	CNGL Frosted Head	$125
	Collectors TFP 90-1	$100
	Collectors TFP 90-4	$100
	DX	$20
	267 Dorado II	$40
	268 Dorado III	$40
	Jim Foulis	$10
	Jim Foulis Yellow Shaft	$100
	Jerry Glynn Ironmaster	$125

MacGregor Frank Sinatra Putter 1/200

MacGregor Tommy Armour IMGL
Ironmaster Putter

MacGregor Tommy Armour IMG
Ironmaster Putter

COMPANY PUTTER	VALUE
MacGregor(cont.):	
Golden Bear	$20
Bruce Herd Ironmaster	$75
IMG5 Carbon Steel Iron Master 1996 Ltd. Edition	$175
Ironmaster CNGL Black Chrome	$100
Ironmaster IMG TCP (Made For Japan)	$150
Ironmaster IMG5	$75
Ironmaster IMGL No XXX's	$100
Ironmaster IMGN	$250
Krook	$40
M2 Brass	$100
M3 Brass	$75
Mity Mite	$20
Mity Mite 100 GP	$20
N201 Smoothie	$20
N307	$20
N410	$15
Nelson Grad-U-Wate	$75
Nelson Par 72	$20
Jack Nicklaus 108	$25
Jack Nicklaus 275 White Fang	$35
Jack Nicklaus JN 100	$100
Jack Nicklaus JN 106 Silver	$75
Jack Nicklaus JN 271 Division	$125
Jack Nicklaus N207	$40
Jack Nicklaus Tourney Classic Black Shaft	$300
Jack Nicklaus VIP	$60
Nicklaus Muirfield	$95
Nicklaus/Low Black	$325
Nicklaus/Low Satin	$325
P502	$25
Pacemaker	$20
Charlie Penna Ironmaster	$400
Tony Penna B-Up Mallet 143	$50
Tony Penna B-Up Mallet 144	$50
Response	$45
Response 1986 Masters Winner (1986 Made)	$175
Response Jack Nicklaus 20th M1615 Black	$125
Response M1799	$100
Response M1880S Pat. Pending Black	$125
1963 Frank Sinatra Invitational Copper Plated (200 Made)	$15,000
Smoothie N201	$75
Smoothie N203	$75
Smoothie N204	$75
Smoothie SMG1	$45
Smoothie SMG5 Milled Black	$50
Souchak K100	$40

MacGregor Tommy Armour Ironmanster
Putter

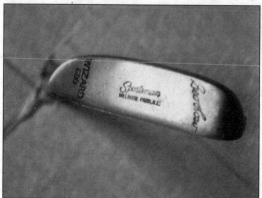

Melrose Park George Low Sportsman
Wizard 600 Putter

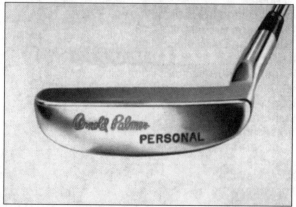

Arnold Palmer Personal Putter

COMPANY PUTTER	VALUE
MacGregor(cont.)**:**	
Spur	$65
Spur 10	$20
St. Andrews	$20
TFP 91-1 VIP	$100
Bob Toski GP Mighty Might	$65
Bob Toski T016	$30
Tourney Classic IMG Ironmaster Black Shaft	$150
Tourney Classic Jack Nicklaus (Made For Japan)	$250
Tourney M5 Copper Face	$75
VIP	$100
VIP 600 Black Milled Limited Edition	$175
VIP Offset	$50
Lew Worsham	$40
Lew Worsham Mallet	$75
Chico Martinez:	
Tomahawk	$80
MatchPlay:	
Ladies Hand Forged	$10
Matzie:	
Hickory Velvet Touch	$30
Maxfli:	
Tad Moore: TM-1	$35
Tad Moore: TM-2	$35
Tad Moore: TM-3	$65
Tad Moore: TM-4	$65
Tad Moore: TM-5	$65
Tad Moore: TM-6	$65
Tad Moore: TM-7	$65
Tad Moore: TM-8	$65
Tad Moore: TM-9	$65
Tad Moore: TM-10	$65
Tad Moore: TM-11	$65
Tad Moore: TM-12	$65
Tad Moore: TM-13	$65
Tad Moore: TM-14	$65
Tad Moore: TM-15	$65
Tad Moore: TM-16	$65
T-Bone Mallet	$60
T-Bone II Mallet	$50
Yipstick	$35
T.P Mills:	
Handmade	$400
Mizuno:	
0606 Mallet	$35
8804	$75
M100 By Scotty Cameron	$40
M200 By Scotty Cameron	$45

COMPANY	PUTTER	VALUE

Mizuno(cont.)**:**

	M400 By Scotty Cameron	$200
	Scotty Cameron	$175
	Scotty Cameron 1993 Pebble Beach Pro Am	$500

Tad Moore:

	Augusta Winner	$250
	Damascus II	$750
	Handmade	$900
	Peach Model 01	$250
	Peach Model 02	$250
	Peach Model 03	$500
	Pro 1	$375
	Pro 1 Damascus	$800
	Pro 1S	$300
	Pro 2	$300
	The Woosnam	$75

K.W. Murray:

	IMG5	$100
	Scottsdale	$150
	USA Bullseye	$50

Natural Golf:

	The Thing	$35

Nicklaus:

	Limited	$150
	TCP-1	$75

Nomad:

	B3	$10

Odyssey:

	550	$60
	992	$50
	Rossie I	$50
	Rossie II	$50

Old Master:

	SIH III	$30

Orizaba:

	Basakwerd	$50

Palmer:

	AP14	$80
	AP20	$40
	AP30	$40
	AP30R	$75
	AP40	$65
	AP44 Chrome Blade	$60
	The Original	$60
	The Original Black	$60
	The Original Chrome	$60

Peerless:

	504	$30

COMPANY PUTTER	VALUE
Peerless(cont.)**:**	
AP1	$30
AP2	$30
Dave Pelz:	
3 Ball Teaching Putter Series	$275
The Teacher #300	$400
Toney Penna:	
The Original IM G-7	$95
PGA Golf:	
The Dundee Mallet	$75
Overspin	$75
Overspin Pat. Pending	$55
Ram V-Line Copper	$500
Ryder Cup	$30
Scrambler	$30
Silver Scott Collection	$40
Texan Mallet	$35
T-Line Designer Model XXIII	$80
T-Line Ladies	$20
T-Line Series	$20
V-Ram	$20
Ping:	
A Blade 029	$75
ADX 50	$95
35th Anniversary Anser	$250
Anser 2 8.5 Inch First Step	$120
Anser 2 BeCu Pat. Pending	$200
Anser 2 Pat. Pending	$200
Anser 2 Pat. Pending Black	$200
Anser 2 Stainless Steel	$45
Anser 3 BeCu	$60
Anser 4 Stainless	$45
Anser 85020 With 6 Inch Step Black Band	$200
Anser 85020 With 9 Inch Step	$175
Anser 85029 With 6 Inch Step	$175
Anser 85029 With 9 Inch Step	$300
Anser 85068 Black Band Wide Top Line	$125
Anser 85068 With 6 Inch Step	$75
Anser Cabot BeCu	$5,500
Anser Dale Head	$450
Anser Karsten Co.	$1,200
Anser Magnesium Bronze	$65
Auld	$75
Ayd 85029 Black Band	$75
Cushin 029 Big Z Bend Shaft	$65
Cushin 029 Stainless Steel Big Z Bend Shaft	$50
Cushin 3	$50
Cushin 4	$45

Dave Pelz The Teacher Putter

Ping Model III Scottsdale

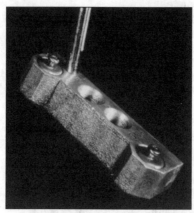

Ping Trainer Putter

COMPANY	PUTTER	VALUE
Ping(cont.):		
	Cushin Copper Color	$40
	Dancer Laminated Mallet	$75
	Day 020	$50
	Echo 1	$35
	Echo 1 029	$75
	Echo 1 Black Band	$75
	Echo 2 Siteline	$70
	Eye 53 Black Satin	$50
	Go Win	$100
	H Blade	$50
	H Blade 029	$75
	J Blade	$35
	J Blade Magnesium Bronze	$75
	Karsten Co. Anser	$850
	Karsten Co. Anser Slazenger/Nicklaus	$3,200
	KBI Anser BeCu	$5,500
	KBI Anser BeNi	$7,500
	MLT 029	$45
	Model 1 Redwood City	$2,000
	Model 1A Redwood City	$2,500
	Model 1A Scottsdale	$475
	Model 1A No Numbers Scottsdale	$600
	Model 69 Scottsdale	$600
	Model 69BC Croquet Scottsdale	$1,500
	Model 69BC Scottsdale	$600
	Model 69FT Scottsdale	$600
	Model 69FTL Scottsdale	$600
	Model 69T Scottsdale	$400
	Model 69W Scottsdale	$400
	Model A5 Redwood City	$2,500
	Model AX Redwood City	$3,500
	Model B5-C Redwood City	$4,000
	Model B-60	$35
	Model B-60 068	$35
	Model B-60 Black Satin	$65
	Model B-60 Pat. Pending	$250
	Model B-60 Stainless	$35
	Model B-61 BeCu	$50
	Model B-61 Pat. Pending	$150
	Model B-66	$65
	Model B-67	$65
	Model B-69	$65
	Model B-69 029	$80
	Model B-90	$75
	Model BLD	$65
	Model II Scottsdale	$500
	Model IIA Scottsdale	$500

Ping Zero Putter

Ram-Zebra Adjustable Putter

COMPANY	PUTTER	VALUE

Ping(cont.):

Model IIIA Scottsdale	$500
Model IIIA Transitional Model Scottsdale Xed Out With Phoenix Stamp	$900
Model IVA Scottsdale	$600
Model XA Redwood City	$4,000
My Day	$45
My Day 029	$75
N-Echo	$125
O Blade	$35
O Blade 029	$75
Pal	$60
Pal 2	$45
Pal 2 BeCu	$40
Pal 2 Stainless	$45
Pal 4	$45
Pal 4 BeCu	$40
Pal 6	$65
Pal 6 BeCu	$40
Pal BeCu	$75
Ping-N-Ping	$65
Gary Player Karsten Co.	$2,500
Gary Player Scottsdale 1A	$2,500
Gary Player Scottsdale Anser	$3,500
Gary Player Scottsdale Cushin	$1200
1994 Ping-N-Ping Reproduction	$150
35th Anniversary Ping-N-Ping	$500
Portland Ping Championship Dale Head	$800
Redwood City Anser	$1,200
Rite In	$75
Scottsdale Anser	$3,000
Scottsdale Anser No Hosel	$3,500
1994 Scottsdale Anser Reproduction Serial # On Hosel	$175
1995 Scottsdale Anser Reproduction BeCu	$125
1995 Scottsdale Anser Reproduction Nickel	$125
Scottsdale Cushin	$325
Scottsdale Kushin	$350
Scottsdale Kushin Slazenger/Nicklaus	$400
Scottsdale Trainer	$25,000
Y Blade	$75
Zero 020	$60
Zero 2 020	$45
Zing 020	$80
Zing 029	$100
Zing BeCu	$65

Pinnacle:

Mallet	$35
Solution	$30

COMPANY PUTTER	VALUE
Plop:	
Center Shaft	$25
PowerBilt:	
10J Offset Mallet	$50
45HB Brass Head Hickory Shaft	$50
Model 48 Mallet	$75
Momentum 1	$50
P73W Persimmon Over Brass	$100
P9 Persimmon Mallet	$60
Preceptor Golf:	
The Teacher	$400
Pro Built:	
Custom Blade	$10
Probe:	
20/20 Brass	$35
Ram:	
810	$20
950	$20
Deep Face	$45
Tom Watson 8802	$75
Wizard 300 Copper 600 Head	$500
Wizard 600 Sportsman Original	$350
Zebra	$45
Zebra II Dale Taylor	$125
Zebra Adjustable	$1200
Zebra Big Z	$50
Zebra Flange	$45
Zebra Instructional Plate	$500
Zebra Mid Mallet	$45
Rawlings:	
Ken Giannini Revenge Mallet	$50
John Reuter Jr.:	
Flange	$125
Old Standard	$125
Standard	$175
Royal:	
501 B	$45
5070	$150
5170	$150
5135	$125
Ben Sayers:	
Benny	$30
Roler	$65
Shakespeare:	
Player Black Knight	$40
PO18 Brass Head	$25
Tru-Aim	$25

COMPANY PUTTER	VALUE
Slazenger:	
706 BeCu	$40
The Clipper	$75
Eaglet Brass Head	$40
Gene Donald Brass Head	$40
Precision Brass Head	$50
Slotline:	
Onset Inertial	$25
Topspin	$50
True Touch	$60
Spalding:	
Blue Chip Hickory Shaft	$85
Blue Chip Steel Shaft	$300
Calamity Jane	$75
Cash-In Pat. Applied For	$100
Cash-In Black Shaft	$60
Cash-In Brass	$50
Cash-In Chrome	$45
Cash-In Long Leather Grip	$60
Cash-In Rocker Sole	$45
Cash-In Special	$30
Cash-In Stainless Steel Yellow Sheath Shaft	$75
Cash-In Yellow Sheath Shaft	$65
Dynamiter Smooth Face Black Sheath Shaft	$175
Elite I	$45
Elite IV	$55
HB Steel Shaft	$40
HB Wooden Shaft	$75
HBA	$65
HBA Black Shaft	$65
HBA Pencil Shaft	$75
Hi Efficiency 1	$40
Jackpot	$65
Line Right Blade	$20
Mayfield Ladies	$5
Rabbit Foot	$60
Horton Smith	$50
ST	$25
ST Brass Blade	$30
Synchro-Line FLA Aluminum Brass Mallet	$75
Tournament Blade Model	$25
TPM1	$35
TPM2	$35
TPM3	$35
TPM4	$40
TPM5	$40
TPM6	$35
TPM7	$35

COMPANY PUTTER	VALUE
Spalding (cont.):	
TPM8	$35
TPM9	$85
TPM10	$50
TPM11	$50
TPM12	$50
TPM13	$60
TPM14	$50
TPM15	$50
TPM19	$60
TPM Classic	$70
TPM Gold I	$50
TPM Gold II	$50
TPM Gold III	$50
TPM Gold IV	$50
TPM Tour I	$125
TPM Tour II	$55
TPM Tour III	$60
TPM Tour 15	$50
TPM Tour 16	$50
TPM Tour 17	$50
TPM Tour 18	$75
TPM Tour 18 Graphite Shaft	$50
TPM Tour 19	$50
TPM Tour 19 Graphite Shaft	$50
TPM Tour 7	$60
TPM Tour 9	$85
Standard Golf:	
Tru-Swing	$75
Standard Mills:	
Schenectady Aluminum Block Putter	$250
STX:	
Broom Handle	$35
Regular	$25
Sunmark:	
F. Fenton Milled Model 1	$250
Taylor Made:	
712 Brass	$35
Pro-Formance 107	$40
TPA I	$100
TPA II	$100
TPA III	$300
TPA IV	$100
TPA V	$100
TPA VI	$100
TPA VII	$100
TPA VIII	$300
TPA IX	$100

COMPANY PUTTER	VALUE
Taylor Made (cont.):	
TPA X	$100
TPA XI	$100
TPA XII	$100
TPA XIII	$100
TPA XIV	$100
TPA XV	$100
TPA XVI	$100
TPA XVII	$100
TPA XVIII (Most Valuable Of The TPA Models)	$350
TPA XIX	$75
TPA XX	$75
TPA XXI	$75
TPA XXII	$75
Teardrop:	
Original Tour	$55
Stan Thompson:	
Tailored Wood Head	$20
Tiger Shark:	
B 3200 Mallet	$40
Titleist:	
Bullseye	$20
Bullseye Flange	$20
Cameron Bolero 1st Run	$250
Cameron Bullseye Original SC	$50
Cameron Bullseye Standard SC	$50
Cameron Caliente	$75
Cameron Caliente (1 Of 500)	$600
Cameron Caliente Black	$550
Cameron Caliente Grand Bolero (1 Of 500)	$600
Cameron Caliente Grand Bolero Black	$550
Cameron Caliente Grande	$150
Cameron Caliente Grande (1 Of 500)	$600
Cameron Caliente Grande Bolero	$95
Cameron Catalina	$150
Cameron Catalina (1 Of 500)	$500
Cameron Coronado	$150
Cameron Del Mar	$250
Cameron Grande	$75
Cameron LaCosta	$300
Cameron Laguna	$150
Cameron Napa	$150
Cameron Napa (1 Of 500)	$500
Cameron Newport	$160
Cameron Newport T3 Insert	$650
Cameron Sante Fe	$160
Cameron Sante Fe T3 Insert	$650
Cameron SCM5 Scottymaster (For Japan)	$900

Titleist Cameron Napa

Titleist Cameron Laguna Putter

Titleist Cameron Newport

COMPANY PUTTER	VALUE
Titleist(cont.):	
Cameron Scottsdale Prototype Black	$4,500
Cameron Sonoma	$160
Cameron St. Jude Memphis Winner	$2,000
Cameron Tour XCP	$1,200
Dead Center	$35
T Model	$25
Bob Toski:	
Mighty Might SS	$40
True Shot:	
10W Aluminum Mallet Sheath Shaft	$50
Wilson:	
8800 Jim Ferrier	$75
8802	$750
8802 Black Head	$500
8802 Brass Cavity Back	$35
8802 Chrome	$750
8802 Chrome Head Speed Shaft	$800
8802 Gothic Letters	$875
8802 HS Silver Band	$1,200
8802 Michael Jordan Limited Edition	$500
8802 "The Original"	$50
8802 R. M. Limited Edition	$850
8802 1996 Redesign	$75
8803	$300
8806	$35
8806 Milled	$50
8810 Winsum	$50
8811	$20
8813	$375
8813 345	$400
8813 Australian	$125
8813 Black Head	$400
8823	$275
8823 Black Head	$175
8823-345	$100
8823-345 Black	$225
8823-355	$150
8825	$60
8836	$20
8843	$50
8873 355 Brass Head	$75
Augusta	$35
Augusta 345	$10
Augusta 355	$25
Augusta Brass	$60
Berg	$25
Berg Defender	$25

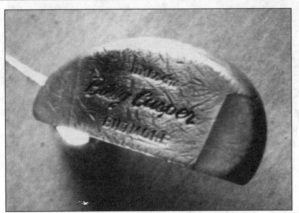

Wilson Casper Biltmore Putter

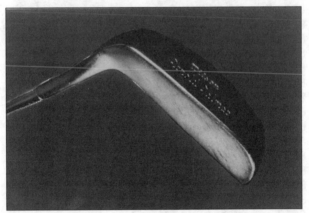

Wilson Arnold Palmer Putter

Wilson 8802 Putter

COMPANY PUTTER	VALUE
Wilson(cont.):	
Berg Signature	$20
Boros Brass Head 8882	$45
Boros Brass Head Speed Shaft	$75
Capital Blade	$25
Capri Brass Head	$40
Casper Biltmore	$50
Casper Personal Aluminum Mallet	$45
GM770 Blade	$15
Hicks Autograph	$25
Helen Hicks	$35
Willie Hoare	$20
Willie Hoare Winsum Brass	$85
Willie Org	$20
Hol Hi Brown Shaft	$50
Hol Hi HS Shaft	$75
George Low 600	$300
Mallet 8800	$40
Mallet 8853	$40
Lloyd Mangrum Mallet	$60
Olympiad Blade	$25
Original 600	$75
Original 600 Fluted Shaft	$200
Arnold Palmer	$1,000
Designed By Arnold Palmer	$1,200
Designed By Arnold Palmer Copper	$3,000
Designed By Arnold Palmer No Offset	$1,500
Gene Sarazen Stroke Master	$10
Seminole Brass Head 8834	$40
Sam Snead Pay Off	$25
Sam Snead Pay Off 355 Brass	$40
Staff 2010	$35
TNT	$30
Tour Special I	$45
Tour Special II	$45
TPA	$50
Winged Foot Mallet	$35
Winton:	
G. Low Sr. Blade Putter: Oval Shaft	$900
Wright & Ditson:	
Cashin	$60
Cashin Long Leather Grip	$70
Lawson Little Blade	$35
Zebra:	
By Taylor Craft Center Shaft	$100
By Taylor Craft Instructional	$1,500
By Taylor Craft Original	$75
By Taylor Craft Toe Connection	$800

COMPANY	PUTTER	VALUE
Zebra(cont.):		
	By Taylor Craft Weighted Blade	$500
	Rosburg Toe Connection	$300
	Rosburg Toe Connection II	$300

Wilson-Designed by Arnold Palmer

IRONS
by JIM BUTLER

A revolution began when clubs were cast, allowing more flexibility in design. Ping was the first company to cast golf clubs, but the last few years have seen a prolific growth in the number of manufacturers.

It is not possible to mention all the manufacturers, therefore, the focus is on collectible clubs. Included here are the collectible clubs from the major manufacturers. None of the component manufacturers are included. This is not indicative of quality, just the editor's choice. Club desirability depends much on Tour success. Just like today, often the Tour player popularized the iron. The older classic collector club prices depend on condition. Reshafting, regripping and rechroming of heads, all lessen the value. Some of the more modern "collectors" clubs are priced for new condition, these include the Dunlop Seve Ballesteros Woods and Irons and the 1981 MacGregor Nicklaus Anniversary Irons.

For this price guide sets are presumed to include the three iron through the pitching wedge. Many earlier sets did not include the pitching wedge and just run three through nine. With few exceptions old blades are very difficult to resell. Modern technology has left them behind. Today the modern player prefers the game enhancing improvements found in the modern irons.

COMPANY IRON	VALUE
Acuform:	
Acuform II	$25
Cavity Back	$50
PTM	$25
Ajay:	
Double Eagle	$25
Invader	$25
Marilyn Miller	$25
Pro Classic	$25
Pro Classic II	$25
San Franciscan	$25
Sandy Shaw	$25
SST	$25
SSV	$25
STD	$25
TFC	$25
VSP Irons	$25
XSP	$25
Tommy Armour:	
Butterfly	$75
Concept 2	$200
E.Q.L.	$250
Emblem	$100
Golden Scott 845C Graphite	$850
Metrilite System	$100
Silver Scott 845S	$250
Silver Scott 986 Tour	$400
T-Line	$150
T-Line BC BeCu	$250
Tour Concept	$240
Auld Golf:	
Agate	$25
Auld Agate	$25
Auld Briar	$25
Auld Classic	$25
Auld Half and Half	$25
Briar	$25
Classic	$25
Classic II	$25
Classic Triax	$25
Classic Troon	$25
Triax II	$25
Troon	$50
Butch Baird:	
Group I	$50
Group II	$50
Group III	$50
Group IV	$50

COMPANY IRON	VALUE
Jerry Barber:	
Goldentouch	$150
Goldentouch 1	$150
Goldentouch 2	$150
Goldentouch 3	$150
Goldentouch 7 (Gemini-1)	$100
GTM-1	$100
Lucky Lady	$200
M1 Goldentouch	$250
M5	$200
M5 Goldentouch	$200
M100 BeCu	$300
M100 Goldentouch	$200
Silver Bullet	$100
X-22	$100
X-22 Goldentouch	$75
Beauwood:	
Cameo	$75
Collectors Edition	$75
Collectors Edition BW 33	$75
Collectors Edition BW 35	$75
Duo Flex	$75
Passage BeCu	$75
Passage CB	$75
Passage EX	$75
Passage Lite	$75
Passage PR	$75
Passage PSS	$75
Passage RE	$75
Passage SPR	$75
Perfect Sweet Spot	$75
Pro	$75
Uniform Flex	$75
BelAir:	
BAI-300	$75
BAI-DX	$75
BeCu-32	$75
Coot	$75
Golden Coot	$75
SST-32	$75
Belmont:	
Belmont Irons	$25
Bridgestone:	
CD Continuous Design Graphite	$150
CD Continuous Design Steel	$150
Ray Floyd Ultimate Weapon	$200
Inceptor	$150
J. Forged Iron	$300

COMPANY	IRON	VALUE
Bridgestone:(cont.)**:**		
Ladies Allure		$100
Precept		$150
Precept 7		$150
Precept 7 Ladies		$150
Precept Bronze		$175
Precept Forged		$250
Precept Pro		$150
Pro 375		$100
Pro Model		$150
Rextar LT-100		$100
Bristol:		
Advisory		$50
Advisory Super Lite		$50
Competitor		$50
Tour Model		$50
Victura 500		$50
Victura VLL		$50
XS1000		$50
Browning:		
440		$100
440 Gold		$100
500		$100
Automatic		$100
Classic Forged		$100
Lady Browning		$100
Maxim		$75
Mirada		$75
Mirage		$75
Panache		$75
Premier		$75
Previa		$75
System 350		$100
TLC		$75
Tour Class		$75
TR500		$75
TR600		$75
Burke:		
Tommy Armour Silver Scot		$250
Bomber		$75
Commander		$75
Compactor		$75
Coronation		$75
Custom		$75
Custom Lady Burke		$75
Golden Chairman		$75
Golden Scot		$75
Chick Harbert Aristocrat		$75

COMPANY	IRON	VALUE
Burke(cont.):		
	Chick Harbert Autograph	$100
	Chick Harbert Bomber	$100
	Chick Harbert Championship	$100
	Chick Harbert Signature	$100
	Larry Hinson Titleholder	$100
	Hy-Speed	$100
	Hy-Speed Fiberglass	$100
	Imperial	$100
	Lady Burke	$75
	Lady Burke Cameo	$75
	Lady Burke Coronation	$75
	Lady Burke Imperial	$75
	Lady Burke Registered	$75
	Lady Burke Signature	$75
	Lloyd Mangrum Custom	$100
	Mark II Punchirons	$175
	Mark III Punchirons	$175
	Miss Burke	$100
	Model 100 Hy Speed	$75
	Sharron Moran	$100
	Sharron Moran Classic	$100
	Sharron Moran Coronation	$100
	Sharron Moran Custom	$100
	Sharron Moran Premier	$100
	Power-Pak	$100
	Premier Cast	$100
	Premier Forged	$100
	Premier Punchirons	$100
	Punchirons	$75
	Recorded	$100
	Registered Model 1000	$100
	Registered Offset	$100
	Riviera	$100
	Silver Scot	$75
	Les Stokes	$75
	Jack Rule Victor	$100
Callaway:		
	Big Bertha	$450
	Big Bertha Graphite	$750
	Hickory Sticks Mazda Champions	$1,500
	Bobby Jones Commemorative	$650
	Bobby Jones Commemorative BeCu	$950
	Bobby Jones S2H2	$250
	Players Blade	$350
	S2H2	$250
	S2H2 Ladies Gems	$350

COMPANY	IRON	VALUE
Cleveland:		
	792 VAS Graphite Shaft	$400
	792 VAS Steel Shaft	$250
	Ladies Tour Action	$200
	Byron Nelson	$250
	Tour Action 588 Blade	$200
	Tour Action 588 Perimeter Weighted	$200
	Tour Action 588P Manganese Bronze	$300
	Tour Action 588P Melonite	$400
	Tour Edition 485	$250
	Tour Edition 485 BeCu	$600
Cobra:		
	Baffler Blade	$100
	Baffler Blade II	$100
	Baffler Blade II Graphite Shafts	$350
	Baffler Blade Senior Graphite	$450
	Baffler Blade TRD	$150
	Baffler Blade TRD II	$100
	Cobralite	$250
	King Cobra	$300
	King Cobra II	$350
	Greg Norman Cavity Back	$300
	Greg Norman Cavity Back Graphite Shafts	$450
	Greg Norman Muscleback Blades	$500
	Greg Norman Muscleback Blades Graphite shafts	$650
	Traditional Baffler Blade	$200
	Traditional Baffler Blade Ladies Model	$200
	Traditional Baffler Blade Seniors Model	$200
	TRD	$150
	TRD Mild Steel	$150
Confidence:		
	CF	$125
	Confidence	$125
	Confidence I	$125
	Confidence II	$125
	Confidence Open	$125
	Confidence Original	$125
	Jerry Heard	$125
	K-81	$125
	K-81 Forged	$125
	Lady Lite	$125
	Lady Lite IV	$125
	Lady Pro	$125
	LP	$125
	Pyramid	$125
	Solid State	$125
	ST-2	$125

COMPANY IRON	VALUE
Confidence(cont.):	
Stature	$125
System 2000	$125
Tour Plus	$125
Visa	$125
Visa II	$125
Visa EZ	$125
Visa Gold	$125
Windsor	$125
Cubic Balance:	
Precision Forging Collector Edition	$625
Diawa:	
Advisor 273	$125
Advisor 8601	$125
Advisor Cavity Blade	$125
Advisor GOH	$125
Balistic	$150
Cats Eye	$150
Chairman	$150
Escala	$150
Exceler G-3	$150
Exceler G-3 AAP	$350
Exceler G-3 Compo	$350
Exceler G-3 Graphite	$350
Exceler II	$150
Hi-Trac	$250
Hi-Trac TCS	$275
Lite Touch	$200
MF110	$275
Monodyne	$150
Monodyne Tour Blade	$150
Protege	$150
SRX-1	$150
SRX-3	$150
Unipower	$150
Dunlop:	
7000	$75
Seve Ballesteros Ltd. Edition 3 Woods 11 Irons	$1,600
Black Max Graphite	$200
Blue Max	$125
Bob Charles	$125
DP-30 Australian Blade	$250
Dynamax	$125
Gundy	$125
John Jacobs System	$125
John Jacobs System 100	$150
John Jacobs System 200	$150
John Jacobs System 300	$150

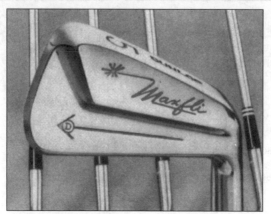

Dunlop Maxfli Iron

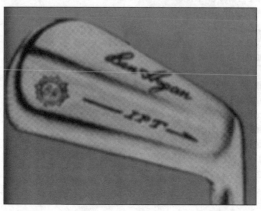

Ben Hogan Golf Company IPT Iron

COMPANY IRON	VALUE
Dunlop(cont.):	
Jan 501	$125
Jan 701	$125
Max 357	$125
Max 357 Maximum Performance	$125
Maxfli	$125
Maxfli Australian Blade	$325
Maxfli Australian Blade Ltd. Edition	$325
Maxfli Australian Blade Standard	$325
Maxfli Cast Irons	$125
Maxfli Lady	$125
Maxfli Power Flange	$125
Maxfli Pro Special	$125
Max-lite	$125
Maxpower	$125
Susie Maxwell	$100
Susie Maxwell Berning	$100
Missile	$100
Model 200	$100
Power Flange	$100
Powermax	$100
Pro Special	$100
Red Max	$100
Jan Stephenson	$100
TM-92 Australian Blade	$250
Tour Limited Cast	$125
Tour Limited Forged	$250
VHL Midsize	$135
Faultless:	
Centra	$100
F-IV	$100
Lady Quantum	$100
Omega System-One	$100
Professional	$100
Quantum	$100
Lee Trevino	$100
Lee Trevino Staff	$100
Fernquest And Johnson:	
Tony Lema Champagne Westerner	$400
Founders Club:	
Fresh Metal	$250
Fresh Metal Ladies	$200
Series 100	$300
Series 200	$300
Foxbat:	
The Blade	$100
F-2	$100
F-3	$100

COMPANY IRON	VALUE
Foxbat(cont.)**:**	
F-4	$100
F-2000	$100
F-5000	$100
Firefox 1000	$100
The Fox	$100
FX-15	$100
Magic	$100
Magic II	$100
Magic Plus	$100
Microlite	$100
Oval	$100
Texas Magic	$100
Golfcraft:	
Custom Built Pro Zone 3858	$275
Willie Low	$200
Walter Hagen:	
American Lady	$100
Crenshaw Grind	$375
Hagen American Lady	$100
Hagen International	$100
Hagen Matrix LP	$100
Hagen Ultra Flex	$125
The Haig	$150
Haig Ultra	$160
Haig Ultra 66	$100
Haig Ultra Contour Sole	$200
Lady Onyx	$100
Lady Ultra 66	$100
Matrix Regular	$100
Star Line	$175
Ultra Power	$165
Ultradyne II	$250
Ben Hogan:	
40th Anniversary 1992	$1,600
Apex	$250
Apex II	$275
Apex II Ladies	$150
Apex PC	$275
Bantam 2442	$250
BAP 2322	$250
Director	$275
Edge	$275
Edge GS	$300
Hogan Bounce Sole	$300
Hogan Bounce Sole 1 Plus	$275
Hogan Round Sole	$200
Ben Hogan 1 Plus	$250

COMPANY IRON	VALUE
Ben Hogan (cont.):	
Ben Hogan Personal With IPT	$300
Lady Hogan	$100
Leader	$150
Magnum	$100
Magnum Plus	$100
Medallion	$350
Model 306	$250
Model 306 306l	$250
Parmaker 1622	$225
Percussion Center	$195
Personal 1982 Ltd. Edition Used	$750
Personal Model 1982 Ltd. Edition	$2,200
Power Thrust	$200
Power Thrust IPT	$300
Precision	$375
Princess	$195
Producer	$200
PTIII	$200
Radial	$250
Saber	$200
Sunburst 1958-59	$200
Vector Lite	$100
Kroydon:	
55 Offset	$150
137 Offset	$125
Louisville Golf:	
Classic 50's	$100
Ladies Personal Model	$100
Level Four	$100
Natural Lite	$100
Personal Model	$100
Personal Model F-55	$100
Personal Model F-70	$100
Personal Model Forged	$100
Progressive	$100
Select CSF	$100
Lynx:	
10 (1981 Ltd. edition)	$300
Liberty Bell 1976	$400
Master Model	$250
Parallax 1990-91	$200
Parallax 1992 On	$350
Precision Lite	$150
Predator Graphite	$300
Predator Plus	$250
Prowler	$150
Radius	$125

COMPANY	IRON	VALUE

Lynx(cont.):

Silver Lynx		$125
Super Predator		$150
Tigress		$125
Tigress G		$125
Tigress SP		$125
Tour Design		$325
USA		$250
USA Low Profile		$200

MacGregor:

Tommy Armour 945 Colokrom		$200
Tommy Armour Black Scot 244		$195
Tommy Armour CF 4000		$300
Tommy Armour Iron Master 235		$100
Tommy Armour Recorded		$275
Tommy Armour Silver Scot		$150
Tommy Armour Silver Scot 905		$250
Tommy Armour Silver Scot 915		$175
Tommy Armour Silver Scot 925		$175
Tommy Armour Silver Scot 945		$275
Tommy Armour Silver Scot 948		$250
Tommy Armour Silver Scot 985		$250
Tommy Armour Silver Scot 990		$250
Tommy Armour Silver Scot A1		$125
Tommy Armour Silver Scot A2		$125
Tommy Armour Silver Scot Recorded		$275
Tommy Armour Silver Scot SS1		$225
Tommy Armour Silver Scot Tourney 915		$175
Tommy Armour Silver Scot Tourney 925		$175
Tommy Armour Silver Scot Tourney 945		$175
Tommy Armour Silver Scot Tourney 985		$185
Tommy Armour Silver Scot Tourney 985T		$275
Tommy Armour SS1		$325
Tommy Armour SS2		$325
Tommy Armour Tourney 985		$175
Tommy Armour VFQ AT1		$325
Tommy Armour VFQ AT2		$250
Tommy Armour VFQ AT3		$150
Jack Burke		$175
CG1800		$100
CG2000		$100
Colokrom Tourney		$300
Ben Crenshaw Texan		$500
DX		$75
DX Tourney		$275
DX Tourney RDX		$275
First Lady 970		$50
Ben Hogan BAP 2332		$350

COMPANY IRON	VALUE
MacGregor(cont.)**:**	
Iron Master	$75
Lady DX	$50
Lady DX RLDX	$75
Lady Finesse	$50
Lady MT	$50
Lady Tourney	$100
Lord Byron 231	$50
Lord Byron 232	$50
MCX	$100
MCX-V	$100
MG Lite	$100
MT	$275
MT Colokrom	$150
MT Split Sole	$150
MT Tourney	$75
MT Tourney Colokrom	$275
MT Tourney Custom	$225
Byron Nelson 215	$100
Byron Nelson 230	$100
Byron Nelson 235	$125
Byron Nelson 240	$125
Byron Nelson 241	$125
Byron Nelson 242	$125
Byron Nelson 245	$125
Byron Nelson 255	$125
Byron Nelson 259	$125
Byron Nelson 269	$125
Byron Nelson 3852	$225
Nicklaus 1981 Limited Edition	$6,500
Nicklaus 1988 Commemorative	$1,200
Nicklaus Heritage	$100
Nicklaus VIP 1967	$750
Nicklaus VIP 1968	$650
Jack Nicklaus Muirfield	$275
Jack Nicklaus Muirfield 20th Anniversary	$300
Jack Nicklaus Muirfield Lite	$150
Jack Nicklaus Personal Forgings	$350
Toney Penna Colokrom 1955-57	$250
Toney Penna VIP 1962-63	$8,000
Toney Penna VIP 1964	$4,000
Toney Penna VIP 1965-67	$1,500
Promaster 940	$100
Reverse Draft	$200
RPM Manganese Bronze	$250
Sprint Lite	$75
Curtis Strange Limited Edition 1989	$1,800
Louise Suggs 215	$75

MacGregor Ben Hogan BAP Iron

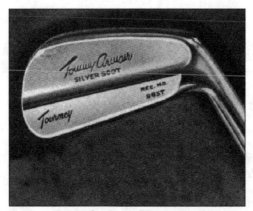

MacGregor Tourney
Silver Scot Iron

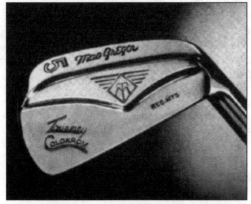

MacGregor MT Tourney
Colokrom Iron

COMPANY IRON	VALUE
MacGregor(cont.):	
Louise Suggs 225	$75
Louise Suggs 258	$75
Louise Suggs 720	$75
Louise Suggs 722	$75
Louise Suggs 780 Tourney	$75
Louise Suggs CF 4000	$75
Louise Suggs Colokrom 980 Tourney	$75
Louise Suggs Empress	$75
Louise Suggs First Lady 258	$75
Louise Suggs First Lady 710	$75
Louise Suggs First Lady 711	$75
Louise Suggs First Lady 712	$75
Louise Suggs First Lady 735	$75
Louise Suggs LS3	$75
Louise Suggs LS3 Empress	$75
Louise Suggs LS4 Empress	$75
Louise Suggs Tourney S3	$75
Louise Suggs Tourney S3T	$75
Louise Suggs Tourney S4	$75
Louise Suggs Tourney S4T	$75
Synchrolite	$150
Tourney 1995 Limited Edition	$450
Tourney CF 4000 MT1	$200
Tourney CF 4000 MT2	$275
Tourney CF 4000 MT3	$300
Tourney CF 4000 MT4	$300
Tourney CF 4000 PT1	$300
Tourney CF 4000 PT2	$300
Tourney CF 4000 PT3	$300
Tourney CF 4000 PT4	$300
Tourney Colokrom	$175
Tourney Custom	$250
Tourney Custom 985	$300
Tourney M55	$100
Tourney M65	$125
Tourney M75	$275
Tourney M85	$350
Tourney M89	$150
Tourney Master 237	$100
Tourney PT1	$300
Tourney PT2	$300
Tourney PT2 Recessed Weight	$325
Tourney PT3	$300
Tourney PT4	$300
VIP	$250
VIP By Nicklaus 1967	$800
VIP By Nicklaus 1968	$700

MacGregor Louise Suggs Tourney
Iron

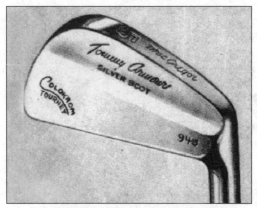

MacGregor Tommy Armour
Silver Scot Tourney Iron

MacGregor Tommy Armour
Recessed Weight Iron

COMPANY IRON	VALUE
MacGregor(cont.):	
VIP Oversize	$250
VIP Oversize Graphite	$450
VIP Split Sole	$225
VIP Tour	$250
Winged MT	$150
Maruman:	
CI-10	$200
Conductor 31 CXII	$600
Conductor 41 CX	$250
DCA II	$150
DCA Kevlar	$150
Elicon	$150
Gracewin	$150
Ladies Suppon	$150
M210	$150
MSC200	$150
MSF	$150
MSL71	$150
Curtis Strange Ltd. Edition	$450
Tap 18	$150
Verity	$150
Verity 21	$150
Merit Golf:	
205	$100
Fusion	$200
PL Graphite Shaft	$300
PL Steel Shaft	$250
TAC	$100
Tour International	$100
Mizuno:	
Altron FWD	$150
Altron SE	$200
Ariel	$100
Black Turbo	$200
Black Turbo II	$250
Cimarron	$200
Grad	$250
Grad MP	$250
MIZ	$150
Mizuno Pro	$250
MP 9 Pro Forge	$400
MP 11 Pro Forge	$450
MP 14	$500
MP 29 Pro Forge	$650
MS 1 Pro Forge	$150
MS 2 Pro Forge	$150
MS 3 Pro Forge	$150

MacGregor Byron Nelson 230 Iron

MacGregor Byron Nelson 240 Iron

MacGregor Tommy Armour
V.F.Q. Irons

COMPANY IRON	VALUE
Mizuno(cont.):	
MS 4 Pro Forge	$150
MS 5 Pro Forge	$150
MS 7 Pro Forge	$150
MS 8 Pro Forge	$150
MS 9 Pro Forge	$150
MST	$200
MSX	$200
MSX Mid Sized	$200
Quad	$200
Silver Cup	$100
SPL	$100
TC 29	$275
Trump	$150
Wings	$150
Nicklaus:	
Bear Offset	$300
Bear Regular Offset	$300
NI Forged Limited Edition Set	$2,200
Northwestern:	
965 Ltd. Edition	$100
Betty Alex	$100
Carrera	$100
Competitor	$100
Pete Cooper Autograph	$100
Pete Cooper Championship	$100
Pete Cooper Signature	$100
Bruce Crampton MP	$100
Custom Power Kick	$100
Stan Dudas Championship	$100
Stan Dudas Deluxe	$100
Dyna Tour	$100
Marty Furgol Personal	$100
Marty Furgol Signature	$100
Gold Signature	$100
GP270	$100
Hubert Green 300CS	$100
Hubert Green RS	$100
Hubert Green RS BeCu	$100
Bob Hagey	$100
Bob Hagey Autograph	$100
Bob Hagey Deluxe	$100
Bob Hagey Gooseneck	$100
Bob Hagey Registered	$100
Bob Hagey Stainless Steel	$100
Chandler Harper Esquire	$100
Chandler Harper Pro Line	$100
Chandler Harper Tournament	$100

MacGregor Jack Burke Iron

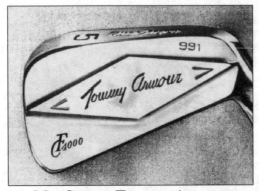

MacGregor Tommy Armour
CF 4000 Iron

MacGregor VIP by Nicklaus Iron

COMPANY IRON	VALUE
Northwestern(cont.):	
Chandler Harper Virginian	$100
Hazel Hixon Autograph	$100
Hazel Hixon Custom Made	$100
Hazel Hixon Deluxe	$100
Hazel Hixon Gooseneck	$100
Hazel Hixon Registered	$100
Betty Jameson	$100
Betty Jameson Gold Signature	$100
Betty Jameson Pro Registered	$100
Betty Jameson Registered	$100
Herman Kaiser Presidential	$100
Ladies Thunderbird II	$100
Ladies Tournament	$100
Lady Nelson Signature	$100
Lady Nelson Tournament	$100
Lady Saga	$100
Lady Ultimate	$100
Lady Ultimate II	$100
Lady Vogue	$100
Lord Byron	$100
Love Stix	$100
Dick Metz Esquire	$100
Mary Mills Championship	$100
Mary Mills Gold Signature	$100
Mary Mills Pro Signature Model	$100
Bob Murphy SST	$100
Al Nelson ProBilt	$100
Byron Nelson Gold Signature	$100
Byron Nelson Hall Of Fame	$100
Byron Nelson Magic Power	$100
Byron Nelson Presidential Model	$100
Byron Nelson Pro Personal Model	$100
Byron Nelson Pro Signature Model	$100
Byron Nelson Professional Model	$100
Byron Nelson Registered	$100
Byron Nelson Senior Model	$100
Byron Nelson Slipstream	$100
NR 60 Tour System	$100
Pro Classic	$100
Pro Master	$100
Pro Master Plus	$100
Pro Signature	$100
Professional	$100
Jackie Pung Autograph	$100
Jackie Pung Championship	$100
Jackie Pung Deluxe	$100
Jackie Pung Personal	$100

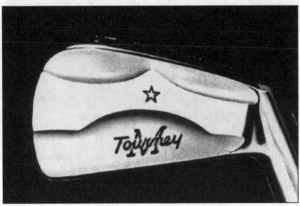

MacGregor Tourney

COMPANY	IRON	VALUE

Northwestern(cont.):

Jackie Pung Pro Line	$100
Jackie Pung Signature	$100
Jackie Pung Tournament	$100
Jackie Pung Virginian	$100
Qualifier Lady Ultimate	$100
Qualifier Lite	$100
RB-68	$100
RB-70	$100
RB-71	$100
RB-200	$100
RB-880	$100
RB-900	$100
Johnny Revolta Magic Power	$100
Johnny Revolta Slipstream	$100
Robbie Robinson	$100
Robbie Robinson Deluxe	$100
Robbie Robinson Signature	$100
Chi Chi Rodriguez Dorado	$100
Chi Chi Rodriguez Pro Signature	$100
Chi Chi Rodriguez Registered	$100
Rosasco Bros.	$100
N. Rosasco	$100
N. Rosasco Pro Made	$100
N. Rosasco Professional	$100
Saga	$100
Saga II	$100
Status XDC Set	$100
Bob Stuart	$100
Bob Stuart Autograph	$100
Superba	$100
Supreme	$100
Team Lopez	$100
Team Player	$100
Team Player Progressive Flow	$100
Team Player Variable Lie	$100
Phil Thomson Gooseneck	$100
Thunderbird	$100
Thunderbird II	$100
Thunderbird II Offset	$100
TNT	$100
Tour II	$100
Tour Model	$100
Tour Select II	$100
Tour Select TS450	$100
Tour Select TSG	$100
Tournament	$100
Jim Turnesa Personal	$100

COMPANY	IRON	VALUE

Northwestern(cont.):

Jim Turnesa Registered	$100
Jim Turnesa Westchester	$100
TW 276	$100
Ultimate	$100
Ultimate II	$100
Ultimate Aluminum Model	$100
Ultimate Square Toe Model	$100
Tom Weiskopf Pro Classic	$100
Craig Wood Gold Signature	$100
Craig Wood Hall Of Fame	$100
X-101	$100
XD-500	$100
XD-660	$100

Arnold Palmer:

FTD	$100
Lady Palmer	$75
Lady Palmer Tru Matic	$75
Palmer Ltd. 1954	$800
Tru Matic	$150

Dave Pelz:

DP1	$250
DP1 Lajet Classic	$250
DP2 Tour Special	$250
Dave Pelz Irons	$250

Toney Penna:

Avenger	$125
Empress	$125
HoneyBee	$125
Innovator	$125
Lady Omega	$125
Original	$125
Penna Lite	$125
Penna Steel	$125
Pinjammer	$125
Powerback	$125
Rawlings RXP	$125
Six + 6	$125
Super Blade	$125
System One	$125
Tip Irons	$125
TP Avenger	$125
TP Blade	$125
TP Irons	$125
TP Stainless Steel	$125
TP1X	$125
TP810	$125
Trevino Professional	$125

COMPANY IRON	VALUE
Toney Penna (cont.):	
Lee Trevino Staff	$125
Lee Trevino TKO	$125
Lee Trevino Tour	$125
Tru Site	$125
Tru Site II Set	$125
USA Forged	$125
PGA Golf:	
Tommy Armour Diamond Scot	$150
Tommy Armour Silver Scot 986 Tour	$300
Tommy Armour Silver Scot Collector 709	$300
Butterfly	$75
Cameron	$125
Champion	$125
Classic	$125
Concept	$125
Concept LCG	$125
Contessa	$125
Contromatic	$125
Contromatic Queen	$125
Coronation	$125
Corvair	$125
The Custom	$125
Emblem	$175
Ladies Custom	$75
Ladies Ryder Cup	$75
Lady Burke	$75
Lady Classic	$75
Lady Contessa	$75
Lady Custom	$75
Lady Par Ex	$75
Lady Par Ex Static Weighted	$75
Lady PGA	$75
Lady Ryder Cup	$75
Mark IV Punchiron	$75
Metrilite System	$75
Mr. President	$75
NUB Iron	$125
Par Ex Static Weighted	$125
Par Ex Swingweighted	$125
Par Excellence	$125
The Performer	$125
Polaris	$125
The Professional	$125
Punchiron	$75
Ryder Cup	$125
Ryder Cup 174	$125
Ryder Cup Deluxe	$125

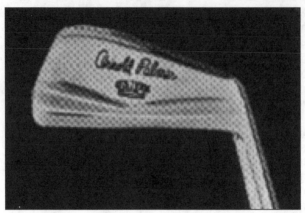

Arnold Palmer Golf Company Iron

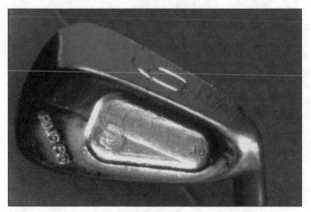

1963 Ping Iron

PowerBilt Citation

COMPANY IRON	VALUE
PGA Golf (cont.):	
Ryder Cup II	$125
Ryder Cup II Over Hosel	$125
Ryder Cup L-100	$125
Ryder Cup LW	$125
Ryder Cup Mark V	$125
Ryder Cup Punch Irons	$125
Ryder Cup RCR	$125
Silver Scot 986 Tour	$125
Thunderbird	$125
T-Line	$125
Tournament	$125
Vardon Cup	$125
Ping:	
1961 Ballmatic Gold Foil In Lower Cavity (100 Made)	$7,500
1963 Large Cavity Back (200 Made)	$4,500
1966 Ping Anser Irons (300 Made)	$6,000
Eye	$400
Eye 2	$375
Eye 2 BeCu	$625
Eye 2 Plus	$300
Eye 2 Plus BeCu	$350
Karsten I	$375
Karsten I 1985 Remake Of The Original	$250
Karsten II	$375
Karsten III	$250
Karsten IV	$250
Ladies Eye	$325
Ping Zing	$300
Zing II	$400
Pinseeker:	
350 RS	$125
Airstream	$125
Black Irons	$125
Bombshell II	$125
Classic	$125
Emerald	$125
Energy Plus	$125
Expeditor	$125
Fireball	$125
Formula 1	$125
Limited Edition Set	$125
Sally Little Autograph	$125
MS	$125
MX	$125
Olympian	$125
Olympian Veri Lite	$125
Pinseeker	$125

COMPANY	IRON	VALUE
Pinseeker(cont.):		
	Pinseeker Over The Hosel	$125
	RB-300	$125
	RB-350	$125
	Rebound	$125
	Rebound II	$125
	Soft Cast	$125
	Tour Classic	$125
	TPW	$125
	TPW II	$125
PowerBilt:		
	Alliance	$100
	Century	$100
	Citation	$200
	Citation 777	$200
	Citation 2292 Scotch Blade	$300
	Citation 2392 Scotch Blade	$250
	Citation 2680T	$200
	Citation 4890	$200
	Citation 4890C	$200
	Citation 6190	$200
	Citation 6192	$200
	Citation 6290	$200
	Citation 6292	$200
	Citation 6390	$200
	Citation 6392	$200
	Citation 6490	$200
	Citation 6492	$200
	Citation 6590	$200
	Citation 6592	$200
	Citation 6645	$200
	Citation 6690	$200
	Citation 6692	$200
	Citation 6790	$200
	Citation 6792	$200
	Citation 6890	$200
	Citation 6892	$200
	Citation 6992	$200
	Citation 7292	$200
	Citation 7492	$250
	Citation 7600	$150
	Citation 7745	$150
	Citation 9935	$150
	Citation 9945	$150
	Citation BeCu Graphite	$450
	Citation C5292	$150
	Citation Forged	$150
	Citation Forged 92	$150

COMPANY IRON	VALUE
PowerBilt(cont.):	
Citation Forged 9825	$150
Citation Light	$150
Citation S7090	$100
Countess 2180T	$125
Countess 2280T	$125
Countess 2380T	$125
Countess 2480T	$125
Countess 2580T	$125
Countess 2680T	$125
Countess 2780T	$125
Countess 2880T	$125
Countess 2980T	$125
Countess 3080T	$125
Countess 3482T	$125
Countess 7680T	$125
Countess 7682T	$125
Countess Cast	$125
Countess Cast 5542T	$125
Countess Cast 555T	$125
Countess Forged	$125
Grand Slam	$150
Imperial	$100
Ladies Pro Sonic A2980	$100
Levelume	$150
Momentum	$200
Momentum 7845	$200
Momentum 9835	$200
PowerBilt 116	$125
PowerBilt 134	$125
PowerBilt 148	$125
PowerBilt 151R	$50
PowerBilt 4190DTC	$100
PowerBilt 4290DTC	$100
PowerBilt 4390	$125
PowerBilt 4490	$125
PowerBilt 4590	$125
PowerBilt 4690	$125
PowerBilt 4790	$125
PowerBilt 4990	$125
PowerBilt 4990C	$125
PowerBilt 5490T	$125
PowerBilt 5590C	$125
PowerBilt 5690C	$125
PowerBilt 5790C	$125
PowerBilt 5890C	$125
PowerBilt 6480C	$150
PowerBilt 6490TC	$150

COMPANY	IRON	VALUE
PowerBilt(cont.):		
PowerBilt 6690TC		$150
PowerBilt 6790T		$150
PowerBilt 6890T		$150
PowerBilt 6990T		$150
PowerBilt 7490		$150
PowerBilt 7590		$150
PowerBilt 8090T		$125
PowerBilt 8190T		$125
PowerBilt Ladies		$100
PowerBilt Ladies 2280TC		$100
PowerBilt Ladies 2380TC		$100
PowerBilt Ladies 2480T		$100
PowerBilt Ladies 2580T		$100
PowerBilt Ladies 2680T		$100
PowerBilt Ladies 2780T		$100
PowerBilt Ladies 6480C		$100
PowerBilt Olin Dutra 201		$50
PowerBilt T2190DTC		$100
PowerBilt T2390DTC		$100
PowerBilt T2490DTC		$100
Pro Sonic A4092		$175
Scotch Blade		$225
Scotch Blade 2092		$225
Scotch Blade 2192		$225
Scotch Blade 2276		$225
Scotch Blade 2492		$225
Scotch Blade 2595		$225
Thoroughbred NTI		$75
Thoroughbred TI		$75
Tournament Players Series		$150
TPS Advanced Players Cavity Back		$150
TPS Advanced Players Forged Blade		$150
TPS Ladies Clubs		$150
TPS Senior Players		$150
TPS Standard Players		$150
ProGroup Inc:		
Axiom		$200
Axiom II		$250
Charger		$100
Fair Lady		$100
First Flight Explo-Flight		$100
First Flight FTD		$100
First Flight Golden Arrow		$100
First Flight Golden Eagle		$100
First Flight Greenmaster		$100
First Flight Lady Golden Eagle		$100
First Flight Mark IV		$100

COMPANY IRON	VALUE
ProGroup Inc(cont.):	
First Flight NALG	$100
First Flight OSS FTD	$100
First Flight Ph.D.	$100
First Flight Phantom	$100
First Flight PT-280	$100
First Flight Standard	$150
First Flight Sterling FX 101	$100
Lady Palmer	$100
Lady Peerless	$250
Original Standard	$250
Palmer Deacon	$150
Palmer Golden Standard	$200
Palmer Peerless	$250
Palmer Personal	$200
Palmer Signature	$200
Palmer Standard	$275
Palmer Tru-Forge	$100
Palmer Tru-Matic	$150
Arnold Palmer Charger	$125
Arnold Palmer Charger II	$125
Arnold Palmer Charger XLF	$100
Arnold Palmer FTD	$150
Arnold Palmer Personal	$100
Arnold Palmer Signature	$100
Arnold Palmer The Boss	$125
Arnold Palmer Tru-Matic	$100
Peerless	$150
Peerless GTW	$275
Peerless PHD	$275
Tony Penna	$100
The Standard	$250
Standard 85	$200
Standard Forged	$300
Tru-Matic	$100
Ram:	
Accubar	$100
Accubar Gold	$100
Accubar Lite	$100
Accubar Low Profile	$100
Accubar Plus	$100
Accucore	$50
Custom 100 Tour Model	$50
Fastback	$75
Fastback Aluminum	$75
Fastback Dynalite	$75
Fastback II	$75
Fullback	$75

COMPANY	IRON	VALUE
Ram(cont.):		
	Golden Girl	$100
	Golden Lady Accubar	$50
	Golden Lady Tribute	$100
	Golden Ram Tour Grind	$250
	Golden Ram Tour Grind Cambered Sole	$250
	Golden Ram Tour Grind Tom Watson	$250
	Golden Ram XPD-100 Aluminum	$100
	Golden Ram XPD-100 Dynalite	$100
	Keith Knox DM-139	$50
	Kroydon Gene Littler Invitational	$100
	Kroydon Jo Ann Prentice Invitational	$50
	Kroydon Thunderbolt	$50
	Kroydon Tommy Bolt Lightning 500	$50
	Lady Accubar Low Profile	$50
	Lady Craigton	$50
	Lady Laser	$100
	Laser Featherlite FLC	$50
	Laser FX	$125
	Laser FX-2	$125
	Laser L X	$150
	Laser X-2	$150
	Laser X-2 BeCu	$200
	Laser Z X	$150
	Gene Littler Invitational	$50
	Milady	$50
	Jo Ann Prentice	$100
	Jo Ann Prentice Invitational	$100
	Pro Set	$300
	Doug Sanders	$75
	Doug Sanders DS	$75
	Doug Sanders Signature	$75
	Doug Sanders Super SST	$75
	Sensor	$100
	Patty Sheehan Tour Grind	$100
	Tour	$200
	Tour Grind	$200
	Tour Grind Axial	$250
	Tour Grind Featherlite	$100
	Tour Grind FLB	$150
	Tour Grind FLC	$150
	Tradition	$100
	TX-2	$100
	XS-100	$100
	XS-1000	$100
Sounder:		
	Classic	$125
	CT600	$125

COMPANY IRON	VALUE
Sounder(cont.):	
Excaliber	$125
First Star	$125
First Star Offset	$125
Silver Star	$125
Silver Star	$125
SMW3	$125
Sonar	$125
Sounder	$125
Sounder Offset	$125
Star	$125
Star Mid-lite	$125
Sun Star	$125
Tour Limited	$150
Tour Star	$150
Triad	$125
Triad BeCu	$200
VS92	$100
Spalding:	
Advance 15	$100
Cannon	$200
Elite	$100
Elite Centurion	$100
Elite Plus	$150
Executive	$150
Executive Limited	$75
Executive XE	$375
Sandra Haynie	$100
Robert T. Jones Kroflite	$150
Robert T. Jones Yellow Sheath Shaft	$200
Gene Littler Pro Model	$100
MV2	$150
Top Flite	$200
Top Flite Auxiliary Windjammers	$50
Top Flite Dynertial	$200
Top Flite Executive	$100
Top Flite Ladies	$100
Top Flite Legacy	$125
Top Flite Mary Lena Faulk	$100
Top Flite Plus	$225
Top Flite Small Bird	$200
Top Flite Synchro-Dyned	$225
Top Flite Tournament Model	$175
Tour Edition	$275
Tour Edition Custom Crafted	$175
Tour Edition Ltd.	$150
XL4	$100

Spalding Top-Flite Iron

Spalding Elite Iron

Spalding Executive Iron

COMPANY IRON	VALUE
Square Two:	
Excalibur	$100
Lady Petite	$100
LPGA	$100
LPGA Forged	$100
LPGA II	$100
LPGA Professional	$100
LPGA Tour Blade	$100
Onyx	$100
PCX	$100
S2 Forged	$100
S2 Professional	$100
S2 Tour Blade	$100
Sabre	$100
Sabre II	$100
Square Two	$100
Square Two Forged	$100
TMP	$100
XGR	$100
ZCX	$100
Taylor Made:	
ICW5	$300
ICW11	$200
Iron Cleek	$275
Technician	$150
Technician Lite	$100
Tour Preferred	$250
Stan Thompson:	
Air Force	$75
Ginty	$75
Ginty II BeCu	$75
Lady Thompson	$75
Personal Model	$75
Pro Motion	$75
RC-20X	$75
ST-50	$75
Titleist:	
Accu-Flow	$100
Accu-Flow Plus Offset	$100
Acushnet AC-108	$240
Acushnet Pro 100	$100
Acushnet Pro Am	$100
Acushnet Titleist	$100
Club Special	$100
DCI	$300
DCI Offset	$300
DCI Oversize	$300
DCI Players Club	$375

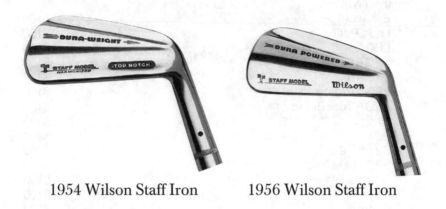

1954 Wilson Staff Iron   1956 Wilson Staff Iron

1960 Wilson Staff Iron   1969 Wilson Staff Iron

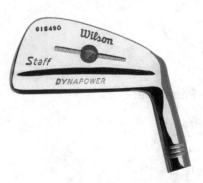

1971 Wilson Staff Iron

Photographs Courtesy of Wilson Sporting Goods.

COMPANY	IRON	VALUE
Titleist(cont.):		
	DTR	$250
	Finalist	$100
	Lite 100	$100
	Model 100	$100
	Model 90	$100
	Pinnacle	$75
	Titleist	$150
	Tour Model	$250
	Tour Model 821	$275
	Tour Model 841	$325
	Tour Model Box Blade	$250
	Tour Model Square Toe	$250
Bob Toski:		
	BTC HP Iron	$100
	BTC SP Iron	$100
	Peter Koskis SGS	$100
	Lady Toski	$100
	Perfect Match	$100
	Perfect Match Bantamweight	$100
	Perfect Match Forged	$100
	Perfect Match II	$100
	Swingprint	$100
	Target	$100
	Target Forged Cavity Back	$100
	Toski Forged	$100
	Toski Target Forged	$100
	Toski Target Cast	$100
	Unifit	$100
	VEC 960	$100
	VEC Tour	$125
Wilson:		
	1200	$125
	1200 GE	$150
	1200 Gear Effect	$150
	1200 Gear Effect Mid Size	$150
	1200 LT	$100
	1200 Power Sole	$100
	1200 TN Gear Effect	$150
	Accurace	$100
	Aggressor	$100
	Berg Staff	$125
	Patty Berg Staff	$100
	Julius Boros Tournament	$125
	Dyna-Power II Cast	$75
	Dyna-Power II Forged	$100
	Dyna-Weight 1951-53	$150
	Dyna-Weight 1954-55	$100

1973 Wilson Staff Iron   1976 Wilson Staff Iron

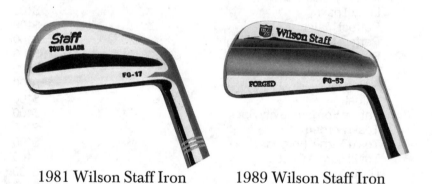

1981 Wilson Staff Iron   1989 Wilson Staff Iron

1995 Wilson Staff Iron

Photographs Courtesy of Wilson Sporting Goods.

COMPANY	IRON	VALUE
Wilson(cont.):		
Lady K-28		$75
Libra		$100
Mystique		$100
Reflex		$150
Gene Sarazen Strokemaster		$75
Sam Snead Championship		$100
Sam Snead Signature		$100
Staff 1995		$225
Staff 1986 Ltd. Edition Remake Of 1971 Staff		$175
Staff 69 Blade (1993 Remake)		$150
Staff 71 Blade (1993 Remake)		$150
Staff Dyna-Powered 1956-57		$175
Staff Dyna-Powered 1958-59		$350
Staff Dyna-Powered 1960-61		$260
Staff Dyna-Power 1962-63		$225
Staff Dyna-Power 1964		$200
Staff Dyna-Power 1965		$200
Staff Dyna-Power 1966		$250
Staff Dyna-Power 1967-68		$200
Staff Dynapower 1969-70		$450
Staff Dynapower 1971-72		$350
Staff Dynapower 1973-75		$250
Staff FG-17 Irons		$185
Staff FG-51 Tour Blade		$250
Staff FG-53 Gooseneck		$200
Staff Gooseneck		$350
Staff Patty Berg Dynapowered		$100
Staff Progressive		$325
Staff Tour Blade		$225
Staff Ultra 45		$100
Sweepstakes		$75
Tiara		$75
Top Notch 1951-52		$75
Top Notch Goose Neck 1951-52		$75
Turfrider		$100
Ultra		$100
Ultra Senior		$100
Ultra W		$100
Ultralite		$100
Ultralite Tour		$100
Ken Venturi		$225
X-31 Forged		$250
X-31 Plus		$100
Yamaha:		
EOS-Z		$150
EX-22 Hollow		$150
EX-Gold		$200

COMPANY	IRON	VALUE
Yamaha(cont.):		
	FD-20	$100
	Image	$150
	Secret	$250
	Secret III	$175
	Secret Mid Size	$175
	ST-30	$175
	ST-30 Gold	$150
	ST-30 SM	$150
	SX-25	$150
	XAM-10	$150
	XAM-8	$150
Yonex:		
	ADX 100	$300
	ADX 200	$300
	ADX FL	$300
	ADX FL 100	$300
	ADX Tour	$300
	Boroniron	$250
	Boroniron II	$250
	Carbonex FL	$250
	Carboniron	$300
	Carboniron FL	$250
	Carboniron II	$250
	Graphlex	$250
	Graphlex FL	$250
	Tournament SP	$250

Wilson Staff X-31 Iron

Wedges
by Jim Butler

From the collector's point of view Wilson wedges are the most desirable. Some newer models have three different lofts available and those differing lofts are not noted. Many wedge prices depend on lie angles. This is especially true in the Ping series with the black and orange dot being the most sought after.

Many old sets carried on the numerical system, a ten iron = wedge and eleven iron = sand iron. Those are noted in the text. The dates that the clubs were issued are four digit numerals. Degrees of loft are only two digit numerals. BeCu indicates that the wedge is made from Beryllium Copper. More and more modern alloys are being used in wedges as the manufacturers search for the perfect feel.

As with putters, older used clubs are sold on a scale of one through ten with ten being new condition. Most fall into the seven, eight, or nine range. Nearly all modern sets include the pitching wedge with a matching sand wedge available. It is impossible to list them all. I have attempted to make sure all the collectible wedges are included in the following price guide. Condition is everything.

Cleveland Tour Edition 485 Wedge

Hagen Haig Ultra Wedge

Hagen Sand Wedge

COMPANY WEDGE	VALUE
Acushnet:	
AC108 PW	$40
Alien:	
Ultimate SW	$40
Tommy Armour:	
845 BC BeCu SW	$95
845 PW	$25
855 SW	$45
945 PW	$25
945 SW	$30
Collector Silver Scot 1987 11 Iron	$30
Collector Silver Scot 1987 SW	$50
D20 Sand Iron	$30
Easy Out SW	$45
R91 Sand Iron	$30
R91 Sand Iron BeCu	$125
RTA Silver Scot Sand Iron	$45
S20 Sand Iron	$30
S20 SW BeCu	$125
Sand Genie	$30
Silver Scot 986 SW	$75
Tour Concept II PW	$30
Tour Concept II SW	$40
Auld Golf:	
Gorce Wedge	$15
Heather Wedge	$15
Jerry Barber:	
Diamond Face Wedge	$10
Heel Spur 52°	$10
Heel Spur 56°	$10
Heel Spur 60°	$10
Beckley Ralston:	
Trapshooter Large Head	$55
Walloper	$50
Big Tex:	
Super Oversize SW	$10
Bridgestone:	
Ray Floyd SW Blade	$50
Ray Floyd SW Cavity Back	$50
Pro Model SW Loomis Graphite Shaft	$75
Bullet:	
444 SW Graphite Shaft	$20
Burke:	
Escalator 400 Brown Shaft	$60
PGA SW	$35
Punch Iron Super Wedge	$50
Sav-A-Shot Blaster Dot face Brown Shaft	$45
Sav-A-Shot Pitcher Sheath Shaft	$35

Ben Hogan Apex Equalizer

Ben Hogan-Medallion Equalizer

Ben Hogan Producer Wedge

COMPANY WEDGE	VALUE
Callaway:	
BAAPI 46° Wedge	$45
Billet Series Milled Hickory Stick	$75
Contempo 50° Wedge	$40
Contempo 55° Wedge	$40
Contempo 60° Wedge	$40
Hickory Stick 3rd Wedge 59°	$75
Hickory Stick Approach Iron	$75
Hickory Stick BeCu Wedges	$150
Runyan Bouncer	$40
S2H2 48° PW	$75
S2H2 52° AW	$75
S2H2 56° SW	$75
S2H2 60° LW	$75
Checkmate:	
Carbite LW	$40
Carbite SW	$40
CS1000 LW	$40
Cleveland:	
485 Tour Action 60°	$75
485 Tour Action 60° No CC Logo	$250
485 Tour Action BeCu 1985 SW	$150
485 Tour Action SW 56° No CC Logo	$250
485 Tour Action Tour Grind Regular 60°	$75
485 Tour Edition 60°	$175
485 Tour Edition PW BeCu	$150
485 Tour Edition SW BeCu	$175
588 Tour Action BeCu 1988 SW	$150
588 Tour Action Regular Satin	$60
588 Tour Action SW Black Mellonite	$125
588 Tour Action SW Magnesium Bronze	$60
690 SW	$45
691 L-Wedge 58°	$65
Hickory Stick 2nd Wedge (Pepsi Logo)	$40
Byron Nelson 50th Anniversary 56° SW BeCu	$100
VAS SW	$45
Cobra:	
Baffler Blade II SW	$15
Flop Wedge	$50
King Cobra Ladies SW Graphite Shaft	$65
King Cobra SW	$25
Greg Norman 54° SW	$25
Greg Norman 60° LW	$25
Greg Norman Sand Iron 60° Graphite Shaft	$50
Rodgers Rusty Cast Aluminum Bronze SW	$50
Rodgers Wedge Series Cast Aluminum Bronze	$50
Rodgers Wedge Series Steel	$50
SW BeCu Graphite Shaft	$75

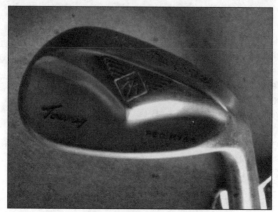

MacGregor Tourney Wedge

MacGregor Double Duty Wedge

Ping Karsten I Wedge

COMPANY WEDGE	VALUE
Confidence:	
Bandit	$10
Boss Sand Iron	$10
Console:	
007 SW	$60
Ladies PW	$25
PW	$40
SW Pat. Pending	$60
Ray Cook:	
Precision Milled 60° Wedge	$50
Otey Crisman:	
PP Brass SW Selma	$35
Red Currie:	
Winged Wedge	$40
Diawa:	
DG903 PW	$40
Excellor 11 Iron Graphite Shaft And Head	$60
Hi Trac SW	$10
Dubow:	
Betty Hicks Xploder	$75
Jock Hutchison Xploder	$75
Dunlop:	
Blue Max PW	$25
Blue Max SW	$25
Dead Eye SW	$25
Fernquest & Johnson:	
Champagne Tony Dual Wedge	$100
Founders Club:	
Defense Series	$60
Defense Series G Loomis Graphite Shaft	$75
Judge Defense Series	$55
Goldsmith:	
Sand Iron Brown Sheath Shaft And Dot Face	$35
Goldwin:	
Blow Out Wedge Graphite Shaft	$75
Golfcraft:	
Leo Diegel 88 Iron	$45
Eddie Hurz Sand Iron	$50
Mangrum PW Glass Shaft	$45
Walter Hagen:	
19MO Sand Iron	$60
Haig 11 Iron	$40
Haig TPW PW	$40
Haig TPW Sand Iron	$45
Haig Ultra All Purpose Wedge	$75
Haig Ultra Contour Sole 385 PW	$40
Haig Ultra Contour Sole Sand Iron Aluminum Shaft	$35
Haig Ultra Dual Wedge	$60

COMPANY	WEDGE	VALUE

Walter Hagen (cont.):

Haig Ultra PW	$40
Haig Ultra SW	$65
Haig Ultra TPW PW	$25
Haig Ultra TPW SW	$45
Ironman Brown Sheath Shaft	$75
Sand Iron	$50
Sandy Andy With Yellow Shaft	$120
Ultra TPW PW	$40
Ultra TPW SW	$45
Ultradyne II PW	$35
Ultradyne II Sand Iron	$40
Ultradyne II Sand Iron Flex Twist Shaft	$40
Ultradyne PW	$35
Ultradyne Sand Iron	$65
WH66 Sand Iron	$35

Head:

Premise SW	$25

Ben Hogan:

47° Wedge	$75
53° Sand Iron	$65
Apex Equalizer	$25
Apex II Equalizer Black Cameo	$50
Apex PC SW	$100
Apex SW	$60
Bounce Sole Equalizer	$50
Bounce Sole Plus One Equalizer	$40
Commemorative 25th Anniversary 1979 SW	$125
Copper Medallion Equalizer	$30
Director Equalizer	$40
Edge SW	$50
HM40 SW	$30
IPT Equalizer	$60
Legend SW 58°	$70
Magnum PW	$30
Medallion Sand Iron Copper Logo	$50
Medallion Wedge	$35
PC SW	$35
Percussion Equalizer Round Toe	$50
Precision 306-L Equalizer	$15
Precision Equalizer Crescents On Hosel	$60
Princess Equalizer	$15
Producer PW	$30
Sand Iron	$45
Sand Iron BeCu	$125
Sand Iron Green Paint	$95
Special 51° PW	$40
Special 55° BeCu PW	$75

COMPANY WEDGE	VALUE
Ben Hogan (cont.):	
Special 55° PW	$40
Special 60°	$60
Special Sand Iron	$75
Special Sand Iron BeCu	$90
Special Sure Out II SW	$45
Special W Grind SW	$40
Special Wadkins Grind Sand Iron	$60
Sure On	$50
Sure Out	$50
Tom Kite K Grind Wedge 51°	$50
Tom Kite K Grind Wedge 56°	$50
Tom Kite K Grind Wedge 62°	$50
Tour Series Wedges	$40
Hornung & Louis:	
Commemorative Caesar Palace BeCu SW	$150
Jaws:	
Wedges BeCu	$50
Kroydon:	
Blaster SW	$70
Lynx:	
Black Cat LW Graphite Shaft	$95
Cat PW	$40
Liberty Bell SW	$100
Master Model PW	$50
Master Model SW	$150
Parallax PW Mellonite And Graphite Shaft	$70
Parallax SW	$50
Parallax SW Mellonite	$95
Parallax Tour Design SW	$50
Predator Plus PW	$40
Predator Plus SW	$40
USA PW	$45
MacGregor:	
99 Sand Iron	$50
152 Double Duty	$50
152 Double Serial Numbers Patent Pending	$65
152 Double Service SW	$50
Tommy Armour 1950's DS	$75
Tommy Armour 1950's SW	$75
Tommy Armour 1960's DS	$75
Tommy Armour 1960's SW	$75
Tommy Armour 3852 1938 SW Green Shaft	$60
Tommy Armour Double Duty 11 Iron	$50
Tommy Armour Double Duty 156 Model 11 Iron	$50
Tommy Armour Double Duty 945 11 Iron	$50
Tommy Armour Double Service SW	$50
Tommy Armour Silver Scot DD Niblick	$40

COMPANY WEDGE	VALUE
MacGregor(cont.):	
Tommy Armour Silver Scot DD Niblick Green Shaft	$75
Tommy Armour Tourney 909 DD Niblick	$35
CF4000 152T Double Service Wedge	$25
CF4000 Tommy Armour SS2 DS Wedge Copper Face	$75
CF4000 Byron Nelson SS1 11 Iron	$50
CF4000 Penna TP1 Wedge	$35
CF4000 Tourney PT2 11 Iron	$45
Ben Crenshaw SW	$45
Expediter MT	$50
Great Scot Chipping Wedge	$45
Great Scot Ladies Sand Iron	$35
Great Scot PW	$45
Great Scot SW	$45
JNP PW	$50
JNP SW	$100
M75 MT Tourney 11 Iron	$30
M75 Tourney Colokrom DS	$60
M85 11 Iron	$70
M85 Colokrom SW	$65
M85 Tourney Colokrom Sand Iron	$60
MCX 10 Iron	$40
Mr. Flipper 157	$50
Jack Nicklaus Golden Bear SW	$30
Jack Nicklaus Muirfield PW	$35
Jack Nicklaus Muirfield SW	$75
Jack Nicklaus Personal 50° PW	$50
Jack Nicklaus Personal 56° SW	$50
Jack Nicklaus Personal 60° LW	$50
Jack Nicklaus Player Of The Century SW	$80
Jack Nicklaus R271 11 Iron	$75
Jack Nicklaus R271 JNW 11 Iron	$100
Jack Nicklaus R271 PW	$75
Jack Nicklaus R271 SW	$125
Penna Wedge TPL	$40
Tony Penna 1950-60 SW	$75
Tony Penna 1962-63 VIP SW	$350
Tony Penna 1964-67 VIP SW	$250
PT1 DS Wedge Recessed Weight	$40
PT2 Tourney Copper Face	$75
PT3 DS Wedge Recessed Weight	$40
REC-MD Double Trouble Wedge	$75
RLDX SW	$20
RPM M1 Jack Nicklaus Manganese Bronze PW	$40
RPM M2 Jack Nicklaus Manganese Bronze SW	$40
RPM M3 Jack Nicklaus Manganese Bronze SW	$40
RPM M4 Jack Nicklaus Manganese Bronze SW	$40
RPM M5 Jack Nicklaus Manganese Bronze SW	$40

COMPANY	WEDGE	VALUE

MacGregor(cont.):

Louise Suggs 720 11 Iron	$30
Louise Suggs Double Duty 156 Model 11 Iron	$30
Louise Suggs Double Service SW	$25
Louise Suggs Tourney Colokrom 156L 11 Iron	$45
Tourney 1950-60 Double Service Wedge	$50
Tourney 1950-60 SW	$50
Tourney Charley Penna Recorded Double Serial Number Niblick	$40
Tourney Custom Jack Nicklaus 25th Anniversary Sand Iron	$100
Tourney MT 11 Iron Black Face	$40
Tourney MT Double Duty 11 Iron Copper Face	$60
Tourney MT Double Duty 11 Iron	$40
Tourney MT Double Service SW	$50
Tourney RMT PW	$45
TP TXA Silver Scot Expediter	$45
VIP 1967 SW By Nicklaus	$350
VIP 1968 SW By Nicklaus	$300
VIP Oversize LW	$50
VIP Oversize SW	$50
VIP PW	$45
VIP SW By Nicklaus Cast	$45
VIP Tour CB92 SW	$45
Worsham Wedge	$15

Maruman:

Verity SW BeCu	$30

Maxfli:

Tad Moore TM53°	$35
Tad Moore TM57°	$35
Tad Moore TM61°	$35
VHL Sand Iron	$30

Mizuno:

Faldo LW	$45
Faldo PW	$45
Faldo SW	$45
Grad MP SW	$50
Grad SW	$35
MP 14 SW	$50
Pro Tour Model 56°	$35
Pro Tour Model 60°	$35

Nicklaus:

The Bear SW	$50

Northwestern:

Easy Out	$10
RB 290	$10
Tomahawk PW	$10

COMPANY WEDGE	VALUE
Northwestern(cont.):	
Tomahawk SW	$15
Palmer:	
AP SW	$45
Axiom II PW	$45
Axiom PW	$45
Original SW Forged	$50
Standard SW	$45
Toney Penna:	
Pin Grabber 11	$30
PGA Golf:	
Tommy Armour 11 Iron	$50
Tommy Armour Sand Iron	$50
D-20 Sand Iron	$50
D-20 SW	$50
R-81 PW	$50
R-91 Aluminum Shaft SW	$50
R-91 Sand Iron	$50
R-91 SW	$50
S-20 Sand Iron	$50
S-80 SW	$50
Triple Threat Utility Wedge	$50
Ping:	
Eye 2 BeCu SW	$95
Eye 2 PW	$40
Eye 2 SW	$45
Eye PW	$75
Eye SW	$75
ISI LW	$50
ISI LW BeCu	$75
ISI LW Stainless Steel	$50
ISI PW	$50
ISI PW BeCu	$75
ISI PW Stainless Steel	$50
ISI SW	$50
ISI SW BeCu	$75
ISI SW Stainless Steel	$50
Karsten I SW	$70
Karsten II PW	$55
Zing II LW	$50
Zing II LW BeCu	$75
Zing II PW	$50
Zing II PW BeCu	$75
Zing II SW	$50
Zing II SW BeCu	$75
Zing LW	$90
Zing PW	$50
Zing SW	$60

COMPANY	WEDGE	VALUE
Pinseeker:		
	RB350 PW	$30
	Sand & 60° Utility Wedge	$30
PowerBilt:		
	1957 Sand Iron	$40
	99 Iron Stainless Steel	$45
	Citation 10 Iron	$35
	Citation Levelume Deluxe 10 Iron	$35
	Citation Pitching Iron	$30
	Citation SW	$35
	Custom Design 99	$35
	Flipper Stainless Steel	$35
	Grand Slam Wedge	$40
	Bill Kratzert Pro Series	$50
	Levelume Pitching Iron 9180C	$40
	Larry Mize SW	$40
	Larry Mize SW Black Head	$30
	Harry Obitz Wedge	$25
	Renewal 60° Wedge	$40
	Renewal Dual Wedge	$40
	Renewal SW	$40
	Scotch Blade Levelume 10 Iron	$25
	Scotch Blade PW	$25
	Scotch Blade PW Pipe Mark	$35
	Scotch Blade SW	$35
	Stainless 10 Iron	$40
	Stainless Sand Blaster	$50
	Stainless Steel Wedge	$35
	Swing True Stainless Sand Blaster	$40
	Thoroughbred SW	$40
	TPS Forged SW	$45
Ram:		
	Golden Ram Tour Grind SW	$50
	Nick Price 56° Wedge	$45
	Nick Price 62° Wedge	$45
	Watson 55° SW BeCu	$125
	Watson 58° Wedge	$45
	Watson Scoring System 53° BeCu SW	$75
	Watson Scoring System 55° BeCu SW	$75
	Watson Scoring System 58° BeCu SW	$85
	Watson Scoring System TW850 PW	$50
	Watson Scoring System TW853 PW Spin Groove Cobalt	$75
	Watson Scoring System TW855 PW	$50
	Watson Scoring System TW855 SW BeCu	$75
	Watson Scoring System TW855 SW Spin Groove Cobalt	$75
	Watson Scoring System TW856 SW Spin Groove Cobalt	$75
	Watson Scoring System TW860 SW	$50
	Watson Scoring System TW864 SW	$50

COMPANY WEDGE	VALUE
Ram(cont.):	
Watson Scoring System TW956 SW	$50
Watson Scoring System TW958 SW	$50
Watson Scoring System TW958 SW Women's	$20
Watson Shootout Sand Wedge 850	$75
Watson Shootout Sand Wedge 860	$75
Watson Spin Wedge 853	$50
Watson Spin Wedge 855	$50
Watson Spin Wedge 858	$50
Watson Troon Grind 853 PW	$50
Watson Troon Grind 855 SW	$50
Watson Troon Grind 858 SW	$50
Watson 860 SW	$50
Royal:	
PW	$30
Shakespeare:	
Sigma SW Fiberglass Shaft	$30
Simmons:	
Attila SW	$15
Sure Shot SW	$20
Slazenger:	
Jack Nicklaus US Open PW	$40
Snake Eyes:	
10	$125
11	$125
12	$125
Sounder:	
Star SW	$10
Spalding:	
Cannon II PW	$20

Spalding Top Flite Wedge

COMPANY WEDGE	VALUE
Spalding (cont.):	
Dynamiter Angle Groove Wedge	$35
Dynamiter Angle Wedge	$45
Dynamiter Custom Forged Wedge	$20
Dynamiter PDN 1940's SW	$75
Dynamiter Robert T. Jones Jr.	$60
Dynamiter Smooth Face Black Sheath Shaft	$175
Dynamiter Stainless	$40
Dy-Nertial SW	$35
Executive PW	$35
Executive PW Small Bird On Ball	$25
Executive SW	$45
Executive XE PW	$50
J. Hebert Pro Sand Club Spade Face	$60
J. Hebert Spade Face Wedge	$50
Jimmy Sheath Shaft	$70
Kro Flite Sweet Spot 19 Iron Steel Shaft	$40
Johnny Miller Classic Wedge	$30
Johnny Miller Finesse Wedge	$30
Johnny Miller Lob Wedge 60°	$30
Johnny Miller Tour Wedge 56°	$30
Johnny Miller Tour Wedge 56° BeCu	$50
Johnny Miller Utility Wedge	$30
Par Saver	$30
Personal Model Sand Club	$25
Personal Model Sand Club Aluminum Shaft	$45
Signature Wedge	$30
Super Dynamiter Yellow Shaft	$70
Top Flite AP99 Wedge	$40
Top Flite Dynamiter Tournament Model	$35
Top Flite EVA PW	$30
Top Flite EVA SW	$30
Top Flite Pro Model 10 Iron	$30
Top Flite Professional PW	$50
Top Flite Tour Edition SW	$30
Top Flite Tour Edition SW II	$30
Top Flite Tour Edition SW III	$30
Tournament Model Wedge Stainless Steel	$35
Springfield:	
Pinehurst 99	$35
Taylor Made:	
Copper Face SW	$65
Tommy Jacobs TJ30 PW	$40
Tommy Jacobs TJ31 SW	$40
Tour Preferred LW	$30
Tour Preferred SW	$30
Tour Preferred SW TD	$75

COMPANY WEDGE	VALUE
Stan Thompson:	
SW	$15
Titleist:	
5004 PW	$30
5616 SW	$30
6000 SW	$30
6010 SW	$35
DCI Oversize SW	$65
DCI Players Club PW	$50
DCI Wedge BeCu	$75
DTR SW	$60
Tour Model SW	$50
Wilson:	
3-D Wedge PW	$30
3-D Wedge SW	$30
8640 Sand Iron	$40
Berg Defender SW	$15
Patty Berg Signature Model 1930's	$250
Bomber 1934 SW	$250
Billy Casper SW	$30
Leo Diegel Contestant Model 1930's SW	$250
Leo Diegel SW	$300
Dual Wedge PW	$45
Dual Wedge SW	$75
Dynapower SW	$100
Dynapower Zaharias PW	$40
Dynapower Zaharias SW	$50
Harmonized Dual Wedge PW	$30
Harmonized Dual Wedge SW	$30
Harmonized R90 SW	$50
Harmonized SW	$30
Helen Hicks National Champ SW	$175
Helen Hicks National Champ SW Brown Sheath Shaft	$275
Helen Hicks SW	$100
JP Custom PW	$40
JP Custom SW	$75
JP II Custom PW	$40
JP II Custom SW	$75
Cary Middlecoff Autograph SW	$30
Music Note Pitcher Brown Shaft	$75
Original R-90 Sand Iron BeCu	$75
Original R-90 SW Brown Sheath Shaft	$75
Pitching Iron Brown Shaft Dot Face	$150
R-9 1930's PW	$225
R-20 1930's SW	$250
R-22 1930's PW	$225
R-30 1930's SW	$250
R-36 Pitcher Model A Dot Face Brown Shaft	$75

COMPANY WEDGE	VALUE
Wilson(cont.):	
R-61 Sandy Andy	$75
R90 Gene Sarazen SW	$50
R90 Sand Iron Brown Shaft	$75
R90 SW	$50
R91 Sand Iron	$50
Johnny Revolta Championship 1930 SW	$250
Johnny Revolta Highlander 1940's SW	$250
Johnny Revolta Sand Iron	$75
Sand Iron	$75
Sand Iron 21 Lines Music Note	$75
Sand Iron Brown Sheath Shaft Dot Face	$125
Sand Iron Music Note 19 Lines	$50
Gene Sarazen 1930's SW	$500
Gene Sarazen R20 Special Wedge Brown Shaft	$75
Gene Sarazen R20 SW	$50
Denny Shute Personal Model Medallist 1930's SW	$250
Sam Snead Blue Ridge SW	$35
Sam Snead Championship SW	$50
Staff 1976-77 SW	$125
Staff 1991 Remake Of 1971 SW	$55
Staff 1992 Remake Of 1958 SW	$50
Staff Dynapower 1956-58 Dual Wedge	$150
Staff Dynapower 1957 SW	$550
Staff Dynapower 1957 Triple Duty Wedge	$300
Staff Dynapower 1958 SW (Most Popular)	$500
Staff Dynapower 1959 SW	$400
Staff Dynapower 1960 SW	$350
Staff Dynapower 1960 Triple Duty Wedge	$125
Staff Dynapower 1961-2 Triple Duty Wedge	$125
Staff Dynapower 1962 Dual Wedge	$100
Staff Dynapower 1962 SW	$175
Staff Dynapower 1964 SW	$150
Staff Dynapower 1965 Dual Wedge	$125
Staff Dynapower 1965 SW	$150
Staff Dynapower 1966 SW	$150
Staff Dynapower 1967 Dual Wedge	$100
Staff Dynapower 1967-68 SW	$150
Staff Dynapower 1969-70 SW	$200
Staff Dynapower 1971-72 SW	$175
Staff Dynapower 1973-75 SW	$125
Staff Dynapower 1992 Remake Of 1958 SW	$75
Staff Dynapower PW 1969 Bullet Back	$50
Staff FG17 1980-83 SW	$125
Staff JP 1984 PW	$40
Staff JP IV 1991 SW BeCu	$60
Staff JP SW	$40
Staff JP55 1993 SW	$40

COMPANY	WEDGE	VALUE
Wilson(cont.):		
Staff Lob Wedge		$75
Staff Patty Berg 1974 SW		$75
Staff Patty Berg SW		$60
Staff Tour Blade FG51 1991 SW		$50
Staff Tour Blade Patty Berg 1978-80 SW		$50
TK 60°		$20
Top Notch Gooseneck 1950's SW		$40
Top Notch Pitching Niblick		$40
Top Notch 1950 PW		$45
Top Notch 1954-55 SW		$75
Top Notch Dynaweight Blade 1950 PW		$95
Top Notch TNT 31420 1950 10 Iron Brown Shaft		$75
Triple Duty 1955 Wedge		$65
Triple Duty 1970 Wedge		$40
Triple Duty SW		$30
Triple Duty Wedge		$30
X-31 1968 PW Aluminum Shaft		$40
X-31 1970-71 PW		$35
X-31 SW		$40
Yamaha:		
800 Alum/Bronze Series 841 Wide Flange 60°		$15
800 Alum/Bronze Series 842 Narrow Flange 60°		$15
800 Series W843		$20

Woods
by Jim Butler

Wooden headed clubs are difficult to resell unless they are a recognized "classic." Sets of woods used to be the norm. They were usually sold in sets of three or four with the customary set being 1-3-4-5 in sets of four or 1-3-5 in sets of three. Some sets are more valuable with the two or four woods included. Unfortunately, sets are not common and the most desirable clubs are now sold individually, mainly due to the price of each club.

Most of the information needed to identify a club is on the sole plate, crown, and the tip of the sole. Different inserts can help identify specific models. Some wood models are the same except for the face inserts or the number of screws in the face. Often sets with the same name are made from Persimmon and Laminated. Where possible I have indicated the difference as it does affect the price.

The bracketed numeral after the individual listing is the original number of clubs issued in each set. Price depends on original condition. A club that has been reshafted, regripped, and refinished other than in original condition is severely penalized as to desirability and price.

COMPANY	WOODS (SET NUMBERS)	VALUE
Accuform:		
	89 Model Woods Laminated (3)	$30
	Persimmon Driver (1)	$20
	PTM Laminated (3)	$30
Ajay:		
	Double Eagle Laminated (3)	$30
	Invader Laminated (3)	$30
	Marilyn Miller Laminated (4)	$30
	Pro Classic Laminated (3)	$30
	Pro Classic II Laminated (3)	$30
	San Franciscan Laminated (4)	$30
	Sandy Shore Laminated (4)	$30
	STD Laminated (3)	$30
	TFC Laminated (3)	$30
	VSP Laminated (3)	$30
	XSP Laminated (4)	$30
Tommy Armour:		
	Butterfly Laminated (4)	$50
	Cameron Persimmon (4)	$50
	Concept 2 Laminated (3)	$50
	Emblem Laminated (4)	$50
	Silver Scot 986 Tour Persimmon (3)	$100
	Silver Scot Deep Face Persimmon (1)	$75
Auld Golf:		
	Auld Classic Laminated (4)	$30
	Auld Classic Persimmon (4)	$30
	Briar Classic Laminated (4)	$30
	Classic Persimmon (3)	$30
	Classic Triax Laminated (4)	$30
	Extractor Laminated (1)	$30
Jerry Barber:		
	Golden Touch Laminated (4)	$50
	Golden Touch 1 Laminated (4)	$50
	Golden Touch 2 Laminated (4)	$50
	GTM-1 Laminated (4)	$50
	GTM-2 Laminated (4)	$50
	M-1 Goldentouch Laminated (4)	$50
Beauwood:		
	Beauwood Persimmon (4)	$50
	Bionize 1 Persimmon (4)	$50
	Bionize 2 Persimmon (4)	$50
	Bionize 3 Persimmon (4)	$50
	BW-33 Collectors Edition Persimmon (4)	$50
	BW-33 Persimmon (4)	$50
	BW-35 Persimmon (4)	$50
	Cameo Laminated (4)	$50
	Duo-Flex Persimmon (4)	$50
	Pro Model Persimmon (4)	$50

COMPANY WOODS (SET NUMBERS)	VALUE
Beauwood(cont.)**:**	
SP-2 Persimmon (4)	$50
BelAir:	
Coot Woods Laminated (4)	$30
Golden Coot Laminated (4)	$30
Belmont:	
Belmont Woods Laminated (4)	$30
Bridgestone:	
Inceptor Laminated (3)	$50
Precept Pro Persimmon (3)	$50
Rextar AC Persimmon (4)	$50
Rextar Pro Persimmon (4)	$50
Bristol:	
Advisory Laminated (4)	$25
Advisory Super Lite Persimmon (4)	$25
B-65 Driver Persimmon (1)	$25
B-75 Driver Persimmon (1)	$25
B-85 Driver Persimmon (1)	$25
B-540 Driver Persimmon (1)	$25
Competitor Laminated (4)	$50
Lady Competitor Laminated (4)	$50
Tour Model Persimmon (4)	$50
Victura Laminated (3)	$50
XS1000 Laminated (3)	$50
Browning:	
440 Laminated (4)	$50
Browning 500 Laminated (4)	$50
Lady Browning Laminated (4)	$50
Mirage Laminated (4)	$50
TLC Laminated (4)	$50
Tour Class II Driver Persimmon (1)	$20
Tour Class Persimmon (4)	$50
TR500 Laminated (4)	$50
TR600 Laminated (4)	$50
Tri Power Laminated (4)	$50
Tri Power Offset Laminated (4)	$50
Tri Power Offset Persimmon (4)	$50
Tri Power Persimmon (4)	$50
Burke:	
Tommy Armour Golden Scot Laminated (4)	$50
Tommy Armour Silver Scot Laminated (4)	$50
Bomber Laminated (4)	$50
Burke Bomber Laminated (4)	$50
Burke Bomber Persimmon (4)	$75
Burke Commander Persimmon (4)	$100
Burke Peerless Laminated (4)	$50
Cobra Persimmon (4)	$150
Compactor Persimmon (4)	$40

COMPANY WOODS (SET NUMBERS)	VALUE
Burke:(cont.):	
Coronation Persimmon (4)	$40
Custom Lady Burke Persimmon (4)	$40
Custom Laminated (4)	$40
Golden Chairman Laminated Golden Colored Shafts (4)	$50
Golden Scot Laminated (4)	$50
Chick Harbert Aristocrat Persimmon (4)	$50
Chick Harbert Autograph Persimmon (4)	$50
Chick Harbert Bomber Laminated (4)	$50
Chick Harbert Championship Persimmon (4)	$50
Chick Harbert Signature Persimmon (4)	$50
Larry Hinson Titleholder Laminated (3)	$50
Hy Speed Fiberglass Laminated (4)	$50
Hy Speed Laminated (4)	$50
Hy Speed Model 15 Persimmon (4)	$50
Hy Speed Model 120 Persimmon (4)	$50
Hy Speed Model 150 Persimmon (4)	$50
Hy Speed Persimmon (4)	$50
Imperial Persimmon (4)	$50
Lady Burke Cameo Persimmon (4)	$50
Lady Burke Coronation Persimmon (4)	$50
Lady Burke Imperial Persimmon (4)	$50
Lady Burke Persimmon (4)	$50
Lady Burke Registered Persimmon (4)	$50
Lady Burke Signature Laminated (4)	$50
Lloyd Mangrum Custom Laminated (4)	$50
Miss Burke Persimmon (4)	$50
Model 135 Persimmon (4)	$50
Model 270 Persimmon (4)	$50
Model 500 Persimmon (4)	$50
Sharron Moran Classic Laminated (3)	$50
Sharron Moran Coronation Laminated (4)	$50
Sharron Moran Custom Laminated (4)	$50
Sharron Moran Laminated (3)	$50
Sharron Moran Premier Laminated (4)	$50
Power-Pak Persimmon (4)	$50
Premier Laminated (4)	$50
Recorded Model 151 Persimmon (4)	$50
Recorded Persimmon (4)	$50
Recorded Woods Mark III Persimmon (4)	$50
Registered Model 152 Persimmon (4)	$50
Riviera Laminated (4)	$50
Rocket Mark II Persimmon (4)	$50
Rock-It Mark I Persimmon (4)	$50
Rock-It Persimmon (4)	$50
Silver Scot Laminated (4)	$50
Les Stokes Laminated (4)	$50
Thunderbird Mark I Persimmon (4)	$50

COMPANY	WOODS (SET NUMBERS)	VALUE

Burke(cont.)**:**
Thunderbird Mark II Persimmon (4) — $50
Jack Rule Victor Laminated (4) — $50

Callaway:
Classic Persimmon Graphite Shaft (4) — $150
Bobby Jones Commemorative Persimmon
    Graphite Shaft (4) — $750

Cleveland:
AL44 Persimmon (4) — $100
Big Al Persimmon (1) — $150
BG1W Persimmon (1) — $100
Ben Crenshaw Model Persimmon (4) — $200
DG43 Persimmon (3) — $100
DW52 Persimmon (3) — $100
The Dunaway Persimmon (1) — $50
Jumbo Persimmon (1) — $150
Launcher II Laminated (1) — $50
Launcher IV P Pertanium Persimmon (3) — $75
Byron Nelson Persimmon Steel Shaft (4) — $150
10th Anniversary Persimmon (4) — $200
RC53 Persimmon (4) — $150
RC69 Persimmon (4) — $250
RC75 Persimmon (4) — $250
RC85 Persimmon (4) — $400
RC693 Persimmon (1) — $150
RC945 Persimmon (1) — $150
TA588 Persimmon (4) — $350
TC15 Persimmon (4) — $300
Tour Edition 485 Persimmon (4) — $250

Cobra:
Baffler Laminated (1) — $25
Baffler Woods Laminated (4) — $100
CWL Laminated (4) — $50
CWP Persimmon (4) — $50
Laminated Graphite Shaft (4) — $40
Laminated Steel Shaft(4) — $50
Low Profile Laminated (4) — $50
Greg Norman Series Persimmon Graphite Shaft (3) — $200
Greg Norman Series Persimmon Steel Shaft (3) — $150
Persimmon Graphite Shaft (4) — $75
Persimmon Steel Shaft (4) — $40
Special Driver Persimmon (1) — $10
Stock Laminated (3) — $25
TMP Persimmon (4) — $50
Tour Model Persimmon (4) — $50
TRD Persimmon Graphite Shaft (3) — $60
TRD Persimmon Steel Shaft (3) — $50

Confidence:
Confidence I Laminated (4) — $40

COMPANY	WOODS (SET NUMBERS)	VALUE

Confidence(cont.)**:**

Confidence II Laminated (4)	$40
Custom Laminated (4)	$40
Custom Persimmon (4)	$40
Gacha Laminated (1)	$40
Jerry Heard Laminated (4)	$40
K-81 Laminated (4)	$40
K-81 Persimmon (4)	$40
Lady Lite Laminated (4)	$40
Lady Lite IV Laminated (3)	$40
Lady Pro Laminated (4)	$40
Lady Stature Laminated (4)	$40
LP Laminated (4)	$40
Open Laminated (4)	$40
Original Laminated (4)	$40
Persimmon (4)	$40
Solid State Laminated (4)	$40
Stature State Laminated (4)	$40
Stature State Persimmon (4)	$40
Tour Plus Laminated (4)	$40
Visa CF Laminated (3)	$40
Visa EZ Laminated (4)	$40
Visa Laminated (4)	$40
Windsor Laminated (4)	$40

Daiwa:

Advisor Persimmon Graphite Shaft (3)	$75
Advisor Persimmon Steel Shaft (3)	$40
Chairman Persimmon (4)	$75
DB561 Persimmon Graphite Shaft (4)	$75
DB561 Persimmon Steel Shaft (4)	$75
DB591 Persimmon Graphite Shaft (4)	$75
DB591 Persimmon Steel Shaft (4)	$75
DB610 Persimmon Graphite Shaft (4)	$75
DB610 Persimmon Steel Shaft (4)	$75
DB621 Persimmon Graphite Shaft (3)	$75
DB621 Persimmon Steel Shaft (3)	$75
DB622 Persimmon Graphite Shaft (3)	$75
DB622 Persimmon Steel Shaft (3)	$75
Escala Persimmon Graphite Shaft (4)	$75
Escala Persimmon Steel Shaft (4)	$75
Hi-Trac Laminated (4)	$75
Monodyne Persimmon (4)	$75
Protege Laminated (4)	$75
Protege Persimmon (4)	$75
SRX3 Laminated (4)	$75

Dunlop:

7000 Laminated (4)	$30
901 Persimmon (3)	$30

Cleveland Classic Wood

Dunlop Maxfli DP 901 Wood

COMPANY WOODS (SET NUMBERS)	VALUE
Dunlop(cont.)**:**	
Seve Ballesteros Limited Edition Persimmon (3)	$600
Blue Max Laminated (4)	$50
Bob Charles Laminated (4)	$50
Explo-Flight Laminated (4)	$50
Fair Lady Laminated (4)	$50
First Flight By Toney Penna Persimmon (4)	$50
First Flight FTD Laminated (4)	$50
First Flight Golden Arrow Laminated (4)	$50
First Flight Mark IV Laminated (4)	$50
First Flight NALG Laminated (4)	$50
First Flight OSS FTD Laminated (4)	$50
First Flight PT-280 Laminated (4)	$50
FTD Laminated (4)	$50
Golden Eagle Laminated (4)	$50
Golden Lady Laminated (4)	$50
Greenmaster Laminated (4)	$50
Gundy Laminated (4)	$50
John Jacobs System 200 Laminated (3)	$50
John Jacobs System 200 Persimmon (3)	$50
John Jacobs System 300 Persimmon (3)	$50
John Jacobs System Laminated (3)	$50
Lady Golden Eagle Laminated (4)	$50
Lady Maxfli Woods Laminated (4)	$50
Lady Palmer Laminated (4)	$50
Max 357 Laminated (3)	$50
Max Lite Maple (3)	$50
Maxfli Australian Laminated (4)	$50
Maxfli Australian Ltd. Edition (4)	$50
Maxfli Australian Persimmon (4)	$50
Maxfli Australian Standard (4)	$50
Maxfli DP 901 (4)	$75
Maxfli Power Flange Laminated (3)	$50
Maxfli Pro Special Persimmon (4)	$50
Maxfli Woods Laminated (4)	$50
Maxpower Laminated (4)	$50
Susie Maxwell Berning Laminated (4)	$50
Susie Maxwell Laminated (4)	$50
Model 200 Laminated (4)	$50
Arnold Palmer Charger II Laminated (4)	$50
Arnold Palmer FTD Laminated (4)	$50
Arnold Palmer Personal Laminated (4)	$50
Arnold Palmer Signature Laminated (4)	$50
Arnold Palmer Tru-Matic Laminated (4)	$50
Toney Penna Persimmon (4)	$50
Power Flange Laminated (3)	$50
Pro Special Persimmon (3)	$50
Sterling FX-101 Laminated (4)	$50

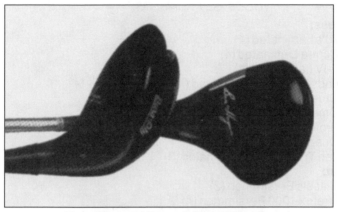

Ben Hogan Speed Slot Woods

Ben Hogan Wood

Ben Hogan Apex Wood

COMPANY	WOODS (SET NUMBERS)	VALUE
Faultless:		
	70's Laminated (4)	$50
	Centra Laminated (4)	$50
	F-IV Laminated (4)	$50
	Lady Faultless Laminated (4)	$50
	Omega Laminated (4)	$50
	Omega Tunnel Sole Laminated (4)	$50
	Professional Laminated (4)	$50
	Quantum Laminated (4)	$50
	Lee Trevino Staff Laminated (3)	$50
Foxbat:		
	Classic Persimmon (3)	$40
	Firefox 1000 Persimmon (4)	$40
	The Fox Persimmon (4)	$50
	FW-B Persimmon (4)	$40
	FW-BL Persimmon (4)	$40
	FW-C Persimmon (4)	$40
	FW-D Persimmon (4)	$40
	FW-E Persimmon (4)	$50
	FW-F Persimmon (4)	$50
	FX-15 Persimmon Graphite Shaft (3)	$50
	FX-15 Persimmon Steel Shaft (3)	$50
	G Model Persimmon (3)	$50
	Magic III Persimmon Graphite Shaft (3)	$50
	Magic III Persimmon Steel Shaft (3)	$50
	Tour Model Persimmon (4)	$50
Walter Hagen:		
	American Lady Laminated (4)	$50
	Hagen American Lady Laminated (4)	$50
	Hagen Ultra Flex Laminated (4)	$50
	The Haig Laminated (4)	$50
	Haig Ultra 66 Laminated (4)	$80
	Haig Ultra 75 Laminated (4)	$100
	Haig Ultra Persimmon (4)	$50
	Haig Ultra Persimmon Driver (1)	$50
	International Laminated (4)	$100
	Lady Onyx Laminated (4)	$50
	Lady Ultra 66 Laminated (4)	$50
	Matrix LP Laminated (4)	$50
	Matrix Regular Laminated (4)	$50
	Pro Consul 105 Laminated (3)	$195
	Ultradyne II Laminated (4)	$100
	Ultradyne III Laminated (4)	$100
Ben Hogan:		
	Apex 1070 Laminated (4)	$75
	Apex 5000 Laminated (4)	$75
	Apex 6010 Laminated (4)	$75
	Apex 7040 Laminated (4)	$75

COMPANY	WOODS (SET NUMBERS)	VALUE
Ben Hogan (cont.)**:**		
Apex 8040 Laminated (4)		$75
Apex 8080 Persimmon (4)		$75
Apex 9080 Persimmon (4)		$75
Apex Ladies 6050 Laminated (4)		$75
Apex Ladies 7050 Laminated (4)		$75
Apex Low Profile 5090 Laminated (4)		$75
Apex Low Profile 6090 Laminated (4)		$75
Apex Master 5080 Laminated (4)		$75
Apex Persimmon (3)		$150
Apex Personal Driver 5100 Laminated (1)		$75
Apex Speed Slot 5020 Laminated (4)		$75
Apex Speed Slot 5040 Laminated (4)		$75
Big Edge Driver Laminated (1)		$50
Commemorative 1978 Persimmon (4)		$375
Companion 1050 Laminated (4)		$50
Companion 2050 Laminated (4)		$50
Companion 3010 Laminated (4)		$50
Companion 4050 Laminated (4)		$50
Companion 8050 Laminated (4)		$50
Companion Laminated (3)		$50
Curved Sole 4010 Laminated (4)		$50
Curved Sole Laminated (4)		$50
Deepface Driver 509 Persimmon (1)		$60
Deepface Driver 609 Persimmon (1)		$60
Deepface Driver 706 Persimmon (1)		$60
Deepface Driver 1060 Persimmon (1)		$60
Deepface Driver 3060 Laminated (1)		$60
Deepface Driver 4060 Laminated (1)		$60
Deepface Driver 8060 Persimmon (1)		$60
Deepface Driver 9060 Persimmon (1)		$60
Director 1039 Laminated (4)		$50
Director 7030 Laminated (4)		$50
Director 8030 Laminated (4)		$50
Director 9030 Laminated (4)		$50
Director Laminated (4)		$50
Driver 2060 Persimmon (1)		$50
Duraply Combination 3060 Laminated (4)		$20
Duraply Combination 4030 Laminated (4)		$20
Edge Laminated Graphite Shaft (3)		$75
Edge Laminated Steel Shaft (3)		$75
Ladies Speed Slot 107 Laminated (4)		$75
Ladies Speed Slot 205 Laminated (4)		$75
Ladies Speed Slot 405 Laminated (4)		$75
Ladies Speed Slot 505 Laminated (4)		$75
Ladies Speed Slot 606 Laminated (4)		$75
Ladies Speed Slot 705 Special Laminated (4)		$75
Ladies Speed Slot 705 Standard Laminated (4)		$75

COMPANY	WOODS (SET NUMBERS)	VALUE

Ben Hogan (cont.):

Ladies Speed Slot 1051 Laminated (4)	$75
Ladies Speed Slot 2050 Laminated (4)	$75
Ladies Speed Slot 3050 Laminated (4)	$50
Ladies Speed Slot 4050 Laminated (4)	$50
Ladies Speed Slot 8050 Laminated (4)	$50
Ladies Speed Slot 9050 Laminated (1)	$50
Ladies Speed Slot Curved Sole 605 Laminated (4)	$75
Ladies Speed Slot Fashion Color 405 Laminated (4)	$75
Ladies Woods 5050 Laminated (4)	$50
Leader Laminated (3)	$50
Magnum Laminated (4)	$95
Medallion 1060 (4)	$50
Medallion Laminated (4)	$50
Model 306 Persimmon (4)	$50
Model 306W Laminated (4)	$50
Model 306W Persimmon (4)	$50
Persimmon 1080 (4)	$100
Personal 3070 Laminated (4)	$50
Personal 3170 Laminated (4)	$50
Personal 4179 Laminated (4)	$50
Personal 5070 Laminated (4)	$50
Personal 6000 Laminated (4)	$50
Personal 6040 Laminated (4)	$50
Personal 6060 Laminated (4)	$50
Personal 6070 Laminated (4)	$50
Personal 7000 Laminated (4)	$50
Personal 7060 Laminated (4)	$50
Personal 7070 Laminated (4)	$50
Personal 7090 Laminated (4)	$50
Personal Laminated (3)	$50
Personal Laminated 1955 (4)	$50
Personal Persimmon 1955 (4)	$250
Precision Persimmon (4)	$250
Princess Laminated (4)	$50
Producer 1019 Laminated (4)	$50
Producer 7010 Laminated (4)	$50
Producer 8010 Laminated (4)	$50
Producer 9019 Laminated (4)	$50
Producer Driver 8060 Laminated (1)	$25
Producer Driver 8070 Laminated (1)	$25
Producer Driver 8090 Laminated (1)	$25
Radial 3.5 Laminated (4)	$30
Radial Laminated (4)	$30
Saber 100 Persimmon 1957-58 (4)	$80
Saber 200 Laminated 1957-58 (4)	$30
Saber Laminated 1974-77 (4)	$30
Saber Laminated 1987-88 (1)	$30

COMPANY	WOODS (SET NUMBERS)	VALUE
Ben Hogan (cont.):		
	Special Sure Out Laminated (1)	$20
	Speed Slot 100 Persimmon (4)	$75
	Speed Slot 101 Persimmon (4)	$75
	Speed Slot 102 Laminated (4)	$50
	Speed Slot 103 Laminated (4)	$50
	Speed Slot 104 Laminated (4)	$50
	Speed Slot 105 Persimmon (4)	$75
	Speed Slot 200 Laminated (4)	$50
	Speed Slot 201 Persimmon (4)	$100
	Speed Slot 202 Laminated (4)	$50
	Speed Slot 203 Persimmon (4)	$100
	Speed Slot 204 Laminated (4)	$50
	Speed Slot 300 Persimmon (4)	$75
	Speed Slot 301 Persimmon (4)	$10
	Speed Slot 302 Laminated (4)	$50
	Speed Slot 303 Persimmon (4)	$100
	Speed Slot 304 Laminated (4)	$50
	Speed Slot 305 Laminated (4)	$50
	Speed Slot 400 Laminated (4)	$100
	Speed Slot 400 Persimmon (4)	$200
	Speed Slot 401 Laminated (4)	$50
	Speed Slot 402 Laminated (4)	$50
	Speed Slot 403 Persimmon (4)	$50
	Speed Slot 500 Laminated (4)	$100
	Speed Slot 501 Laminated (4)	$100
	Speed Slot 502 Laminated (4)	$100
	Speed Slot 601 Laminated (4)	$100
	Speed Slot 602 Laminated (4)	$100
	Speed Slot 702 Laminated (4)	$100
	Speed Slot 708 Laminated (4)	$100
	Speed Slot 709 Laminated (4)	$50
	Speed Slot 2030 Persimmon (4)	$150
	Speed Slot 2070 Persimmon (4)	$150
	Speed Slot 5030 Laminated (4)	$100
	Speed Slot 8030 Laminated (4)	$100
	Speed Slot 8100 Laminated (4)	$50
	Speed Slot Curved Sole 404 Laminated (4)	$75
	Speed Slot Curved Sole 504 Laminated (4)	$75
	Speed Slot Curved Sole 603 Laminated (4)	$75
	Speed Slot Curved Sole 604 Laminated (4)	$75
	Speed Slot Curved Sole 703 Laminated (4)	$75
	Speed Slot Curved Sole 704 Laminated (4)	$75
	Speed Slot Curved Sole 1040 Laminated (4)	$75
	Speed Slot Curved Sole 2020 Laminated (4)	$75
	Speed Slot Curved Sole 2040 Laminated (4)	$75
	Speed Slot Curved Sole 4040 Laminated (4)	$75
	Speed Slot Curved Sole 8040 Laminated (4)	$75

COMPANY	WOODS (SET NUMBERS)	VALUE
Ben Hogan (cont.):		
	Speed Slot Curved Sole 9040 Laminated (4)	$75
	Speed Slot Deep Face 500 Persimmon (4)	$200
	Speed Slot Deep Face 600 Persimmon (4)	$200
	Speed Slot Deep Faced Driver 2060 Persimmon (1)	$100
	Speed Slot Driver DFD Persimmon (1)	$100
	Speed Slot Laminated (4)	$50
	Speed Slot Low Profile 1091 Laminated (4)	$75
	Speed Slot Low Profile 2090 Laminated (4)	$75
	Speed Slot Low Profile 3090 Laminated (4)	$75
	Speed Slot Low Profile 4090 Laminated (4)	$75
	Speed Slot Low Profile 8090 Laminated (4)	$75
	Speed Slot Low Profile 9090 Laminated (4)	$75
	Speed Slot Persimmon (4)	$175
	Speed Slot Personal 507 Persimmon (4)	$100
	Speed Slot Personal 607 Persimmon (4)	$100
	Speed Slot Personal 707 Persimmon (4)	$100
	Speed Slot Personal 1070 Persimmon (4)	$100
	Speed Slot Personal 2030 Persimmon (4)	$100
	Speed Slot Personal 2030 Persimmon (4)	$100
	Speed Slot Personal 2070 Persimmon (4)	$100
	Speed Slot Personal 3070 Persimmon (4)	$100
	Speed Slot Personal 4070 Persimmon (4)	$100
	Speed Slot Personal 8070 Persimmon (4)	$100
	Speed Slot Personal 9070 Persimmon (4)	$100
	Speed Slot Personal Persimmon (4)	$150
	Speed Slot Thin 1100 Laminated (4)	$40
	Speed Slot Thin 2100 Laminated (4)	$40
	Speed Slot Thin 9100 Laminated (4)	$40
	Speed Slot True Set 1080 Laminated (4)	$50
	Speed Slot True Set Laminated (4)	$50
	Tour Woods 2030 Persimmon (4)	$150
	Tour Woods 3030 Persimmon (4)	$150
	Tour Woods 4030 Persimmon (4)	$150
	Tour Woods Persimmon (4)	$150
	Vector Light Laminated (4)	$50
Louisville Golf:		
	Authentic 50's Persimmon	$25
	Classic 50's Air Dried Persimmon (4)	$125
	Classic 50's Laminated (4)	$50
	Classic 50's Persimmon (3)	$75
	Custom Classic Persimmon (4)	$75
	Dogwood Series (1)	$40
	Level Four Laminated (4)	$50
	Level Four Persimmon (4)	$75
	Natural Lite Laminated (4)	$30
	Natural Lite Persimmon (4)	$50
	Niblick Laminated (1)	$20

MacGregor Tommy Armour
Wood

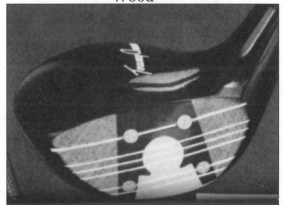

MacGregor Tommy Armour Tourney
Wood

MacGregor Jimmy Demaret

COMPANY WOODS (SET NUMBERS)	VALUE
Louisville Golf(cont.):	
Niblick Persimmon (1)	$20
Personal Laminated (3)	$25
Personal Persimmon (3)	$50
Progressive (3)	$25
Select NDP Persimmon (4)	$75
Lynx:	
10 Aluminum-Laminated Limited Edition (4)	$100
Chiseler Laminated (1)	$20
Classic Persimmon Graphite Shaft (3)	$50
Classic Persimmon Steel Shaft (3)	$50
CR Laminated (4)	$30
Elegance Aluminum Laminated (4)	$50
Ladies Chiseler Laminated (1)	$20
Liberty Laminated (4)	$50
Lynx Laminated Plastic (4)	$50
Master Laminated Plastic (4)	$50
Pecan Laminated (4)	$50
Persimmon Jumbo Classic (1)	$50
Precision Lite Laminated (4)	$40
Predator Plus Aluminum Laminated (4)	$60
Predator Plus Claw Aluminum Laminated (1)	$25
Pro Wood Laminated (4)	$50
Prowler Laminated (4)	$50
Seville Persimmon (4)	$50
Tigress Elegance Aluminum Laminated	$50
Tigress Laminated (4)	$50
USA Persimmon (4)	$50
MacGregor:	
300 Laminated Uniblock (4)	$50
693 Persimmon (4)	$800
693W Driver Persimmon (1)	$500
945 Persimmon (4)	$750
945T Driver Persimmon (1)	$550
Tommy Armour 108T Persimmon Driver (1)	$700
Tommy Armour 403 Persimmon (4)	$400
Tommy Armour 405 Persimmon (4)	$400
Tommy Armour 4367 Persimmon (4)	$300
Tommy Armour 4368 Persimmon (4)	$300
Tommy Armour 4371 Persimmon (4)	$450
Tommy Armour 69 Speedwood Persimmon (4)	$350
Tommy Armour 915W Persimmon (4)	$250
Tommy Armour 925KW Persimmon (4)	$425
Tommy Armour 925W Persimmon (4)	$375
Tommy Armour 945KW Persimmon (4)	$250
Tommy Armour 945W Persimmon (4)	$900
Tommy Armour A1W Persimmon (4)	$325
Tommy Armour A2W Persimmon (4)	$250

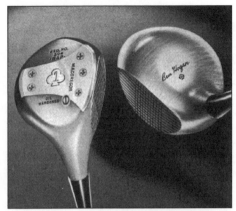

MacGregor Ben Hogan BAP Wood

MacGregor Jack Nicklaus
VIP Wood

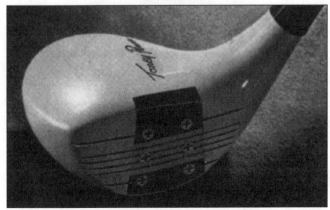

MacGregor Toney Penna Wood

COMPANY	WOODS (SET NUMBERS)	VALUE
MacGregor(cont.):		
	Tommy Armour AT1FW Persimmon (4)	$450
	Tommy Armour AT1W Persimmon (4)	$450
	Tommy Armour AT1WH Persimmon (4)	$450
	Tommy Armour AT2FW Persimmon (4)	$325
	Tommy Armour AT2W Persimmon (4)	$325
	Tommy Armour AT2WH Persimmon (4)	$325
	Tommy Armour AT3W Persimmon (4)	$125
	Tommy Armour AT3WH Persimmon (4)	$125
	Tommy Armour Ben Hogan Model 4353 Persimmon (4)	$850
	Tommy Armour Ben Hogan Model 4378 Persimmon (4)	$850
	Tommy Armour Ben Hogan Model 4393 Persimmon (4)	$850
	Tommy Armour Demaret Model 2347 Persimmon (4)	$400
	Tommy Armour Demaret Model 4376 Persimmon (4)	$350
	Tommy Armour Demaret Model 4377 Persimmon (4)	$400
	Tommy Armour Ed Dudley Persimmon (4)	$325
	Tommy Armour Iron Master 234 Persimmon (4)	$100
	Tommy Armour Iron Master 234W Persimmon (4)	$100
	Tommy Armour Iron Master 235 Persimmon (4)	$100
	Tommy Armour Iron Master Persimmon (4)	$100
	Tommy Armour Jumbo Persimmon Driver (1)	$700
	Tommy Armour Model 202 Persimmon (4)	$300
	Tommy Armour Model 65 Persimmon (4)	$400
	Tommy Armour Professional Persimmon (4)	$400
	Tommy Armour Silver Scot A1W Persimmon (4)	$325
	Tommy Armour Silver Scot A1WH Persimmon (4)	$325
	Tommy Armour Silver Scot A2W Persimmon (4)	$250
	Tommy Armour Silver Scot A2WH Persimmon (4)	$250
	Tommy Armour Silver Scot Jumbo Persimmon Driver (1)	$700
	Tommy Armour Silver Scot Persimmon (4)	$300
	Tommy Armour Silver Scot Tourney T693 Persimmon (4)	$100
	Tommy Armour Silver Scot Tourney T915 Persimmon (4)	$300
	Tommy Armour SS1KW Persimmon (4)	$600
	Tommy Armour SS1TW Eye-O-Matic 60 Persimmon (4)	$450
	Tommy Armour SS1TW Persimmon (4)	$400
	Tommy Armour SS1W Eye-O-Matic 60 Persimmon (4)	$450
	Tommy Armour SS1W Persimmon (4)	$600
	Tommy Armour SS2KW Persimmon (4)	$400
	Tommy Armour SS2TW Eye-O-Matic 60 Persimmon (4)	$450
	Tommy Armour SS2TW Persimmon (4)	$400
	Tommy Armour SS2W Eye-O-Matic 60 Persimmon (4)	$450
	Tommy Armour SS2W Persimmon (4)	$400
	Tommy Armour TDA-40 4302 Persimmon (4)	$275
	Tommy Armour TDA-41 4151 Persimmon (4)	$275
	Tommy Armour Toney Penna Model Persimmon (4)	$550
	Tommy Armour Tourney 4151 Persimmon (4)	$300
	Tommy Armour Tourney 4311 Persimmon (4)	$300
	Tommy Armour Tourney 4371 Persimmon (4)	$300

MacGregor Wood

MacGregor Tourney
Velocitized Wood

MacGregor MT Tourney Wood

COMPANY WOODS (SET NUMBERS)	VALUE
MacGregor(cont.):	
Tommy Armour Tourney 4375 Persimmon (4)	$300
Tommy Armour Tourney 653 Persimmon (4)	$450
Tommy Armour Tourney 653HK Persimmon (4)	$450
Tommy Armour Tourney 653KW Persimmon (4)	$450
Tommy Armour Tourney 653T Persimmon (4)	$450
Tommy Armour Tourney 653W Persimmon (4)	$450
Tommy Armour Tourney 653WH Persimmon (4)	$450
Tommy Armour Tourney 655 Persimmon (4)	$450
Tommy Armour Tourney 693	
Jumbo Persimmon Driver (1)	$1,200
Tommy Armour Tourney 693 Persimmon (4)	$850
Tommy Armour Tourney 693T Persimmon (4)	$850
Tommy Armour Tourney 695 Persimmon (4)	$850
Tommy Armour Tourney 883T Persimmon (4)	$600
Tommy Armour Tourney 945TW Persimmon (4)	$450
Tommy Armour Tourney 945W Persimmon (4)	$1,000
Tommy Armour Tourney P59W Persimmon (4)	$400
Herman Barron Persimmon (4)	$400
George Bayer Driver B1W Persimmon (1)	$150
George Bayer Driver BW1WH Persimmon (1)	$550
George Bayer Driver DX300KW Persimmon (1)	$550
George Bayer Driver DX300W Persimmon (1)	$550
George Bayer Driver GB1KW Persimmon (1)	$550
George Bayer Driver GB1W Persimmon (1)	$575
Armour Black Scott 244 Persimmon (4)	$100
CDX Tourney CDX2W Persimmon (4)	$100
CDX Tourney CDX2WH Persimmon (4)	$100
CG1800 Laminated Graphite (3)	$50
CG1800 Laminated Steel (3)	$50
Classic Driver 693W Persimmon (1)	$100
Classic Reproduction 3 Wood 945 Persimmon	$50
Classic Reproduction 3 Wood M85 Persimmon	$50
Classic Reproduction 3 Wood PT35 Persimmon	$50
Classic Reproduction Driver 945 Persimmon	$75
Classic Reproduction Driver M85 Persimmon	$75
Classic Reproduction Driver MT Aluminum Persimmon	$50
Classic Reproduction Driver MT Keysight Persimmon	$50
Classic Reproduction Driver PT35 Persimmon	$50
Classic Woods 693 Persimmon (4)	$150
Classic Woods Eye-O-Matic Persimmon (4)	$125
Classic Woods M40 Persimmon (4)	$125
Classic Woods M65 Persimmon (4)	$125
Classic Woods M85 Persimmon (4)	$150
Constant T1W Cycolac (4)	$50
Constant T1WH Cycolac (4)	$50
Constant T2W Cycolac (4)	$50
Constant TW2H Cycolac (4)	$50

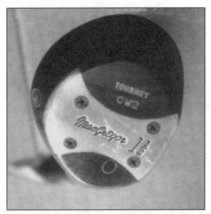

MacGregor Tourney

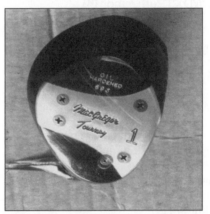

MacGregor Tourney Wood

MacGregor Eye-O-Matic 60

COMPANY	WOODS (SET NUMBERS)	VALUE

MacGregor(cont.):

Jimmy Demaret 1B32 Persimmon (4)	$400
Jimmy Demaret Master 352CW Persimmon (4)	$250
Jimmy Demaret Master 3552 Persimmon (4)	$250
Jimmy Demaret Pace Maker 382W Persimmon (4)	$250
Jimmy Demaret Pace Maker 3882 Persimmon (4)	$250
Jimmy Demaret Par Wind Persimmon (4)	$400
DX Laminated (4)	$50
DX Tourney WCDX2 Persimmon (4)	$100
DX Tourney WCDX2H Persimmon (4)	$100
DX Tourney WDX1 Persimmon (4)	$100
DX Tourney WDX1H Persimmon (4)	$100
DX Tourney WDX2 Persimmon (4)	$100
DX Tourney WDX2H Persimmon (4)	$100
DX Tourney WDX3 Persimmon (4)	$100
DX Tourney WDX3H Persimmon (4)	$100
DX Tourney WDX9H Persimmon (4)	$100
DX1 Tourney DX1W Persimmon (4)	$100
DX1 Tourney DX1W Persimmon (4)	$100
DX1 Tourney DX1WH Persimmon (4)	$100
DX2 Tourney DX2W Persimmon (4)	$100
DX2 Tourney DX2WT Persimmon (4)	$100
DX3 Persimmon (4)	$100
DX5 Persimmon (4)	$100
DX9 Tourney DX9WH Persimmon (4)	$100
DXLW Tourney DXLWH (4)	$100
DXW1 Persimmon (4)	$100
DXW1H Persimmon (4)	$100
DXW2 Persimmon (4)	$100
DXW2H Persimmon (4)	$100
DXW9H Persimmon (4)	$100
Finesse Persimmon (4)	$50
First Lady 734 Persimmon (4)	$50
Five Wood A1W Persimmon (1)	$50
Five Wood A1WH Persimmon (1)	$50
Five Wood Byron Nelson Persimmon (1)	$50
Five Wood Louise Suggs Persimmon (1)	$75
Five Wood M05 Persimmon (1)	$150
Five Wood M1W Persimmon (1)	$50
Five Wood M1WH Persimmon (1)	$50
Five Wood M9W Persimmon (1)	$50
Five Wood M9WH Persimmon (1)	$50
Five Wood Nelson Tourney Persimmon (1)	$50
Five Wood R1W Persimmon (1)	$50
Five Wood R1WH Persimmon (1)	$50
Five Wood Suggs Tourney Persimmon (1)	$75
Five Wood T1W Persimmon (1)	$50
Five Wood T1WH Persimmon (1)	$50

MacGregor Super Eye-O-Matic
Tourney Wood

COMPANY	WOODS (SET NUMBERS)	VALUE
MacGregor(cont.):		
	Hi Loft Wood Laminated (1)	$50
	Ben Hogan 1425 Persimmon (4)	$400
	Ben Hogan 693 Persimmon (4)	$1,400
	Ben Hogan Bantam 2432C Persimmon (4)	$325
	Ben Hogan BAP 1452 Persimmon (4)	$425
	Ben Hogan BAP 2312 Persimmon (4)	$325
	Ben Hogan Par Master 1552 Laminated (4)	$325
	Ben Hogan Par Master 1612 Laminated (4)	$325
	Ben Hogan Pro Model Persimmon (4)	$600
	Iron Master Woods Persimmon (4)	$100
	Jumbo Classic - M09T Persimmon	$250
	Ladies Tourney Laminated (4)	$50
	Lady DX WLDX3 Persimmon (4)	$100
	Lady DX WLDX3H Persimmon (4)	$100
	Lady DX WLDX4 Persimmon (4)	$100
	Lady DX WLDX4H Persimmon (4)	$100
	Lady Finesse Laminated (3)	$50
	Lady MTWL3H Persimmon (4)	$50
	Lady MTWL4H Persimmon (4)	$50
	Lady Tourney Persimmon (3)	$50
	Long Jacks Laminated Graphite Shaft (3)	$100
	Lord Byron 231W Persimmon (4)	$150
	Lord Byron 232W Persimmon (4)	$150
	M09T Driver Persimmon (1)	$550
	M65 Driver Persimmon (1)	$100
	M65T Driver Persimmon (1)	$150
	M65TW Driver Persimmon (1)	$150
	M85T Driver Persimmon (1)	$600
	M88 Persimmon (3) Graphite	$100
	M88 Persimmon (3) Steel	$50

COMPANY	WOODS (SET NUMBERS)	VALUE
MacGregor(cont.)**:**		
	MCX Laminated (4)	$50
	MCX-V Laminated (4)	$50
	MG Lite Laminated (4)	$50
	MT C2W Persimmon (4)	$50
	MT C2WH Persimmon (4)	$50
	MT Compact Laminated (4)	$50
	MT CW2 Persimmon (4)	$50
	MT CW2H Persimmon (4)	$50
	MT Jumbo Driver Laminated (1)	$50
	MT Laminated TW1A Laminated (4)	$50
	MT Laminated TW1AH Laminated (4)	$50
	MT Laminated TW2A Laminated (4)	$50
	MT Laminated TW2AH Laminated (4)	$50
	MT Laminated TW3AH Laminated (4)	$50
	MT M1TW Persimmon (4)	$125
	MT M1TWH Persimmon (4)	$125
	MT M1W Persimmon (4)	$125
	MT M1WH Persimmon (4)	$125
	MT M2TW Persimmon (4)	$125
	MT M2W Persimmon (4)	$125
	MT M2WH Persimmon (4)	$125
	MT M3TW Persimmon (4)	$50
	MT M3TWH Persimmon (4)	$50
	MT M3W Persimmon (4)	$50
	MT M3WH Persimmon (4)	$50
	MT M5TW Persimmon (4)	$125
	MT M5W Persimmon (4)	$125
	MT M9TW Persimmon (4)	$125
	MT M9TWH Persimmon (4)	$125
	MT M9W Persimmon (4)	$125
	MT M9WH Persimmon (4)	$125
	MT Regular Laminated (4)	$50
	MT Super Eye-O-Matic M65KW Persimmon (4)	$125
	MT Super Eye-O-Matic M65W Persimmon (4)	$125
	MT Super Eye-O-Matic M75KW Persimmon (4)	$150
	MT Super Eye-O-Matic M75W Persimmon (4)	$150
	MT Super Eye-O-Matic M80KW Persimmon (4)	$125
	MT Super Eye-O-Matic M80W Persimmon (4)	$125
	MT Super Eye-O-Matic M85KW Persimmon (4)	$250
	MT Super Eye-O-Matic M85W Persimmon (4)	$250
	MT Tee Sole Laminated (4)	$50
	MT Tourney Five Wood Persimmon (1)	$25
	MT Tourney M19W Persimmon (4)	$300
	MT Tourney M19WH Persimmon (4)	$300
	MT Tourney M35W Persimmon (4)	$300
	MT Tourney MT1W Persimmon (4)	$300
	MT Tourney MT1WH Persimmon (4)	$300

COMPANY WOODS (SET NUMBERS)	VALUE
MacGregor(cont.):	
MT Tourney MT2W Persimmon (4)	$300
MT Tourney MT2WH Persimmon (4)	$300
MT Tourney MT3W Persimmon (4)	$300
MT Tourney MT3WH Persimmon (4)	$300
MT Tourney Persimmon (4)	$75
MT Tourney RT2W Persimmon (4)	$300
MT Tourney RT2WH Persimmon (4)	$300
MT TW1 Persimmon (4)	$125
MT TW1H Persimmon (4)	$125
MT TW2 Persimmon (4)	$125
MT TW2H Persimmon (4)	$125
MT TW9H Persimmon (4)	$125
MT WMT1 Persimmon (4)	$250
MT WMT1H Persimmon (4)	$250
MT WMT2 Persimmon (4)	$250
MT WMT2H Persimmon (4)	$250
MT Woods Persimmon (4)	$50
MT1W Persimmon (4)	$125
MT1WH Persimmon (4)	$125
MT2W Persimmon (4)	$125
MT2WH Persimmon (4)	$125
MTW1 Persimmon (4)	$125
MTW1H Persimmon (4)	$125
MTW2 Persimmon (4)	$125
MTW2H Persimmon (4)	$125
MTW3H Persimmon (4)	$125
Byron Nelson 230W Persimmon (4)	$275
Byron Nelson 231W Persimmon (4)	$275
Byron Nelson 232W Persimmon (4)	$275
Byron Nelson 240W Persimmon (4)	$375
Byron Nelson 241W Persimmon (4)	$375
Byron Nelson 242W Persimmon (4)	$275
Byron Nelson 255W Persimmon (4)	$325
Byron Nelson 259W Persimmon (4)	$400
Byron Nelson 269W Persimmon (4)	$325
Byron Nelson 403W Persimmon (4)	$400
Byron Nelson 405W Persimmon (4)	$400
Byron Nelson 563 Persimmon (4)	$300
Byron Nelson 663 Persimmon (4)	$400
Byron Nelson 663BP Persimmon (4)	$400
Byron Nelson 693 Persimmon (4)	$900
Byron Nelson Open Champion Persimmon (4)	$350
Byron Nelson Professional Model Persimmon (4)	$400
Byron Nelson Texan Persimmon (4)	$450
Nicklaus Heritage Laminated (4)	$50
Nicklaus Muirfield Persimmon (4)	$200
Nicklaus VIP Laminated (4)	$100

COMPANY WOODS (SET NUMBERS)	VALUE
MacGregor(cont.):	
Nicklaus VIP Persimmon (4)	$300
1982 Jack Nicklaus Limited Edition Woods (4)	$1,000
Jack Nicklaus 1988 Commemorative 3 Wood Persimmon (1)	$125
Jack Nicklaus 1988 Commemorative Driver Persimmon (1)	$175
Jack Nicklaus 271 Driver Persimmon (1)	$200
Jack Nicklaus Muirfield 20th Graphite (3)	$50
Jack Nicklaus Muirfield 20th Steel (3)	$75
Toney Penna 106T Persimmon (4)	$700
Toney Penna 403 Persimmon (4)	$425
Toney Penna 403PT Persimmon (4)	$425
Toney Penna 693 Persimmon (4)	$800
Toney Penna 945 Persimmon (4)	$1,300
Toney Penna 4377 Persimmon (4)	$450
Toney Penna GB1TW Persimmon (1)	$175
Toney Penna GB1W Persimmon (1)	$175
Toney Penna P1W Persimmon (4)	$200
Toney Penna P40KW Persimmon (4)	$350
Toney Penna P40W Persimmon (4)	$350
Toney Penna P83KW Persimmon (4)	$175
Toney Penna P83TW Persimmon (4)	$175
Toney Penna P83W Persimmon (4)	$425
Toney Penna P403PT Persimmon (4)	$1,000
Toney Penna Rocker Sole Woods R1W Persimmon (4)	$200
Toney Penna Rocker Sole Woods R1WH Persimmon (4)	$200
Toney Penna Rocker Sole Woods R2W Persimmon (4)	$200
Toney Penna Rocker Sole Woods R2WH Persimmon (4)	$200
Toney Penna RS2W Persimmon (4)	$200
Toney Penna RS2WH Persimmon (4)	$200
Toney Penna TP Persimmon (4)	$425
Toney Penna TP1KW Persimmon (4)	$450
Toney Penna TP1TW Persimmon (4)	$450
Toney Penna TP1W Persimmon (4)	$450
Toney Penna TPS Persimmon (4)	$400
Toney Penna TPT Persimmon (4)	$425
Toney Penna VIP Persimmon (4)	$550
Toney Penna WW1 Persimmon White Finish (4)	$6,000
Promaster 726W Persimmon (4)	$100
Six Wood M06 Persimmon (1)	$200
Louise Suggs 104L Five Wood Persimmon (1)	$200
Louise Suggs 615 Persimmon (4)	$200
Louise Suggs 642 Persimmon (4)	$200
Louise Suggs 712W Persimmon (4)	$200
Louise Suggs 720W Persimmon (4)	$200
Louise Suggs 721W Persimmon (4)	$200
Louise Suggs 722W Persimmon (4)	$200

COMPANY	WOODS (SET NUMBERS)	VALUE
MacGregor(cont.):		
	Louise Suggs Empress 744 Persimmon (4)	$200
	Louise Suggs Empress LS3W Eye-O-Matic 60 Persimmon (4)	$300
	Louise Suggs Empress LS3W Persimmon (4)	$300
	Louise Suggs Empress LS4W Eye-O-Matic 60 Persimmon (4)	$300
	Louise Suggs First Lady 642 Persimmon (4)	$300
	Louise Suggs First Lady 645 Persimmon (4)	$300
	Louise Suggs First Lady 710W Persimmon (4)	$250
	Louise Suggs First Lady 711W Persimmon (4)	$250
	Louise Suggs First Lady 712W Persimmon (4)	$250
	Louise Suggs First Lady 735 Persimmon (4)	$250
	Louise Suggs Tourney 712 Persimmon (4)	$300
	Louise Suggs Tourney 712T Persimmon (4)	$300
	Louise Suggs Tourney 780KW Persimmon (4)	$300
	Louise Suggs Tourney 780W Persimmon (4)	$300
	Louise Suggs Tourney 782 Persimmon (4)	$250
	Louise Suggs Tourney S3TFW Persimmon (4)	$250
	Louise Suggs Tourney S3TW Persimmon (4)	$250
	Louise Suggs Tourney S3TWH Persimmon (4)	$250
	Louise Suggs Tourney S3W Persimmon (4)	$250
	Louise Suggs Tourney S3WH Persimmon (4)	$250
	Louise Suggs Tourney S4TW Persimmon (4)	$250
	Louise Suggs Tourney S4TWH Persimmon (4)	$250
	Louise Suggs Tourney S4W Persimmon (4)	$250
	Louise Suggs Tourney S4WH Persimmon (4)	$250
	Louise Suggs Tourney ST3W Persimmon (4)	$250
	Louise Suggs Tourney ST3WH Persimmon (4)	$250
	Louise Suggs Tourney ST4W Persimmon (4)	$250
	Louise Suggs Tourney ST4WH Persimmon (4)	$250
	Super Eye-O-Matic Persimmon (4)	$200
	Super Eye-O-Matic Tourney B75KW Persimmon (4)	$250
	Super Eye-O-Matic Tourney B75W Persimmon (4)	$250
	Super Eye-O-Matic Tourney M45KW Persimmon (4)	$300
	Super Eye-O-Matic Tourney M45W Persimmon (4)	$300
	Super Eye-O-Matic Tourney M55KW Persimmon (4)	$200
	Super Eye-O-Matic Tourney M55W Persimmon (4)	$200
	Super Eye-O-Matic Tourney M60KW Persimmon (4)	$250
	Super Eye-O-Matic Tourney M60W Persimmon (4)	$250
	Super Eye-O-Matic Tourney M65KW Persimmon (4)	$250
	Super Eye-O-Matic Tourney M65W Persimmon (4)	$250
	Super Eye-O-Matic Tourney M85KW Persimmon (4)	$900
	Super Eye-O-Matic Tourney M85W Persimmon (4)	$900
	Super Eye-O-Matic Tourney R75KW Persimmon (4)	$300
	Super Eye-O-Matic Tourney R75W Persimmon (4)	$300
	Synchrolite Persimmon (4)	$100
	Tourney BT2KW Persimmon (4)	$200

COMPANY	WOODS (SET NUMBERS)	VALUE
MacGregor(cont.)**:**		
Tourney BT2W Persimmon (4)		$200
Tourney Custom Laminated (4)		$350
Tourney M06B Persimmon Six Wood (1)		$200
Tourney M06M Persimmon Six Wood (1)		$200
Tourney M09 Jumbo Persimmon Driver (1)		$375
Tourney M09 Persimmon Driver (1)		$700
Tourney M09T Persimmon Driver (1)		$700
Tourney M23 Persimmon (4)		$375
Tourney M23T Persimmon (4)		$375
Tourney M33 Persimmon (4)		$450
Tourney M33T Persimmon (4)		$450
Tourney M35 Persimmon (4)		$450
Tourney M35T Persimmon (4)		$450
Tourney M43 Persimmon (4)		$600
Tourney M43T Persimmon (4)		$600
Tourney M45W Eye-O-Matic Persimmon (4)		$350
Tourney M55W Eye-O-Matic Persimmon (4)		$400
Tourney M65W Eye-O-Matic Persimmon (4)		$425
Tourney M70TW Eye-O-Matic Persimmon (4)		$475
Tourney M70W Eye-O-Matic Persimmon (4)		$475
Tourney M75TW Eye-O-Matic Persimmon (4)		$700
Tourney M75W Eye-O-Matic Persimmon (4)		$700
Tourney M80TW Eye-O-Matic Persimmon (4)		$650
Tourney M80W Eye-O-Matic Persimmon (4)		$650
Tourney M85TW Eye-O-Matic Persimmon (4)		$900
Tourney M85W Eye-O-Matic Persimmon (4)		$900
Tourney Master Persimmon (4)		$150
Tourney MT1FW Persimmon (4)		$300
Tourney MT1W Persimmon (4)		$300
Tourney MT2FW Persimmon (4)		$200
Tourney MT2W Persimmon (4)		$350
Tourney MT3FW Persimmon (4)		$200
Tourney MT3W Persimmon (4)		$200
Tourney MT4FW Persimmon (4)		$250
Tourney MT4W Persimmon (4)		$200
Tourney MT19W Persimmon (4)		$200
Tourney MT35W Persimmon (4)		$200
Tourney P25W Persimmon (4)		$250
Tourney Persimmon (4)		$100
Tourney PT1KW Persimmon (4)		$250
Tourney PT1TW Eye-O-Matic 60 Persimmon (4)		$400
Tourney PT1W Eye-O-Matic 60 Persimmon (4)		$400
Tourney PT1W Persimmon (4)		$250
Tourney PT2TW Eye-O-Matic 60 Persimmon (4)		$375
Tourney PT2W Eye-O-Matic 60 Persimmon (4)		$375
Tourney PT3W Eye-O-Matic 60 Persimmon (4)		$350
Tourney PT3W Persimmon (4)		$250

COMPANY WOODS (SET NUMBERS)	VALUE
MacGregor(cont.)**:**	
Tourney PT4W Eye-O-Matic 60 Persimmon (4)	$450
Tourney PT4W Persimmon (4)	$250
Tourney PT25KW Persimmon (4)	$250
Tourney PT25W Eye-O-Matic 60 Persimmon (4)	$375
Tourney PT35W Eye-O-Matic 60 Persimmon (4)	$350
Tourney PT35W Persimmon (4)	$250
Tourney RT2FW Eye-O-Matic 60 Persimmon (4)	$375
Tourney RT2KW Persimmon (4)	$250
Tourney RT2TW Eye-O-Matic 60 Persimmon (4)	$375
Tourney RT2W Eye-O-Matic 60 Persimmon (4)	$375
Tourney RT2W Persimmon (4)	$250
Tourney Velocitized BT2TW Persimmon (4)	$400
Tourney Velocitized BT2W Persimmon (4)	$400
Tourney Velocitized PT1TW Persimmon (4)	$550
Tourney Velocitized PT1W Persimmon (4)	$550
Tourney Velocitized PT3W Persimmon (4)	$375
Tourney Velocitized PT4W Persimmon (4)	$350
Tourney Velocitized PT25W Persimmon (4)	$450
Tourney Velocitized PT35W Persimmon (4)	$375
Tourney Velocitized RT2TW Persimmon (4)	$400
Tourney Velocitized RT2W Persimmon (4)	$400
VIP By Nicklaus Laminated (4)	$100
VIP By Nicklaus Persimmon (4)	$300
VIP Laminated (4)	$100
VIP Persimmon (4)	$250
W25MT Persimmon (4)	$125
Winged MT Persimmon (4)	$150
Winged MT Velocitized Persimmon (4)	$150
Maruman:	
Conductor Pro Persimmon (1)	$75
Conductor Pro Persimmon Graphite Shaft (1)	$100
Merit:	
Tour International Persimmon (3)	$50
Mizuno:	
Altron Laminated (3)	$40
Ariel Persimmon (4)	$50
Champion Flag Maple (4)	$50
Cimmarron Persimmon (4)	$150
Grand Monarch Persimmon (4)	$50
MS-2 Persimmon (4)	$100
MS-4 Persimmon (4)	$100
MS-5 Persimmon (4)	$100
MS-7 Persimmon (4)	$100
MS-8 Persimmon Graphite Shaft (3)	$150
MS-8 Persimmon Steel Shaft (4)	$100
MS-194 Persimmon (3)	$75
Pro Original Persimmon (4)	$150

COMPANY WOODS (SET NUMBERS)	VALUE
Mizuno (cont.)**:**	
Pro Persimmon (4)	$150
Silver Cup Laminated (3)	$50
Silver Cup Maple (4)	$50
SPL Persimmon (4)	$75
Wings Laminated (3)	$50
Northwestern:	
241 Tour Model Persimmon (1)	$25
965 Laminated (4)	$40
965 Limited Edition Persimmon (3)	$50
Betty Alex Persimmon (4)	$50
Autograph Laminated (4)	$50
Blue Ash Ash (3)	$50
Bombardier Driver Persimmon (1)	$50
Competitor Laminated (4)	$50
Pete Cooper Autograph Persimmon (4)	$50
Pete Cooper Championship Persimmon (4)	$50
Pete Cooper Signature Laminated (4)	$50
Bruce Crampton MP+ (4)	$50
Custom Power Kick Laminated (3)	$50
Stan Dudas Championship Persimmon (4)	$50
Stan Dudas Deluxe Laminated (4)	$50
Marty Furgol Personal Laminated (4)	$50
Marty Furgol Signature Laminated (4)	$50
Gold Signature Laminated (3)	$50
Hagey Matched Woods Persimmon (4)	$50
Bob Hagey Autograph Persimmon (4)	$50
Bob Hagey Deluxe Persimmon (4)	$50
Bob Hagey Deluxe Registered Persimmon (4)	$50
Bob Hagey Registered Persimmon (4)	$50
Chandler Harper Esquire Laminated (4)	$50
Chandler Harper Pro Line Laminated (4)	$50
Chandler Harper Signature Laminated (4)	$50
Chandler Harper Tournament Laminated (4)	$50
Chandler Harper Virginian Laminated (4)	$50
Hazel Hixon Autograph Persimmon (4)	$50
Hazel Hixon Custom Made Persimmon (4)	$50
Hazel Hixon Deluxe Persimmon (4)	$50
Hazel Hixon Deluxe Registered Persimmon (4)	$50
Hazel Hixon Registered Persimmon (4)	$50
Herman Kaiser Presidential Laminated (4)	$50
Betty Jameson Laminated (3)	$50
Betty Jameson Gold Signature Laminated (4)	$50
Betty Jameson Pro Registered Laminated (4)	$50
Betty Jameson Registered Laminated (3)	$50
Betty Jameson Utility Wood Laminated (1)	$50
Ladies Tournament Laminated (4)	$50
Lady Nelson Pro Built Persimmon (4)	$50

COMPANY	WOODS (SET NUMBERS)	VALUE
Northwestern(cont.)**:**		
	Lady Nelson Signature Laminated (4)	$50
	Lady Nelson Tournament Laminated (4)	$50
	Lady Saga Laminated (4)	$50
	Lady Thunderbird Laminated (4)	$50
	Lady Ultimate Laminated (3)	$50
	Lady Ultimate II Laminated (4)	$50
	Lady Vogue Laminated (3)	$50
	Lord Byron Laminated (4)	$50
	Dick Metz Esquire Laminated (4)	$50
	Mary Mills Championship Persimmon (4)	$50
	Mary Mills Gold Signature Laminated (4)	$50
	Mary Mills Pro Signature Laminated (4)	$50
	Bob Murphy SST Laminated (4)	$50
	Bob Murphy Tournament (4)	$50
	Al Nelson Pro Built Persimmon (4)	$50
	Byron Nelson Gold Signature Laminated (4)	$50
	Byron Nelson Hall Of Fame Laminated (4)	$50
	Byron Nelson Magic Power Laminated (4)	$50
	Byron Nelson Presidential Laminated (4)	$50
	Byron Nelson Pro Personal Laminated (4)	$50
	Byron Nelson Pro Signature Laminated (4)	$50
	Byron Nelson Professional Laminated (4)	$50
	Byron Nelson Registered Laminated (4)	$50
	Byron Nelson Senior Model Laminated (4)	$50
	Byron Nelson Slipstream Laminated (4)	$50
	Byron Nelson Utility Wood Laminated (1)	$50
	Pro Signature Laminated (4)	$50
	Professional Persimmon (4)	$50
	Jackie Pung Autograph Persimmon (4)	$50
	Jackie Pung Championship Persimmon (4)	$50
	Jackie Pung Deluxe Laminated (4)	$50
	Jackie Pung Gold Signature Laminated (4)	$50
	Jackie Pung Personal Laminated (4)	$50
	Jackie Pung Pro Line Laminated (4)	$50
	Jackie Pung Signature Laminated (4)	$50
	Jackie Pung Tournament Laminated (4)	$50
	Jackie Pung Virginian Laminated (4)	$50
	Qualifier Laminated (4)	$50
	RB-115 Utility Laminated (1)	$50
	RB-200 Laminated (4)	$50
	RB-68 Laminated (4)	$50
	RB-70 Laminated (4)	$50
	RB-71 Laminated (4)	$50
	RB-880 Laminated (4)	$50
	Johnny Revolta Magic Power Laminated (4)	$50
	Johnny Revolta Personal Laminated (4)	$50
	Johnny Revolta Slipstream Laminated (4)	$50

COMPANY WOODS (SET NUMBERS)	VALUE
Northwestern(cont.):	
Robbie Robinson Persimmon (4)	$50
Robbie Robinson Registered Deluxe Persimmon (4)	$50
Robbie Robinson Regular Persimmon (4)	$50
Robbie Robinson Signature Persimmon (4)	$50
Chi Chi Rodriguez Dorado Laminated (4)	$50
Chi Chi Rodriguez Pro Registered Laminated (4)	$50
Chi Chi Rodriguez Pro Signature Laminated (4)	$50
Chi Chi Rodriguez Registered Laminated (4)	$50
Rosasco Bros. Laminated (4)	$50
N. Rosasco Persimmon (4)	$50
N. Rosasco Pro Made Persimmon (4)	$50
N. Rosasco Professional Persimmon (4)	$50
Saga Laminated (4)	$50
Bob Stuart Autograph Persimmon (4)	$50
Bob Stuart Persimmon (4)	$50
Superba Laminated (4)	$50
Team Player Progressive Flow Persimmon (3)	$50
Phil Thomson Registered Persimmon (4)	$50
Thunderbird Laminated (4)	$50
Thunderbird II Laminated (4)	$50
TNT Laminated (3)	$50
Tour Model Laminated (4)	$50
Tour Model Persimmon (4)	$50
Tour Select Laminated (1)	$50
Tournament Laminated (4)	$50
Turf Glider Laminated (1)	$50
Jim Turnesa Personal Laminated (4)	$50
Jim Turnesa Registered Laminated (4)	$50
Jim Turnesa Westchester Laminated (4)	$50
Ultimate Laminated (4)	$50
Ultimate Laminated Aluminum Shaft (4)	$50
Ultimate Square Toe Laminated (4)	$50
Craig Wood Gold Signature Laminated (4)	$50
Craig Wood Hall Of Fame Laminated (4)	$50
Craig Wood Utility Laminated (1)	$50
X-101 Laminated (4)	$50
Arnold Palmer:	
Arnie's Own Driver Laminated (1)	$50
FTD Laminated (4)	$50
Lady Palmer Laminated (4)	$50
Sears Arnold Palmer Persimmon (4)	$50
Tru-Matic Laminated (4)	$50
Dave Pelz:	
Dave Pelz Woods Laminated (4)	$75
DP1 Lajet Classic Laminated (4)	$75
DP1 Persimmon (3)	$150
DP2 Persimmon (3)	$150

COMPANY WOODS (SET NUMBERS)	VALUE
Dave Pelz (cont.):	
DP2 Tour Special Laminated (4)	$75
Toney Penna:	
Avenger Laminated (3)	$50
Bicentennial Driver Persimmon (1)	$250
Classic Persimmon Woods (3)	$150
Empress Persimmon (4)	$75
Honeybee Laminated (4)	$50
Jupiter Slugger Persimmon (4)	$75
Lady Omega Laminated (3)	$50
Limited Edition Persimmon (1)	$150
Model 1 Driver Persimmon (1)	$100
Model 1 Persimmon (3)	$125
Model 1A Driver Laminated (1)	$50
Model 2 Driver Persimmon (1)	$100
Model 2A Laminated (4)	$75
Model 3 Persimmon (4)	$150
Model 4A Laminated (4)	$50
Model 12 Driver Persimmon (1)	$100
Model 12 Persimmon (3)	$150
Model 29 Driver Persimmon (1)	$100
Model 59 Driver Persimmon (1)	$100
Model 59 Persimmon (4)	$175
Model 65 Driver Persimmon (1)	$100
Model 65 Persimmon (3)	$150
Model 65A Driver Laminated (1)	$50
Model 65A Laminated (4)	$50
Model 75 Persimmon (1)	$100
Model 78A Driver Laminated (1)	$50
Model 79 Driver Persimmon (1)	$100
Model 79 Persimmon (4)	$150
Model 79-S Driver Persimmon (1)	$100
Model 80 Persimmon (4)	$125
Model 85 Persimmon (1)	$125
Model JS Driver Persimmon (1)	$100
Model JS Persimmon (4)	$125
The Natural Persimmon (1)	$50
Omega Laminated (4)	$50
Original Model 65 Persimmon (4)	$150
Penna Eyesite Laminated (4)	$50
Penna Original Persimmon (4)	$150
Powerback Laminated (4)	$75
Rawlings RXP Laminated (4)	$75
Rawlings RXP Persimmon (4)	$75
Six + 6 Laminated (6)	$125
Special Edition II Persimmon (4)	$125
Special Edition III Persimmon (4)	$125
Super Woods Model 1 Persimmon (4)	$75

COMPANY	WOODS (SET NUMBERS)	VALUE
Toney Penna (cont.):		
	Super Woods Model 1A Laminated (4)	$50
	Super Woods Model 2 Persimmon (4)	$125
	Super Woods Model 2A Laminated (4)	$75
	Super Woods Model 4 Persimmon (4)	$125
	Super Woods Model 4A Laminated (4)	$75
	Super Woods Model 12 Persimmon (4)	$125
	Super Woods Model 12A Laminated (4)	$50
	Super Woods Model 65 Persimmon (4)	$100
	Super Woods Model 65A Laminated (4)	$50
	TP Avenger Laminated (3)	$50
	TP1X Persimmon (4)	$125
	TP-201 Laminated (4)	$75
	TP810 Persimmon (4)	$125
	Trevino Professional Laminated (3)	$100
	Lee Trevino Staff Laminated (3)	$100
	Lee Trevino Tour Grind Laminated (4)	$100
	Lee Trevino Woods Laminated (3)	$100
Ping:		
	Eye 2 Laminated Graphite Or Titanium (4)	$300
	Eye 2 Laminated Steel Shaft (4)	$250
	Eye Laminated (4)	$250
	Karsten I Laminated (4)	$250
	Karsten II Laminated (4)	$250
	Karsten IIA Laminated (4)	$250
	Karsten III Laminated (4)	$250
	Karsten IIIA Laminated (4)	$250
	Zing Laminated Graphite Or Titanium (4)	$300
	Zing Laminated Steel Shaft (4)	$250
Pinseeker:		
	350-RS Laminated (4)	$50
	Deep Faced Driver Persimmon (1)	$50
	Emerald Laminated (4)	$50
	Fireball 350 Deep Faced Driver Persimmon (1)	$50
	Fireball Deep Faced Driver Persimmon (1)	$30
	Fireball Persimmon Driver (1)	$30
	Formula 1 Laminated (4)	$50
	Formula 1 Persimmon (4)	$75
	Limited Edition Persimmon (4)	$100
	MS Laminated (4)	$75
	Persimmon (3)	$75
	Pinseeker Laminated (4)	$50
	RB-300 Laminated (4)	$50
	RB-300 Persimmon (4)	$75
	RB-350 Laminated (4)	$50
	RB-350 Persimmon (4)	$75
	Rebound Laminated (4)	$20
	Silver Spoon Persimmon (1)	$20
	Trouble Wood Laminated (1)	$20

COMPANY WOODS (SET NUMBERS)	VALUE
PGA Golf:	
Tommy Armour Collector Driver (4)	$150
Tommy Armour Laminated (4)	$75
Tommy Armour Persimmon (4)	$125
Butterfly Laminated (4)	$100
Cameron Persimmon (4)	$150
Champion Persimmon (4)	$100
Classic Laminated (4)	$75
Cobra Laminated (4)	$75
Concept Laminated (4)	$75
Concept LCG Laminated (4)	$75
Contromatic Queen Persimmon (4)	$75
Contromatic X-100 Persimmon (4)	$125
Contromatic X-200 Persimmon (4)	$125
Contromatic X-300 Persimmon (4)	$125
Contromatic X-90 Persimmon (4)	$125
Coronation Laminated (4)	$50
Coronation Persimmon (4)	$75
Corvair Persimmon (4)	$75
Cutlass Persimmon (4)	$75
Emblem Laminated (4)	$75
Emblem Persimmon (4)	$150
Lady Burke Persimmon (4)	$50
Lady Classic Laminated (4)	$50
Lady Contessa Laminated (4)	$50
Lady Custom Laminated (4)	$50
Lady Par Ex Laminated (4)	$50
Lady Par Excellence Laminated (4)	$50
Lady PGA Laminated (4)	$50
Lady Ryder Cup Laminated (4)	$50
Metrilite System Laminated (4)	$50
Model 159 Mark II Persimmon (4)	$75
Mr. President Laminated (4)	$50
Par Ex Static Weighted Laminated (4)	$50
Par Ex Swingweighted (4)	$50
Par Excellence Laminated (4)	$50
Par Excellence Persimmon (4)	$75
Performer Laminated (4)	$50
PGA Ryder Cup II Laminated (4)	$50
PGA Ryder Cup Titan Persimmon (4)	$75
PGA Thor Persimmon (4)	$75
Polaris Persimmon (4)	$75
Professional Persimmon (4)	$75
Rapier Laminated (4)	$50
Ryder Cup 174 Laminated (4)	$50
Ryder Cup Classic Laminated (4)	$50
Ryder Cup Deluxe Laminated (4)	$50
Ryder Cup II Laminated (4)	$75

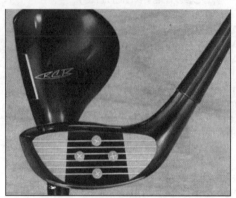

PGA RCR Woods

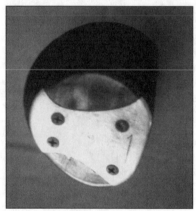

Original Ping Wood

COMPANY	WOODS (SET NUMBERS)	VALUE

PGA Golf (cont.)**:**

Ryder Cup L-100 Laminated (4)	$50
Ryder Cup Laminated (4)	$50
Ryder Cup LW Persimmon (4)	$75
Ryder Cup Mark I Persimmon (4)	$75
Ryder Cup Mark II Laminated (4)	$75
Ryder Cup Mark V Laminated (4)	$75
Ryder Cup Persimmon (4)	$100
Ryder Cup RCR Persimmon (4)	$125
Scrambler 7 Wood Laminated (4)	$25
Silver Scot 986 Tour (4)	$175
The Custom Laminated (4)	$50
Thunderbird Persimmon (4)	$50
T-Line Laminated (4)	$50
Tournament Persimmon (4)	$50
Vardon Cup Laminated (4)	$50
Viking Persimmon (4)	$50

PowerBilt:

5 Wood Persimmon (1)	$50
6 Wood Persimmon (1)	$50
Alliance Laminated (4)	$50
Auxiliary Persimmon Drivers (1)	$100
Bomber Driver Persimmon (1)	$100
Century Persimmon (4)	$75
Citation 305 Persimmon (4)	$250
Citation 306 Persimmon (4)	$250
Citation 307 Persimmon (4)	$250
Citation 308 Persimmon (4)	$250
Citation 309 Persimmon (4)	$250
Citation 310 Persimmon (4)	$250
Citation 311 Persimmon (4)	$250
Citation 312 Persimmon (4)	$250
Citation 313 Persimmon (4)	$250
Citation 314 Persimmon (4)	$250
Citation 315 Persimmon (4)	$250
Citation C316 Persimmon (4)	$250
Citation 317 Persimmon (4)	$250
Citation 318 Persimmon (4)	$250
Citation 319 Persimmon (4)	$250
Citation 320 Persimmon (4)	$250
Citation 323 Persimmon (4)	$250
Citation 324 Persimmon (4)	$250
Citation 3245 Persimmon (4)	$250
Citation 326 Persimmon (4)	$250
Citation 423 Laminated (4)	$75
Citation 424 Laminated (4)	$75
Citation 511 Laminated (4)	$75
Citation 512 Laminated (4)	$75

COMPANY	WOODS (SET NUMBERS)	VALUE

PowerBilt(cont.):

Citation 513 Laminated (4)		$75
Citation 514 Laminated (4)		$75
Citation 515 Laminated (4)		$75
Citation 517 Laminated (4)		$75
Citation 518 Laminated (4)		$75
Citation 519 Laminated (4)		$75
Citation 523 Laminated (4)		$75
Citation 524 Laminated (4)		$75
Citation 5245 Laminated (4)		$75
Citation Driver Persimmon (1)		$75
Citation Laminated (4)		$75
Citation Light Laminated (4)		$75
Citation Ltd. Persimmon (4)		$125
Citation Persimmon Graphite Shaft (3)		$100
Citation Persimmon Steel Shaft (3)		$125
Citation Plus Persimmon (4)		$125
Citation Pro Persimmon (1)		$100
Citation S600 Laminated (4)		$50
Citation T500L5 Laminated Driver Titanium Shaft (1)		$50
Countess Laminated (4)		$50
Countess Persimmon (3)		$50
Countess W458 Persimmon (4)		$100
Countess W459 Persimmon (4)		$100
Countess W460 Persimmon (4)		$100
Countess W463 Persimmon (4)		$100
Countess W464 Persimmon (4)		$100
Countess W465 Persimmon (4)		$100
Countess W466 Laminated (4)		$50
Countess W467 Laminated (4)		$50
Countess W468 Laminated (4)		$50
Countess W469 Laminated (4)		$50
Countess W4702T Laminated (4)		$50
Countess W4712T Laminated (4)		$50
Countess W4722T Laminated (4)		$50
Countess W4732T Laminated (4)		$50
Grand Slam Laminated (4)		$50
Imperial 405 Persimmon (4)		$75
Imperial 406 Persimmon (4)		$75
Imperial 407 Persimmon (4)		$75
Imperial 408 Persimmon (4)		$100
Imperial 409 Persimmon (4)		$100
Imperial Persimmon (4)		$75
Ladies 5 Wood Persimmon (1)		$50
Ladies 650 Persimmon (4)		$50
Ladies 651 Persimmon (4)		$50
Ladies Pro Sonic WA269 Laminated (4)		$50
Ladies W450 Persimmon (4)		$50

COMPANY	WOODS (SET NUMBERS)	VALUE
PowerBilt(cont.)**:**		
	Ladies W451 Persimmon (4)	$50
	Ladies W452 Persimmon (4)	$50
	Ladies W453T Persimmon (4)	$50
	Ladies W454 Persimmon (4)	$50
	Ladies W455 Persimmon (4)	$50
	Ladies W456 Persimmon (4)	$50
	Ladies W457 Persimmon (4)	$50
	Ladies W850 Persimmon (4)	$50
	Ladies W851 Persimmon (4)	$50
	Orbit Driver (1)	$50
	PowerBilt 14R Persimmon (1)	$50
	PowerBilt 30W Persimmon (1)	$50
	PowerBilt 43 Persimmon (1)	$50
	PowerBilt 48 Persimmon (1)	$50
	PowerBilt 51 Persimmon (1)	$50
	PowerBilt 104 Persimmon (4)	$125
	PowerBilt 200 Laminated (4)	$75
	PowerBilt 200 Persimmon (4)	$200
	PowerBilt 302 Persimmon (4)	$200
	PowerBilt 303 Persimmon (4)	$175
	PowerBilt 304 Persimmon (4)	$175
	PowerBilt 400 Persimmon (4)	$175
	PowerBilt 401 Persimmon (4)	$175
	PowerBilt 402 Persimmon (4)	$175
	PowerBilt 403 Persimmon (4)	$175
	PowerBilt 404 Persimmon (4)	$175
	PowerBilt 500 Persimmon (4)	$175
	PowerBilt 501 Persimmon (4)	$175
	PowerBilt 502 Persimmon (4)	$175
	PowerBilt 600 Persimmon (4)	$175
	PowerBilt 603 Persimmon (4)	$175
	PowerBilt 700 Persimmon (4)	$175
	PowerBilt 701 Persimmon (4)	$175
	PowerBilt 702 Persimmon (4)	$175
	PowerBilt 703 Persimmon (4)	$175
	PowerBilt 703T Persimmon (4)	$175
	PowerBilt 704 Persimmon (4)	$175
	PowerBilt 705 Persimmon (4)	$175
	PowerBilt 801 Persimmon (4)	$175
	PowerBilt 802 Persimmon (4)	$175
	PowerBilt 803 Persimmon (4)	$175
	PowerBilt 804 Persimmon (4)	$175
	PowerBilt 805 Persimmon (4)	$175
	PowerBilt Laminated (4)	$100
	Pro Sonic A340 Persimmon (4)	$350
	Riviera 510 Laminated (4)	$50
	Super Cleek Persimmon (1)	$50

COMPANY	WOODS (SET NUMBERS)	VALUE
PowerBilt(cont.):		
	Thoroughbred NTW Laminated (4)	$100
	ThoroughbredTW Laminated (4)	$100
	ThoroughbredTWL Laminated (4)	$100
	TPS Advanced Players Persimmon Graphite Shaft (3)	$150
	TPS Advanced Players Persimmon Steel Shaft (3)	$125
	TPS Large Driver Persimmon (1)	$100
	TPS Standard Players Pro Sonic Persimmon Graphite Shaft (3)	$150
	TPS Standard Players Pro Sonic Persimmon Steel Shaft (3)	$125
	TPSL Driver Persimmon (1)	$100
ProGroup:		
	Arnie's Own Driver Laminated (1)	$50
	Arnie's Own Persimmon (1)	$100
	Axiom Persimmon (4)	$125
	First Flight FTD Laminated (4)	$50
	First Flight FTD Persimmon (4)	$125
	First Flight Golden Eagle Laminated (4)	$50
	First Flight Jumbo Driver Persimmon (1)	$75
	First Flight NALG Laminated (4)	$100
	First Flight OSS FTD Laminated (4)	$50
	First Flight Ph.D. Laminated (4)	$100
	First Flight Phantom Laminated (4)	$100
	First Flight PT-280 Laminated (4)	$100
	First Flight Standard Laminated (4)	$150
	First Flight Standard Persimmon (4)	$150
	Lady Palmer Laminated (4)	$150
	Original Standard Persimmon (3)	$150
	P31 Persimmon (1)	$75
	P32 Persimmon (1)	$75
	P33 Persimmon (1)	$75
	P61 Persimmon (1)	$75
	P62 Persimmon (1)	$75
	P63 Persimmon (1)	$75
	Palmer Deacon Persimmon (4)	$150
	Palmer Golden Standard Persimmon (4)	$150
	Palmer Jumbo Driver Persimmon (1)	$75
	Palmer Laminated (4)	$50
	Palmer Original Persimmon (1)	$75
	Palmer Peerless Driver Persimmon (1)	$125
	Palmer Persimmon (4)	$200
	Palmer Personal Laminated (4)	$50
	Palmer Rough Rider Laminated (1)	$20
	Palmer Signature Laminated (4)	$50
	Palmer Standard Laminated (4)	$50
	Palmer Standard Persimmon (4)	$125
	Palmer Tru-Forge Laminated (4)	$50

COMPANY WOODS (SET NUMBERS)	VALUE
ProGroup(cont.):	
Palmer Tru-Matic Laminated (4)	$50
Arnold Palmer The Boss Laminated (4)	$150
Arnold Palmer Charger II Laminated (4)	$150
Arnold Palmer Charger Laminated (3)	$150
Arnold Palmer FTD Laminated (4)	$150
Arnold Palmer Personal Laminated (4)	$150
Arnold Palmer Signature Laminated (4)	$150
Peerless Persimmon (4)	$175
Peerless Pete Persimmon (1)	$150
PTM Persimmon (1)	$50
Standard 85 Persimmon (4)	$125
Standard Persimmon (4)	$125
Tru-Matic Laminated (4)	$50
Ram:	
Accubar Laminated (3)	$50
Accubar Low Profile Laminated (4)	$50
Accubar Plus Laminated (4)	$50
Custom 100 Tour Model Laminated (4)	$50
Custom 800 Series Persimmon (4)	$100
Fastback Dynalite Laminated (4)	$50
Fastback Laminated (4)	$50
Fastback Laminated Aluminum Shafts (4)	$50
Fastback II Laminated (4)	$50
Fullback Laminated (4)	$50
Golden Girl Laminated (3)	$50
Golden Lady Tribute Laminated (4)	$50
Golden Ram Classic 65 Driver Persimmon (1)	$50
Golden Ram Classic 85 Driver Persimmon (1)	$100
Golden Ram Laminated (4)	$50
Golden Ram Tour Grind Laminated (4)	$50
Golden Ram Tour Grind Persimmon (4)	$125
Golden Ram Tour Grind Standard Laminated (4)	$50
Golden Ram Tour Grind Standard Persimmon (4)	$125
Golden Ram Tour Model Laminated (4)	$50
Golden Ram XPD-100 Laminated (4)	$50
Keith Knox DM-139 Laminated (4)	$50
Kroydon Gene Littler Invitational Laminated (4)	$30
Kroydon Jo Ann Prentice Invitational Laminated (4)	$30
Kroydon Thunderbolt Laminated (4)	$30
Kroydon Tommy Bolt Lightning 500 Laminated (4)	$30
Lady Accubar Low Profile Laminated (4)	$30
Lady Craigton Laminated (4)	$30
Lasert Featherlite FLC Laminated (3)	$30
Gene Littler Invitational Laminated (4)	$30
Jo Ann Prentice Invitational Laminated (4)	$30
Jo Ann Prentice Laminated (4)	$30
Ram Milady Laminated (4)	$30

COMPANY	WOODS (SET NUMBERS)	VALUE
Ram(cont.):		
	Ram Pro TW800 Persimmon (3)	$150
	Ram Pro TW801 Persimmon (3)	$150
	Ram Pro TW802 Persimmon (3)	$150
	Ram Pro TW805 Persimmon (3)	$150
	Ram Tour Grind Axial Persimmon (4)	$125
	Ram Tour Grind FLC Laminated (3)	$30
	Ram Tour Grind FLC Persimmon (3)	$100
	Ram Tour Grind Persimmon (4)	$125
	Ram Tour Laminated (4)	$30
	Recovery Woods Laminated (1)	$10
	Doug Sanders DS Laminated (4)	$30
	Doug Sanders Laminated (4)	$30
	Doug Sanders Signature Laminated (4)	$30
	Doug Sanders Super SST Laminated (4)	$30
	Sensor Laminated (4)	$30
	Super Ram Dyna-Wood Driver Laminated (1)	$10
	Tour Grind Axial Persimmon (3)	$100
	Tour Grind Persimmon (3)	$100
	Tradition Laminated (3)	$30
	Tradition Persimmon (4)	$125
	TX-2 Laminated (4)	$30
	Tom Watson Woods 800 Persimmon (4)	$150
	Tom Watson Woods 801 Persimmon (4)	$150
	Tom Watson Woods Persimmon (4)	$150
	XS-1000 Laminated (4)	$30
Sounder:		
	Excalibur Laminated (3)	$50
	Joe Powell Limited Edition Persimmon (1)	$75
	Sounder Persimmon (4)	$50
	Sounder Laminated (3)	$30
	Star Laminated (3)	$30
	Star Mid-Lite Laminated (3)	$30
	Tour Limited Persimmon (3)	$60
	Triad Laminated (3)	$30
Spalding:		
	Cannon Laminated (3)	$30
	Elite Centurion Laminated (4)	$40
	Elite Laminated (4)	$40
	Elite Plus Laminated (4)	$40
	Executive Laminated (3)	$30
	Executive XE Laminated (3)	$40
	Sandra Haynie Laminated (4)	$30
	Sandra Haynie Persimmon (4)	$50
	Gene Littler Pro Model Persimmon (4)	$80
	MV2 Laminated (4)	$30
	MV2 Persimmon (4)	$80
	Syncro-Dyned Persimmon (4)	$80

Spalding (cont.):

Top-Flite 79 Persimmon (4)	$100
Top-Flite 121 Persimmon (4)	$100
Top-Flite 131 Laminated (4)	$30
Top-Flite 131 Persimmon (4)	$100
Top-Flite Center Powered Persimmon (4)	$80
Top-Flite EVA Driver Persimmon (1)	$50
Top-Flite Executive Persimmon (4)	$80
Top-Flite Ladies Woods Laminated (4)	$30
Top-Flite Laminated (4)	$30
Top-Flite Legacy Laminated (4)	$30
Top-Flite Mary Lena Faulk Model 28 Persimmon (4)	$50
Top-Flite Mary Lena Faulk Model 76 Persimmon (4)	$50
Top-Flite Men's Woods Laminated (4)	$30
Top-Flite Model 14 Persimmon (4)	$80
Top-Flite Model 18 Persimmon (4)	$80
Top-Flite Model 28 Persimmon (4)	$80
Top-Flite Model 56 Persimmon (4)	$100
Top-Flite Model 57 Persimmon (4)	$100
Top-Flite Model 74 Persimmon (4)	$100
Top-Flite Model 76 Persimmon (4)	$100
Top-Flite Model 83 Persimmon (4)	$100
Top-Flite Model 84 Persimmon (4)	$100
Top-Flite Model 87 Persimmon (4)	$100
Top-Flite Persimmon (4)	$80
Tour Edition Custom Crafted Persimmon (3)	$80
Tour Edition Laminated (3)	$30
Tour Edition Persimmon (3)	$60
Tournament Model Persimmon (4)	$80
XL4 Laminated (3)	$30
XL4 Persimmon (4)	$80

Square Two:

Lady Petite Laminated (4)	$30
LPGA Imperial Jade Laminated (4)	$30
LPGA Laminated (4)	$30
LPGA II Laminated (3)	$30
S2 Persimmon (4)	$60
S2 Professional Laminated (4)	$30
S2 Professional Persimmon (4)	$60
S2 Saber Laminated (3)	$30
Saber II Laminated (3)	$30
Square Two Laminated (4)	$30
Square Two Persimmon (4)	$60

Stan Thompson:

Ginty Laminated (1)	$50
Ginty Steamer Laminated (1)	$50
Personal Laminated (4)	$30
Pro Motion Laminated (4)	$30
RC-20X Laminated (3)	$30

COMPANY	WOODS (SET NUMBERS)	VALUE
Titleist:		
	Accu-Flo Laminated (4)	$30
	Acushnet Pro 100 Laminated (4)	$30
	Acushnet Pro Am Laminated (3)	$30
	Acushnet Titleist Laminated (4)	$30
	Acushnet Titleist Persimmon (4)	$60
	Club Special Laminated (4)	$30
	Club Special Persimmon (4)	$50
	Finalist Laminated (3)	$30
	Jumbo Driver Persimmon (1)	$75
	Persimmon (4)	$75
	Pinnacle Laminated (3)	$40
	Ruffian Laminated (1)	$20
	Special Persimmon Driver (1)	$50
	Titleist AC-108 Laminated (4)	$30
	Titleist Lite 100 Laminated (4)	$40
	Titleist Model 100 Laminated (4)	$40
	Titleist Model 90 Laminated (4)	$40
	Titlette Laminated (3)	$20
	Tour Model 821 Persimmon (4)	$125
	Tour Model 841 Persimmon (4)	$125
	Tour Model Laminated (4)	$50
	Tour Model Persimmon (4)	$100
	Tour Model Persimmon Driver (1)	$75
Bob Toski:		
	Driver And A Half Persimmon (1)	$20
	Penetrator Persimmon (1)	$20
	Penetrator Plus Laminated (4)	$40
	Penetrator Plus Persimmon (4)	$80
	Perfect Match Persimmon (3)	$60

Titleist Tour Model Wood

COMPANY	WOODS (SET NUMBERS)	VALUE
Bob Toski(cont.):		
	Target Bantamweight Persimmon (4)	$80
	Target Laminated (4)	$30
	Target Persimmon (3)	$60
	Toski Bantamweight Laminated (4)	$30
	Toski Target Woods Laminated (4)	$30
	Toski Target Woods Persimmon (4)	$80
Wilson:		
	300 Driver Laminated (4)	$40
	1200 GE Laminated (4)	$40
	1200 Gear Effect Laminated (4)	$40
	1200 LT Laminated (3)	$30
	1200 Power Sole Laminated (4)	$40
	Berg Staff Laminated (4)	$20
	Patty Berg Laminated (4)	$20
	Patty Berg Staff Laminated (4)	$20
	Black Heather Laminated (4)	$40
	Dyna-Power II Laminated (4)	$40
	Foremaster Laminated (4)	$40
	Jet Laminated (4)	$40
	Lady K-28 Laminated (4)	$30
	Libra Laminated (4)	$30
	Model 7 Laminated (4)	$30
	Mystique Laminated (4)	$30
	Pro Graphite Laminated Driver (1)	$25
	Reflex Laminated (4)	$40
	Roughneck Laminated (1)	$20
	Gene Sarazen Strokemaster Laminated (4)	$30
	Sam Snead Championship Laminated (4)	$30
	Sam Snead Signature Laminated (4)	$30
	Staff 11 Laminated (4)	$150
	Staff 11 Persimmon (4)	$150
	Staff 13 Laminated (4)	$50
	Staff 13 Persimmon (4)	$125
	Staff 21 Laminated (4)	$50
	Staff 41 Laminated (4)	$50
	Staff Compact Model Laminated (4)	$50
	Staff JP Persimmon (4)	$150
	Staff JP5 Laminated (4)	$50
	Staff JP5 Persimmon (4)	$150
	Staff Laminated (4)	$50
	Staff Persimmon (4)	$300
	Staff Series 11 Laminated (4)	$50
	Staff Series 11 Persimmon (4)	$200
	Staff Series 21 Laminated (4)	$50
	Staff Tour Block Persimmon Driver (1)	$75
	Top Notch Compact Laminated (4)	$50
	Top Notch Woods Laminated (4)	$50

COMPANY	WOODS (SET NUMBERS)	VALUE
Wilson(cont.):		
	Turf Rider Laminated (4)	$50
	Ultralite Laminated (3)	$30
	Whale Laminated (1)	$125
	X31 Laminated (3)	$75
	X31 Plus Laminated (4)	$100
	Babe Zaharias Top Notch Laminated (4)	$50
Wood Bros.:		
	All American Persimmon Driver (1)	$250
	The Corker Persimmon (1)	$125
	The Texan Persimmon (1)	$250
Yamaha:		
	AR-1 Persimmon (4)	$75
	Hal Sutton Signature Persimmon (3)	$100
	Y-45 Persimmon (4)	$125

Wood Shafted Clubs

T he golf boom in the United States during the 1920s and 1930s saw the manufacture of millions of hickory shafted clubs. Unfortunately only a few are desirable to collectors. Clubs from the late 20s and 30s still have some value but not necessarily to collectors. Weird generally means collectible, irons with no facemarkings are good collectibles as they were generally made before 1910. Clubs with "Patent" markings are more collectible than those with none since there tends to be less of them. Putters are generally more valuable than the other clubs. Clubs with "Made In Scotland" command a premium due to the roots of this great pastime, and the fact that many were made by the famous and historic names involved with the game. Metal shafted clubs painted to look like hickory have no value to the hickory collector.

Collectors and dealers feel that fewer than five percent of all hickory shafted clubs have added interest or value above their decorative or playable worth. A club has value due to its demand by collectors. The higher demand, the higher the value.

Millions of "common" hickory golf clubs were made during the 1920s and 1930s. They were sold through department stores, hardware stores, and sporting goods stores. These clubs are very common and have no real value other than as decorating accessories, as conversation pieces, or as playable clubs. Many of these clubs can be identified by their manufacturer's name, such as Ace, Biltmore, Thistle,

Hollywood, Columbia, Majestic, Metropolitan, and Bonnie; by metal caps at the top end of the grip; by yardage ranges stamped on the back of the club head; by a chromed, chromium, or stainless steel head; by numbered irons from sets or matched set irons; or especially by irons with dots, hyphens, lines or other scoring on the face of the club.

The more collectible clubs generally have some of the following characteristics: the irons have no, or very unusual, face markings or club head shapes; the putters have unusual or wooden heads; woods have thick, curved, oval necks covered with four or five inches of string whipping. Smooth faced irons with names like Anderson, Army & Navy, Ayres, Carrick, Forgan, Gray Morris, Park, White, and certain Spalding, MacGregor, Condie, Nicoll, Stewart, Gibson, and Wright & Ditson clubs are the more desirable collectible.

The world of hickories has a language all of its own. Terms like mashie, niblick and spoon leap out at the reader. A driver is the same today. A brassie approximates the two wood of today while a spoon was used as a three wood is today. A driving iron or driving cleek was used as a one iron. A mid iron is the equivalent of a two iron. A mid mashie is the equivalent of a three iron. A mashie fits today's four and five irons. A spade mashie was used as a modern six iron. A mashie niblick is today's seven iron. The niblick is the equivalent of today's eight and nine irons. A jigger was used as a chipper, a sammy was a round backed pitching club, and a spring faced iron had a thin steel face with a cavity behind. There are many other terms for individual clubs but these dominate.

The earlier long nosed clubs have names such as play club, grassed driver, driving putter, and baffing spoon. They had spliced heads and were made from the wood of beech, apple, thorn, and pear trees. These were the primary clubs before the 1890s. Transitional headed wooden clubs were clubs with heads of reduced length and were spliced to the shaft. The Bulger shaped heads popular at this time bulged out instead of the concave face prior to this period. Heads slowly became smaller and the socket head, where the head was drilled to accept the shaft, became popular. As the ball changed from feathers to the Rubber Gutta Percha ball, clubs needed a harder face to protect the wood from damage. Face inserts became the norm. Some really fancy inserts are very desirable as collectibles. Ivory, fancy woods, and fibers were all used successfully.

The irons were scored with some unusual marking. Dots, hyphens, dashes, dot and hyphen combinations, scored lines, crisscrosses, crisscross with dots, deep groves, and corrugated and ribbed faces predominate. The backs of the irons are just as varied. Diamond backed clubs have the back coming to a point in the center. A musselback resembles a mussel shell. A Carruthers style hosel has holes drilled through the hosel. A rounded back iron is just that, a slightly rounded back. A flanged sole has a wider sole than normal. A concentric or centrajet back has most of the weight behind the sweet spot. A hollow backed iron is similar to the modern perimeter weighted iron. An anti shank iron has a bent neck to prevent shanking. Center shafted putters and woods have the shaft in the center.

On some clubs all the information needed is stamped on the head. Special markings on the head may designate the maker or period when that particular club was made. All these cleek marks have special meaning to the collector, and prices vary as to the marks on individual clubs.

This particular selection of hickory shafted clubs is listed by maker. Many of the very expensive early clubs are not listed here. I have listed clubs more readily found just to give you an indication of their value and more importantly the names to look for.

One thing you will notice is that modern clubs all have borrowed ideas from the past. Aluminum putters, drivers with shafts towards the center of the head, cavity backed irons, face inserts and different face scorings all have been tried before.

Just as with other collectibles condition is everything. Rust, and peeling chrome is not good, cracked and broken shafts do not help a club's value either. Clubs that still look all original and slightly used bring premium prices. If a club has been restored, refinished, or cleaned; clubs that have warped or cracked shafts, hosels, or heads; heads that are pitted and rusted; and clubs with grips missing or in very poor condition bring much less than the listed prices.

COMPANY	HICKORY	VALUE

Abercrombie & Fitch:
Hi Model Jigger Dot Face		$60
Kroydon Made Mashie		$50
Master Model Driver		$175
Monel Lined Face Mashie		$75
Stainless Mashie Niblick Lined Face		$455

Aberdeen:
Mashie		$35
Mid Iron Lined Face		$500
Splice Head Driver		$325

Abraham & Strauss:
Lined Face Stainless Mashie		$35

Ace:
Klin Bros. K-70 Lofter		$45

David Adams:
Blade Putter		$75
Dot Faced Mashie		$65
Lined Face Diamond Backed Mashie		$75
Splice Head Driver		$225

Jeff Adams:
Center Shafted Boat Shaped Putter		$550

Alex Aiken:
Deep Faced Short Hosel Putter		$500
Smooth Faced Iron		$125
Socket Head Driver		$100
Splice Head Short Driver Face Insert		$225

G. Alexander:
Hammer Head Wood with Dual Striking Surfaces		$2,250

George Alexander & Co.:
Dot Faced Mashie		$45

John Allan:
Long Spoon Beech Head		$4,250
Play Club		$5,250
Short Spoon with Lofted Face		$5,000
Transitional Head Driver		$1,350

Allaway:
Oval Headed Putter Vulcanite Insert		$525

P.G. Allday Co.:
Gun Metal Blade Putter		$100
Mallet Head Putting Cleek		$130

Seales Allen:
Pegasus Diamond Backed Mashie Lined Face		$35

Tom Allen:
Persimmon Head Spliced Neck Brassie		$275

Allied Golf Co.:
Socket Head Driver Stripe Top		$60

B. Altman & Co.:
Everbrite Stainless Mashie Dot Face		$50

COMPANY	HICKORY	VALUE
B. Altman & Co. (cont.):		
Stainless Mashie Dot Face		$35
AMPCO Metal Golf Club Co.:		
AMPCO Metal Head Mashie Lined Face		$100
Bronze Alloy Head Jigger Lined Face		$110
Dow Metal Head Driver Bronze Insert		$225
Gold Medal Troon Spade Mashie		$80
The An Company:		
Blade Putter Lined Face		$75
Anderson, Anderson & Anderson:		
Lined Face Mashie		$285
Putting Cleek		$275
Smooth Faced Driving Iron		$395
Smooth Faced Oval Head Mashie Niblick		$1,955
Anderson of Anstruther:		
A of A Mark On a Pyramid Back Weighted Iron		$75
Deep Smooth Faced Putter		$85
Ladies Iron Sold By "The Gamage"		$75
Ladies Lofter		$50
Ridge Backed Blade Putter		$250
Rustless Mashie		$55
Smooth Faced Blade Putter		$95
Smooth Faced Lofting Iron		$65
Special Putting Cleek		$150
G.S. Sprague Lofting Iron		$75
Straight Blade Brass Putter		$100
Anderson & Blythe:		
Deep Faced Iron Dot Face		$135
Lined Face Cleek		$75
Socket Head Brassie		$110
Socket Head Driver		$110
R.E. Weymess Pat No. 16070 Two Level		
Back Dot Faced Iron		$90
Wood Splice Head Putter Brass Face Insert		$425
Wood Splice Head Putter Fiber Sole		$375
Anderson & Gourlay:		
Driving Iron Lined Face		$85
Lined Face 3 Iron		$90
Carl H. Anderson:		
Socket Head Brassie		$65
D. Anderson & Sons:		
Anti Shank Mashie Crisscross Face Scoring		$275
Anti Shank Mashie Stamped "G Bres Minchin Hampton"		$225
Bulge Back Putter Dot Face		$100
Concentric Back Weighted Lofter		$60
Dot Punched Face Monarch Jigger		$65
Driving Iron Dot Face		$75
Excelsior Putter		$100

COMPANY	HICKORY	VALUE

D. Anderson & Sons(cont.):

Glory Model Mashie	$135
Glory Putter Bent Neck Dot Punched Face	$95
Large Size Niblick Lined Face	$85
Large Socket Brassie Driver	$125
George Lowe Anti Shank Mashie	$195
Medium Size Niblick Dot Face	$100
Model 100 Putter Offset	$110
Premier Series Stainless Mashie	$75
Rustless M 8 Mashie Niblick	$65
Rustless Mashie Niblick	$60
Smith's Anti Shank Mashie	$225
Smooth Faced Cleek	$135
Smooth Faced Compact Blade Mashie	$195
Smooth Faced Lofting Iron	$165
Spliced Head Driver	$425
Supreme Model Socket Head Driver Ivorine Insert	$135
Zenith Model Driving Iron Dash Face	$75

James Anderson:

ANCSL Hold Fast Iron 11F	$150
ANCSL Long Faced Shallow Blade Cleek	$150
Approaching Cleek #38 Dot Faced	$75
Cleek #3 Dot Face	$75
Coaxer Model Iron Blade Bent Neck Putter	$165
Concave Face Niblick #33 Dash Face	$250
Concave Face Smooth Faced Lofting Iron	$950
Convex Back Cleek	$100
Diamond Back Mashie #21	$65
Dished Face Thick Hosel Smooth Faced Lofting Iron	$795
Driving Iron #121 Dot Face	$65
Farlie Model Mashie Iron	$250
G. Forrester Smooth Blade Putter	$75
Gun Metal Small Head Putter Steel Face Insert	$325
Gun Metal Small Head Putter Wood Face Insert	$465
Iron Blade Putter #105B	$90
Iron Blade Putter #91 Hosel Notch	$135
Kurtos Convex Face And Back Putter	$400
Long Faced General Purpose Iron	$125
Long Thin Smooth Faced Cleek	$1,500
G. Lowe Anti Shank Smooth Faced Small Head Niblick	$325
Mashie #22	$50
Mashie #24 Ribbed Face	$165
Maxwell Pattern Mashie Niblick #115	$100
Medium Head Smooth Faced Niblick	$200
Musselback Jigger #88 Dot Face	$75
Offset Blade Putter #151	$90
Oval Headed Mashie Niblick #136 Ribbed Face	$185
Patented Auchterlonie Dot Faced Putter	$250

COMPANY HICKORY	VALUE
James Anderson(cont.):	
Putter #68 Dot Face	$135
Round Back Sammy #5A Dot Faced Iron	$90
Round Sole Driving Iron #85 Lined Face	$75
Round Sole Pitcher #41	$125
Sammy #2 Dot Faced Iron	$85
Sammy Iron #133 Dot Face	$90
Short Blade Smooth Faced Mashie	$100
Short Head Deep Face Blade Heavy Hosel	
Smooth Faced Mashie	$475
Small Head Smooth Faced Niblick	$950
Smooth Faced General Purpose Iron	$135
Smooth Faced Iron	$95
Steel Bladed Putter #51	$65
Thick Blade And Hosel Smooth Faced Putter	$300
Thick Soled Sammy #6 Iron	$90
Twisted Neck Smooth Faced Putter	$200
Jamie Anderson:	
Beech Headed Play Club Thin Shaft	$4,800
Green Heart Shafted Putter	$5,250
Joe Anderson:	
Mallet Head Offset Putter Extreme Goose Neck	$375
O. K. Brand Mid Iron Lined Face	$50
O. K. Brand Stainless Niblick Dot Face	$75
Rounded Top Shallow Faced Putter	$135
Rustless 2 Iron	$75
Rustless Mashie	$55
Smooth Faced Mid Iron	$100
Splice Wood Head Putter	$350
R.C.B. Anderson:	
Rex Model Socket Head Driver	$100
Smooth Faced Mid Iron	$100
Splice Head Spoon Deep Face	$395
Robert Anderson & Sons:	
Aluminum Headed Brassie Small Headed Cleek	$200
Compact Smooth Blade Mashie	$115
Crescent Head Lofter	$2,250
Gun Metal Blade Putter	$195
Heavy Hosel Putter	$125
Lofted Smooth Face Iron	$165
Short Head Through Bore Center Shaft Driver	$4,500
Smooth Faced Brass Putter	$125
Smooth Faced Cleek	$185
Willie Anderson:	
Iron Blade Putter	$95
Socket Head Driver	$195
Argyle:	
Smooth Faced Iron	$75

COMPANY HICKORY	VALUE
Argyle (cont.)**:**	
Socket Head Brassie	$75
Arlington Manufacturing Co.:	
Composition Socket Head Driver Black Pyralin	$750
Army & Navy Cooperative Stores Ltd.:	
Blade Putter	$325
Hold Fast Putter Iron Blade	$265
Long Nosed Beech Driver	$2,500
Medium Size Head Smooth Faced Lofter	$475
Medium Size Head Smooth Faced Lofter	
Heavy Thick Blade	$395
Putter	$900
Smooth Deep Faced Mashie	$225
Smooth Faced Iron	$300
Smooth Faced Lofter	$375
Smooth Faced Mashie	$300
Arrow:	
Stainless Mashie Lined Face	$45
Arrowflite:	
Stainless Mashie Ribbed Face	$100
Arrowline:	
Par Model Mid Iron Line Face	$35
W. & G. Ashford:	
Beech Head Putter	$1,125
Combination Wood/Aluminum Head Driver	$3,750
Smooth Faced Blade Putter Mild Steel	$375
Smooth Faced Cleek Mild Steel	$300
Smooth Faced Lofter	$325
Smooth Faced Mashie	$495
Transitional Beech Head Brassie	$900
Ashland Manufacturing Co.:	
Ribbed Face Mashie Niblick	$135
Auchterlonie & Crothwaite:	
Center Shafted Smooth Faced Iron	$3,650
Gun Metal Blade Putter	$275
Smooth Faced Lofter	$450
Smooth Faced Mashie	$225
D. & W. Auchterlonie:	
2 Iron	$60
Brown Head Baffing Spoon	$1,450
Lined Face Putter	$75
Long Blade Putting Cleek Dot Face	$755
Musselback Lined Face Cleek	$135
Putting Cleek Chain Link Face	$275
Smooth Faced Approaching Cleek	$265
Smooth Faced Iron	$100
Smooth Faced Medium Head Niblick	$130
Smooth Flat Face Mashie Niblick	$1,255

COMPANY	HICKORY	VALUE

D. & W. Auchterlonie (cont.):

Socket Head Brassie	$75
Splice Head Driver	$265
Splice Head Putter	$750
Splice Head Putter Slip Sole	$165
Alex Taylor Socket Head Driver	$75
Transitional Beech Head Driver	$625
Wanamakers Socket Head Brassie	$75
Wood Head Putter The Balance Model	$650

Laurence Auchterlonie:

Top Spin Putter Concentric Weighted Blade	$145

Tom Auchterlonie:

Anti Shank Mashie Niblick	$195
Ellice Series Putter Offset Blade	$75
Ellice Series Stripe Top Driver	$100
Lined Face 2 Iron	$60
Lined Face Mashie	$75
Lined Face Spade Mashie	$75
Persimmon Head Long Nose Style Socket Putter	$350
Prism Shaped Head Putter	$600
Socket Head Brassie	$85
Stainless 5 Iron Line Face	$60
Stainless Blade Putter	$75
Stainless Mashie Niblick Lined Face	$75
Wood Socket Head Putter	$295

Robert Auld:

Iron Blade Putter	$70
Small Splice Head Spoon Leather Face Insert	$250
Smooth Face Driving Iron	$75
Socket Head Spoon	$135

F.H. Ayres:

Aluminum Square Headed Putter	$1,450
Archie Compston Deep Faced Mashie	$60
Beech Wood Head Semi Long Nosed Putter	$950
Cleek Marked F H Ayres B C	$175
Deep Faced Mashie Dot Punched Face	$55
Dot Punched Face Anti Shank Iron	$250
The Fascet Straight Blade Dot Faced Putter	$90
Goosenecked Socket Headed Driver	$995
Gun Metal Blade Putter Thick Hosel	$225
Heavy Headed Niblick Smooth Face	$750
Ladies Mashie	$50
Lofting Iron	$150
Long Iron Blade Putting Cleek	$175
Mashie Iron	$150
Oak Brand Putter	$85
Olympic Model Socket Headed Driver	$150
Rounded Sole Iron Marked F Cheshire Delta	$65

COMPANY HICKORY	VALUE
F.H. Ayres(cont.):	
Semi Long Nosed Driver	$1,750
Smooth Faced 1 Iron	$160
Smooth Faced Cleek	$85
Smooth Faced Driving Iron	$185
Smooth Faced Large Cleek	$185
Smooth Faced Lofter	$150
Smooth Faced Lofter Heavy Hosel	$175
Smooth Faced Lofter Thick Compact Blade	$175
Socket Head Driver	$1,250
Tru Put Putter Fiber Face Insert	$365
P. A. Vaile Model Iron Swan Neck Hosel Dot Face	$750
Wooden Square Headed Putter	$3,250
W. Ayrton:	
Gun Metal Cleek Gutta Percha Insert	$4,250
B.A.M. Company:	
Smooth Faced Iron	$175
Socket Head Brassie	$225
Socket Head Driver	$225
Tom Ball:	
Beech Headed Semi Long Nosed Driver	$750
Baltimore Putter Co.:	
Triangular Shaped Adjustable Loft Aluminum Putter	$3,250
Banner:	
Center Shafted Putter	$700
Leo Diegel Chromed Niblick	$45
Driving Iron Diagonal Lined Face	$60
H.H. Barker:	
Socket Threaded Driver White Face Insert	$100
Jim Barnes:	
Adjustable Putter	$1,850
Medium Round Shaped Head Niblick Lined Face	$100
N. Barnes:	
Birco Mashie	$55
James Batley:	
Mashie Niblick Lined Face	$50
Socket Headed Driver	$65
Tom Bendelow:	
Lined Face Mashie Iron	$75
Bentefink & Co.:	
Concentric Series Iron Dot Face	$75
Offset Blade Putter	$75
Socket Headed Driver	$100
The Berkley Ralston Co.:	
Jock Hutchison Socket Head Brassie	$75
Long Head Putter	$70
James Beveridge:	
Long Nosed Spoon	$6,850

COMPANY HICKORY	VALUE
James Beveridge (cont.):	
Semi Long Nosed Transitional Deep Faced Driver	$2,800
Wooden Niblick Lofted Face And Short Head	$3,850
H.N. Billet:	
Wood Head Putter Cylindrical Shape	$4,250
Billing Co.:	
Mashie Circular Scored Face	$135
Billings & Spencer:	
5 Mashie Through Hosel Shafted Dot Punched Iron	$60
Dot Punched Face Mashie Carruthers Hosel	$90
Birdie:	
Thick Bladed Putter	$40
Andrew Bisset:	
Socket Headed Brassie	$75
J.L. Black:	
Dot Faced Driving Iron	$50
Thomas Black:	
Wood Mallet Socket Head Putter Rollers In Sole	$5,250
Blackheath Golf Co.:	
Coronet Series Jigger Dash Face	$55
Arthur Boggs:	
Iron Man Mashie Dot Face	$95
F. Bonner:	
The Scot Mid Iron	$55
Bonnie B:	
Heavy Blade Putter Lined Face	$35
Percy Boomer:	
Autograph Jigger Dot Face	$75
Harry Bowler:	
Pear Shaped Spoon Socket Wood	$90
Tom Boyd:	
Blade Putter	$60
Driving Iron Lined Face	$50
Boyden:	
Iron Patented Fork Splice In The Shaft	$195
Boye:	
Adjustable Putter	$850
Charles Boyle:	
Dot Faced Niblick	$95
Driver Fancy Face Insert	$100
Square Toed Putter Flat Sided Hosel	$225
Edwin Bradbeer:	
Smooth Faced Putter	$75
James Bradbeer:	
Jay Bee 2 Iron	$75
Top Line Iron	$325
Thomas Braddell & Sons:	
Aluminum Head Driver Leather Face and Horn Insert	$1,450

COMPANY HICKORY	VALUE
Thomas Braddell & Sons (cont.):	
Smooth Concave Faced Niblick	$600
Smooth Faced Cleek Long Blade	$450
Smooth Faced Mashie	$325
Splice Head Brassie Leather Face	$450
Splice Head Driver Leather Face	$450
Frank Brady:	
Overspin Gun Metal Putter Curved Face Hollow Back	$995
Brae Burn:	
Lined Face Mashie Niblick	$35
J. Burnes & Co.:	
Dot Faced Niblick	$125
Butchard-Nichols:	
#11 Niblick Dot Punched Face	$150
BTN Mid Iron	$150
BTN Putter	$225
Model 12 Putter	$190
Model 120 Driver	$225
Model H Spliced Neck Driver	$250
James Braid:	
Dot Faced Cleek	$135
Mid Iron	$75
Orion Putter Broad Sole	$195
W. & G. Braid:	
Smooth Faced Niblick Thick Sole	$1,000
Charles Brand:	
Diamond Faced Iron	$65
Large Headed Niblick	$100
Lined Face Mashie	$65
Lofted Face Semi Long Nosed Baffing Spoon	$3,750
Small Headed Niblick	$625
Smooth Deep Faced Mashie	$250
Smooth Faced Cleek	$325
Smooth Faced Cleek Long Thin Blade	$750
Special Putter with Crisscross Scoring Face	$70
J. Breare:	
Stainless Steel Mid Iron Lined Face	$50
G. Brodie Breeze:	
Dash Faced Mid Iron	$60
Excelsior Iron Bladed Putter	$65
George Brews:	
Semi Long Nosed Shallow Faced Driver	$2,750
Smooth Faced Cleek	$190
Smooth Faced Iron	$150
Splice Headed Brassie	$450
Trusty Putter Wood Mallet Head Brass Backweight	$225
Francis Brewster:	
Simplex Center Shafted Driver Boat Shaped Head	$2,750

COMPANY	HICKORY	VALUE

Francis Brewster(cont.):
| Simplex Center Shafted Niblick | $2,995 |
| Simplex Center Shafted Putter | $2,500 |

Briarcliff:
| Blade Putter Lined Face | $45 |

Bridgeport Gun & Implement Co.:
Brooklawn Splice Headed Driver	$2,25
Centrajet Model Mashie	$125
Chevy Chase Model Socket Head Driver	$150
Chevy Chase Model Splice Head Driver	$325
Cleek	$120
Concave Face Lofting Cleek	$185
Convex Back Mashie	$135
Deep Face Putting Cleek	$150
Deep Smooth Faced Approaching Mashie Carruthers Hosel	$75
Deep Smooth Faced Putter	$100
Driving Cleek Carruthers Hosel	$225
Driving Mashie	$125
Dundonald Socket Head Driver	$225
Dunn Model Driving Iron	$100
Dunn Model Splice Head Bulger Face Driver	$275
Dunn Model Splice Head Driver	$325
Fork Splice Head Driver Leather Face Insert	$750
Gooseneck Putting Cleek	$165
Gun Metal Blade Putter	$135
Hibbard Model Splice Head Driver	$275
Kilgour Deep Faced Splice Head Brassie	$325
Kilgour Model Socket Headed Driver	$165
Kilgour Socket Head Niblick Brassie	$325
Kilgour Splice Head Niblick Brassie	$675
Lofting Iron	$100
Lofting Mashie	$75
McEwan Socket Head Driver	$195
McEwan Splice Head Driver	$295
Medium Mashie	$75
Mid Mashie	$60
Moore Splice Headed Brassie	$250
Tom Morris Socket Head Brassie	$195
Tom Morris Socket Head Driver	$250
Tom Morris Spliced Driver	$450
One Piece Bulger Face Brassie	$1,800
One Piece Bulger Faced Driver	$1,750
One Piece Straight Faced Brassie	$1,750
One Piece Straight Faced Driver	$1,800
Putting Cleek	$125
Rounded Head Niblick	$75
Short Blade Cleek	$100

COMPANY	HICKORY	VALUE

Bridgeport Gun & Implement Co. (cont.):

Simpson Model Approaching Mashie	$150
Simpson Model Brassie	$235
Simpson Model Socket Headed Driver	$175
Simpson Model Splice Headed Driver	$175
Smooth Face Lofting Iron	$75
Smooth Faced Approaching Cleek	$65
Smooth Faced Mashie	$95
Smooth Faced Putter	$125
Socket Headed Brassie Straight Face	$160
Splice Head Brassy Niblick	$600
Splice Headed Driver Bulger Face	$275
Splice Headed Straight Faced Driver	$275
St. Andrews Splice Head Driver	$225
Straight Blade Standard Putter	$150
Taylor Deep Faced Medium Mashie	$150
Taylor Lofting Mashie	$175
Taylor Model Mashie	$150
Through Hosel Shafted Socket Head Lofted Spoon	$195
Twisted Neck Putting Cleek	$135
Wooden Splice Head Putter	$750

James W. Brine:

Dreadnaught Mashie Niblick	$75
Lined Face Mid Iron	$50

British Golf Co.:

Center Shaft Boat Shaped Putter	$325
Offset Smooth Bladed Putter	$900
Offset Smooth Faced Putter	$75
Smooth Faced Cleek	$325

R. Brodie & Sons:

Tom Morris Stainless Mashie Niblick	$100
Stainless Iron	$65
Stainless Mashie Lined Face	$65

Robert Brodie:

Extended Blade Iron with Dot Face Scoring	$250

W. & D. Brodie Co.:

Dash Faced Stainless Mid Iron	$60

Reginald T. Brougham:

Transitional Shaped Aluminum Driver Wood Face Insert	$1,650

Brown & Smart:

Iron Blade Putter	$75

Daniel Brown:

Smooth Faced Cleek	$65

George Brown:

Long Nosed Mid Spoon	$9,500

Harry Brown:

Lined Face Niblick	$50

COMPANY	HICKORY	VALUE

J. Brown:
Semi Long Nosed Putter $1,500
Wallace Brown:
Long Nosed Beech Headed Play Club $4,500
William Brown:
Socket Headed Brassie $65
George W. Bryant:
Rustless Mashie $65
R. H. Buhrke Mfg. Co.:
Baxpin Mashie Deep Ribbed Face $150
Burr-Key Dot Faced Mid Iron $45
Classic Driving Iron Brass Disk In Face $125
Finalist Blade Putter $45
Majestic Blade Putter $45
Majestic Lined Face Mid Iron $45
Majestic Socket Headed Driver $60
Medallist Stainless Niblick Lined Face $50
Mohawk Mashie Dot Face $45
Mohawk Putter $45
Princess Pat. Mashie Lined Face $50
Princess Pat. Mid Iron Lined Face $50
Rambler Thick Bladed Putter $45
Regal Brassie Wood Face Insert $85
Robertson Lined Face Mashie Niblick $45
Andy Robertson Chrome Mashie $60
Andy Robertson Spade Mashie $70
Spade Mashie Niblick $50
Speedway Chrome Blade Putter $45
Stylist Chrome Putter $45
Stylist Mashie $45
Stylist Stainless Mid Mashie Dot Face $45
R.A. Bunker:
Mallet Headed Putter $75
C.S. Burchart:
Lined Face Mashie $75
Splice Head Driver Aluminum Face Insert $375
U.S. Patented Driver $300
U.S. Patented Driver Striped Top and Fiber Face Insert $125
Charles Burgess:
Gun Metal Putter Round Top $225
Burke Manufacturing Co.:
#28 Niblick Hyphen Scored Face $100
Mike Brady Mashie Dash Face $100
Mike Brady Mashie Niblick Dash Face $100
Burke Special Mashie Niblick $75
Burke Stainless Mashie Dot Face $45
Columbia Blade Putter $40
Columbia Deep Faced Mashie Dash Face $40

COMPANY	HICKORY	VALUE

Burke Manufacturing Co. (cont.):

Columbia Driving Iron Dash Face	$40
Columbia Gooseneck Blade Putter	$50
Columbia Mashie Deep Inverted Waffle Mesh Face	$225
Columbia Mashie Niblick	$55
Columbia Mashie Niblick Dash Face	$40
Columbia Mashie Niblick Deep Ribbed Face	$100
Columbia Mid Iron Dash Face	$40
Columbia Niblick Dash Face	$40
Columbia Plain Faced Driver	$50
Columbia Regular Mashie Dash Face	$40
Columbia Special Jigger	$55
Deluxe Brassie Black Fiber Insert Aluminum Backweight	$75
Deluxe Driver Black Fiber Insert Aluminum Backweight	$75
Deluxe Spoon Black Fiber Insert Aluminum Backweight	$75
Dot Faced Putter	$60
Duncan Gray Brassie Wood Six Peg Face	$145
End Grain Wooden Headed Putter	$525
Gimbal Bros. Special Niblick	$50
Glencoe Mashie Ribbed Face	$95
Glencoe Putter Line And Dot Face Scorings	$90
Gold Smith Putter Line Scored Face	$150
Golfrite Brassie Pegged Face Aluminum Backweight	$120
Golfrite Driver Pegged Face Aluminum Backweight	$120
Golfrite Mid Iron Dot And Line Face Scoring	$95
Golfrite Spoon Pegged Face Aluminum Backweight	$135
Grand Prize Approaching Cleek	$90
Grand Prize Approaching Cleek Dot Face	$85
Grand Prize Blade Putter Lined Face	$65
Grand Prize Blade Putter Pointed Top Edge	$125
Grand Prize Blade Putting Cleek	$70
Grand Prize Brassie Bulls Eye Face Insert	$135
Grand Prize Brassie Face Insert	$195
Grand Prize Brassie Plain Face	$70
Grand Prize Brassie Sliced Head	$175
Grand Prize Brassie Thick Face Insert	$120
Grand Prize Broad Flange Sole Putter Square Toe	$125
Grand Prize Bulger Faced Monel Metal Mashie Niblick	$150
Grand Prize Bulger Faced Monel Metal Putter	$175
Grand Prize Bulldog Head Spoon Deep Face	$150
Grand Prize Cleek Lined Face	$60
Grand Prize Concave Face Niblick	$125
Grand Prize Concentric Back Deep Faced Mid Iron	$75
Grand Prize Concentric Back Mid Iron Dash Face	$70
Grand Prize Concentric Backed Mashie	$70
Grand Prize Deep Faced Mashie	$60
Grand Prize Deep Faced Mashie Flange Sole	$80
Grand Prize Deep Faced Mashie Niblick Lined Face	$60

COMPANY	HICKORY	VALUE

Burke Manufacturing Co. (cont.):

Grand Prize Deep Faced Niblick	$90
Grand Prize Deep Faced Straight Necked Putter	$80
Grand Prize Deep Ribbed Face Cleek	$150
Grand Prize Deep Ribbed Face Mashie	$125
Grand Prize Deep Ribbed Face Niblick	$185
Grand Prize Deep Ribbed Face Offset Mashie Niblick	$125
Grand Prize Deep Slotted Face Mashie Niblick	$150
Grand Prize Deep Slotted Face Monel Mashie Niblick	$145
Grand Prize Diamond Backed Cleek Lined Face	$75
Grand Prize Diamond Backed Mashie	$95
Grand Prize Driver Bulls Eye Face Insert	$135
Grand Prize Driver Face Insert	$195
Grand Prize Driver Thick Face Insert	$120
Grand Prize Driving Iron Round Sole and Lined Face	$70
Grand Prize Driving Mashie	$70
Grand Prize Flanged Sole Putter	$125
Grand Prize Gooseneck Putter	$70
Grand Prize Gooseneck Putter Flange Sole	$80
Grand Prize Gun Metal Blade Putter	$95
Grand Prize Gun Metal Blade Putter Flange Sole	$100
Grand Prize Gun Metal Straight Necked Putter Wide Sole	$95
Grand Prize Heavy Bladed Mashie Iron Dash Face	$70
Grand Prize Jigger Musselback	$80
Grand Prize Jigger Scored Face Line	$50
Grand Prize Large Head Brassie	$125
Grand Prize Large Head Niblick	$75
Grand Prize Large Head Spoon	$145
Grand Prize Lined Face Mashie Niblick	$60
Grand Prize Long Blade Deep Face Flange Sole	$95
Grand Prize Long Blade Driving Iron	$60
Grand Prize Long Blade Mashie Flange Sole	$75
Grand Prize Long Narrow Head Brassie	$150
Grand Prize Long Narrow Head Driver	$150
Grand Prize Mashie Offset Head	$65
Grand Prize Mashie Rounded Sole Short Blade	$70
Grand Prize Medium Blade Mashie Lined Face	$60
Grand Prize Medium Head Niblick Dash Face	$65
Grand Prize Medium Length Blade Mid Iron Lined Face	$60
Grand Prize Mid Iron Deep Faced Short Blade	$60
Grand Prize Mid Iron Diamond Back Dash Face	$75
Grand Prize Mid Iron Offset Blade Lined Face	$60
Grand Prize Mid Iron Round Sole	$70
Grand Prize Monel Metal Approaching Cleek	$100
Grand Prize Monel Metal Bulger Face Driving Iron	$150
Grand Prize Monel Metal Bulger Face Mid Iron	$150
Grand Prize Monel Metal Cleek	$80
Grand Prize Monel Metal Driving Iron	$75

COMPANY	HICKORY	VALUE

Burke Manufacturing Co. (cont.)**:**

Grand Prize Monel Metal Jigger	$90
Grand Prize Monel Metal Mashie	$75
Grand Prize Monel Metal Mashie Niblick	$125
Grand Prize Monel Metal Mid Iron	$75
Grand Prize Monel Metal Niblick	$80
Grand Prize Monel Metal Pitcher	$90
Grand Prize Monel Metal Putting Cleek	$95
Grand Prize Monel Putter	$125
Grand Prize Musselback Mid Iron	$75
Grand Prize Musselbacked Cleek Lined Face	$75
Grand Prize Musselbacked Mashie	$85
Grand Prize Narrow Faced Cleek Lined Face	$75
Grand Prize Narrow Faced Mashie	$60
Grand Prize Offset Head Deep Face Cleek	$70
Grand Prize Offset Head Lined Face	$65
Grand Prize Pear Shaped Brassie Semi Bulger Face	$195
Grand Prize Pear Shaped Driver Semi Bulger Face	$195
Grand Prize Pitcher Lined Face	$80
Grand Prize Plain Faced Spoon	$75
Grand Prize Putter Extreme Gooseneck	$95
Grand Prize Putter Round Sole Straight Neck	$65
Grand Prize Putter Round Top Broad Sole	$125
Grand Prize Putting Cleek	$70
Grand Prize Round Backed Mashie Lined Face	$50
Grand Prize Round Sole Driving Mashie Short Blade	$80
Grand Prize Round Sole Spoon	$125
Grand Prize Sargeant Round Backed Monel Putter	$125
Grand Prize Sargeant Round Backed Steel Putter	$100
Grand Prize Schenectady Putter	$225
Grand Prize Semi Bulldog Head Brassie	$125
Grand Prize Semi Bulldog Head Driver	$125
Grand Prize Semi Gooseneck Mashie Niblick Dash Face	$70
Grand Prize Semi Gooseneck Musselback Putter	$75
Grand Prize Short Bladed Mashie	$75
Grand Prize Short Bladed Mid Iron	$60
Grand Prize Short Bladed Niblick	$65
Grand Prize Slight Gooseneck Narrow Blade	$75
Grand Prize Slight Gooseneck Putter	$75
Grand Prize Small Bulldog Head Spoon Fancy Face Insert	$145
Grand Prize Small Head Driver Deep Face	$95
Grand Prize Socket Headed Driver Plain Face	$60
Grand Prize Splice Head Driver	$160
Grand Prize Spoon Fiber Face Insert	$125
Grand Prize Taylor Brassie	$150
Grand Prize Taylor Mid Iron Lined Face	$95
Grand Prize Taylor Spoon	$185

COMPANY	HICKORY	VALUE

Burke Manufacturing Co. (cont.):

Grand Prize Victory Model Brassie	$150
Grand Prize Victory Model Driver	$150
Grand Prize Victory Spoon	$175
Grand Prize Wooden Cleek Bulls Eye Face Insert	$295
Grand Prize Wooden Cleek Fiber Face Insert	$195
Walter Hagen Monel Metal Mashie Lined Face	$150
Walter Hagen Monel Metal Mashie Niblick Dot Face	$150
Hutchison Brassie Fiber Face	$150
Hutchison Deep Slotted Face Monel Metal Niblick	$300
Hutchison Deep Slotted Face Niblick	$150
Hutchison Driver Fiber Face	$150
Hutchison Mashie Niblick Deep Slotted Face	$150
Hutchison Mid Iron Flange Sole Lined Face	$125
Hutchison Monel Blade Putter	$125
Hutchison Monel Metal Lined Face Mashie	$95
Hutchison Monel Metal Mashie	$115
Hutchison Monel Metal Mid Iron Lined Face	$95
Hutchison Monel Offset Deep Slot Faced Mashie Niblick	$225
Hutchison Spade Mashie Monel Metal Deep Slot Face	$250
Hutchison Spoon Fiber Face	$175
Ladies Diamond Back Mid Iron	$55
Lady Burke Blade Putter	$50
Lady Burke Brassie	$75
Lady Burke Brassie Face Insert	$60
Lady Burke Brassie Fancy Face Insert	$145
Lady Burke Brassie Fiber Face Insert	$145
Lady Burke Cleek	$45
Lady Burke Driver	$60
Lady Burke Driver Face Insert	$125
Lady Burke Driver Fiber Face Insert	$145
Lady Burke Driving Iron Lined Face	$50
Lady Burke Gooseneck Blade Putter	$75
Lady Burke Gun Metal Blade Putter	$95
Lady Burke Jigger Lined Face	$60
Lady Burke Mashie Lined Face	$50
Lady Burke Mashie Niblick	$50
Lady Burke Mid Iron Lined Face	$50
Lady Burke Niblick Lined Face	$50
Lady Burke Round Backed Mashie	$75
Lady Burke Spade Mashie Lined Face	$50
Lady Burke Spoon	$75
Lady Burke Square Toe Putter Broad Sole	$125
Lady Burke Wooden Cleek Fancy Face	$300
Lady Burke Wooden Cleek Fiber Face	$175
Long Burke Mid Mashie	$55
Long Hosel Monel Metal Blade Putter	$225
Mashie Heavy Dot Punched Face	$55

COMPANY	HICKORY	VALUE

Burke Manufacturing Co. (cont.):

McLean Cleek Dot Face	$100
McLean Niblick	$100
Monarch Putter Flanged Back	$45
Monel Mashie Flanged Back	$55
Monel Mid Iron Hyphen Face Scoring	$45
Monel Non Corrodable Metal Niblick	$45
Monel Slot Groove H 7 Special Mashie Niblick	$145
Mussel Backed Mid Iron	$55
Dave Ogilvie Mashie Niblick	$100
Parplay: Brassie Black Fiber Insert Brass Sole Plate	$70
Parplay: Driver Black Face Insert	$70
Parplay: Spoon Black Fiber Insert Brass Sole Plate	$75
Plus Four Brassie Red Fiber Insert Aluminum Sole Plate	$70
Plus Four Driver Red Fiber Insert Aluminum Sole Plate	$70
Plus Four Spoon Red Fiber Insert Aluminum Sole Plate	$70
Prestwick Deep Ribbed Face Mashie	$125
Prestwick Irons Chrome Lined Face	$45
Prestwick Irons Lined Face	$50
Prestwick Socket Head Brassie Plain Face	$60
Prestwick Socket Head Driver Plain Face	$60
Prestwick Socket Head Spoon Plain Face	$60
Ranger Brassie Aluminum Face Insert and Sole Plate	$65
Ranger Driver Aluminum Face Insert and Sole Plate	$65
Ranger Spoon Aluminum Face Insert and Sole Plate	$65
Ted Ray Brassie Bulger Face	$175
Ted Ray Cleek Monel Metal Dash Face	$125
Ted Ray Driver Bulger Face	$175
Ted Ray Mashie Monel Metal	$125
Ted Ray Mashie Monel Metal Dash Face	$125
Ted Ray Mid Iron Monel Metal Line Face	$125
Ted Ray Monel Metal Jigger	$135
Ted Ray Mongrel Iron Monel Metal	$150
Ted Ray Mongrel Mashie Monel Metal	$150
Ted Ray Pitcher Monel Metal	$135
Red Faced Brassie	$95
Regal Mid Iron	$60
Rotary Model Mashie Deep Groove Checkered Face	$325
Rotary Model Mashie Niblick Deep Groove Checkered Face	$325
Rotary Model Mashie Niblick Half Checkered Half Slot Face	$600
George Sargent Monel Mashie Lined Face	$100
George Sargent Monel Mashie Niblick	$200
George Sargent Monel Mid Iron	$100
Sportsman Brassie Plain Face with Striped Top	$60
Sportsman Driver Plain Face with Striped Top	$60
Sportsman Long Head Brassie	$65

COMPANY	HICKORY	VALUE
Burke Manufacturing Co. (cont.):		
Sportsman Long Head Driver		$75
Sportsman Spoon Plain Face with Striped Top		$70
St. Andrews Special Mid Iron		$50
St. Andrews Special Putter Dot Punched Face		$50
Stainless Blade Putter		$50
Standard Blade Putter		$60
Standard Concentric Back Mid Iron		$60
Standard Deep Faced Mashie Lined Face		$50
Standard Deep Faced Niblick		$60
Standard Deep Faced Putter		$60
Standard Diamond Back Mid Iron Lined Face		$60
Standard Gooseneck Putter		$75
Standard Jigger Lined Face		$50
Standard Lined Face Cleek		$50
Standard Lined Face Driving Iron		$80
Standard Lined Face Mashie Niblick		$50
Standard Mashie Deep Grooved Face		$95
Standard Mashie Iron with Plain Back		$50
Standard Mashie Lined Face		$45
Standard Mashie Niblick		$50
Standard Mashie Niblick Deep Ribbed Face		$95
Standard Mashie Niblick Plain Back		$50
Standard Mashie Round Back		$55
Standard Medium Head Niblick		$50
Standard Mid Iron Lined Face		$45
Standard Mid Iron Offset		$55
Standard Mid Iron Round Back Lined Face		$60
Standard Niblick Plain Back		$50
Standard Plain Faced Brassie		$60
Standard Plain Faced Spoon		$60
Standard Putter Round Top Broad Sole		$75
Standard Putter Square Toe and Broad Sole		$95
Standard Putting Cleek		$50
Standard Round Back Cleek		$60
Standard Series Driver Plain Face		$60
Standard Spade Mashie Plain Back		$50
Harry Vardon Splice Headed Driver		$375
Harry Vardon Approach Mashie		$225
Harry Vardon Brassie Face Insert		$225
Harry Vardon Bulger Faced Brassie Fiber Face		$190
Harry Vardon Bulger Faced Driver		$190
Harry Vardon Driver Face Insert		$225
Harry Vardon Driving Iron		$150
Harry Vardon Fiber Faced Spoon		$265
Harry Vardon Jigger		$190
Harry Vardon Lined Face Cleek		$150
Harry Vardon Mashie		$150

COMPANY HICKORY	VALUE
Burke Manufacturing Co. (cont.):	
Harry Vardon Mashie Niblick	$150
Harry Vardon Mid Iron	$150
Harry Vardon Monel Metal Approach Mashie	$280
Harry Vardon Monel Metal Driving Iron	$190
Harry Vardon Monel Metal Jigger	$225
Harry Vardon Monel Metal Mashie	$190
Harry Vardon Monel Metal Mashie Niblick	$190
Harry Vardon Monel Metal Mid Iron	$190
Harry Vardon Monel Metal Mogrel Iron	$350
Harry Vardon Monel Metal Mongrel Mashie	$350
Harry Vardon Monel Metal Niblick	$190
Harry Vardon Mongrel Iron	$300
Harry Vardon Mongrel Mashie	$300
Harry Vardon Niblick	$150
Harry Vardon Plain Faced Brassie	$190
Harry Vardon Plain Faced Spoon	$250
Harry Vardon Splice Head Brassie	$375
W.C. Sherwood Large Head Niblick	$100
Zenith Brassie Plain Faced Striped Top Aluminum Backweight	$60
Zenith Driver Plain Faced Striped Top Aluminum Backweight	$60
Zenith Spoon Plain Faced Striped Top Aluminum Backweight	$60
J. Burnes & Co.:	
Dot Faced Niblick The Falcon	$955
George G. Bussey:	
Patented Gun Metal Bladed Putter Steel Hosel	$600
Patented Iron Blade Putter	$500
Patented Long Blade Lofting Iron Smooth Face	$500
Patented Smooth Faced Mashie Compact Blade	$450
Patented Steel Socket Cleek Short Smooth Face	$500
Patented Steel Socket Mashie	$300
Transitional Beech Headed Brassie	$750
J.H. Busson:	
Socket Headed Driver	$75
Striped Top Brassie	$75
XLALL Iron Blade Putter Square Socket	$150
Peter Cafferty:	
Top Spin Stainless Putter	$375
Adam Caird:	
Diamond Backed Driving Iron Diamond Dot Face	$90
Caledonia:	
Dot Faced Driving Iron	$40
Callan Brothers:	
Stainless Leaf Brand Putter	$90

COMPANY HICKORY	VALUE
Alex Campbell:	
Nipper Putter	$125
Stainless Mashie Lined Face	$125
Jamie Campbell:	
Smooth Faced Mid Iron	$150
W.W. Campbell:	
Jigger	$75
Willie Campbell:	
Wm. Campbell Smooth Faced Mid Iron	$175
Franklin Park Gun Metal Blade Putter	$375
Gun Metal Blade Putter	$150
Smooth Faced Mashie	$125
Socket Headed Brassie	$150
Socket Headed Driver	$150
Special Mashie	$150
Splice Headed Driver	$275
Cann & Taylor:	
Long Splice Bulldog Shaped Head Brassie	$250
Richmond Smooth Faced Mashie	$300
Short Splice Spoon	$375
Splice Headed Driver	$450
Straight Blade Ladies Putter	$165
"J.H. Taylor" Bent Blade Putter	$150
"J.H. Taylor" Confidus Driver	$125
"J.H. Taylor" Confidus Spoon	$150
"J.H. Taylor" Cynosure Mid Iron Lined Face	$90
"J.H. Taylor" Deep Faced Mashie Iron	$75
"J.H. Taylor" Dot Faced Mashie Niblick	$65
"J.H. Taylor" Driver	$150
"J.H. Taylor" Flywheel Dot Faced Mashie	$65
"J.H. Taylor" Flywheel Putter	$125
"J.H. Taylor" Hyphen Scored Niblick	$55
"J.H. Taylor" Lined Face Mashie	$65
"J.H. Taylor" Mascot Mid Iron	$95
"J.H. Taylor" Mules Patent Spring Faced Mashie	$700
"J.H. Taylor" Quickstop Oval Headed Mashie	
Dash Dot Face	$90
"J.H. Taylor" Short Blade Mashie Lined Deep Face	$125
"J.H. Taylor" Smooth Faced Cleek	$75
"J.H. Taylor" Smooth Faced Lofter Long Blade	$125
"J.H. Taylor" Smooth Faced Mashie	$95
"J.H. Taylor" Smooth Faced Mashie Heavy Blade	$125
"J.H. Taylor" Smooth Faced Mashie Short Deep Face	$125
"J.H. Taylor" Smooth Faced Mid Iron	$95
"J.H. Taylor" Smooth Faced Niblick Small Heavy Head	$300
"J.H. Taylor" Stripe Head Brassie Socket Head	$125
"J.H. Taylor" Striped Top Driver Socket Head	$125
Winchester Smooth Faced Iron	$375

COMPANY HICKORY	VALUE
Cann & Taylor (cont.):	
Winchester Smooth Faced Lofter	$300
William K. Cannon:	
Flanged Sole Mashie Lined Face	$95
J. Carr:	
Dot Faced Mashie Niblick Short Blade	$50
F. & A. Carrick:	
Cleek	$350
Deep Faced Mashie	$450
Iron Long Hosel	$900
Long Blade Lofter	$500
Long Faced Cleek Long Hosel	$750
Mashie	$500
Short Blade Wide Toe Mashie	$550
Small Circular Headed Niblick Thick Heavy Hosel	$2,750
Thomas Carruthers:	
Smooth Convex Face Putter Drilled Through Hosel	$650
Smooth Faced Cleek Short Blade Drilled Through Hosel	$450
Smooth Faced Mashie Drilled Through Hosel	$400
Smooth Faced Niblick Drill Through Hosel	$400
George Carter:	
Lined Face Mashie	$75
Socket Headed Driver	$100
J.L. Cassidy:	
Aluminum Head Mallet Putter	$125
Starbeck Socket Headed Driver	$100
A. Catlin:	
Socket Headed Driver	$75
Harry Cawsey:	
Angsol Spoon	$300
Hypen Faced Niblick	$75
Lined Face Spade Mashie	$65
Socket Headed Brassie Round Sole	$175
Spli Sok Brassie	$650
F. Chambers:	
Socket Headed Driver	$65
Splice Head Driver	$175
J. Chambers:	
Beech Headed Putter Pointed Toe	$450
Champion:	
Putter	$50
Chattell Co.:	
Spade Mashie Dot Face	$45
Stainless Mashie Niblick	$50
Harry Chestney:	
Small Socket Headed Spoon	$70
James Churchill:	
Dot Faced Mashie	$275

COMPANY	HICKORY	VALUE
Clan Golf Company:		
Compact Blade Mashie Smooth Face		$350
Light Colored Head Brassie		$650
Long Deep Bladed Iron Smooth Face		$450
Putter		$75
Semi Long Nosed Transitional Shaped Head Driver		$900
Splice Headed Transitional Bulger Brassie		$450
A. Clark:		
Smooth Faced Mashie		$175
D.W. Clark:		
Putter		$60
J. & D. Clark:		
Bent Blade Putter		$325
Blade Putter		$95
Dot Faced Mashie		$125
Semi Long Nosed Wooden Headed Putter		$1,150
Short Spliced Head Driver Bulger Face		$500
Small Headed Niblick Long Hosel Smooth Face		$850
Smooth Concave Faced Lofter		$400
Smooth Faced Cleek Short Round Back Blade		$300
Smooth Faced Lofting Iron		$75
Smooth Faced Mashie Compact Blade		$225
Peter Clark:		
Diamond Faced Mashie Niblick		$75
Climax Fife:		
Putter		$45
J. Clucas:		
Iron Bladed Putter		$45
Clydesdale Rubber Company:		
Smooth Faced Lofter		$125
R.T. Cobb:		
Long Nosed Brassie		$650
George Coburn:		
Medium Head Niblick Lined Face		$50
Socket Headed Brassie		$65
J.P. Cochrane & Company:		
Dedli Grooved Face Pitcher		$175
Walter Hagen 2 Iron		$135
Walter Hagen Brassie Socket Head		$150
Walter Hagen Stainless Blade Putter		$100
JPC Putting Cleek		$90
Joe Kirkwood Brassie Wood Red Face Insert		$145
Lined Face Mashie		$50
Mammoth Model Niblick Huge Face		$1,500
T. & G. McKenzie Deep Faced Mid Iron		$75
Model Z Broad Flange Sole Putter Flat Side On Hosel		$100
Nigger Model Long Thin Blade And Hosel Putter		$400
Nigger Model Putter Deep Faced Blade		$400

COMPANY HICKORY	VALUE

J. P. Cochrane & Company (cont.):

Oval Headed Mashie Niblick Extra Large Head	$2,500
Travers Putter Rectangular Wooden Head Center Shaft	$700
U.O.T. Putter with Cut Out Section at Toe	$650
U.O.T. Putter with Knight Mark at the Toe	$600

William Collins:

Smooth Faced Mashie	$90

Archie Compston:

A. Patrick Five Iron	$45
Socket Headed Driver	$50

Robert Condie:

Auchteronie Mashie	$55
Diamond Dot Scored Cleek	$75
Dot Faced Mid Iron	$50
Excelsior Model Blade Putter	$70
Gun Metal Blade Putter	$70
Iron with Gutta Percha Face Insert	$1,950
J. Smart & Co. Lofting Iron	$65
Smooth Deep Face Blade Putter	$80
Smooth Faced Cleek	$90
Smooth Faced Cleek Short Hosel	$165
Smooth Faced Ladies Iron	$145
Smooth Faced Lofting Iron	$70
Straight Blade Brass Putter	$125

Connellan & Campbell:

Smooth Faced Driving Iron	$125

Connellan Brothers:

Smooth Faced Mid Iron	$90

Thomas J. Conroy:

Smooth Faced Cleek	$85
Smooth Faced Mashie Niblick	$100
Splice Headed Driver	$25

S.J. Cooper:

Bulger Brassie Spliced Wood	$275

Corey & Savage:

Center Shafted Putter	$165

Corona:

Lined Face Niblick	$30

E. Cosby:

Wm. Gibson Mid Iron	$140
Wm. Gibson Socket Headed Driver	$225

Cowan Golf Company:

Mills Style Fairway Brassie Cross Hatch Face Markings	$275

Cox & Sons:

Dot Faced Mashie Niblick	$50

J. & W. Craigie:

Comet Putter Iron Blade	$90
Comet Small Headed Brassie	$175

COMPANY	HICKORY	VALUE

J. & W. Craigie (cont.):

Hyphen Face Mashie	$90
Ladies Driving Iron	$60
Large Head Niblick Lined Face	$120
Lined Face Mashie	$80
Smooth Faced Mid Iron	$120
Smooth Faced Niblick Small Head	$425
Socket Headed Brassie	$200
Splice Headed Driver	$425

Crawford Bartlett Company:

Child's Mashie	$60

J. & R. Crighton:

Dot Faced Cleek	$85
Oval Shaped Head Mashie Niblick Lined Face	$90

Jack Croke:

Dot Faced Niblick	$60
Driver	$60

Henry Crook:

Lined Face Iron	$65

Crosthwaite & Lorimer:

Semi Long Nosed Brassie Transitional Shaped Head	$350
Smooth Face Heavy Blade Iron	$225

Crusader:

Putter	$50

George Cumming:

Corrugated Face Mashie Niblick	$150

William Cunningham:

Dreadnaught Style Large Socket Head Driver	$75
Gullen Model Socket Headed Brassie	$75
Socket Headed Brassie Striped Top	$65

J.D. Currie:

Child's Socket Headed Driver	$65

H.L. Curtis:

Anti Shank Niblick Smooth Face	$190
Lined Face Mashie	$50
Round Backed Sammy Iron Dot Face	$75
Socket Headed Brassie	$95
Socket Headed Driver	$90
Wooden Putter Center Shaft And Brass Sole	$325

J. Cuthbert:

Dot Faced Driving Iron	$40
Premier Putting Cleek	$95

George Dagnall:

Bobby Low Profile Putter Dot Face Sloped Back	$90
Handy Andy Kutspin Highball Mashie Dot Dash Face	$650

Allan Dailey:

Socket Head Driver Stripe Top	$50

COMPANY HICKORY	VALUE
J. Dalgleish:	
Blade Putter	$65
Missouri Topspin Putter Top Flange	$275
Old Elm Offset Blade Putter	$60
Splice Head Driver	$165
Walter Dalrymple:	
Duplex Club Cylindrical Aluminum Head	
Dual Striking Surfaces	$2,250
Duplex Club Cylindrical Brass Head	
Dual Striking Surfaces	$5,000
Dame, Stoddard & Co.:	
Dot Face Blade Putter	$60
Gun Metal Blade Putter	$140
Smooth Faced Lofter	$50
Trimount Smooth Faced Mid Iron	$65
Dame, Stoddard & Kendall:	
Socket Headed Driver	$60
Daniel:	
Rectangular Headed Putter Adjustable Toe Weights	$2,500
J.H. Dargo:	
Lined Face Mashie	$40
Lined Face Mid Iron	$45
Socket Headed Driver	$60
Davega:	
Tommy Armour Putter	$60
Tommy Armour Two Iron	$50
Baxspin Deep Ribbed Face Mashie	$95
Cameo Niblick	$40
Dot Face Mashie	$35
Gairlock Blade Putter	$35
Gairlock Lined Face Driving Iron	$35
Imperial Mashie Niblick Lined Face	$40
La Salle Mashie	$35
Metropolitan Chromed Mid Iron Dot Face	$35
Metropolitan Socket Headed Driver	$40
Wicklow Blade Putter Lined Face	$35
Wicklow Chromed Mid Iron	$35
Ashley Davey:	
Excelsior Dot Faced Mashie	$70
Gun Metal Blade Putter	$95
Gun Metal Niblick Two Surface Concave Face	
Top Extension	$4,250
Lined Face Mashie	$60
Smooth Faced Cleek	$125
Robert Davidson:	
Long Nosed Baffing Spoon	$7,000
Long Nosed Driving Putter	$8,500

COMPANY HICKORY	VALUE
Robert Davidson(cont.):	
Long Nosed Play Club	$9,500
W. Davidson:	
Splice Head Driver	$275
W.F. Davis:	
Smooth Faced Cleek	$225
Dayton's:	
Flange Sole Putter	$90
Arthur Day:	
Special 6 EEZE Scored Lofted Iron	$55
A. De La Torre:	
Lined Face Mashie	$50
The Deamon:	
Fred Blaisdell Smooth Faced Iron	$120
H.E. Dean:	
Mashie	$40
R.M. Dean:	
Smooth Faced Child's Cleek	$140
Deluxe:	
Maxwell Pattern Putter	$60
Andrew Denholm:	
Splice Headed Driver Leather Face Insert	$225
A. Des Jardins:	
Laval Driver Stripe Top	$60
Hugh Dewar:	
Lined Face Mashie Niblick	$60
Diamond Manufacturing Co.:	
Dot Face Mashie	$70
Diamond State Brand:	
Reid Corrugated Face Mashie	$125
J. & A. Dickson:	
Bent Hosel Blade Putter	$175
Convex Face Mashie	$450
Dot Punch Face Jigger	$60
Gun Metal Blade Putter	$175
Small Headed Niblick Smooth Face	$450
Dint Patent Golf Company Ltd.:	
Socket Headed Brassie Silver Sole and Face Plate	$450
Frank Doleman:	
Semi Long Nosed Beech Headed Putter	$700
Semi Long Nosed Spliced Transitional Head Driver	$700
Smooth Faced Iron	$150
Smooth Faced Mashie	$125
Splice Head Transitional Driver	$475
J. Donald & Son:	
Dot Faced Mashie	$70
J. Donaldson & Co.:	
Birdie Stainless Iron Lined Face	$70

COMPANY HICKORY	VALUE
J. Donaldson & Co. (cont.):	
Bunny Stainless Mallet Head Putter Brass Face Insert	$175
Rangefinder Blade Putter Dot Face	$70
Rangefinder Lined Face Mashie	$60
Rapier Mid Iron Dot Face	$50
Skelpie Iron Pointed Toe and Lined Face	$80
J.T. Donaldson:	
1 Iron Dot Face	$40
E.S. Douglas:	
Bent Necked Putter Line Dash Face	$65
Robert Dow:	
Splice Head Driver	$550
Draper Maynard Co.:	
Doggie Series Spade Mashie Dot Face	$50
Ideal Stainless Mid Iron Dot Face	$40
Kingswood 3 Chrome Iron Dot Face	$50
Lucky Dog Brassie	$90
Lucky Dog Mashie Deep Corrugated Face	$125
Lucky Dog Stainless Mashie Dot Face	$50
J.A. Dubow:	
Silver Cup Offset Putter	$40
A.M. Duncan:	
Perfector Driver Triangular Face Insert	$100
George Duncan:	
Duncan Mashie Niblick	$85
Socket Headed Brassie Face Insert	$90
William Duncan:	
Greenock Socket Head Brassie	$75
Dunn Brothers:	
Dunn Selected Smooth Faced Lofter	$95
Smooth Faced Mashie Iron	$275
John Duncan Dunn:	
British Golf Co. Lofter	$80
British Golf Co. Smooth Faced Niblick	$95
Ladies Ionic Mid Iron	$75
Splice Headed Brassie Fiber Face Insert	$200
Seymour Dunn:	
Splice Headed Brassie	$165
Viet Arte Mashie	$55
Viet Arte Mid Mashie	$60
Thomas Dunn:	
Beech Head Baffing Spoon	$5,750
Compact Blade Short Hosel Smooth Faced Cleek	$175
Long Blade Lofting Iron Hooked Face	$490
Long Nosed Mid Spoon	$2,995
Long Nosed Play Club	$2,650
Long Nosed Short Spoon Leather Face Insert	$3,500
Semi Long Nosed Beech Headed Brassie	$1,500

COMPANY HICKORY	VALUE
Thomas Dunn(cont.):	
Transitional Head Brassie	$600
Transitional Head Spoon	$1,250
William Dunn:	
Long Nosed Spoon	$8,000
William Dunn Jr.:	
Aluminum/Wood Headed Driver	$1,650
Approaching Cleek	$175
Child's Splice Headed Driver	$350
Cleek	$275
Dunn Select Splice Head Brassie	$300
Dunn Selected Putter Bent Neck Blade	$195
Dunn Selected Smooth Face Iron	$200
Dunn-Macgregor Short Blade Smooth Faced Iron	$300
Mallet Headed Center Shafted Chipper	
Dual Striking Surfaces	$275
One Piece Driver	$2,500
Persimmon Headed Short Splice Brassie	$325
Short Splice Head Driver	$600
Smooth Faced Lofter	$200
Smooth Faced Niblick Small Head	$775
Splice Headed Brassie Round Sole	$550
Splice Headed Bulger Faced Brassie	$425
Durexo:	
Patrick Socket Headed Driver	$65
Alex Duthie:	
Dot Faced Heavy Iron	$75
Dot Faced Light Iron	$65
Dot Faced Medium Iron	$65
J.W. Dwight:	
Boat Shaped Head Center Shaft Mashie Dot Faced	$3,750
Conic Shaped Head Driver Brass Backweight	$4,650
Peter Eagan:	
Socket Head Brassie	$55
Eager Special:	
Offset Blade Putter	$45
Eagrow Company:	
Arrow Stainless Mashie Line Face	$40
Edco:	
Dash Faced Niblick	$50
Edinboro:	
Smooth Faced Mashie	$80
Edinburgh Club:	
Smooth Faced Mashie	$65
Elm Ridge:	
Chrome Mid Iron Lined Face	$30
Elvery's:	
Shallow Faced Putter Curved Top	$165

COMPANY	HICKORY	VALUE

Emperor:
  Wooden Socket Headed Putter Bent Hosel $750
Esto Perpetua:
  Gun Metal Blade Putter $65
Eureka:
  Johnson Socket Head Driver $55
Everbrite:
  Dot Faced Mashie Niblick $60
  Stainless Mashie Dot Face $65
Fairfield:
  Approaching Mashie $125
  Centrajet Mashie $125
  Child's Driving Mashie $125
  Child's Putting Cleek $125
  Child's Spliced Head Brassie $225
  Child's Spliced Head Driver $225
  Concave Face Lofting Cleek $165
  Convex Back Mashie $125
  Deep Faced Medium Mashie $125
  Deep Faced Putting Cleek $140
  Driving Cleek $90
  Driving Iron $90
  Driving Mashie $125
  Gooseneck Putting Cleek $140
  Iron $75
  Light Mid Iron $125
  Lofting Iron $90
  Lofting Mashie $125
  Long Blade Driving Mashie $125
  Medium Mashie $90
  Putting Cleek $125
  Short Bladed Cleek $125
  Smooth Faced Child's Cleek $125
  Smooth Faced Child's Iron $125
  Smooth Faced Child's Lofting Iron $125
  Splice Headed Brassie Bulger Face $250
  Splice Headed Brassie Straight Face $250
  Splice Headed Driver Bulger Face $285
  Spliced Headed Driver Straight Face $275
  Thick Soled Niblick $140
  Twisted Neck Putting Cleek $125
Fairview:
  Smooth Faced Iron $80
Faith Manufacturing Co.:
  Big Ball Chromed Head Iron Lined Face $30
  Superflight Chromed Head Iron Dot Face $30
Far & Sure Golf Co.:
  Smooth Faced Iron $250

COMPANY HICKORY	VALUE
Far & Sure Golf Co. (cont.):	
Splice Head Driver Short Narrow Head	$800
Transitional Splice Head Brassie	$635
Transitional Wood Splice Head Putter	$965
Feild:	
Child's Mashie	$35
Child's Mid Iron	$30
Feltham & Co.:	
Smooth Faced Mashie	$125
William Fergie:	
Semi Long Nosed Spliced Headed Putter	$650
Semi Long Nosed Transitional Spliced Head Brassie	$500
Short Spliced Head Driver	$225
Smooth Faced Lofter	$225
Wood Socket Head Putter Fiber Face Insert	$280
A. Ferguson:	
Hyphen Scored Mid Iron	$75
Fernie & Ross:	
Eden Niblick Lined Face	$90
Ross's Own Cleek Carruthers Hosel Dot Face	$125
George Fernie:	
Semi Long Nosed Transitional Spoon Brass Sole Plate	$825
John Fernie:	
Par 4 Stainless Iron Dot Face	$30
Tom Fernie:	
Wooden Socket Head Baffy	$265
Willie Fernie:	
Short Splice Headed Brassie	$165
Smooth Faced Cleek	$125
Splice Head Driver	$225
Steel Blade Putter	$125
Fife Golf Co.:	
Lined Face Mid Iron	$45
Fitzjohn Brothers:	
Smooth Faced Iron	$90
Ed Fitzjohn:	
Adjustable Putter Shaft Attached to Back of Blade	$2,500
Val Fitzjohn:	
Short Splice Head Driver	$225
Niblett Flanders:	
Stainless Dot Faced Iron	$65
W. Fletcher:	
Gravitum Socket Headed Driver	$225
Hornby Brassie Face Insert	$70
Iron Blade Putter Dot Face	$45
W.S. Flite:	
Lined Face Niblick	$50

COMPANY HICKORY	VALUE
Val Flood:	
Splice Headed Driver	$295
Andrew Forgan:	
Anderson Smooth Faced Niblick Small Head	$625
Gun Metal Blade Putter	$225
Semi Long Nosed Splice Wooden Head Putter	$700
Semi Long Nosed Spliced Head Driver	$595
Smooth Faced Diamond Backed Cleek	$175
Smooth Faced Lofter Long Blade and Hosel	$325
Smooth Faced Mashie Compact Blade	$165
Spliced Neck Driver	$350
Robert Forgan:	
2 Iron	$60
4 Scotia Iron Line Scored Face	$60
Angle Shaft Brassie	$190
Anti Shank Lofter	$375
Approching Cleek Musselback Dot Face	$50
Boys Iron Blade Putter	$50
Boys Niblick Dot Face	$70
Celtic Lined Face Niblick	$55
Clan Mid Iron Lined Face	$35
Concave Face Lofter	$145
Crown Socket Headed Brassie	$75
Crown Socket Headed Driver	$95
Crown Stainless Iron Lined Face	$35
Dash Faced Niblick	$45
Diamond Backed Mashie	$65
Dot Faced Cleek	$50
Dot Faced Mashie	$70
Dot Faced Spade Mashie	$70
Dot Punched Face Jigger	$55
Dot Punched Mashie Iron	$60
Driving Iron Dot Face	$55
Eeze Lined Face Iron	$35
Forganite Socket Headed Brassie	$140
Forganite Socket Headed Driver	$135
Gem Rounded Back Dot Faced Putter	$80
General Purpose Iron	$475
General Purpose Iron Square Hosel	$250
Gold Medal Lined Face Iron	$35
Gold Medal Socket Headed Brassie Striped Top	$65
Gold Medal Socket Headed Driver Striped Top	$65
Gold Medal Socket Headed Spoon Striped Top	$65
Gun Metal Blade Putter	$195
Iron Bladed Putter	$55
Kirkaldy Driving Iron Dot Face	$95
Ladies Diamond Back Iron	$60
Ladies Smooth Faced Lofter	$95

COMPANY	HICKORY	VALUE

Robert Forgan(cont.):

Large Socket Headed Driver Face Insert	$75
Lined Face Iron	$45
Lined Face Mashie	$55
Lined Face Mashie Niblick	$65
Long Blade And Hosel Putting Cleek Lined Face	$80
Long Blade Lofting Iron	$175
Long Nose Beech Head Putter	$1,250
Long Nose Putter	$2,450
Long Nosed Baffy	$3,995
Long Nosed Play Club	$5,500
Long Nosed Spoon	$3,650
Long Thin Hosel James B. Batley Putter	$190
Maxmo Mallet Head Putter	$95
Maxmo Wood Mallet Headed Putter	$225
Meteor Socket Headed Brassie	$65
Meteor Socket Headed Driver	$65
Meteor Socket Headed Spoon	$65
Oval Headed Mashie Niblick Lined Face	$70
Oversize Socket Headed Driver	$125
Scotia Iron	$30
Scotia Stainless Iron	$35
Scotia Striped Top Brassie	$60
Scotia Striped Top Driver	$60
Scotia Striped Top Spoon	$60
Smooth Deep Faced Mashie	$125
Smooth Faced Cleek Long Hosel	$450
Smooth Faced Compact Blade Lofting Iron	$225
Smooth Faced Compact Blade Mashie	$150
Smooth Faced Iron Long Hosel	$390
Smooth Faced Lofter Long Hosel	$375
Smooth Faced Lofting Iron	$225
Smooth Faced Niblick Small Head Long Hosel	$650
Socket Driver Stamped Pastone & Sons	$95
Splice Headed Wood Putter	$550
Spliced Beech Wood Club Red Face Insert	$975
Steel Blade Putter	$195
Straight Blade Brass Putter	$190
Straight Faced Brass Blade Putter	$145
Tolley Forganite Socket Head Putter	$265
Tolley Wood Socket Head Putter	$225
Transitional Head Brassie	$550
Transitional Head Driver	$550
Whee Putter	$750

Charles Forrest:

Smooth Faced Lofter	$125

J. Forrest:

Spliced Headed Brassie Face Insert	$140

COMPANY HICKORY	VALUE
George Forrester:	
Composite Fiber Head Driver	$595
Concentric Back Weighted Iron	$135
Concentric Backed Mashie	$175
General Smooth Faced Iron	$150
Little Gem Putter Small Blade	$75
Long Nosed Spoon	$7,500
Putter Top Edge Bent Over Face	$1,250
Round Backed Iron	$295
Semi Long Nosed Brassie Bulger Shaped Splice Head	$475
Short Splice Head Brassie	$300
Smooth Faced Cleek	$125
Smooth Faced Cleek Bulbous Toe	$575
Smooth Faced Lofter	$150
Smooth Faced Mashie Two Humps On Back	$750
Smooth Faced Niblick Small Head	$275
Socket Headed Brassie	$265
Socket Headed Driver Patented	$225
James Forrester:	
Socket Head Brassie Stripe Top	$90
Forth Rubber Company Ltd.:	
Semi Long Nosed Transitional Head Driver Bulger Face	$435
Semi Long Nosed Transitional Splice Head Putter	$850
Smooth Faced Mashie	$225
Smooth Faced Niblick	$175
Fortnum & Mason:	
Fort Mason Giant Headed Stainless Niblick Dot Face	$1,950
Fort Mason Stainless Mashie Dot Face	$45
Small Socket Headed Spoon Fiber Face Insert	$65
Socket Headed Driver Stripe Top	$50
Foster Brothers:	
Bogee Square Hosel Rectangular Head Putter Broad Sole	$225
Dot Faced Driving Iron	$90
Lined Face Jigger	$120
Socket Headed Driver Ridged Sole Plate	$95
James Foulis:	
Concave Face Mashie Niblick Flat Sole	$550
Small Headed Niblick Slight Concave Face	$325
Smooth Faced Cleek	$250
Smooth Faced Cleek Octagon Back	$425
Splice Headed Brassie Leather Face Insert	$550
A. Fovargue:	
Concentric Back Mid Iron	$65
C. Fox:	
Mid Iron	$60
Chick Fraser:	
Lined Face Driving Iron	$45

COMPANY	HICKORY	VALUE
James Fryer:		
	Forrester Splice Headed Driver	$135
Harry Fulford:		
	Sammy Dot Faced Iron	$125
Charles Gadd:		
	Mallet Head Putter Beveled Top	$90
Alexander Gair:		
	Midget Marvel 2 Sided Approach Cleek	$275
Thomas Galloway:		
	Dot Faced Mashie	$55
A.W. Gamage Company:		
	Duncan Adjustable Head Putter/Chipper	$1,500
	Kromwell Dot Faced Mid Iron	$45
	Semi Long Nosed Transitional Splice Head Brassie	$375
	Smooth Faced Cleek	$95
	Splice Headed Driver	$150
Jean Gassiat:		
	Large Square Wood Socket Head Putter	$900
P.J. Gaudin:		
	Socket Head Driver Stripe Top	$55
Gee Bee:		
	Child's Mashie	$25
Gibson & Gadd:		
	Rounded Sole Socket Wood	$125
C.H. Gibson Jr.:		
	Socket Headed Driver	$55
Charles Gibson:		
	3 Iron Line Scored Face	$75
	Beech Headed Brassie Leather Face Insert	$950
	Child's Diamond Backed Iron Dash Face	$120
	Dash Faced Niblick Flange Sole	$65
	Geo. Duncan Akros Model Superior Rustless 2 Iron	$55
	Excellar 1 Iron Lined Face	$65
	Lofting Iron	$75
	Nippy Spoon Fiber Insert	$275
	Offset Blade Putter Hyphen Face Scoring	$110
	Scored Face 1 Iron	$45
	Semi Long Nosed Driver Wood Face Insert	$1,350
	Short Bladed Mashie Iron Deep Face	$90
	Smooth Face Niblick	$95
	Smooth Faced Rounded Sole Iron	$75
	Socket Wood Driver	$95
	Special Offset Blade Putter	$125
	Star Maxwell Rustless Mid Iron	$65
	Star Maxwell Starona Stainless Mid Iron	$75
	Jack White 2 Iron Stainless	$55
R.J. Gibson:		
	Excellar 1 Iron	$70

COMPANY HICKORY	VALUE
R.J. Gibson(cont.):	
Triplex Mid Iron	$90
William Gibson & Co.:	
Accurate Bent Neck Putter	$75
Aluminum Putter	$95
Aluminum Schenectady Putter	$200
Anti Shank Mashie Concave Back	$175
Anti Shank Smooth Face Medium Iron	$225
Baxspin Mashie Diamond Dot Face	$75
Baxspin Mashie Stainless Mashie Niblick	$90
Bent Neck Blade Putter	$75
Bent Neck Putter	$75
Boomer Shallow Faced Jigger Lined Face	$70
Braid Musselbacked Dot Faced Cleek	$90
Braid Musselbacked Dot Faced Driving Cleek	$90
Braid Musselbacked Dot Faced Heavy Iron	$90
Braid Musselbacked Dot Faced Light Iron	$90
Braid Musselbacked Dot Faced Mashie	$90
Braid Musselbacked Dot Faced Medium Iron	$90
Braid Musselbacked Dot Faced Niblick	$90
Braid Musselbacked Dot Faced Putter	$90
Carruthers Hosel Iron	$120
Cheshire Dot Faced Mashie Niblick	$95
Cleek Leather Face Insert	$1,950
Dandy Mashie Niblick Diamond Back Dot Face	$95
De Montmorencie Dot Faced Push Iron	$125
Dead'un Mashie Niblick Holes Drilled In Face	$750
Deep Faced Mashie	$70
Deep Faced Socket Driver	$125
Domine Round Back Putter	$135
Dot Faced Light Iron	$80
Duncan Dot Faced Mid Iron	$95
Duncan Driving Iron	$70
George Duncan Akros Model Mashie Niblick	$50
George Duncan Akros Model Medium Iron	$55
George Duncan Deep Slotted Face Mashie Niblick	$185
ESKIT Offset Hosel Blade Dot Faced Putter	$165
Flanged Back Medium Iron	$55
Frostick's Anti Shank Mashie Niblick	$190
Gem Dot Faced Putter	$90
Goosenecked Putter	$75
Horn Mid Iron	$50
Jerko Corrugated Deep Grove Mashie	$235
Jerko Deep Ribbed Face Pitcher	$175
Jonko Flat Sole Putter Large Hump At Sweet Spot	$2,650
Kilgour Match Blade Putter	$95
Kinghorn Large Head Persimmon Socket Driver	$110
Kinghorn Mashie Dash Face	$40

COMPANY	HICKORY	VALUE

William Gibson & Co. (cont.):

Kinghorn Socket Head Driver Stripe Head	$75
Kirkaldy Lined Face Mashie	$90
Ladies R. Hutton Smooth Faced Cleek	$70
Lined Face Full Iron	$50
Lined Face Medium Iron	$90
Logan's Genii Lined Face Mashie	$65
Logan's Genii Lined Face Mashie Cleek	$65
Logan's Genii Lined Face Mashie Niblick	$65
Logan's Genii Lined Face Medium Iron	$65
Logan's Genii Lined Face Putting Cleek	$65
Logan's Genii Lined Face Stainless Cleek	$50
Logan's Genii Lined Face Stainless Mashie	$50
Logan's Genii Lined Face Stainless Mashie Cleek	$50
Logan's Genii Lined Face Stainless Mashie Niblick	$50
Logan's Genii Lined Face Stainless Medium Iron	$50
Logan's Genii Smooth Faced Cleek Notched Hosel	$165
Logan's Genii Smooth Faced Mashie Cleek Notched Hosel	$165
Logan's Genii Smooth Faced Mashie Notched Hosel	$165
Logan's Genii Smooth Faced Medium Iron Notched Hosel	$165
Logan's Genii Smooth Faced Putting Cleek Notched Hosel	$165
Logan's Smooth Mashie Niblick Notched Hosel	$165
Massy Cleek	$90
Massy Deep Faced Mashie	$100
Massy Iron	$90
Massy Jigger	$90
Massy Long Faced Mashie	$100
Massy Mashie Niblick	$90
Massy Niblick	$90
Massy Putter	$90
Massy Round Backed Iron	$100
Mignon Socket Head Driver Bulger Face	$120
Monel Metal Patented Putter	$265
Offset Hosel Dot Faced 2 Iron	$60
Orion Broad Flange Sole Putter	$85
Pixie Cleek Offset Head Dot Face	$95
Pixie Sammy Lined Scored Specialty Club	$85
Princeps Top Edge Weighted Putter	$325
Sargent Lined Face Spade Mashie	$90
Semi Long Nosed Aluminum Putter	$175
Shallow Bladed Jigger Dot Face	$65
Jack Shannon Mongrel Mashie	$75
Short Socket Head Spoon	$120
Simpson Smooth Faced Mashie	$125
Skart Lined Face Mashie Niblick	$55

COMPANY	HICKORY	VALUE

William Gibson & Co. (cont.):

Skinner Protruding Face Putter	$275
Skoogee Concave Niblick	$500
Small Socket Head Baffy Spoon	$140
Smooth Faced Cleek	$120
Smooth Faced Cleek Carruthers Hosel	$95
Socket Head Brassie Stripe Stop	$75
Socket Head Driver	$75
Special Kinghorn Smooth Faced Oval Head Lofter	$90
Stainless Jigger	$50
Star Maxwell Stainless Mashie Dot Face	$75
Starona Stainless Mid Iron Lined Face	$65
Stella Stainless Mid Iron Lined Face	$40
Straight Blade Brass Putter	$175
Straight Blade Putting Iron Heavy Dot Punch Face	$75
Superior Stainless Iron	$40
Superior Stainless Niblick Dash Face	$45
Tate Putting Cleek	$90
Triple Star Stainless Offset Blade Putter	$65
Winchester Deep Ribbed Face Niblick	$175

Glasgow Golf Company:

Dot Faced Blade Putter	$55
Socket Headed Driver	$375

Glencoe:

Corrugated Face Mashie	$90

Glover Specialty Co.:

Driver Metal Face Insert	$100
Socket Head Balance Brassie	$65
Square Wood Headed Mallet Putter Metal Face Insert	$700

Goick:

Center Shafted Putter	$750

Gold Smith Company:

Gun Metal Blade Putter	$35
Hyde Park Mashie Lined Face	$30
Lined Face Mid Iron	$30

Golden Eagle:

Lined Face Mashie Niblick	$55

Golf Goods Manufacturing Co.:

Small Headed Niblick	$900
Smooth Faced Cleek	$200
Smooth Faced Mashie Thick Blade	$225
Socket Headed Driver	$275
Splice Headed Driver	$550
Thick Bladed Putting Cleek	$225

The Golf Shop:

Deep Faced Mashie	$40
Dot Faced Mid Iron	$35
Hold Em Mashie Deep Corrugated Face	$175

COMPANY HICKORY	VALUE
The Golf Shop (cont.):	
Musselbacked Jigger Dot Face	$55
Golf Specialty Shop:	
Arroflite Deep Ribbed Face Mashie	$90
Goodrich Sales Co.:	
Adjustable Iron	$2,250
Goudie & Co.:	
Convex Backed Cleek	$80
Gun Metal Blade Putter	$120
Patented Hosel Putter Smooth Face	$140
Semi Long Nosed Transitional Beech Headed Driver	$450
Bert Gourlay:	
Socket Headed Driver	$55
James Gourlay:	
Bent Neck Putter	$90
Concentric Back Mashie Diamond Face	$65
Deep Face Mashie	$60
Diamond Backed Mid Iron	$65
Large Headed Niblick Dot Face	$125
Oval Headed Mashie Niblick Diamond Dot Face	$65
Rounded Sole Sammy Iron	$60
Smooth Face Round Backed Putter	$100
Smooth Faced Cleek	$80
Smooth Faced Rounded Back Putter	$95
Vaile Swan Necked Putter	$450
Walter Gourlay:	
Dot Faced Blade Putter	$50
Grampian Range:	
Mashie Weight Holes in Upper Edge of Blade	$140
Grand Leader:	
Gun Metal Blade Putter	$90
Frank Grant:	
Deep Faced Socket Head Driver	$60
Gravitator Golf Ball Co.:	
Multi Faced Putter Four Interchangeable Inserts	$3,750
A. Gray:	
Deep Faced Short Bladed Niblick	$6,500
Heavy Hosel Iron	$5,750
Long Nosed Cleek	$3,250
Ernest Gray:	
Socket Headed Driver	$60
John Gray:	
Concave Face Long Hosel Lofter	$2,650
Long Hosel Cleek Smooth Face	$1,950
Long Hosel Lofter Deep Face	$1,950
Long Thick Hosel Niblick Small Thick Head	$3,250
Great Lakes Company:	
Tommy Armour 5 Iron	$45

COMPANY HICKORY	VALUE
Great Lakes Company (cont.):	
Baltic Mid Iron Dot Face	$125
Blade Putter	$35
Glen Eagle Socket Headed Driver	$45
New Yorker Chrome Bladed Putter	$40
Socket Headed Driver Stripe Top	$40
Stainless Niblick	$35
Great Lakes Golf Corp.:	
Al Watrous Straight Eight 5 Mashie	$40
Grosse Ile Putter Co.:	
Stailess Putter Flanged Sole	$65
George Grove & Co.:	
Hawk Stainless Mid Iron	$60
F. Guise:	
Small Musselback Putter	$140
Gyroscope:	
Deep Diagonal Grooved Mashie	$225
Otto Hackbarth:	
Aluminum Headed Coat Hanger Hosel Putter	
Brass Weight Insole	$575
Small Splice Head Spoon	$450
J. Hagen:	
Brassie with Black Face Insert	$95
Walter Hagen:	
Belleair Iron	$30
Diplomat Socket Head Brassie	$55
Diplomat Socket Head Driver	$55
Diplomat Socket Head Spoon	$55
Diplomat Stainless Iron Dot Face	$35
Getaway Socket Head Brassie Stripe Top	$55
Getaway Socket Head Driver Stripe Top	$55
Getaway Socket Head Spoon Stripe Top	$55
Getway Iron Lined Face	$35
Hagen Autograph Brassie Bulls Eye	
Insert Brass Backweight	$90
Hagen Autograph Driver Bulls Eye	
Insert Brass Backweight	$90
Hagen Autograph Spoon Bulls Eye	
Insert Brass Backweight	$90
Hagen Autograph Socket Headed Brassie	
Brass Face Insert	$90
Hagen Autograph Socket Headed Driver	
Brass Face Insert	$90
Hagen Autograph Socket Headed Spoon	
Brass Face Insert	$90
Hagen Deluxe Stainless Iron	$40
The Haig Mallet Head Putter	$175
The Haig Mallet Head Putter with Paddle Grip	$275

COMPANY	HICKORY	VALUE

Walter Hagen (cont.):

Heatherdowns Socket Head Brassie Striped Top	$55
Heatherdowns Socket Head Driver Striped Top	$55
Heatherdowns Socket Head Spoon Striped Top	$55
International Iron	$35
Ironman Sand Iron Flat Lined Face Large Flange	$225
Lucky Len Wooden Head Putter	$275
Smooth Concave Faced Sand Iron Large Flanged Sole	$525
St. James Stainless Iron	$35
Staybrite Stainless Iron	$35
Tom Boy Stainless Iron	$35
Triangle Brassie Plain Face	$60
Triangle Brassie Plug Face Insert	$75
Triangle Compact Head Iron Duro Chrome Lined Face	$40
Triangle Driver Plain Face	$60
Triangle Driver Plug Face Insert	$75
Triangle Putter	$45
Triangle Spoon Plain Face	$60
Triangle Spoon Plug Face Insert	$75
Ultra Stainless Iron	$35
"WH" Lined Face Iron	$40
"WH" Socket Headed Brassie Plain Face	$60
"WH" Socket Headed Driver Plain Face	$60
"WH" Socket Headed Spoon Plain Face	$60

Willie Hall:

Mallet Headed Putter	$225

James B. Halley & Co.:

28 Maxwell Mashie Niblick	$85
Child's Gum Metal Blade Putter	$125
Child's Iron	$45
Dot Faced Mid Iron	$50
Dreadnought Niblick	$90
Gun Metal Shallow Faced Putter	$90
Ideal Putter	$85
Lined Face Mid Iron	$55
Malley Headed Putter	$125
Maxwell Mid Iron Hyphen Face	$75
Mid Iron Concentric Back Weighted Dot Faced	$50
Small Headed Mallet Gun Metal Putter	$150
Stainless Mashie	$50
Two Sided Putter	$75

Arthur Ham:

Dot/Dash Faced Sammy Iron	$100
Hamsole Niblick Shallow Cuts In The Sole	$3,250
Lined Face Mashie	$45

Handkraft:

Chrome Headed Mashie Dot Face	$35

COMPANY	HICKORY	VALUE
Con Harders:		
	Chrome Head Mashie Lined Face	$35
	Flange Sole Mid Iron Lined Face	$50
Edward Hardman:		
	Socket Headed Brassie	$60
Hardright:		
	Vulcanite Head Driver Brass Hosel Ferrule	$450
T. Harris:		
	Lined Face Mashie	$55
E.V. Hartford:		
	Gun Metal Putter Center Shafted Aiming Device on Top	$6,500
Haskins & Sons:		
	Smooth Faced Iron	$90
	Stainless Niblick Dot Face	$50
Arthur Havers:		
	Socket Head Driver Stripe Top	$60
Hawco:		
	Large Socket Head Driver	$65
	Offset Blade Putter	$65
	Willie Park Iron Smooth Face	$225
Charles Haywood:		
	Stainless Mid Iron Lined Face	$75
J.H. Hearn:		
	Niblick Stainless Mashie	$50
Heather Brand:		
	Maxwell Stainless Mashie.	$50
Thomas Hemming & Son:		
	Oval Blade Mashie Niblick Thick Sole	$175
Hemming Golf Co.:		
	Offset Putter	$175
William Henderson:		
	Beech Transitional Play Club Spliced Neck	$975
Hendry & Bishop Ltd.:		
	The Bert Oval Headed Mid Iron	$65
	Cardinal 2 Iron Dot Face	$75
	Cardinal Child's Giant Niblick	$1,400
	Cardinal Dreadnought Extra Large Headed Niblick	$175
	Cardinal Driving Iron	$55
	Cardinal Giant Headed Niblick Dot Face	$1,950
	Cardinal Large Headed Niblick Lined Face	$90
	Cardinal Lined Faced Iron	$45
	Cardinal Mashie Dot Punched Face	$55
	Cardinal Oval Headed Mashie Niblick Lined Face	$65
	Compston Smooth Concave Faced Niblick	$375
	Diamond Back Putting Cleek	$90
	Diamond Faced Pitching Mashie	$75
	Dot Punched Face Blade Putter	$75
	Dot Punched Face Jigger	$50

COMPANY HICKORY	VALUE
Hendry & Bishop Ltd. (cont.):	
Eagle Special Iron Blade Putter	$75
Long Faced Putting Cleek Dot Face	$75
The Master Round Back Niblick Lined Face	$95
Miter Dot Faced Cleek	$55
Miter Dot Faced Mashie	$60
Miter Lined Face Mashie	$55
Offset Blade Iron Putter	$65
Per Whit Round Blade Hollow Back Putter	$475
Pitch Em Mashie Niblick Lined Face	$90
Scottie Dot Faced Niblick	$75
Slog Em Iron Threaded Nut to Tighten Hosel	$750
Smooth Concave Faced Sand Iron Very Thick Sole	$425
Sniper Long Thin Hosel and Blade Putter	$295
Henley:	
Short Splice Head Driver	$165
Hugh Henry:	
Socket Head Brassie	$75
James Hepburn:	
Socket Headed Driver	$75
Herd & Herd:	
Champion Splice Head Driver	$175
Flange Sole Putter	$75
Long Narrow Socket Head Baffy	$50
Herd & Yeoman:	
Lined Face Mid Iron	$60
Socket Head Brassie	$75
Socket Head Spoon	$95
Alexander Herd:	
Dot Faced Niblick	$100
Semi Long Nosed Putter Fiber Slip	$225
Semi Long Nosed Splice Head Brassie	$425
Semi Long Nosed Splice Head Putter	$700
Short Splice Headed Driver Leather Face Insert	$200
Trusty Iron Blade Putter	$65
James Herd:	
St. Andrews Socket Head Driver	$75
George Heron:	
Short Blade Mashie Cross Face	$75
Socket Head Driver	$75
Walter Hewitt:	
Bent Neck Putter	$100
Hiatt & Co.:	
Compact Head Smooth Faced Lofting Iron	$150
Smooth Faced Mashie Short Blade	$175
Straight Blade Brass Putter	$125
Hillerich & Bradsby:	
9 X Chipping Iron	$60

COMPANY	HICKORY	VALUE

Hillerich & Bradsby (cont.):

Backspin Mashie Deep Ribbed Face	$100
Backspin Pitcher Stag Dot Face	$65
Center Shafted Mallet Head Putter	$150
Child's Mashie	$35
Child's Mid Iron	$35
Deep Grooved Face Mashie Niblick	$125
Diamond Back Cleek	$55
Flanged Back Dot Punched Face 2P Putter	$75
Grand Slam Iron	$35
Hindsdale Iron	$30
Invincible Iron Chrome Duo Flange Head	$45
Invincible Mid Iron	$60
Invincible Socket Head Wood	$55
Kernal Iron Blade Putting Cleek	$65
Kernel Socket Head Driver	$75
Lady Lo Skore	$35
Lined Face Approach Putter	$120
Lo Skore 11A Driver	$100
Lo Skore Iron	$35
Lo Skore Two Tone Socket Brassie	$95
Musselback Approach Iron Dash Dot Face	$75
Par X Driving Iron	$55
Par X L Driving Iron	$60
Par X L Mashie Deep Ribbed Face	$90
Par X L Mid Iron Kork Grip	$150
Par X L Mid Iron Scored Face with Dots And Dashes	$50
Par X Mallet Head Putter	$100
Par X Schenectady Putter Cork Grip	$250
S C I Slotted Hosel Mashie Niblick	$100
Socket Head Brassie Kork Grip	$150
Stainless Putter	$100

Percy Hills:

Large Head Lined Face Niblick	$65

Jack Hobens:

Short Splice Driver	$175

A.J. Hobley:

Lined Face Iron	$90

J.A. Hockey:

Splice Headed Persimmon Brassie	$175

Tom Hood: (Scotland)

Long Nosed Play Club	$5,250
Long Nosed Spoon	$4,750
Semi Long Nosed Driver	$1,995

Tom Hood: (Ireland)

Lined Face Mashie	$75
Lined Face Niblick Medium Head	$80

COMPANY	HICKORY	VALUE
E.A. Hooker:		
Socket Headed Brassie		$65
The Horn:		
Lined Face Niblick		$60
Chester Horton:		
Socket Headed Brassie		$65
Socket Headed Spoon Stripe Top		$75
Waverly Horton:		
Mid Iron		$60
Pay Me Schenectady Head Putter		$250
Spence & Gourlay Niblick		$75
Wonder Aluminum And Wood Driver		$750
Hoylake:		
Concave Smooth Faced Mashie Niblick		$100
Jigger		$50
The Hub:		
Child's Putting Cleek		$65
Iron Blade Putter		$50
Hunt:		
Smooth Faced Driving Iron		$175
Splice Head Driver		$275
C. & J. Hunter:		
Iron Bladed Putter		$75
Charles Hunter:		
Long Nosed Play Club		$7,000
Long Nosed Putter		$3,750
Long Nosed Spoon		$1,750
Semi Long Nosed Splice Headed Brassie		$925
Semi Long Nosd Splice Headed Bulger		$450
Socket Headed Brassie		$125
Dave Hunter:		
Large Headed Spoon Bulger Face		$150
Harry Hunter:		
Bent Neck Blade Putter		$100
Ramsey Hunter:		
Gooseneck Blade Putter		$135
Semi Long Nosed Splice Headed Driver		
Leather Face Insert		$650
Short Splice Headed Driver		$175
Huntly:		
Aluminum Mallet Putter		$150
D.H. Hurry:		
Smooth Faced Child's Mashie		$125
H. Hurry:		
Broad Splice Head Brassie		$175
W. Hutchings:		
Socket Head Brassie		$75

COMPANY HICKORY	VALUE
J.H. Hutchison:	
Gun Metal Blade Putter	$200
Long Neck Beech Head Sliced Neck Putter	$1,950
Semi Long Nosed Brassie	$2,250
Semi Long Nosed Driver Leather Face Insert	$2,750
Semi Long Nosed Spoon	$2,000
Two Level Smooth Faced Mashie	$1,350
R. Hutton:	
Transitional Bulger Spoon	$290
Illini:	
Chrome Head Putter Long Gooseneck Hosel	$120
Imperial Golf Co.:	
Aluminum Putter "The Verden"	$145
Aluminum Putter "U Model"	$170
Brassie	$225
Checkered Face Mid Iron	$225
Putter	$275
Ionic:	
Socket Headed Driver	$45
A.J. Isherwood:	
Socket Headed Driver	$65
John Jackson:	
Long Nosed Play Club Ash Shaft and Long Thin Head	$27,500
Long Nosed Short Spoon Ash Shaft	$35,000
Charles Jacob:	
Socket Headed Baffy Spoon Fiber Face Insert	$175
Rowland James:	
Medium Head Smooth Faced Niblick	$225
Putting Cleek	$185
Socket Headed Driver	$100
Jarvis And White:	
Lined Face Mashie Niblick	$45
Ben Jeffrey:	
Stainless Mid Iron Lined Face	$60
Charles Johns:	
Manor Socket Headed Brassie	$75
Round Soled Cleek Dot Face	$50
The A.L. Johnson Co.:	
Dot Faced Iron	$50
Large Head Niblick Smooth Face	$195
Socket Headed Driver	$65
Frank A. Johnson:	
Premier Anti Shank Niblick	$175
Premier Lined Face Putter	$125
Smooth Faced Mashie	$100
Smooth Faced Niblick	$125
Iver Johnson Sporting Goods Co.:	
Smooth Faced Iron	$125

COMPANY HICKORY	VALUE
W. Claude Johnson:	
Round Headed Driver Removable Weights	$2,250
Charles Johnston:	
Diamond Faced Mashie	$45
Socket Headed Driver	$55
Johnstone Bros.:	
Lined Face Mashie	$125
R. Johnstone:	
Splice Headed Driver	$200
Ernest Jones:	
Socket Headed Driver	$125
H.I. Jones:	
Lined Face Mashie	$35
T.W. Jones:	
Lined Face Driving Iron	$55
James Kay:	
Socket Driver with Bone Slip	$125
Karl Keefer:	
Mallet Headed Putter	$90
Kempshall Manufacturing Co.:	
Duplex Club Twin Striking Faces Brassie and Spoon	$1,450
Mallet Headed Putter Center Shaft and	
Brass Face Black Pyralin	$500
Mallet Headed Putter Center Shaft and	
Brass Face White Pyralin	$750
Schenectady Headed Putter Black Pyralin	$5,755
Socket Headed Driver Black Pyralin	$950
Daniel Kenny:	
Socket Headed Spoon Fiber Face Insert	$75
Kilty Kersten Co.:	
Kilty Kersten Iron	$35
Kilty Kersten Wood	$45
Lady Lucky Strike Iron	$35
King Hardware Co.:	
King Bee Mashie	$55
King Horn:	
Lined Face Mid Iron	$45
J.B. & Co.:	
Falcon Niblick Lined Face	$65
J.B. Kinnear:	
Deep Faced Mashie	$45
David Kinnell:	
Splice Headed Spoon	$235
James Kinnell:	
Socket Headed Brassie Deep Face	$90
R. Kirk:	
Fruitwood Head Putter	$13,500

COMPANY	HICKORY	VALUE
R.W. Kirk:		
	Smooth Faced Iron	$125
	Splice Head Driver	$400
	Splice Headed Driver Short Thick Head	$185
Andrew Kirkaldy:		
	Wm. Gibson Lined Face Mashie	$100
	Kirkaldy Dreadnought Large Head Driver	$195
	Splice Headed Putter Fiber Slip	$250
Joe Kirkwood:		
	Lined Face Spade Mashie	$65
Kismet:		
	Long Rectangular Metal Headed Putter Heel Shaft	$225
Charles J. Klees:		
	MacGregor Driving Iron Dot Faced	$75
	Socket Headed Brassie	$55
Willie Klein:		
	Dot Faced Mashie Niblick	$65
Klin Brothers:		
	Dash Faced Mashie	$50
	Drive Rite Driver Brass Backweight Face Insert	$75
	Klin Club Socket Headed Brassie	$55
	Socket Headed Driver	$50
	Socket Headed Driver Striped Top Bulger Face	$55
	Stainless Dot Faced Iron	$40
	Thick Bladed Offset Putter	$65
Eddie Klin:		
	Dot Faced Mashie	$45
Mike Klin:		
	MacGregor Putter	$150
A.H. Knight:		
	Aluminum Schenectady Center Shafted Putter Diamond Face	$750
Ben Knight:		
	Vertically Slotted Face Mashie Open On The Bottom Rake Style	$10,750
G.P. Knox:		
	Socket Headed Driver	$55
Kroydon:		
	50 Degree Niblick Vertical Line Face Scoring	$275
	Ball Faced Blade Putter	$90
	Ball Faced Mashie	$90
	Ball Faced Mashie Niblick	$100
	Ball Faced Mid Iron	$100
	Ball Faced Niblick	$65
	Ball Faced Spade Mashie	$90
	Blade Putter	$100
	Center Shafted Putter	$175
	Dot Faced 4 Iron	$55

COMPANY	HICKORY	VALUE
Kroydon(cont.):		
Dot Faced Driving Iron		$65
Dot Faced Mashie		$60
Dot Faced Mid Iron		$100
Dot Faced Niblick		$65
Gun Metal Dash Faced Putter		$175
Hy Power Socket Headed Brassie Face Insert		$75
M 8 Jigger Broken Line Face Scoring		$50
Mallet Headed Putter		$125
Mallet Headed Putter Recessed Top Chamber		$150
Panther Blade Putter Dash Diamond Face		$90
S 30 A Aluminum Putter		$115
Shallow Blade Lined Face Putter		$65
Short Stop Spade Mashie Brick Face		$400
Spoon Brass Star In Sole Plate		$60
Striped Top Socket Headed Driver		$60
Super Kroydonite Black Finish Driver		$100
Tiny Waffle Faced Spade Mashie		$125
Vertical Lined Face Niblick		$250
Waffle Faced Mashie Niblick		$125
Laclede Brass Works:		
Doer Topem Stainless Putter Top Flange		$175
Lakewood:		
Socket Headed Driver		$65
Lambert Bros.:		
Walter Hagen Sterling Silver Putter		$1,250
Lamino Golf Co.:		
Laminated Head Driver		$800
Laminated Large Headed Driver		$1,650
Bennet Lang:		
Beech Headed Play Club		$4,750
William Large:		
Offset Blade Stainless Putter		$50
Lee & Underhill:		
Dot Faced Driving Iron		$45
Hammer Head Schenectady Putter		$175
Kilgour Match Putter		$125
George Sargent Dot Faced Mashie		$90
George Sargent Socket Headed Brassie		$115
Split Socket Headed Driver Leather Face Insert		$585
Harry Lee & Co.:		
Aluminum Schenectady Headed Baffy Lofted Face		$2,750
Aluminum Schenectady Putter Patent No. 976267		$235
Aluminum Schenectady Putter Patent Pending		$750
Iron Bladed Putter		$55
Lined Face Mashie		$45
Neptune Stainless Dot Faced Iron		$45
Neptune Stainless Lined Face Mid Mashie		$45

COMPANY HICKORY	VALUE
Harry Lee & Co. (cont.)**:**	
Smooth Faced Mid Iron	$60
Square Punch Face Driving Iron	$75
Stainless Lined Deep Faced Mashie	$45
Stainless Lined Deep Faced Mid Iron	$45
Stainless Lined Face Mashie Niblick	$45
Stainless Lined Face Mashie Offset	$45
Stainless Lined Face Mid Iron	$45
Stainless Lined Face Mid Mashie	$50
Stainless Lined Face Niblick Large Head	$55
Stainless Lined Face Putter	$50
Stainless Lined Face Putter Offset Blade	$45
Stainless Lined Face Round Sole Mid Iron	$45
Robert Legg:	
Maxwell Niblick	$75
R. & W. Leslie & Co.:	
Patented Putter with Step Down Back	$175
Patented Step Down Back Putter	$190
Robert Leslie:	
Gun Metal Blade Putter	$125
Thick Top of Blade Putter	$400
W. Leslie:	
Smooth Faced Cleek	$175
John Letters & Co.:	
Newbridge Jigger Shallow Face and Dot Blade	$90
Rustless Mashie Niblick	$95
Rustless Mid Iron	$95
Socket Headed Driver Stripe Top	$100
Stainless Lined Face Mashie Niblick	$75
Leyland & Birmingham Rubber Co.:	
Century Iron Bladed Putter	$55
Century Lined Face 2 Iron	$45
Dot Faced Mashie	$50
Lined Face 5 Iron	$50
Rustless Mashie Niblick	$65
J. Lillywhite Frowd & Co.:	
Blade Putter Wood Insert	$975
V-Groove Splice Headed Driver	$595
Lindgren Bros.:	
Adjustable Center Shafted Putter Set Screw in Face	$875
Litchfield Manufacturing Co.:	
Smooth Faced Driving Mashie	
Deep Faced Gun Metal Blade	$465
N. Littledale:	
Socket Head Brassie Pear Shaped	$75
Joe Lloyd:	
Smooth Faced Lofter	$250

COMPANY HICKORY	VALUE
Lockwood & Brown:	
Anti Shank Stainless Mashie Niblick	$175
Dot Faced Spade Mashie	$60
Giant Headed Niblick Dot Face	$1,800
Large Wooden Headed Putter	$950
A.G. Lockwood:	
Lined Face Mid Iron	$60
The Sampson Fiber Face Driver	$150
Hugh Logan:	
Aluminum Mallet Headed Putter T Aiming Bar	$525
Splice Headed Brassie	$175
I.R. Longsworth:	
Adjustable Boat Shaped Putter	$1,750
John P. Lovell Arms Co.:	
Diamond Smooth Faced Mashie	$175
Iron Bladed Putter	$175
Splice Headed Brassie	$350
Splice Headed Driver	$365
Low & Hughes:	
Sure Shot Swan Necked Putter	$300
George Low:	
Gem Putter	$90
Mashie	$75
Socket Headed Brassie	$125
Socket Headed Driver	$125
Lowe & Campbell:	
Ace Iron	$35
Dot Faced Stainless Iron	$35
Fairview Socket Headed Driver	$55
Sterling Forged Iron	$35
Wilson Range Iron	$35
D. Lowe:	
Gourlay Anti Shank Mashie	$175
George Lowe:	
James Anderson Anti Shank Iron	$235
Hawkins Never Rust Anti Shank Cleek	$275
Semi Long Nosed Dished Face Spoon	$950
Small Headed Niblick	$275
Steel Bladed Putter Raised Top Edge	$350
Lumley's Ltd.:	
Scottish Champion Dot Faced Mashie	$60
Scottish Champion Magic Putter	$75
Semi Long Nosed Driver	$950
Murray Lurcock:	
Socket Headed Putter	$135
John Lurie:	
Burke Mashie	$65

COMPANY	HICKORY	VALUE

The Henry Lytton Co.:

Child's Putting Cleek — $75

Hub Iron Bladed Putter — $55

M.L. Co.:

Iron Blade Putter — $35

Mac & Mac Co.:

Back Spin Mashie Deeply Drilled Holes In Face — $450

Back Spin Mashie Niblick Wide Slots Cut Through Face — $1,750

Brass Headed Putter Lead Center — $600

The MacDonald:

Aluminum Headed Putter Long Head
with Removeable Weights — $4,650

MacGregor:

492 Pear Shaped Persimmon Socket Brassie — $100

Airway AR-1 Mashie Niblick with a Concave Face — $55

Airway AR-2 Mashie Niblick Concave Face — $125

Airway Slight Concave Dot Faced Iron — $95

Aluminum Mallet Head Putter Lead Face Insert — $495

Aluminum Mallet Head Putter Vulcanite T-line — $375

Aluminum Schenectady Putter — $225

Aluminum Short Mallet Head Dot Faced Putter — $150

Backspin Gun Metal Blade Putter Deep Ribbed Face — $295

Backspin Pitcher Wide Slot Deep Grooves — $150

Bakspin Mashie Niblick Deep Grooved Face — $150

Bakspin Mashie Niblick Deep Ribbed Face — $245

Bakspin Mashie Niblick Radite Ribbed Face — $150

Bakspin Mashie Niblick Stagdot Face — $80

Bakspin Mashie Radite Ribbed Face — $150

Bakspin Mashie Slot Grooved Face — $150

Bakspin Mashie Stagdot Face — $90

Bakspin Niblick Stagdot Face — $90

Bakspin Ribbed Face Jigger — $225

Brass Backweighted Brassie Spoon Face Insert — $150

Brassie Fiber Face Insert — $90

Brassie with Fibber Lock Face Insert — $150

Brassie with Red and White Fiber Face Insert — $90

Bulldog Short Socket Headed Spoon Face Insert — $175

Chieftain Brassie Ivory Backweight Top Inlaid — $450

Chieftain Driver Ivory Backweight Top Inlaid — $450

Chieftain Spoon Ivory Backweight Top Inlaid — $450

Child's Driving Cleek — $65

Child's Driving Mashie — $65

Child's Lofter — $60

Child's Lofting Mashie — $65

Child's Mashie — $50

Child's Mid Iron — $65

Child's Putting Cleek — $55

Child's Socket Headed Brassie — $85

COMPANY	HICKORY	VALUE

MacGregor(cont.):

Child's Socket Headed Driver	$85
Climax Fife Smooth Faced Iron	$65
Corrugated Deep Grove Mashie	$175
Deep Smooth Faced Mashie	$175
Dot Faced Brassie	$325
Down It Wooden Headed Mallet Putter Brass Face	$375
Dreadnought Large Headed Brassie	$150
Dreadnought Large Headed Driver	$150
Driver Dovetailed Face Insert	$225
Driver Fiber Face Insert	$125
Driver Fiber Lock Insert	$150
Driving Iron Wide Spaced Dot Punches	$60
Driving Mashie	$95
Dunn One Piece Driver Leather Face Insert	$2,250
Willie Dunn Iron Blade Putter	$265
Willie Dunn Short Bladed Cleek	$265
Willie Dunn Smooth Faced Iron	$225
Willie Dunn Smooth Faced Lofter	$265
Willie Dunn Smooth Faced Mashie	$225
Willie Dunn Smooth Faced Small Headed Niblick	$600
Willie Dunn Spliced Head Driver	$450
Duralite 1 Driving Iron	$60
Duralite 5 Mashie	$45
Duralite Mid Iron	$50
Duralite Stainless Iron	$45
Edgemont Approach Mashie Shallow Dot Face	$55
Edgemont Deep Dot Faced Mashie Thick Sole	$50
Edgemont Dot Faced Driving Iron	$50
Edgemont Dot Faced Lofter	$60
Edgemont Dot Faced Mashie	$55
Edgemont Dot Faced Mashie Centrajet Back	$60
Edgemont Dot Faced Mid Iron	$50
Edgemont Driving Cleek Dot Faced	$50
Edgemont E 1 Socket Brassie	$100
Edgemont Goosenecked Blade Putter	$75
Edgemont Mashie Niblick	$50
Edgemont Plain Faced Socket Headed Driver	$90
Edgemont Putting Cleek	$50
Edgemont Round Medium Headed Niblick	$65
Edgemont Socket Driver Plain Face	$95
Fiber Faced Brassie	$175
Fiber Faced Driver	$185
Flanged Sole Mashie Stagdot Face	$90
Flanged Sole Mid Iron Stagdot Face	$90
Flanged Sole Niblick Stagdot Face	$90
Flanged Sole Stagdot Face Putter	$95
Go-Sum Stainless Iron	$40

COMPANY HICKORY	VALUE
MacGregor(cont.):	
Go-Sum 2 Ladies Mid Iron	$45
Go-Sum 5 Ladies Mashie	$45
Go-Sum 6 Ladies Mashie Niblick	$45
Gun Metal Blade Putter	$100
Gun Metal Blade Putter Round Face Insert	$300
Gun Metal Extra Wide Blade Putter	$180
Gun Metal Flanged Sole Top Edge Weight	$150
Gun Metal Goosenecked Putter	$225
Gun Metal Round Backed Putter	$325
Iron Bladed Putter	$250
Lady Mac Stainless Iron	$40
J. MacGregor Socket Driver	$115
Nokorade Stainless Iron	$45
Par Centrajet Back Lofter	$125
Par Concave Face Mashie Jigger	$195
Par Dot Faced Mashie	$125
Par Dot Faced Mashie Deep Face	$125
Par Dot Faced Mid Iron	$125
Par Driving Cleek Long Blade Dot Face	$125
Par Driving Cleek Short Blade and Dot Faced	$125
Par Driving Iron Dot Faced	$125
Par Driving Mashie Medium Blade Dot Face	$125
Par Heavy Blade Mid Iron Dot Face	$125
Par Large Headed Niblick	$155
Par Narrow Bladed Putter Flange Sole and Dot Face	$155
Par Putting Cleek Dot Faced	$125
Peerless Approach Iron Dash Faced	$85
Peerless Dash Faced Jigger	$85
Peerless Dash Faced Mashie	$65
Peerless Dash Faced Mid Iron	$65
Peerless Dash Faced Niblick	$75
Peerless Driving Cleek	$75
Peerless Driving Iron Dash Faced	$75
Peerless Goosenecked Blade Putter Dash Faced	$90
Perfection Centrajet Approach Iron Stagdot Face	$125
Perfection Centrajet Approach Jigger Stagdot Face	$125
Perfection Centrajet Backed Mashie	$125
Perfection Centrajet Driving Cleek Stagdot Face	$125
Perfection Centrajet Driving Iron Stagdot Face	$125
Perfection Concave Faced Mashie Niblick	$165
Perfection Concave Faced Mid Iron	$165
Perfection Concave Faced Niblick Round Sole	$165
Perfection Concave Faced Pitcher	$185
Perfection Concave Faced Sammy Iron Round Back	$185
Perfection Flanged Sole Putter Stagdot Face	$195
Perfection Plain Faced Brassie	$100
Perfection Plain Faced Brassie Spoon	$125

COMPANY	HICKORY	VALUE
MacGregor(cont.):		
Perfection Plain Faced Driver		$100
Perfection Putting Cleek		$185
Perfection Round Backed Bobbie Iron Stagdot Face		$175
Perfection Spoon		$95
Persimmon Schenectady Symmetric Putter		$375
Pilot Lined Face Putter		$65
Pilot Concave Faced Mashie Niblick		$225
Pilot Driving Cleek Lined Face		$50
Pilot Driving Iron Lined Face		$50
Pilot Lady's Lined Face Driving Cleek		$50
Pilot Lady's Lined Face Mashie		$60
Pilot Lady's Lined Face Niblick		$50
Pilot Lady's Plain Faced Brassie		$75
Pilot Lady's Plain Faced Driver		$75
Pilot Lined Face Mashie		$50
Pilot Lined Face Mid Iron		$50
Pilot Lined Face Niblick		$50
Pilot Lined Face Putter		$65
Pilot P-1 Putter		$45
Pilot Plain Faced Brassie		$75
Pilot Plain Faced Brassie Spoon		$95
Pilot Plain Faced Driver		$75
Plain Faced Brassie		$120
Plain Faced Brassie Cleek		$150
Plain Faced Brassie Cleek Wide Head		$100
Plain Faced Driver		$100
Plain Faced Spoon		$125
Popular Approach Mashie Carruthers Hosel		$100
Popular Approach Mashie Centrajet Back		$75
Popular Carruthers Hosel Mid Iron		$100
Popular Centrajet Back Dot Faced Driving Iron		$65
Popular Centrajet Back Dot Faced Mid Iron		$65
Popular Centrajet Back Lofter		$75
Popular Centrajet Back Short Socket Driving Cleek		$65
Popular Concave Faced Jigger		$150
Popular Concave Faced Mashie Niblick		$225
Popular Concave Faced Round Backed Mashie Niblick		$160
Popular Contraject Jigger		$75
Popular Deep Faced Putting Iron		$75
Popular Diamond Backed Approach Mashie		$90
Popular Diamond Backed Dot Faced Driving Cleek		$70
Popular Diamond Backed Driving Iron Dot Face		$60
Popular Diamond Backed Mid Iron Dot Face		$75
Popular Diamond Backed Putting Cleek Dot Face		$90
Popular Dot Faced Driving Iron		$65
Popular Dot Faced Driving Mashie Diamond Back		$75
Popular Dot Faced Driving Mashie Weighted Top Edge		$75

COMPANY	HICKORY	VALUE

MacGregor(cont.):

Popular Dot Faced Mashie	$75
Popular Dot Faced Mashie Niblick	$100
Popular Dot Faced Mid Iron	$50
Popular Dot Faced Mid Mashie	$100
Popular Dot Faced Niblick	$60
Popular Dot Faced Putting Cleek	$75
Popular Dual Faced Putting Iron	$75
Popular E Ladies Mid Iron	$60
Popular Extra Wide Blade Lofting Mashie	$90
Popular Goosenecked Putter	$125
Popular Goosenecked Putter Narrow Blade	$90
Popular Half Jigger	$60
Popular Heavy Bladed Mid Iron	$65
Popular Large Head Dot Faced Niblick	$75
Popular Large Heavy Bladed Niblick	$75
Popular Long Bladed Putting Cleek Dot Face	$75
Popular Musselback Approach Cleek Dot Faced	$90
Popular Musselbacked Putting Cleek	$75
Popular Plain Faced Brassie	$75
Popular Plain Faced Brassie Cleek	$125
Popular Plain Faced Brassie Spoon	$125
Popular Plain Faced Driver	$75
Popular Round Back Approach Iron Dot Faced	$75
Popular Round Back Approach Mashie	$75
Popular Round Back Driving Cleek Dot Faced	$65
Popular Round Back Driving Iron Dot Faced	$50
Popular Round Back Lofter	$75
Popular Shallow Bladed Putter	$75
Popular Short Blade Driving Cleek Dot Faced	$50
Popular Slight Goosenecked Putter Dot Face	$75
Popular Small Head Concave Smooth Faced Niblick	$175
Popular Straight Back Approach Iron Dot Faced	$75
Popular Straight Backed Jigger	$75
Popular Straight Backed Lofter	$75
Popular Straight Backed Mid Iron	$60
Popular Thick Toed Approach Mashie	$100
Popular Top Edgeweight Putter	$90
Popular Wide Backed Putter Beveled Edge	$60
Popular Wide Toe Mashie Niblick	$70
Premier Deep Corrugated Face Iron	$150
Premier Lined Face Iron	$50
Putting Cleek	$60
Radite Stainless Iron	$45
Radite Wont Rust Mid Mashie	$45
Rustless Metal Putting Cleek Lined Face	$165
Sampson Faced Driver	$365
Sampson Faced Brassie	$385

COMPANY HICKORY	VALUE
MacGregor(cont.):	
Shallow Faced Bent Neck Semi Putter Thick Toe	$225
Short Bulldog Headed Brassie Face Insert	$175
Short Bulldog Headed Driver Face Insert	$175
Short Spliced Neck Brassie	$250
Sink Em Wooden Mallet Putter	
Aluminum Face Brass Backweight	$350
Sink It Wooden Headed Mallet Putter Aluminum Face	$295
Slotted Hosel Stag Dot Scored Bobbie Iron	$300
Slotted Hosel Stag Dot Scored Cleek	$250
Smooth Faced Iron	$225
Smooth Faced Lofter	$265
Smooth Faced Mashie	$225
Smooth Faced Medium Headed Niblick	$225
Smooth Faced Niblick	$525
Smooth Faced Short Bladed Cleek	$280
Smooth Faced Straight Blade Putter	$50
Socket Brassie	$95
Socket Spoon	$95
Splice Headed Driver	$475
Spliced Neck Brassie	$350
Steel Faced Brassie	$120
Steel Faced Driver	$120
Superior Broad Sole Slotted Hosel Putter Stagdot Face	$300
Superior Niblick	$50
Superior Plain Faced Brassie Brass Backweight	$125
Superior Plain Faced Driver Brass Backweight	$125
Superior Slotted Hosel Approach Iron Stagdot Face	$225
Superior Slotted Hosel Blade Putter Stagdot Face	$250
Superior Slotted Hosel Diamond Backed Driving Iron	$250
Superior Slotted Hosel Jigger Stag Dot Face	$150
Superior Slotted Hosel Mashie Niblick Stagdot Face	$175
Superior Slotted Hosel Mashie Stagdot Face	$225
Superior Slotted Hosel Mid Iron Stag Dot Face	$195
Superior Slotted Hosel Mid Mashie Stag Dot Face	$250
Superior Slotted Hosel Niblick Stagdot Face	$250
Swan Necked Gun Metal Blade Putter	$350
Tomahawk Brand T-2 Mashie Niblick	$200
Tomahawk Soft Steel Iron	$90
Wooden Head Mallet Putter Fiber Face Insert	$300
Wooden Schenectady Putter with Brass Face	$275
Yardsmore Brassie Black And White Face Insert	$125
Yardsmore Driver Black And White Face Insert	$125
Yardsmore Spoon Black And White Face Insert	$125
Yardsmore Stainless Iron	$90
MacKay:	
Socket Headed Brassie Stripe Top	$75
Socket Headed Driver	$75

COMPANY HICKORY	VALUE
J. Mackie:	
Lined Face Mid Iron	$55
Mackrell & Simpson:	
Lined Face Mashie	$50
James Mackrell:	
Flanged Sole Mashie Lined Face	$90
Medium Headed Niblick Smooth Face	$225
Dan MacNamara:	
Socket Headed Driver	$100
A.F. MacPherson:	
Dot Faced Niblick	$5050
Duncan MacPherson:	
Lined Face Putter	$75
J. MacPherson:	
Lined Face Niblick	$75
R.H. Macy:	
Riverside Stainless Mashie Dot Faced	$50
Supremacy Stainless Spade Mashie Lined Face	$50
Stewart Maiden:	
Stainless Blade Putter	$100
Stainless Iron	$55
Harry Malpass:	
Dot Faced Mashie	$50
Socket Headed Driver Ivorine Face	$120
Marathon:	
Stainless Lined Face Iron	$35
Marling & Smith:	
Dot Faced Mashie Niblick	$65
Splice Headed Driver	$225
Alick Marling:	
Magic Putter Bent Neck Dot Punched Face	$90
Martin & Kirkaldy:	
Elite Dot Faced Mashie	$75
Elite Large Headed Niblick Lined Face	$100
Elite V-Shaped Back Putter	$150
Kirkaldy Dot Faced Mid Iron	$100
Andrew Kirkaldy Dreadnought Socket Headed Driver	$250
Short Socket Headed Brassie Thick Toe	$175
Sovereign Socket Headed Brassie	$100
Splice Headed Spoon	$250
Martin & Patrick:	
Sovereign Socket Headed Driver	$100
R.B. Martin:	
The Golf Depot Dot Faced Mashie	$100
Martin's Velometer Golf Clubs:	
Socket Headed Brassie	$350
Socket Headed Driver	$350

COMPANY HICKORY	VALUE
Arnaud Massy:	
Iron	$125
Dick May:	
Bulge Face Blade Putter Lined Face	$225
Charles Mayo:	
Socket Headed Driver	$65
Martin McDaid:	
Aluminum Compact Head Driver	$325
Small Splice Headed Driver Horn Slip	$275
W. McDonald:	
Long Nosed Driving Putter Slender Head	$7,500
William McDonald:	
Short Splice Head Driver	$225
J. McDowall:	
Mashie	$50
McEwan & Sayner:	
Short Socket Headed Brassie	$95
McEwan & Son:	
Feather Ball Long Nosed Play Club	$9,750
Feather Ball Long Nosed Play Club Thistle Stamp	$37,500
Feather Ball Long Nosed Putter Slight Hook Face	$12,500
Feather Ball Long Nosed Spoon	$7,750
Guttie Ball Bent Bladed Putter	$225
Guttie Ball Gun Metal Blade Putter	$225
Guttie Ball Iron Blade Putter	$150
Guttie Ball Long Nosed Long Spoon	$5,500
Guttie Ball Long Nosed Play Club Leather Face Insert	$4,750
Guttie Ball Long Nosed Play Club Shorter Head	$1,750
Guttie Ball Long Nosed Putter Broader Head	$2,450
Guttie Ball Long Nosed Putter Long Slender Head	$4,500
Guttie Ball Long Nosed Short Spoon Broad Head	$5,500
Guttie Ball Long Nosed Spoon Well Lofted Face	$6,000
Guttie Ball Medium Headed Niblick	$495
Guttie Ball Semi Long Nosed Brassie	$950
Guttie Ball Semi Long Nosed Driver Short Head Leather Face Insert	$1,250
Guttie Ball Semi Long Nosed Putter	$1,000
Guttie Ball Small Headed Niblick	$495
Guttie Ball Smooth Faced Cleek	$250
Guttie Ball Smooth Faced Iron	$300
Guttie Ball Smooth Faced Lofter	$250
Guttie Ball Smooth Faced Mashie	$300
David McEwan:	
Birkdale Small Socket Headed Driver	$135
Persimmon Head Bulger Spliced Neck Brassie	$245
Peter McEwan:	
Lined Face Mashie Niblick	$65

COMPANY HICKORY	VALUE
Stewart McEwan:	
Dot Faced Mashie	$50
Dot Faced Mashie Centrajet Back	$55
Smooth Faced Mashie	$100
Socket Headed Driver Steel Face Insert	$125
Klin McGill Golf Manufacturing Co.:	
Backspin Mashie Stagdot Face	$55
Corrugated Face Bronze Alloy Mid Iron	$250
Lined Face Bronze Alloy Niblick	$125
Rustless Bronze Alloy Mashie	
Corrugated and Brick Face	$450
David McIntosh:	
Gun Metal Blade Putter	$100
Smooth Faced Driving Iron	$100
Smooth Faced Pitcher	$225
J. McKenna:	
Splice Headed Brassie	$125
Meadowlark:	
Dot Faced Niblick	$35
R.H. Meaker:	
Splice Headed Driver	$135
Jack Melville:	
Socket Headed Driver Stripe Top	$60
A. Miles:	
Handcraft Socket Headed Brassie	$60
Millar & Taylor:	
Concave Face Mashie Niblick Half Dot Face	$325
Charles L. Millar:	
Rustless Steel Cleek Dot Punched Face	$50
Smooth Faced Back Weighted Iron	$125
Smooth Faced Iron	$95
Smooth Faced Mashie	$65
Smooth Faced Offset Putter	$95
Smooth Faced Offset Blade Putter	$100
Smooth Faced Short Bladed Mashie	$100
John Milne:	
Socket Headed Driver	$100
Mitchell & Ness:	
Lined Face Mashie Niblick	$65
Socket Headed Driver Stripe Top	$75
Mitchell & Weidenkopf:	
Socket Headed Brassie Circular Face Insert	$150
Joe Mitchell:	
Smooth Faced Mid Iron	$90
Socket Headed Driver	$90
W. Mitchell:	
Brass Sole Plate Socket Spoon	$95

COMPANY HICKORY	VALUE
Monarch:	
Dash Faced Mashie	$35
Iron Bladed Putter	$45
Arthur Monk:	
Stainless Dot Faced Mashie	$45
Morehead Co.:	
Lined Face Mid Iron	$100
Socket Headed Driver Vulcanite Face Insert	$225
Stainless Dot Faced Mashie	$35
E. Morgan:	
Oval Headed Mashie Niblick Dot Face	$65
Morris & Youds:	
Anti Shank Mashie	$375
Jack Morris:	
Lined Face Iron	$75
Socket Headed Driver	$125
Tom Morris:	
Concave Faced Niblick	$565
Cylindrical Iron Headed Putter	$2,950
Dot Faced Driving Iron	$90
Dot Faced Iron	$75
Dot Faced Jigger	$125
Dot Punched Face 1 Iron Portrait at the Toe	$145
Driving Iron Dot Punched Face Portrait at the Toe	$145
General Purpose Iron Squared Hosel and Blade Top	$350
Gun Metal Blade Putter	$175
Guttie Ball Long Nose Beech Head Putter	$1,975
Guttie Ball Long Nosed Brassie Leather Face Insert	$2,000
Guttie Ball Long Nosed Compact Deeper Head Putter	$2,650
Guttie Ball Long Nosed Driver Leather Face Insert	$2,250
Guttie Ball Long Nosed Play Club Narrow Head	$4,500
Guttie Ball Long Nosed Play Club Wider Head	$3,000
Guttie Ball Long Nosed Shallow Headed Putter	$3,250
Guttie Ball Long Nosed Spoon Narrow Head	$3,950
Guttie Ball Long Nosed Spoon Wider Head	$3,000
Guttie Ball Long Nosed Spooned Face Baffy	$2,000
Guttie Ball Semi Long Nosed Brassie Shorter Head	$650
Guttie Ball Semi Long Nosed Driver Leather Face Insert	$700
Guttie Ball Transitional Shaped Head Putter	$650
Lined Face Mashie	$90
Lined Face Mashie Niblick	$90
Mid Iron Lined Scored Face	$145
Morris Dot Faced Mashie Niblick	$90
Morris Putter	$90
Old Tom Niblick	$100
Old Tom Stainless Spade Mashie Lined Face	$75
Short Splice Brassie	$225
Short Splice Head Driver	$325

COMPANY HICKORY	VALUE
Tom Morris(cont.):	
Smooth Faced Cleek	$325
Smooth Faced Cleek Rounded Sole	$425
Smooth Faced Mashie	$295
Smooth Faced Medium Size Head Niblick	$295
Smooth Faced Small Headed Niblick	$500
Socket Headed Brassie	$90
Socket Headed Driver	$165
Socket Wood Head Putter	$325
St. Andrean Musselback Stainless Mashie	$90
Wellington Putter	$135
J.G. Motion:	
Splice Head Driver	$235
W. Mules:	
Driver with Leather Cushioned Metal Face Plate	$950
R. Munro:	
Large Socket Headed Driver	$90
Semi Long Nosed Large Splice Headed Putter	$750
D. Murray:	
Splice Headed Brassie	$125
J. Murray:	
Iron Bladed Putting Iron Lined Face	$50
Murrie & Sons:	
Concentric Backed Offset Putter Hyphen Scored Face	$90
Concentric Backed Putter Dash Face	$75
Smooth Faced Mid Iron	$90
David Myles:	
Nipper Driving Iron	$465
Paxie Driving Iron	$450
Placer Driving Iron	$575
Rexor Driving Iron	$575
Nassau:	
Gun Metal Blade Putter	$125
Charles Neaves:	
Genii Smooth Faced Mashie Niblick	$90
Long Tom Large Socket Head Driver	$75
Smooth Faced Cleek	$95
Smooth Faced Mid Iron	$65
Socket Headed Driver Fiber Insert	$90
J. Neilson:	
Putting Cleek Dot Punched Face	$95
Spoon with Full Brass Sole Plate Red Face Insert	$275
Robert Neilson:	
Dot Faced Iron	$65
Lined Face Cleek	$75
Smooth Faced Niblick	$95
Splice Headed Driver	$175

COMPANY	HICKORY	VALUE
Nesco:		
Brass Headed Putter Aluminum Insert Aiming Fin		$1,950
New York Sporting Goods Co.:		
Gun Metal Blade Putter		$125
Small Headed Concave Smooth Faced Niblick		$565
Splice Headed Driver		$325
O.M. Ness:		
Top Weighted Putter		$195
Ernest Newbery:		
Half Moon Shaped Putter Crescent Shaped Weight on Back		$450
George Nicoll:		
Able Lined Face Niblick		$50
Big Ball Stainless Deep Faced Mashie Niblick		$45
Big Shooter Stainless Lined Face Mashie Niblick		$45
Braid Driving Iron Mussel Back and Hyphen Scored Face		$70
Braid Musselbacked Mashie Dot Faced		$100
Cleek with Gutta Percha Insert		$2,650
Cleek with Leather Insert		$2,500
Clinker Oval Headed Iron		$75
Compaction Blade Dot Faced Iron		$45
Corrugated Face Mashie Niblick		$90
Corrugated Face Pitcher		$125
Cracker Jack Carruthers Hosel Dot Faced Iron		$85
Dot Punched Face 1 Iron		$65
Gray Lined Face Putter		$65
Indicator 3 Iron		$55
Indicator Dot Faced Niblick		$50
Indicator Mashie		$55
Lined Face Driving Iron		$65
Long Hosel Putter		$75
Mashie Dot Punched Face		$50
Niblick		$55
Nicoll Patented Putter		$285
Nicoll Stainless Lined Face Iron		$45
Park Bent Necked Putter		$175
Precision Stainless Driving Iron Flanged Sole		$45
Precision Stainless Iron Flanged Sole		$45
Putter		$75
Recorder Iron		$50
Recorder 1 Iron		$60
Recorder Long Blade Putter Dot Face		$65
Recorder Mashie Dot Faced		$50
Recorder Niblick		$50
Scored Face Precision Mashie		$55
Small Headed Niblick		$400
Smith Stainless Iron		$50
Smooth Faced Cleek		$175

COMPANY HICKORY	VALUE
George Nicoll (cont.):	
Smooth Faced Iron	$225
Smooth Faced Long Blade Lofter	$325
Spade Mashie	$50
Sure Dot Faced Mid Iron	$50
Swan Necked Putter	$275
Tait Dot Faced Cleek	$125
Tait Putter	$175
Vicking Iron	$45
Zenith Corrugated Face Pitcher	$125
Zenith Deep Faced Mashie	$55
Zenith Long Bladed Putter	$90
Zenith Mashie	$55
Zenith Mashie Niblick	$55
Zenith Oval Headed Mashie Niblick Dot Faced	$55
Nicholls Brothers:	
Gun Metal Blade Putter	$100
Smooth Faced Lofting Iron	$150
Smooth Faced Niblick	$175
Smooth Faced Nickel Plated Cleek	$100
Socket Headed Driver	$100
Splice Headed Driver	$225
F. Bernard Nicholls:	
Iron Blade Putter	$75
Smooth Faced Rustless Cleek	$100
Socket Headed Driver Steel Face Insert	$135
Special Bead Spliced Headed Driver	$325
Nicholson Bros.:	
Stainless Mashie	$75
T. Nicholson:	
Lined Face Iron	$100
Severely Bent Neck Ladies Putter	$170
Smooth Faced Mashie	$145
Thomas Norton:	
Smooth Faced Lofter	$125
William Norton:	
Dot Faced Mashie	$55
Smooth Concave Faced Small Round Head Niblick	$425
Noyes Bros.:	
Transitional Splice Headed Driver	$325
O.V.B.:	
Carruthers Hosel Cleek	$125
Gun Metal Blade Putter	$90
Iron Bladed Putter	$75
Line Dot Faced Niblick	$75
Lined Face Mid Iron	$65
Mashie Niblick	$60
Socket Headed Brassie	$90
Socket Headed Driver	$90

COMPANY	HICKORY	VALUE
James Ocenden:		
Socket Headed Driver		$65
J.H. Oke:		
Offset Blade Putter		$60
Smooth Faced Mashie		$90
W.G. Oke:		
Dot Faced Mashie		$55
Oak Brand Putter		$90
Stainless Head Putter Long Thin Hosel		$190
R. Ollarton:		
Small Splice Headed Brassie		$125
Olympia:		
Lined Face Putter		$35
Osborn:		
Rustless Mid Iron		$75
Ouimet & Sullivan:		
Socket Headed Driver		$225
Outing Goods Manufacturing Co.:		
Semi Long Nosed Brooklawn Special Splice Headed Driver		$1,500
Overman Wheel Co.:		
Smooth Faced Cleek		$325
Smooth Faced Gun Metal Head Niblick		$2,250
Straight Bladed Smooth Face Putter		$275
Victor Straight Blade Smooth Faced Putter		$135
P.G. Manufacturing:		
Cleek with Large Dot Punched Face		$75
Homewood Smooth Faced Niblick		$75
Mitchell Made Mashie		$75
Smooth Faced Lofter		$75
Mungo Park:		
Long Nosed Beech Headed Putter		$2,500
Long Nosed Play Club		$3,000
William Park:		
Long Nosed Play Club		$5,250
Long Nosed Putter		$4,250
Long Nosed Spoon		$4,750
William Park Jr.:		
1900 Patented Bent Neck Putter		$425
Bent Neck Blade Putter		$125
Compact Deep Smooth Faced Lofting Iron		$225
Compressed Patent Splice Headed Brassie		$375
Extra Deep Face Driving Mashie		$825
General Purpose Iron		$190
Gun Metal Blade Putter		$225
Iron Bladed Putter		$175
Lined Face Iron		$125
Long Faced Rounded Toe General Purpose Iron		$190

COMPANY HICKORY	VALUE
William Park Jr. (cont.):	
Medium Headed Smooth Faced Niblick	$285
Patent Lofter Concave Smooth Face	$450
Patent Smooth Faced Round Backed Driving Cleek	$325
Pik Up Grooved Sole Brassie	$475
Semi Long Nosed Bowed Face Brassie Bulger Face	$1,750
Semi Long Nosed Bowed Face Driver Bulger Face	$1,750
Semi Long Nosed Transitional Head Putter	$1,750
Shallow Blade Cleek	$150
Smooth Blade Offset Putter	$155
Smooth Faced Cleek	$225
Smooth Faced General Purpose Iron	$150
Smooth Faced Iron	$175
Smooth Faced Ladies Iron	$190
Smooth Faced Lofter	$195
Smooth Faced Mashie	$150
Smooth Faced Offset Blade Putter Special Patent	$145
Smooth Faced Small Headed Niblick	$425
Spliced Head Driver	$225
Step Faced Mashie Niblick	$2,950
Thick Heavy Bladed Smooth Faced Mashie	$200
Transitional Splice Head Baffy	$675
William Parker:	
Blade Putter	$90
Defiance Mashie	$75
Royal Crown Dot Faced Mid Iron	$65
J.D. Parr:	
Dot Faced Mashie	$45
Oval Head Excelsior Mashie Niblick	$55
Oval Headed Mashie Niblick	$50
Socket Headed Spoon Fiber Face Insert	$75
Tom Parr:	
Gun Metal Blade Putter Center Balanced	$90
Socket Headed Driver Face Insert	$75
S. Parr:	
Stainless Lined Face Mashie	$35
Horace Partridge Co.:	
Diamond Backed Mashie	$50
Hyphen Faced Mid Iron	$50
Oval Headed Mashie Niblick	$75
Socket Headed Brassie	$65
Alex Patrick & Son:	
Acme Brassie Fiber Face Insert	$125
Apex Short Headed Spoon Fiber Face Insert	$140
Approach Mashie	$50
Gun Metal Blade Putter	$175
Leven Iron	$95
Lined Face Mashie	$90

COMPANY HICKORY	VALUE
Alex Patrick & Son (cont.):	
Long Nosed Beech Headed Putter	$2,350
Long Nosed Play Club Shallow Face	$3,250
Long Nosed Spoon	$3,000
Mashie Niblick	$65
Oval Headed Ladies Mashie Niblick	$600
Perfector Brassie Triangle Face Insert	$235
Popular Niblick	$90
Popular Socket Head Brassie Fiber Face Insert	$65
Robbie Socket Headed Driver Aluminum Face Insert	$175
Robbie Wood Socket Head Putter Steel Face Plate	$335
Semi Long Nosed Bulger Headed Driver	$1,450
Semi Long Nosed Splice Headed Putter	$1,450
Semi Long Nosed Transitional Head Bassie	$1,350
Short Splice Head Driver	$275
Smooth Faced Mashie	$65
Socket Headed Driver	$95
Socket Headed Spoon	$100
Splice Headed Driver Leather Face Insert	$325
Tivoli Thick Toed Driving Iron	$140
Transitional Beech Headed Semi Long Nosed Bulger	$1,150
D.M. Patrick:	
Foster Wood Socket Head Putter	$325
Iron Bladed Putter	$95
Socket Headed Driver	$125
Spliced Head Brassie	$345
James Paxton:	
Socket Head Brassie	$150
Wooden Spoon Triangular Face Insert	$150
Peter Paxton:	
Anderson Smooth Faced Mashie	$395
Ealing Socket Headed Driver	$150
Gun Metal Blade Putter	$165
Long Iron Bladed Putter	$300
Long Nosed Play Club	$2,250
Semi Long Nosed Brassie Bulger Head	$1,650
Semi Long Nosed Short Spoon Well Lofted Face	$1,850
Semi Long Nosed Transitional Headed Brassie	$950
Semi Long Nosed Transitional Headed Driver	$1,250
Semi Long Nosed Transitional Headed Putter	$875
Smooth Faced Cleek	$350
Smooth Faced Iron	$295
Smooth Faced Mashie	$295
Wilson Smooth Faced Cleek	$595
Wilson Smooth Faced Lofter	$695
Peacock:	
Lined Face Mashie	$30
J.M. Peacock:	
Gun Metal Blade Putter	$90

COMPANY HICKORY	VALUE
J.S. Pearson:	
Mashie Niblick Slots Cut Through the Face	$2,350
Pederson:	
Convex Lined Face Mashie Niblick	$265
Convex Lined Face Niblick	$335
Putter Two Dials on Top of Head	$265
Thomas Peebles:	
Smooth Faced Cleek	$265
Smooth Faced Mashie	$225
Rogers Peet Co.:	
Offset Blade Putter	$35
PGA Golf:	
Dot Faced Mashie	$45
Kro Flite Dot Faced Mashie	$35
Kro Flite Putter	$45
Kro Forged Iron	$40
Lined Face Jigger	$45
Lined Face Mashie	$45
Ribbed Face Mashie Niblick	$125
Hugh Philp:	
Long Nosed Play Club	$19,500
Long Nosed Slight Hook Face Putter	$14,500
Phosphor Bronze Smelting Co.:	
Rectangular Head Heel Shafted Putter	$235
Piccadilly:	
Chromed Head Mashie Lined Face	$35
Playgolf Inc.:	
Chrome Headed Mashie	$35
Playwell:	
Chrome Head Lined Face Mashie Niblick	$35
W.R. Pope:	
Center Shafted Square Headed Putter	$265
Short Headed Putter	$135
W.H. Potts:	
Lined Face Mashie	$50
Spalding Gun Metal Mallet Head Putter Cork Face Insert	$1,295
Premier Golf Co.:	
Dot Faced Driving Iron	$90
Jack Pritchard:	
Dot Faced Iron	$40
Pro Made:	
Socket Headed Driver Striped Top	$65
R.D. Pryde:	
Bulldog Socket Headed Driver	$65
Dash Faced Iron	$50
Socket Headed Brassie Aluminum Sole Plate	
And Head Weight	$335
Socket Headed Wooden Cleek	$100

COMPANY HICKORY	VALUE
G. Pullford:	
Beech Deep Faced Bulger Brassie Spliced Wood	$275
J. Purkess:	
Excelsior Lined Face Niblick	$75
Robert Ramsbottom:	
Aluminum Headed Wooden Faced Driver	$995
Concave Smooth Faced Lofter	$325
John Randall:	
Dot Faced Iron	$55
Grand Slam Socket Headed Grass Fiber Face Insert	$145
Long Mallet Headed Aluminum Putter	$250
Short Splice Head Driver	$125
Robert Randall:	
Lined Face Driver	$75
Lined Face Pitcher	$85
True Sight Iron Blade Oval Hosel Putter	$175
Velometer Large Socket Head Driver	$125
Horace Rawlins:	
Smooth Faced Iron	$325
Socket Headed Driver	$225
Splice Headed Brassie	$350
Ted Ray:	
Aluminum Schenectady Putter	$275
Everbrite Stainless Mashie	$90
Socket Headed Driver	$125
Socket Headed Steel Faced Driver	$325
Wilson Mashie	$75
The Rayl:	
Heather Offset Blade Putter	$75
A.J. Reach Co.:	
Check Rite Deeply Corrugated Face Mashie Niblick	$90
Check Rite Deeply Corrugated Face Niblick	$90
Dedstop Deeply Corrugated Face Mashie Niblick	$90
Eagle Stainless Dot Faced Mashie	$45
Hammer Deeply Corrugated Face Niblick	$125
Iron with Hatched Face Scoring	$60
Lined Face Mid Iron	$45
Long Socket Headed Driver	$90
Willie Mack Iron Blade Putter Lined Face	$65
Mid Iron	$50
Putter	$45
Reach Mid Iron	$45
Red Stainless Lined Face Mashie	$45
Socket Headed Driver Double Stripe Top	$50
Super Grade Flanged Sole Putter	$75
Superior Dot Faced Mashie	$45
Wood with Ivorine Face Insert	$125

COMPANY HICKORY	VALUE
Read Golf Co.:	
Spoon with Brass Face Insert	$175
William Read:	
Socket Headed Driver	$75
Splice Headed Driver	$165
Redpath & Co.:	
Dot Faced Mashie	$45
Tom Reekie:	
Iron	$55
Socket Headed Driver Plain Face	$75
John Reid:	
Atlantic City Medium Faced Niblick	$325
Compressed Bulger Splice Headed Brassie	$450
Smooth Faced Mashie	$165
Remson:	
Gun Metal Head Putter Hump In	
Face Center Face Inlay	$425
T.G. Renouf:	
Diamond Faced Cleek	$75
Socket Headed Driver Striped Top Face Insert	$90
Rev O Noc:	
Line Dot Faced Mashie	$70
Smooth Faced Carruthers Hosel Driving Iron	$95
F. Rhodes:	
Patented Cup Faced Baffie	$475
F.E. Rigden:	
Short Splice Head Driver	$175
Turk Righter:	
Aluminum Center Shafted Putter Finger Bar In Grip	$950
W.L. Ritchie:	
Scottish Bluebell Mashie Niblick	$75
The Uncanny Round Topped Blade Putter	
Notched At Hosel	$100
W.L.R. Mashie Niblick	$65
Peter Robertson:	
Large Head Lined Face Niblick	$90
Notched Hosel Cleek	$275
Notched Hosel Dot Faced Mashie	$275
Socket Headed Spoon One Piece Sole	
and Backweight	$275
Robo:	
Mallet Headed Putter Notched Toe	$350
Fred Robson:	
Socket Headed Driver	$65
Stainless Lined Face Mashie	$65
Charles Rodwell & Co.:	
Anti Shank Niblick Diamond Dot Face	$225

COMPANY HICKORY	VALUE
Charles Rodwell & Co. (cont.):	
Flanged Back Mashie Offset Blade	$65
Mallet Headed Putter Aiming Dial On Top	$225
Rollins & Parker:	
Anti Shank Lined Face Mashie	$225
Excelsior Round Backed Mashie Niblick	$90
A.E. Rolls:	
Dot Faced Mashie	$50
Alex Ross:	
Mashie	$65
Pinehurst Socket Headed Driver	$125
Donald Ross:	
Dot Faced Mashie	$125
Iron Bladed Putter	$150
Lined Face Mid Iron	$150
Small Headed Niblick Smooth Face	$550
Small Splice Headed Spoon	$565
Socket Headed Brassie	$175
Socket Headed Driver	$225
John Ross:	
Splice Headed Driver Face Insert	$125
Jack Rowe:	
Small Splice Head Driver	$175
Royal:	
Chrome Headed Mashie Niblick	$35
Lined Face Chrome Headed Mashie	$35
Russo:	
Socket Headed Driver	$55
Rustless Golf Club Co.:	
Smooth Faced Mashie	$75
Thick Toed Mashie	$90
S.B.F.:	
Smooth Faced Mashie	$75
Socket Headed Brassie	$75
S.D. & G.:	
Dot Faced Pitcher	$60
Smooth Faced Iron	$90
Smooth Faced Mashie	$90
Socket Headed Brassie	$90
Splice Headed Brassie	$165
Ernest Sales:	
Wood Socket Head Putter	$140
Ludovic Sandison:	
Long Nosed Putter	$13,000
Fred Saunders:	
Aluminum Putter	$900
Diamond Backed Dot Faced Mashie	$45
Long Iron Blade Putter	$65
Socket Headed Driver Red Fiber Face Insert	$75

COMPANY HICKORY	VALUE
J.J. Saville Ltd.:	
Stainless Dot Faced Mashie	$60
Ben Sayers:	
Benny Putter Registered 718956 Putter	$190
Craig Pointed Toe Lined Face Iron	$50
Crest Stainless Iron Lined Face	$45
Domesole Stainless Iron	$50
Grooved Sole Stainless Putter	$165
Gun Metal Blade Putter	$140
Large Socket Headed Dreadnought Driver	$140
Large Stainless Head Niblick Lined Face	$55
Lofter	$90
Redan Mid Iron	$75
Regent Stainless Iron	$45
Semi Long Nosed Splice Headed Putter Brass Sole	$325
Socket Headed Driver	$75
Socket Headed Wooden Cleek	$240
Socket Headed Wooden Cleek Grooved Sole Plate	$200
Splice Headed Brassie Protruding Sole Front Edge	$550
Stainless Iron	$50
Stop Um Deep Corrugated Face Mashie Niblick	$225
Waverley Stainless Iron	$45
Wooden Mallet Headed Putter	$325
Wooden Socket Head Putter Fiber Slip Sole	$85
G. Sayers:	
Two Tone Head Socket Brassie	$125
Schmelzer's:	
Dot Faced Mashie	$40
Schoverling, Daly & Gales:	
Ladies Lofter	$75
Mashie 1 Dot Punched Face	$70
Smooth Deep Faced Lofter	$75
Wide Soled Offset Pitcher	$75
F.A.O. Schwarz:	
Child's Lofter	$90
Child's Mid Iron	$90
A.H. Scott:	
2 Iron	$75
4 Iron	$75
Blade Putter Top Edge Weight	$165
Fork Splice Headed Brassie	$425
Fork Spliced Head Driver	$425
Invincible Smooth Faced Iron	$225
Lined Face Lofter	$90
Lined Face Spade Mashie	$60
A Davey Margate Offset Lofting Iron	$55
Monarch Aluminum Mallet Headed Putter	$125
Short Bladed Mashie	$125

COMPANY HICKORY	VALUE
A.H. Scott (cont.):	
Smooth Faced Cleek	$165
Smooth Faced General Purpose Iron	$95
Socket Headed Driver	$75
Straight Line Putter Registered No. 349407	$85
James Scott:	
Ladies Smooth Faced Cleek	$95
Scottish Golf Club Manufacturing Co. Ltd.:	
Gun Metal Blade Putter	$275
Iron Bladed Putter	$225
Long Bladed Lofter Smooth Face	$235
Rounded Back Smooth Faced Cleek	$225
Semi Long Nosed Splice Headed Putter	$225
Semi Long Nosed Transitional Splice Head Driver	$900
Short Hosel Rounded Back Iron	$190
Smooth Faced Cleek	$165
Splice Headed Driver Face Insert	$395
Scotty:	
Socket Headed Driver	$35
Shaler Co.:	
Over Brook Chromed Iron	$30
Tailor Made Lined Face Iron	$40
Sheffield Steel Products Ltd.:	
Lined Face Mid Iron	$60
Alex Shepherd:	
Lined Face Mashie	$90
H.G. Sherlock:	
Socket Brassie Triangular Sole Plate	$95
James Sherlock:	
Bent Neck Semi Putter	$60
Montmorencie Iron	$90
Small Bar Shaped Head Putter	$140
Smooth Faced Mashie	$90
Socket Headed Brassie	$70
Ray & Turner Sherlock:	
Metal Faced Brassie	$325
Stainless Mid Iron	$75
Robert Silton:	
Semi Long Nosed Splice Headed Driver Fiber Insert	$375
Silverite:	
Stainless Mashie	$50
Simmons Hardware Co.:	
Deeply Corrugated Face Mashie	$90
Lined Face Mid Iron	$40
Alex Simpson:	
Iron Bladed Putter Square Hosel	$265
Archie Simpson:	
Offset Blade Putter	$90

COMPANY HICKORY	VALUE
Archie Simpson (cont.):	
Small Smooth Faced Niblick	$385
Small Splice Headed Driver	$325
G. O. Simpson:	
Stop Em Deeply Corrugated Face Mashie	$90
J. & A. Simpson:	
Lined Face Putter	$60
Musselbacked Cleek Carruthers Hosel	$140
Smooth Faced Iron	$75
Robert Simpson:	
Ball Face Mashie Oversize Round Sweet Spot on Face	$1,450
Ballingall's Smooth Faced Flanged Sole Lofter	$325
Compressed Driver	$150
Concentrated Mashie V-Shaped Thicked Back	$175
Gem Vertical Face Lined Putter	$95
Iron Bladed Putting Cleek	$90
Ivorex Brassie Face Insert	$125
Ivorex Socket Headed Driver Face Insert	$90
Laminated Splice Headed Driver	$750
Long Nosed Play Club Medium Length Head	$2,250
Long Nosed Spoon	$2,250
Malinka Socket Headed Driver	$90
Matchless Socket Headed Driver	$90
Medallist Socket Headed Brassie Aluminum Face Insert	$125
Paragon Socket Headed Driver	$90
Perfect Balance Iron Large Bulge Behind Sweet Spot	$500
Perfect Balance Putter Large Bulge In Back Center	$550
Perfect Balance Socket Headed Driver	
Brass Backweight .	$125
Premier Hollow Steel Headed Putter	$500
Reliance Socket Headed Brassie	$125
Semi Long Nosed Bulger Splice Headed Brassie	$900
Semi Long Nosed Driver Spliced Head	$950
Semi Long Nosed Laminated Splice Headed Brassie	$750
Semi Long Nosed Putter Fiber Slip Sole	$395
Semi Long Nosed Putter Transitional Head	$875
Semi Long Nosed Transitional Splice Headed Brassie	$750
Semi Long Nosed Wooden Socket Headed Putter	$335
Short Splice Headed Driver Face Insert	$225
Simplex Socket Headed Spoon Brass Backweight	$75
Socket Headed Driver	$125
Teacher Offset Putter	$175
Tom Simpson:	
Propellor Stainless Mid Iron	$55
W.H. Skelly:	
Socket Headed Brassie	$7
F. Slater:	
Propellor Lined Face Mashie Niblick	$55

COMPANY	HICKORY	VALUE
Slazenger:		
Threaded Socket Patented Screw In Shaft Spoon		$375
Slazenger & Sons:		
Concave Faced Thick Soled Stainless Niblick		$75
Concave Head Centrajet Back Niblick		$650
Deamon Driver		$900
Dreadnought Driver Threaded Socket and Screw in Shaft		$450
Iron Bladed Putter		$75
Mackrell Autograph Brassie		$100
One Piece Driver Leather Face Insert		$1,950
Screw Socket Head		$400
Screw Socket Head Driver Large Dreadnought Size		$425
Semi Long Nosed Elongated Socket Headed Brassie		$125
Small Smooth Faced Head Niblick		$325
Smooth Faced Cleek		$150
Special Persimmon Headed Socket Brassie		$100
Vardon Small Spliced Head Brassie		$325
W.G. Smalldon:		
Tru Flite Stainless Lined Face Niblick		$35
J. Smart:		
Smooth Faced Iron Bladed Putter		$60
Smethwick Golf Co.:		
Valor Lined Face Mid Iron		$90
E. Smith:		
Anti Shank Mashie		$175
J.C. Smith & Sons:		
Lined Face Mashie		$50
W.B. Smith:		
Dot Faced Sammy Iron		$55
W.P. Smith:		
Maxmi Model Mallet Headed Putter		$95
Willie Smith:		
Putter		$100
Andrew Sommerville:		
Semi Long Nosed Transitional Spliced Head Driver		$550
Southern Cross:		
Stainless Dot Faced Mid Iron		$90
Spalding, Scotland:		
Gold Medal #1 Iron		$60
Gold Medal Mashie		$75
James McDowell Rustless Mashie		$65
Mid Iron "A"		$65
Rustless Calamity Jane "Robt. T. Jones" in Script		$375
Rustless Kro-flite Sweet Spot #5 Mashie		$65
Lewis Scott Cleek		$60
SR Putter Long Radial Blade Lines And Dots On Face		$190
Aluminum Brassie		$325
Aluminum Cleek		$325

COMPANY	HICKORY	VALUE
Spalding, USA (cont.)**:**		
Aluminum Cleek Spring Face		$850
Aluminum Driver		$265
Aluminum Driver Wooden Face		$2,750
Aluminum Driving Iron		$225
Aluminum Lofter		$275
Aluminum Mashie		$225
Aluminum Mid Iron		$200
Aluminum Offset Malleted Headed Putter		$275
Aluminum Putter		$125
Aluminum Schenectady Putter		$175
Bent Neck Putter		$75
Harry Bowler Special Bent Neck Blade Putter		$65
Brassie Wood Laminated Face Plate Insert		$125
Bronze Mashie Niblick		$375
Centra-Ject Back Weighted Lofting Iron		$60
Child's Brassie		$45
Child's Dot Faced Iron		$50
Child's Driver		$45
Child's Lined Face Niblick		$75
Child's Putter		$50
Child's Smooth Faced Mashie		$50
Compact Head Pat. Dec 7 1910 Socket Wood		$125
Compact Smooth Faced Cleek Carruthers Hosel		$125
Crescent Smooth Faced Iron		$55
Crescent Smooth Faced Lofting Iron		$65
Crescent Socket Headed Brassie		$95
Dedstop Deep Waffle Faced Mashie Niblick		$325
Dedstop Deeply Ribbed Face Mashie		$95
Dedstop Deeply Ribbed Face Mashie Niblick		$90
Dedstop Mashie Niblick C-92 Slot Grooved Face		$175
Deep Smooth Faced Lofter Short Blade		$125
Deeply Ribbed Face Mashie Iron		$125
Deeply Ribbed Face Mid Iron		$125
Duncan Model Brassie Wood Black Face Insert		$145
Dundee Dot Faced Mashie		$45
Dundee Dot Faced Mashie Niblick		$45
Dundee Dot Faced Mid Iron		$45
Dundee Dot Faced Niblick		$45
Dundee Iron Bladed Putter		$45
F-3 Mashie Niblick Deep Scoring Lines		$50
Fire Brand Hyphen Scored Blade Putter		$70
Fire Brand Socket Driver		$135
Firebrand Lined Face Niblick		$65
Gold Medal 1 Cleek Carruthers Hosel		$175
Gold Medal 1 Ladies Mid Iron		$45
Gold Medal 1 Putter Dot Ball Face Scoring		$70
Gold Medal 1 Putter Random Dot Face Punching		$65

COMPANY	HICKORY	VALUE

Spalding, USA (cont.):

Gold Medal 1 Putting Cleek	$75
Gold Medal 1 Putting Cleek Dot Punched Face	$90
Gold Medal 1 Smooth Faced Niblick	$85
Gold Medal 1 Socket Brassie	$125
Gold Medal 1 Socket Driver	$125
Gold Medal 2 Ladies Dot Punch Face Iron	$45
Gold Medal 2 Mashie	$50
Gold Medal 3 Ball Face Mashie	$60
Gold Medal 3 Concave Smooth Faced Mashie Niblick	$275
Gold Medal 3 Mid Iron	$75
Gold Medal 5 Socket Brassie	$95
Gold Medal 7 Spoon	$120
Gold Medal A Cleek	$85
Gold Medal Aluminum Mallet Headed Putter	
Lead Face Insert	$675
Gold Medal Brass Blade Putter	$75
Gold Medal Brass Headed Mallet Putter	
Cork Face Insert	$1,500
Gold Medal Broad Soled Putter	$140
Gold Medal Cleek Carruthers Hosel and Centrajet Back	$125
Gold Medal Cleek Spring Face	$850
Gold Medal Compressed Socket Head Driver	$425
Gold Medal Concave Faced Mashie Niblick	$125
Gold Medal Deeply Corrugated Face Mashie	$125
Gold Medal Driver	$75
Gold Medal Driver Brass Backweight	$325
Gold Medal Driver Ivory Face Insert	$450
Gold Medal Fanged Sole Driving Iron Dash Face	$225
Gold Medal Gun Metal Blade Putter	$75
Gold Medal Gun Metal Flanged Sole Putter	$75
Gold Medal J Shallow Faced Spoon Wood	$350
Gold Medal Mashie Niblick Patent Date	$225
Gold Medal Mashie Niblick Three Step Face	$3,500
Gold Medal Mashie Twin Angled Face	$650
Gold Medal Oval Hosel Rounded Dot Faced Putter	$300
Gold Medal Putting Cleek	$75
Gold Medal RN Socket Driver	$90
Gold Medal Rounded Back Putter	$175
Gold Medal Smooth Faced Mid Iron	$75
Gold Medal Smooth Faced Niblick	$90
Gold Medal Socket Headed Driver	$150
Gold Medal Splice Headed Driver	$140
Gold Medal V Ladies Lofting Iron	$70
Heather Driver	$100
Heather Lined Face Niblick	$50
Heavy Lined Face Mashie	$75
Heavy Lined Face Mid Iron	$60
Robt. T. Jones Stainless Dot Faced Iron	$100

COMPANY	HICKORY	VALUE

Spalding, USA (cont.)**:**

Robt. T. Jones Jr. Calamity Jane Putter	$300
Jacobus Triple Insert Driver	$275
Jigger	$75
Kro Flite Dedstop Deeply Ribbed Face Pitcher	$90
Kro Flite Deeply Corrugated Face Mashie Niblick	$100
Kro Flite Deeply Corrugated Face Pitcher	$100
Kro Flite Deeply Ribbed Face Sky Iron	$90
Kro Flite Deeply Waterfall Faced Pitcher	$425
Kro Flite Double Waterfall Face Mashie Niblick	$3,500
Kro Flite Lined Face Driving Iron	$50
Kro Flite Lined Face Mashie	$45
Kro Flite Lined Face Mid Iron	$35
Kro Flite Lined Face Mid Mashie	$50
Kro Flite Lined Face Niblick	$50
Kro Flite Lined Face Putter	$55
Kro Flite Lined Face Sky Iron	$90
Kro Flite R F Blade Putter	$50
Kro Flite Socket Headed Brassie Fancy Face Insert	$175
Kro Flite Socket Headed Driver Fancy Face Insert	$175
Kro Flite Socket Headed Spoon Fancy Face Insert	$175
Kro Flite Waterfall Face Mashie Niblick	$375
Kro-flite Sweet Spot #17 Pitcher	$60
Kro-Flite Sweet Spot Pitcher	$70
Ladies Smooth Faced Cleek	$75
Ladies Special Smooth Faced Compact Head Lofting Iron	$85
Ladies The Spalding Lofting Iron	$60
Lined Face Niblick	$50
Long Square Headed Putter Brass Face	$325
M 1 Driving Iron	$60
M-3 Monel Metal Mashie	$65
M-8 Sky Iron	$55
Mallet Headed Putter	$275
Harry Collis Maxwell Hosel Cleek	$95
Medal 2 Small Head Brassie	$110
Medal 7 Socket Spoon	$95
Medal 23 Socket Spoon	$110
Medal Dedstop Corrugated Face Mashie Niblick	$90
Medal Deeply Corrugated Face Niblick	$90
Mid Iron	$50
Mid Iron Small Dots on the Face	$125
Model B Cleek Dot Punched Face	$60
Monel Metal Mashie Niblick	$65
Morristown Bulger Spliced Head Driver	$325
Morristown Gun Metal Blade Putter	$90
Morristown Round Headed Smooth Concave Faced Niblick	$550
Morristown Smooth Faced Cleek	$75

COMPANY	HICKORY	VALUE

Spalding, USA (cont.):

Morristown Smooth Faced Driving Mashie	$125
Parputta Iron Bladed Putter Hollow Back	$350
Pro Golfers Ass'n Offset Lined Face Putter	$45
Riveted Hosel Iron	$700
Severe Bent Neck Park Style Putter	$135
Severe Bent Neck Putter	$75
Small Socket Headed Driver	$65
Smooth Concave Faced Mashie Niblick	
Boat Shaped Head	$275
Smooth Face Brass Blade Putter "Morristown"	$95
Smooth Faced Cleek	$225
Smooth Faced Compact Head Lofting Iron	$95
Smooth Faced Lofter	$95
Smooth Faced Mid Iron	$60
Socket Headed Brassie	$65
Socket Headed Driver	$125
Socket Headed Driver One Piece Sole and Backweight	$100
Socket Headed Spoon	$65
Spalding 2 Persimmon Socket Driver	$95
Spalding Special Cleek	$140
Spalding Special Driving Iron	$275
Spalding Special Gun Metal Blade Putter	$225
The Spalding Center Shafted Lofting Mashie	$3,250
The Spalding Cleek Iron Head And Wood Face	$850
The Spalding Convex Back Smooth Faced Iron	$150
The Spalding Deep Faced Gun Metal Blade Putter	$275
The Spalding Gun Metal Blade Putter Diamond Back	$200
The Spalding Large Headed Smooth Faced Niblick	$165
The Spalding Lofter Concave Smooth Face	$90
The Spalding Offset Blade Putting Cleek	$200
The Spalding Short Heavy Blade Smooth Faced Mashie	$125
The Spalding Smooth Concave Faced Niblick	$550
The Spalding Smooth Faced Cleek Carruthers Hosel	$165
The Spalding Smooth Faced Driving Mashie	$125
The Spalding Smooth Faced Niblick Oval Head	$3,000
The Spalding Splice Headed Driver	$275
Special Concave Smooth Faced Lofting Iron	$70
Special Heavy Lofting Mashie	$175
Splice Headed Bassie Niblick	$1,400
Splice Headed Driver	$225
Spoon	$900
Spring Faced Iron	$900
Stop Em Deeply Ribbed Face Mashie	$125
Stop Em Deeply Ribbed Face Mashie Niblick	$125
Stop Em Deeply Ribbed Face Niblick	$125
Straight Blade Brass Putter	$70
Striped Top Driver Face Insert	$75

COMPANY HICKORY	VALUE
Spalding, USA (cont.):	
Sweet Spot Jigger	$50
Tong Putting Cleek	$225
Triple Splice Brassie	$450
Triple Splice Headed Spoon	$450
Two Sided Straight Brass Blade Putter	$95
Vardon Diamond Faced Cleek	$165
Vardon Iron Bladed Putter	$125
Vardon Lined Face Mid Iron	$90
Vardon Offset Blade Putting Cleek	$125
Vardon Short Splice Headed Brassie	$275
Vardon Small Headed Smooth Faced Niblick	$550
Vardon Small Splice Headed Driver	$325
Vardon Smooth Faced Driving Iron	$140
Vardon Smooth Faced Jigger	$90
Vardon Smooth Faced Lofting Mashie	$125
Vardon Smooth Faced Mashie Short Blade	$125
Vardon Smooth Faced Mid Iron	$125
H. Vardon Light Mid Iron Angled Line Face Scoring	$125
Harry Vardon Cleek	$125
Wooden Headed Brass Face Plate Putter	$225
George Sparling:	
Gun Metal Blade Putter	$225
Spence & Gourlay:	
Deeply Corrugated Face Mashie Niblick	$135
Dot Faced Iron	$55
Dot Faced Mashie	$55
Dot Faced Putter	$55
Medium Headed Dot Faced Niblick	$65
Small Headed Lofter Daisy Shaped Face Scoring	$165
T.H. Stone Long Hosel Putter	$85
James Spence:	
Iron Bladed Putter	$90
Lined Face Iron	$50
Lined Face Mashie Niblick	$60
Long Thin Blade And Hosel Putter	$150
Oval Headed Lined Face Mashie Niblick	$60
David Spittle:	
Socket Headed Driver	$800
Sport Mart:	
Chromed Head Lined Face Iron	$30
Sports & Games Association Ltd.:	
Lined Face Mashie	$75
Sports Depot:	
Stainless Dot Faced Mashie	$55
The Sportsman's Emporium:	
Long Smooth Bladed Putting Cleek	$90

COMPANY	HICKORY	VALUE
G.S. Sprague:		
Deep Faced Mashie		$70
Driver Bore Through Sole Shafting		$135
St. Andrew Golf Co.:		
Aluminum Putter Black Sight Line		$120
Anti Shank Lined Face Niblick		$165
Bent Neck Lined Face Putter		$60
Challenge Stainless Mashie Niblick		$50
Child's Gun Metal Blade Putter		$50
Child's Socket Headed Driver		$50
Choix Stainless Iron		$40
D F Mashie Hyphen Scored Face		$65
Deep Corrugated Face Mashie Niblick		$125
Dot Faced Mid Iron		$60
Drilled Hosel Mashie		$65
Driver		$65
Hawkins Never Rust Cleek		$95
Hawkins Never Rust Mashie		$60
Jupiter Heavy Iron Blade Putter		$60
Lined Face Mid Iron		$50
Dick May Convex Faced Putter		$165
Niblick		$60
Scottie Stainless Mashie Lined Face		$45
Smooth Faced Iron		$65
Socket Headed Brassie Patented Grypta Grip		$365
Special Rustless Niblick		$75
Standard Lined Face Mashie		$50
Striped Top Driver Ivory Face and Backweight		$225
Super Stag Brassie Striped Top		$55
Super Stag Stainless Cleek Lined Face		$45
Suxes Stainless Spade Mashie		$50
Synchromatic Socket Headed Driver		$75
Thick Soled Niblick		$50
St. Andrews Special:		
Convex Backed Jigger		$45
Iron Bladed Putter		$50
St. Regis:		
Chromed Head Mid Iron		$30
Stadium Golf Co.:		
Approach Putter		$250
Dot Faced Pointed Sole Niblick		$300
Korecta Mashie Niblick		$250
Korecta Niblick		$300
Korecta Putter		$250
Offset Blade Putter		$75
Pointed Sole Brassie Baffy		$400
Putting Cleek 2 Dot Faced Blade Putter		$75
Round Blade Solid Backed Putter		$550
Stainless Lined Face Mid Iron		$75

COMPANY HICKORY	VALUE
Standard Golf Co.:	
Aluminum Fairway Club Mills Medium Lofter	$325
Bent Necked Putter	$90
Brassie Spoon	$300
Center Shafted Aluminum Putter	$245
Cotton Mills Mallet Headed Putter	$100
Duplex Dual Sided Head	$650
Hooked Face Baffy	$550
Long Nosed Putter	$475
M. N. G. Bent Neck Aluminum Putter	$190
Mallet Headed Cylindrical Hammer Headed Putter	$1,400
The Mills L Model Medium Lie Aluminum Putter	$125
Braid Mills Mallet Headed Putter	$65
Braid Mills Medium Lie Aluminum Putter	$75
Braid Mills R B B Model Aluminum Putter	$125
Braid Mills Semi Long Nosed Putter	$150
Edgar Mills Small Mallet Headed Putter	$125
R S R Model Aluminum Putter	$275
Semi Long Nosed Putter	$495
Semi Long Nosed Spoon	$300
Short Headed Spoon	$375
Special X Aluminum Putter	$160
Standard Aluminum Driver Fancy Wooden Face Insert	$850
Steel Bladed Putter	$150
Wooden Faced Driver	$400
Wooden Faced Spoon	$400
Y Model Long Nose Aluminum Putter	$225
J.A. Steer:	
Large Headed Brassie Fiber Face Insert	$90
Fred Stephens:	
Stainless Dash Faced Mashie	$75
James Stephens:	
Stainless Dot Faced Mashie	$50
Sterling & Gibson:	
Smooth Deep Faced Mashie	$100
Smooth Faced Medium Headed Niblick	$125
Smooth Faced Short Bladed Cleek	$125
Rufus Stewart:	
Lined Face Niblick	$90
Thomas Stewart:	
Anti Shank Iron	$300
Anti Shank Mashie	$250
Anti Shank Niblick	$125
Backwards Bent Hosel Putter	$375
Bent Necked Blade Putter	$125
Concentrated Back Putter	$125
Dash Faced Mashie	$90
Deep Lined Face Spade Mashie	$75

COMPANY	HICKORY	VALUE
Thomas Stewart (cont.):		
Deeply Corrugated Face Mashie		$185
Deeply Corrugated Face Mashie Niblick		$225
Deeply Corrugated Face Spade Mashie		$225
Dot Faced Iron		$60
Dot Faced Jigger		$90
Dot Faced Lofting Iron		$75
Dot Faced Lofting Mashie		$100
Dot Faced Mashie		$55
Dot Faced Mid Iron		$60
Driving Iron		$75
Extra Long Heavy Bladed Smooth Faced Cleek Long Hosel		$300
T.R. Fernie Radial Sole Specialty Club		$75
Fred Whiting Lined Scored Iron		$55
Giant Head Lined Face Niblick		$1,750
Gun Metal Blade Putter		$135
Hollow Backed Putter		$400
Iron Bladed Putter		$65
Robert T. Jones Iron		$125
Robert T. Jones Lined Face Mashie		$225
Line Scored Driving Iron		$75
Lined Face Bobby Iron Rounded Sole		$125
Lined Face Driving Mashie		$75
Lined Face Mashie		$65
Lined Scored Face Iron		$50
Long Blade Approaching Cleek Lined Face		$75
Long Blade Beveled Heel and Toe Putter		$100
Mashie Dot Punched Face		$55
J.J. McKenna Malahide Iron		$70
Medium Headed Lined Face Niblick		$65
Offset Blade Putter		$80
Oval Headed Lined Face Mashie Niblick		$65
Oval Headed Lined Face Pitcher		$75
Putter with a Dot Punched Face		$75
Shallow Smooth Faced Mashie		$65
Short Bladed Smooth Faced Cleek		$125
Small Headed Smooth Faced Niblick		$150
Small Iron Headed Mallet Putter		$750
Smooth Faced Cleek		$90
Smooth Faced Cleek Carruthers Hosel		$165
Smooth Faced Iron		$75
Smooth Faced Iron Musselbacked		$125
Smooth Faced Jigger		$100
Smooth Faced Lofter		$50
Smooth Faced Mashie		$90
Smooth Faced Mid Iron		$75
Vardon Lined Face Mashie		$125
M.E. Yates Deep Faced Lofter		$90

COMPANY HICKORY	VALUE
W. Stoddard:	
Bottom Weighted Round Sole Mashie	$175
J. Stoker:	
Offset Musselback Putter	$325
Stokes & Co.:	
Smooth Faced Putter	$75
W. Strachan:	
Semi Long Nosed Transitional	
Headed Spoon Leather Face Insert	$475
Strath & Beveridge:	
Long Nosed Beech Headed Play Club	$9,500
George Strath:	
Center Shafted Putter	$1,850
Long Nosed Beech Headed Driver Grassed Face	$9,500
Long Nosed Beech Headed Play Club	$7,500
Long Nosed Beech Headed Putter	$5,500
Stream-Line Co.:	
Melhorn Metal Headed Driver with Sole Plate	$235
J.G. Stuart:	
Socket Headed Driver	$65
Suggs Ltd.:	
Rustless 1 Iron	$65
R. Sullivan:	
Mid Iron Hyphen Scored Face	$55
Supreme:	
Chromed Head Mid Iron	$35
Sure Thing:	
Triangular Shaped Head Putter	$125
Sure Winner:	
Socket Headed Driver Stripe Top	$65
H.L. Sutton:	
Mallet Headed Putter Rollers In Sole	$2,750
David Swank:	
Musselbacked Lined Face Mid Iron	$45
H.R. Sweeny:	
Center Shafted Splice Headed Driver	$3,750
Smooth Faced Cleek	$195
Sweney Sporting Goods Co.:	
Cavity Back Smooth Faced Lofter	$300
William Sykes:	
Select Dot Faced Mid Iron	$65
T. Tait:	
Smooth Faced Mid Iron	$90
Thick Bladed Putter	$90
Taplow:	
Deeply Corrugated Face Pitcher	$125
Socket Headed Driver	$65

COMPANY HICKORY	VALUE
Alex Taylor Co.:	
Deep Faced Socket Driver	$90
Juvenile Socket Headed Driver	$65
Mashie Niblick Dot Face	$45
Small Head Driver Black Face Insert	$125
Smooth Faced Mashie	$75
Stainless Mashie Lined Face	$35
Two Toned Head Brassie	$85
Taylor Brothers:	
Lined Face Jigger	$60
Josh Taylor:	
Mascot Mashie	$75
Walter Tedder:	
Socket Headed Driver	$75
A. Teen & Co.:	
Bar Back Model Horizontal Weight Along the Back	$1,250
Round Headed Driver	$1,950
Thistle Golf Co.:	
Gun Metal Blade Putter	$90
Splice Headed Spoon Face Insert	$500
Thistle Putter Co.:	
Aluminum Mallet Headed Putter Aiming T on Top	$150
Aluminum Putter T Square Top Removable Head Weights	$750
Thistle Special:	
Smooth Faced Jigger	$90
J. Thompson:	
Semi Long Nosed Transitional Splice Headed Driver	$400
James Thompson:	
Iron Bladed Bent Neck Putter	$65
A. Thomson:	
Socket Headed Brassie	$125
Jimmy Thomson:	
Socket Headed Driver	$300
W. Thomson:	
Socket Spoon	$120
Thornton & Co. Ltd.:	
Bent Necked Dash Faced Putter	$65
Deep Faced Socket Headed Driver	$140
Short Splice Headed Driver	$150
Socket Headed Brassie	$100
Stainless Dot Faced Mashie	$75
Straight Blade Smooth Faced Putter	$75
Tom Thumb:	
Chromed Blade Putter	$65
Timperly:	
Aluminum Small Center Shafted Schenectady Putter	$750
Albert Tiney:	
Semi Long Nosed Socket Headed Putter	$225
Semi Long Nosed Splice Headed Beech Putter	$1,250

COMPANY HICKORY	VALUE
Arner C. Tollifson:	
Mashie	$55
J. Tolmie:	
Smooth Faced Large Headed Iron Long Blade	$325
Alfred Toogood:	
Socket Headed Brassie	$75
Walter Toogood:	
Splice Headed Brassie	$100
A. Tooley & Sons:	
Iron with Two Large Weights on Blade Back	$900
Lined Face Mid Iron	$200
Smooth Concave Faced Jigger	$80
Stainless Iron	$65
Suitall Round Sole Pointed Top Edge Putter	$350
S. Trapp:	
Socket Headed Driver Face Insert	$75
Tom Trapp:	
Dot Faced Iron	$45
Ideal Socket Headed Spoon Face Insert	$75
Jerry Travers:	
Wooden Headed Schenectady Putter	$325
T. Travers:	
Socket Headed Brassie	$75
Splice Headed Spoon	$175
Wooden Headed Mallet Putter	$500
A. Tribble:	
Socket Headed Brassie	$65
D.S. Trimount:	
Smooth Faced Iron	$55
Truhital:	
Aluminum Rectangular Headed Heel Shafted Putter	$300
Tru-Line:	
Putter with Removable Aiming Rod	$3,000
Tru-Put:	
Aluminum Schenectady Putter Fiber Face Insert	$300
Edward K. Tryon Co.:	
Imperial Mashie	$35
Lined Face Mashie	$50
Tip Top Iron Bladed Putter	$60
Tucker Bros.:	
Defiance Short Socket Head Driver	$150
Defiance Short Spliced Head Driver	$200
William Tucker:	
Aluminum Fairway Club	$350
Defiance Approaching Mashie	$150
Defiance Goosenecked Putter	$175
Defiance Gun Metal Blade Putter	$150
Defiance Mid Iron	$125

COMPANY	HICKORY	VALUE

William Tucker (cont.):

Defiance Short Deep Bladed Mashie	$175
Defiance Smooth Faced Driving Cleek	$175
Defiance Smooth Faced Driving Mashie	$125
Defiance Smooth Faced Jigger	$175
Defiance Smooth Faced Lofting Iron	$175
Defiance Smooth Faced Mashie	$150
Defiance Smooth Faced Medium Headed Niblick	$175
Defiance Socket Headed Brassie	$150
Defiance Splice Headed Brassie	$300
Defiance Splice Headed Driver	$350
Iron Bladed Putter	$125
Lined Face Mashie Jigger	$100
Smooth Faced Lofter	$150

J. Tulloch:

Diamond Faced Mashie	$75
Rounded Back Putter	$100

Tom Turnbull:

Splice Headed Driver	$125

John Henry Turner:

Lined Face Mashie Weights In Top of Blade Edge	$150
Socket Headed Driver Center Balanced	$175
Socket Headed Driver Stripe Top	$75

George Turpie:

Smooth Faced Mid Iron	$75

Tuxedo:

Stainless Lined Face Mashie	$35

W.T. Twine:

Splice Headed Driver	$150

R.G. Tyler:

Aluminum/Wood Headed Driver	$175
Schenectady Brass Faced Putter	$250

U.D.S.:

Aluminum Driver with Wood Face Plugs	$300

Gardner F. Underhill:

Aluminum Mallet Headed Putter	$100
Flanged Back Putter	$75

Union Golf Co.:

Shur Putt Chromed Blade Putter	$45

R. Urquhart:

Patented Adjustable Iron	$1,750

U.S. Golf Manufacturing Co.:

Driver	$250
Holdfast Lined Faced Mid Iron	$75
Reliance Straight Putter	$95

V.L. & A.:

Perfect Dot Faced Mashie Centrajet Back	$60
Socket Headed Brassie	$75

COMPANY HICKORY	VALUE
V.L. & A. (cont.):	
Striped Top Socket Headed Driver	$60
Velanay Putter	$60
V.L. & D.:	
Braid Musselback Approaching Cleek	$100
Socket Headed Driver Dreadnought Model	$100
P.A. Vaile:	
Swan Necked Gun Metal Blade Putter	$400
Swan Necked Socket Headed Brassie	$475
Swan Necked Socket Headed Brassie Fancy Face Insert	$600
Harry Vardon:	
Short Spliced Head Driver	$400
Small Splice Headed Brassie	$300
Tom Vardon:	
Bulger Splice Headed Brassie	$400
Deep Lined Face Mashie	$100
Lined Face Mashie	$100
Splice Headed Brassie	$200
Velometer:	
Socket Headed Driver	$300
Jack Venters:	
Splice Headed Brassie	$475
Vickers Ltd.:	
Bamboo Shafted Mashie	$125
Stainless Bladed Putter	$75
Stainless Lined Face Mashie	$75
Stainless Mashie	$50
Stainless Mid Iron	$50
Stainless Niblick	$65
Stainless Spade Mashie	$60
Victor:	
Iron Bladed Putter	$125
Smooth Faced Concentric Backed Iron	$150
Victor-O W C:	
Small Headed Smooth Faced Gun Metal Niblick	$2,500
Vim:	
Chromed Spade Mashie	$35
Greenfield Lined Face Driving Iron	$35
Thick Bladed Putter	$45
L.H. Vorhies:	
Adjustable Iron with Three Selectable Striking Surfaces	$2,750
Vulcan Golf Co.:	
Burma Dot Faced Blade Putter	$50
Lined Face Niblick	$45
Lined Face Stainless Driving Iron	$45
Long Hosel Jigger	$125
Long Hosel Putter	$175

COMPANY HICKORY	VALUE
Vulcan Golf Co. (cont.):	
Long Thin Blade and Hosel Putter	$175
Pirae Stainless Lined Faced Mashie	$45
Socket Headed Driver Face Insert	$100
Socket Headed Driver Fancy Face Insert	$125
Stainless Blade Putter	$65
Stainless Long Hosel Blade Putter	$190
Stripe Top Socket Headed Driver Face Insert	$60
Tom Waggott:	
Short Splice Headed Driver	$175
Wales:	
Chromed Blade Lined Face Putter	$35
Walgreen Co.:	
Chromed Head Lined Face Irons	$35
George Walker:	
Socket Headed Driver Striped Top	$60
Thomas Walker:	
Semi Long Nosed Splice Headed Driver	$450
Semi Long Nosed Spoon Dished Face	$950
S.B. Wallace:	
Talisman Lined Face Iron	$45
Willie Wallis:	
Diamond Dot Faced Niblick	$65
John D. Wanamaker Co.:	
Socket Headed Brassie	$75
Socket Headed Driver	$65
James Watt:	
Lined Face Driving Iron	$45
William Watt:	
Socket Headed Spoon Face Insert	$60
Waverly:	
Lined Face Mashie	$35
W.H. Way:	
Medium Head Smooth Faced Niblick Carruthers Hosel	$165
Smooth Faced Cleek Short Blade	$95
W.H. Webb:	
Anti Shank Lined Face Niblick	$250
One Piece Driver	$1,950
A.N. Weir:	
Socket Headed Driver	$75
Wellington-Stone Co.:	
Lined Face Parlor Putter	$250
Westward Ho:	
Lined Face Mashie	$50
E.R. Whitcombe:	
Dot Faced Iron	$50
J.C. White:	
Ladies Deep Faced Driving Iron Hyphen Scored Face	$90

COMPANY HICKORY	VALUE
Jack White:	
Civic Putter Holes Drilled in Blade	$525
Concave Hooked Face Lofting Iron	$500
Ladies Rustless Putter	$55
Musselbacked Iron	$75
Socket Headed Driver Striped Top	$90
Sunningdale Mashie	$55
James White & Co.:	
Monel A 5 Mid Mashie	$75
Robert White: (Ohio)	
Smooth Faced Driving Iron	$90
Smooth Faced Mashie	$95
Robert White: (St. Andrews)	
Compact Head Smooth Faced Iron	$300
Long Bladed Iron Putter	$400
Medium Headed Niblick	$475
Short Blade Smooth Faced Lofter	$325
Small Headed Niblick	$625
Smooth Faced Cleek	$325
Smooth Faced Iron	$275
Smooth Faced Mashie	$595
Fred Whiting:	
Small Head Lofted Wooden Cleek Full Brass Sole Plate	$250
S. Whiting:	
Socket Headed Driver	$75
William Whittet:	
Dovetail Splice Headed Driver	$650
J.H. Williams:	
Persimmon Socket Head Driver	$125
Smooth Faced Mashie	$175
Tom Williamson:	
Offset Blade Putter	$75
Smooth Faced Mid Iron	$90
Harold A. Wilson:	
Dash Faced Mashie Niblick	$65
James Wilson:	
Long Nosed Beech Headed Play Club	$12,500
R.B. Wilson:	
Accurate Offset Blade Putter	$90
Blade Putter No Hosel	$950
Gun Metal Blade Putter	$100
Iron Bladed Putter Square Hole in Face	$900
Oval Headed Convex Faced Blade Putter	$650
Raised Face Putter Diamond Face Markings	$250
Short Blade Deep Faced Iron Putter	$185
Small Splice Headed Driver	$350
Smooth Face Heavy Headed Niblick	$400
Smooth Face Short Bladed Mashie Cleek	$185

COMPANY	HICKORY	VALUE

R.B. Wilson (cont.):
Smooth Faced Cleek		$125
Smooth Faced Iron		$400
Smooth Faced Mashie		$125
Smooth Faced Wide Toe Mashie		$250

R.G. Wilson:
Long Blade Lined Faced Mashie Niblick		$75
Socket Headed Brassie		$75
Splice Headed Fancy Face Insert Aluminum Backweighted Driver		$300

Robert Wilson:
Concave Faced Lofter		$750
Long Iron Blade Putting Cleek		$600
Small Head Concave Faced Niblick		$1,500
Smooth Concave Faced Cleek		$650
Smooth Faced Iron		$550
Smooth Faced Lofter		$550

Thomas E. Wilson:
Aim Right Jigger		$45
Aim Rite Lined Face Mashie		$35
Aluminum Success Mallet Headed Putter		$90
Baxspin Deeply Corrugated Face Mashie		$225
John Black Super Stroke Mashie		$75
Blue Ribbon Stainless Lined Face Iron		$45
Carnoustie Iron		$35
Carnoustie Wood		$35
Child's Putter		$35
Corrugated Deep Groove Mashie Niblick		$125
Cup Defender Lined Face Iron		$30
Dixie Iron		$30
Dixie Wood		$35
Johnny Farrell Stainless Iron		$35
Jock Hutchison Lined Face Mashie		$65
Ladies Lucky Stroke Lined Face Stainless Iron		$35
Ladies Walker Cup Stainless Steel		$40
Lincoln Park Iron		$30
Lincoln Park Wood		$45
Lined Face Mid Iron		$65
Lined Face Thick Bladed Mashie		$50
Linkhurst Stainless Lined Face Iron		$35
Model Six Plus Success Mid Iron		$65
Open Hearth Iron		$30
Plus Success Iron		$45
Plus Success Socket Headed Wood		$50
Range Stainless Iron		$35
Ted Ray Chromed Iron		$55
Ted Ray Stainless Iron		$60
Ted Ray Wood		$65

COMPANY HICKORY	VALUE

Thomas E. Wilson (cont.):

Red Ribbon Stainless Lined Face Iron	$40
Sarazen Stainless Lined Face Iron	$45
Sarazen Wood	$55
Sarazen Wood Striped Top	$60
Gene Sarazen 8 Niblick Dot Face	$70
Sharpshooter Socket Headed Wood	$45
Skokie Stainless Lined Face Iron	$35
Smooth Faced Niblick with Dot Punched Face	$60
Socket Headed Driver	$65
Streak Stainless Iron	$30
Super Stroke Chromed Iron	$35
Taplow Iron	$40
Taplow Wood	$45
Two Sided Wooden Headed Mallet	$425
Harry Vardon Iron	$75
Harry Vardon Wood	$95
Whiz Driver	$95
The Wilsonian Blade Putter	$65

William Wilson:

Anti Shank Smooth Faced Lofter	$750
Gun Metal Blade Putter	$350
Iron Bladed Putter	$265
Long Blade Deep Faced Iron	$325
Long Blade Smooth Faced Cleek	$450
Long Bladed Lofter	$350
Small Headed Niblick	$1,250
Thick Heavy Bladed Mashie	$425

William C. Wilson:

Solwin Lined Face Mashie	$90

Winchester Arms Co.:

Brae Burn Blade Putter	$90
Brae Burn Round Soles Mid Iron	$90
Deeply Corrugated Face Mashie	$300
Deeply Ribbed Face Niblick	$225
Flanded Sole Dot Faced Mashie	$90
Jock Hutchison Dot Faced Iron	$100
Jock Hutchison Driver Fiber Face Insert	$150
Pickwick Dash Faced Mashie	$90
Socket Headed Driver	$125
Wide Soled Putter	$125

N. Winders:

Socket Headed Brassie	$60

Winfield Special:

Iron Bladed Putter	$55

S. Wingate:

Socket Headed Brassie	$60

COMPANY	HICKORY	VALUE

J. Winton:

Semi Long Nosed Transitional Splice Headed Putter		$325
Socket Headed Brassie		$60

James Winton:

Smooth Faced Lofter		$95

Tom Winton:

Slice Neck Brassie Wood		$225

W.M. Winton Co.:

Anti Shank Dot Faced Mashie Niblick		$225
Anti Shank Mashie		$250
Anti Shank Niblick		$225
Bent Necked Putter		$75
Bogie Cavity Back Smooth Faced Niblick		$300
Bogie Cleek		$195
Brown Patented Bent Necked Horizontally Slotted Face Putter		$7,500
Brown Patented Horizontally Slotted Face Cleek		$8,000
Brown Patented Horizontally Slotted Face Driving Mashie		$7,500
Brown Patented Horizontally Slotted Face Niblick		$7,500
Brown Patented Horizontally Slotted Face Putter		$7,500
Brown Patented Vertically Slotted Face Mashie Niblick		$8,000
Brown Patented Vertically Slotted Face Niblick		$7,500
Centrajet Backed Mid Iron		$75
Cert Concave Faced Mashie		$75
Cert Deeply Corrugated Face Mashie Niblick		$150
Cert Deeply Ribbed Face Mashie		$125
Compact Head Smooth Faced Lofting Iron		$75
Concave Dot Faced Mid Iron		$60
Dot Faced Cleek		$65
Dot Faced Driving Iron		$60
Dot Faced Jigger		$65
Dot Faced Mashie		$50
Dot Faced Mashie Niblick		$65
Dot Faced Mid Iron		$50
Dot Faced Niblick		$75
Dot Faced Putter		$75
Flange Sole Lined Face Mashie		$60
Hunters Scored Blade Putter Severely Bent Hosel		$145
Large Headed Niblick		$75
Lined Face Driving Iron		$60
Lined Face Mashie		$50
Lined Face Mid Iron		$50
Lined Face Spade Mashie		$75
Long Faced Putter		$75
Mashie with Deep Faced Large Dot Punched Head		$150
Niblick Line Scored Face		$50
Niblick with a Round Lined Scored Face		$85

COMPANY HICKORY	VALUE
W.M. Winton Co. (cont.):	
Persimmon Head Spliced Neck Brassie	$190
Ted Ray's Own Niblick	$120
Rounded Back Mashie	$60
Sammy #6	$120
Small Square Punched Face Jigger	$65
Special Mid Iron #89	$55
Special Z Mashie Niblick Stainless Iron	$60
Stainless Mashie	$55
Straight Backed Mid Iron	$50
Super Large Headed Niblick Dot Face	$1,750
Thick Bladed Mashie Niblick	$75
Vardon Jigger	$65
Vardon Musselback Lined Face Mashie	$90
Harry Vardon Iron Bladed Putter	$75
Harry Vardon Putting Cleek	$75
Win On Smooth Faced Sand Iron Niblick	$150
J. Wisden & Co.:	
Gun Metal Blade Putter	$150
Royal Aluminum Mallet Headed Putter	$150
Royal Smooth Faced Mashie	$100
Wood Wand:	
Iron Bladed Putter	$40
Ted Wooley:	
Red Ribbon Stainless Dot Faced Iron	$40
H.W. Wooliscroft:	
Goose Neck Ladies Putter	$55
Worthington Co.:	
Iron Bladed Putter	$75
Socket Headed Driver	$200
Wright & Ditson:	
Aluminum Mallet Headed Putter	$75
Bee Line Deep Waterfall Face Pitcher	$400
Bee Line Deeply Grooved Face Pitcher	$135
Bee Line Double Waterfall Faced Mashie Niblick	$3,500
Bee Line Lined Face Driving Iron	$50
Bee Line Lined Face Jigger	$75
Bee Line Lined Face Mashie	$50
Bee Line Lined Face Mashie Niblick	$50
Bee Line Lined Face Mid Iron	$50
Bee Line Lined Face Niblick	$45
Bee Line Lined Face Pitcher	$50
Bee Line Lined Face Putter	$55
Brassie Fancy Face Insert	$195
Brassie with Brass Backweight	$100
Brassie with One Piece Sole and Backweight	$135
Child's Stainless Dot Faced Iron	$40
Circular Dot Faced Mashie	$75

COMPANY	HICKORY	VALUE

Wright & Ditson (cont.):

Circular Dot Faced Putting Cleek	$75
Concave Faced Mashie Niblick	$195
Cross Dash Faced Niblick	$60
Deep Lined Face Mashie Niblick	$60
Deeply Corrugated Face Mashie Niblick	$90
Deeply Corrugated Face Niblick	$145
Deeply Slotted Face Mashie Niblick	$90
Diamond Backed Mid Iron Diamond/Dot Face	$75
Dot Faced Mashie	$60
Dot Faced Mashie Niblick	$60
Dot Faced Mid Iron	$60
Dot Faced Niblick	$60
Dot Faced Putter	$135
Driver with Brass Backweight	$100
Driver with Fancy Face Insert	$135
Driver with One Piece Brass Sole and Backweight	$135
Driving Mashie	$75
A.H. Findlay Brassie Full Brass Sole Plate	$115
A.H. Findlay Goose Neck Putter	$95
A.H. Findlay Iron Vertical Rows of Dots On The Face	$75
Flange Sole Dot Sole Putter	$75
Gooseneck Beveled Sole with Dash Faced Mashie Niblick	$60
Goosenecked Dash Faced Niblick	$65
Goosenecked Putter	$65
Heavily Offset Head Diamond Faced Putter	$75
Iron Blade Dot Faced Putter	$75
Large Socket Headed Driver	$145
Lined Face Mashie	$60
Lined Face Mid Iron	$60
Lofted Socket Spoon	$90
Long Faced Baffy Spoon	$90
Long Faced Spoon	$75
Long Narrow Bladed Mashie Jigger	$75
Long Narrow Socket Head Wooden Cleek	$165
Monel Metal Mashie	$65
Musselbacked Approaching Cleek	$165
Narrow Blade Lined Face Putter	$65
Narrow Headed Brassie	$75
Narrow Headed Driver	$75
Offset Smooth Faced Blade Iron	$195
Plain Faced Brassie	$65
Random Dot Faced Niblick	$75
Rounded Back Dot Faced Mid Iron	$55
Selected Cleek	$85
Selected Smooth Faced Lofting Iron	$75
Shallow Face Rounded Back Putter	$300
Short Headed Mid Iron	$60

COMPANY HICKORY	VALUE
Wright & Ditson (cont.):	
Small Head Concave Smooth Faced Niblick	$750
Small Headed Driver	$65
Smooth Faced Approaching Cleek	$90
Smooth Faced Cleek	$95
Smooth Faced Iron	$100
Smooth Faced Mid Iron	$65
Smooth Faced Niblick	$75
Socket Head Deep Faced Driver	$75
Socket Headed Brassie	$65
Socket Headed Brassie Fancy Face Insert	$135
Socket Headed Driver	$65
Socket Headed Driver Fancy Face Insert	$135
Socket Headed Driver Steel Face Plate	$145
Socket Headed Spoon	$75
Socket Headed Spoon Fancy Face Insert	$100
Socket Headed Spoon Fiber Face	$75
Splice Headed Brassie Brass Backweight	$145
Splice Headed Driver Brass Backweight	$135
Spliced Neck Bulger Driver	$250
Spring Faced Mashie	$1,100
Spring Faced Mid Iron	$900
St. Andrews Mashie	$50
Triple Splice Headed Brassie	$500
Vertically Open Slotted Face Mashie	$12,500
Victor Special Brassie	$90
Wooden Faced Cleek	$1,050
Philip Wynne:	
Lined Face Mashie	$55
Socket Headed Driver	$65
William Yeoman:	
Dot Faced Iron	$55
Robert T. Jones Lined Face Iron	$145
Short Splice Headed Brassie	$225
Splice Headed Driver	$275
J. Youds:	
Aluminum Mallet Headed Putter Lead Face	$350
Anti Shank Mashie	$225
Dot Faced Mashie	$75
Short Splice Headed Driver	$225
Socket Headed Driver Face Insert	$75
L.A. Young Co.:	
Hagen Getaway L W Putter	$50
Hagen Gettaway Putter	$60
Hagen Graduated 7 Mashie Niblick	$50
Hagen Stainless Concave Faced Sand Iron Flanged Sole	$450
S.A. Zappe:	
Socket Headed Driver	$55

Books

by Eldon P. Steeves

Eldon P. Steeves has been engaged in the full time sale and purchase of quality books for many years. More and more of his efforts were directed towards golf related material until in 1982 it became his sole focus. He issues an incredible catalog that is a source of historic facts as well as material for sale. He can be reached at

> Eldon P. Steeves Rare Books
> PO Box 491
> Syracuse NY 13209

There are thousands of hard cover books written on the topic of golf. In keeping with the classic collectible theme, I have tried to list all the relevant titles. The focus is primarily 1980 and before. If a book is not listed it means nothing. The last decade has seen a huge increase in the number of titles and I had to draw the line somewhere. Some new books are issued strictly as collectibles and a few are listed here.

The books are alphabetized by author and then by book. Usually the first or major printing is listed. The dates of publication are as listed in the title page of the book. Club handbooks present special difficulty in the establishment of a publishing date.

Some books have very lengthy names. T.H. Haultain wrote a book he entitled "The Mystery Of Golf: A Briefe

Account Of Games In Generall; Their Origine; Antique; & Rampancie: And Of The Gameycleped Golf In Particular; Its Uniqueness; Its Curiosness; And Its Difficultie; Its Anatomical, Philosophicall, And Moral Properties; Together With Diverse Concepts On Matters To It, Appertaining." This has been shortened to a more manageable "The Mystery of Golf." Some books are of a regional nature. They may have a greater value in that local area than the world at large

Books without obvious author are listed alphabetically in the body of text using the title as author. For example "A Most Convenient Setting Forth of Much Interesting Information Regarding Golf" with no recognized author is listed under "Most Convenient Setting Forth" as author.

Some titles or subjects are intriguing. There is a book on how to plumb bob greens successfully written by Gene Andrews, titled "Scientific Analysis of The Plumb Bob Method of Reading Greens." The most misguided title belongs to Hack Miller when he titled his book "The New Billy Casper: More Important Things in Life Than Golf". Also included are books on the shadier side of golf such as "How To Cheat and Hustle At Golf" by Tom Ramsey.

The values listed are for books in very good condition. Dust jackets should be present and intact if the book was originally issued with one. The spine should be solid and all pages present and intact. The various printings of books greatly affect the value. Generally a first edition has more value than subsequent issues. A signed copy has more value to some collectors.

AUTHOR TITLE	PUB. DATE	VALUE
A Member:		
"The Duffers Golf Club Papers"	1891	$1,200
"St. Andrews To The Play"	1994	$45
A Novice:		
"On The Links"	1889	$1,700
"Shakespeare On Golf"	1885	$1,200
Abersoch Golf Club:		
"Abersoch Golf Club"	1966	$10
Aboyne Golf Club:		
"Aboyne Golf Club 1893-1983"	1983	$12
Edward C. Acree:		
"Golf Simplified"	1956	$15
Frederick U. Adams:		
"John Henry Smith: A Golfing Romance"	1905	$95
"John Henry Smith: A Humorous Romance Of Outdoor Life"	1905	$100
G. C. Adams:		
"History Of Barwon Heads Golf Club 1907-1973"	1973	$12
Herbert Adams:		
"The 19th Hole Mystery"	1939	$125
"The Body In The Bunker"	1935	$125
"John Brand's Will"	1933	$110
"Death Off The Fairway"	1936	$150
"Death On The First Tee"	1957	$125
"The Golf House Murder"	1933	$100
"One To Play"	1949	$150
"The Perfect Round: Tales Of The Links"	1927	$95
Signed By Adams		$375
"The Secret Of Bogey House"	1924	$135
Signed By Adams		$475
John Adams:		
"Huntercombe Golf Club 1900-1983"	1984	$20
"The Parks Of Musselburgh" Leather Bound Presentation Copy Signed By Adams	1991	$220
Robert W. Adams:		
"Timing Your Golf Swing"	1957	$10
"What Club Fits You?"	1957	$10
Alistair B. Adamson:		
"In The Winds Eye: North Berwick Golf Club"	1980	$85
"Millions Of Mischiefs: Rabbits, Golf And St. Andrews"	1990	$30
"Alan Robertson: His Life and Times"	1985	$60
Leather Bound Limited Edition Of 12		$300
Henry Adamson:		
"The Muses Threnodie"	1774	$600
Aderley Edge Golf Club:		
"Aderley Edge Golf Club"	1960	$15

AUTHOR TITLE	PUB. DATE	VALUE
A Divotee:		
"It's A Moral Beauty"	1923	$475
Ken Adwick:		
"Alphabet Of Golf"	1973	$10
"Dictionary Of Golf"	1974	$10
"Golf"	1975	$10
"X-Ray Way To Master Golf"	1970	$12
George Aikman:		
"A Round Of The Links"	1893	$9,000
Limited Edition Reprint	1980	$275
Thomas S. Aitchison and George Lorimer:		
"A Keen Hand: The Golfers Manual"	1857	$7,000
Limited Edition Reprint Of 750	1947	$350
Reprint	1965	$65
"Reminiscences Of The Old Bruntsfield		
Links Golf Club 1866-1874"	1902	$1,350
E.J.B. Akerman:		
"The Leatherjackets Golfing Society 1928-1949"	1949	$125
Chuck Albury:		
"Dunedin Country Club 1925-1970"	1970	$15
Amy Alcott:		
"Golf Tips From Amy Alcott"	1983	$17
John Alenson:		
"Ten Decades 1882-1982"	1982	$15
Peter Alfano:		
"Grand Slam"	1973	$10
John C. Alicoate:		
"Reference Year Book Of Golf"	1971	$12
"Reference Year Book Of Golf 1972"	1972	$12
"Reference Year Book Of Golf 1972-73"	1972	$12
Frank K. Allen And Others:		
"The Golfer's Bible"	1968	$10
Leslie Allen:		
"Murder In The Rough"	1946	$35
Mark Allen:		
"Royal Portrush Golf Club		
Coastal Erosion Appeal Fund"	1983	$10
Peter Allen:		
"Famous Fairways"	1968	$95
"Play The Best Courses"	1973	$85
Mark Allergen:		
"The Girl On The Green"	1914	$125
"Golf Faults Remedied"	1911	$40
Mark Allergen And Robert Browning:		
"Golf Made Easy"	1910	$215
Jane P. Ales:		
"The History Of The Philadelphia		
Country Club 1890-1965"	1965	$45

AUTHOR TITLE	PUB. DATE	VALUE
All Weather Golf:		
"All Weather Golf Practices"	1927	$25
Benjamin R. Allison:		
"The Rocky Hunting Club"	1952	$30
Willie Allison:		
"The First Golf Review"	1950	$20
Percy Alliss:		
"Better Golf"	1926	$95
"Making Golf Easier"	1933	$35
Peter Alliss:		
"Allis Through The Looking Glass"	1963	$35
"An Autobiography"	1981	$20
"Drive And Bunker Shot"	1955	$25
"The Duke"	1983	$50
"The Golfer's Logbook"	1984	$15
"Lasting The Course"	1984	$20
"More Bedside Golf"	1982	$15
"The Open: The British Open		
Championship Since The War"	1984	$10
"Peter Alliss' Bedside Book"	1980	$15
"Play Golf With Peter Allis"	1977	$25
"The Shell Book Of Golf"	1981	$20
"The Who's Who Of Golf"	1983	$15
Peter Alliss and Alec:		
"The Parkstone Golf Club"	1965	$10
Peter Alliss and Paul Trevillion:		
"Easier Golf"	1969	$12
Alpert, Mothner, And Schonberg:		
"How To Play Double Bogey Golf"	1975	$10
Amazing Golf Ball:		
"The Amazing Golf Ball"	1978	$10
Charles Ambrose:		
"The West Sussex Golf Club And Course"	1938	$25
American Annual:		
"American Annual And Golf Guide		
And Year Book" First Published	1916	$175
American Golf Foundation:		
"Example Golf Club By-Laws"	1947	$15
"A Golf Club Is A Business"	1944	$20
"How To Secure More Members"	1946	$20
"Suggestions For Golf Club By-Laws"	1948	$10
"What Is The American Golf Foundation"	1945	$20
American Golfer Magazine:		
"Twelve Golf Lessons"	1929	$10
American Society Of Golf Course Architects:		
"Master Planning: The Vital First Steps		
In Golf Course Construction"	1977	$15
"Planning The Municipal Golf Course"	1976	$20

AUTHOR TITLE	PUB. DATE	VALUE
American Society Of Golf Course Architects (cont.):		
"Planning The Real Estate		
Development Golf Course"	1977	$15
"Selecting Your Golf Course Architect"	1977	$15
William W. Amick:		
"The Executive Golf Course"	1975	$5
Carlyle E. Anderson:		
"Glen View Club 1897-1982"	1982	$15
Harold A. Anderson And Others:		
"Golf Club Construction: Design, Fitting, Repair"	1968	$10
Robert Anderson:		
"A Funny Thing Happened		
On The Way To The Clubhouse"	1971	$10
"Heard At The Nineteenth"	1966	$15
Thomas Anderson-Davis:		
"The Ryder Cup Heritage"	1983	$15
Richard Andre:		
"Colonel Bogey's Sketch Book"	1897	$1,000
"Golf Plays And Recitations"	1904	$2,500
Dale Andreason:		
"Simplified Golf"	1960	$10
Gene Andrews:		
"Scientific Analysis Of The Plumb Bob Method		
Of Reading Greens"	1968	$5
Julia L. Andrews:		
"Golf: A Play In Two Acts"	1902	$150
Major Angas:		
"The Golf Swing In The Plural"	1962	$5
Anndandale Golf Club:		
"Annandale Golf Club 75th Anniversary		
1906-1981"	1981	$20
Anonymous:		
"200 Funny Golf Stories As Told At The 19th"	1931	$135
Anstruther Golf Club:		
"Anstruther Golf Club"	1953	$10
Greg Anthony:		
"Building Clubhead Speed, Leverage,		
And Centrifugal Force In The Golf Swing"	1985	$10
Apawamis Golf Club:		
"The Apawamis Tradition 1890-1965"	1965	$45
Audrey Apple:		
"History Of Richmond Country Club 1924-1978"	1978	$20
Arboath Golf Club:		
"Arboath Golf Club"	1920	$150
James Arbuckle:		
"Glotta"	1721	$8,000
Angelo Argea:		
"The Bear And I"	1979	$55

AUTHOR TITLE	PUB. DATE	VALUE
J.C. Armitage:		
"The 100th Open Championship Held At Royal Birkdale Golf Club From July 7th-10th 1971"	1971	$10
Richard Armour:		
"Golf Bawls"	1946	$5
"Golf Is A Four Letter Word"	1962	$15
Tommy Armour:		
"Tommy Armour Speaks"	1960	$15
"Tommy Armour Tells You How To Play Your Best Golf"	1956	$15
"Tommy Armour's ABC Of Golf"	1967	$15
"How To Play Your Best Golf All The Time"	1953	$55
Autographed By Armour		$750
"Play Better Golf: The Drive"	1964	$15
"Play Better Golf: The Irons"	1963	$15
"A Round Of Golf With Tommy Armour"	1959	$15
A.E. Arnold:		
"Putting And Spared Shots"	1939	$65
John Arnold:		
"Riversdale Golf Club: A History 1892-1977"	1977	$20
Arran Golf Guide:		
"Arran Golf Guide"	1985	$10
Allan Arthur:		
"The Country Club, Its First 75 Years 1889-1964"	1964	$20
Ashford Manor Golf Club:		
"History Of The Ashford Manor Golf Club"	1966	$10
M.J. Astle:		
"The Principles Of Golf"	1923	$35
Howie Atten:		
"Chatten With Atten On Golf"	1959	$10
Augusta National:		
"Augusta National Yearbook"	1935	$3,000
Augusta National Golf Club:		
"The Masters 1978"	1978	$25
"The Masters 1979"	1979	$25
"The Masters 1980"	1980	$40
"The Masters 1981"	1981	$40
"The Masters 1982"	1982	$40
"The Masters 1983"	1983	$20
"The Masters 1984"	1984	$20
"The Masters 1985"	1985	$25
"The Masters 1986"	1986	$25
"The Masters 1987"	1987	$20
"The Masters 1988"	1988	$20
"The Masters 1989"	1989	$15
"The Masters 1990"	1990	$15
"The Masters 1991"	1991	$15
"The Masters 1992"	1992	$15

AUTHOR TITLE	PUB. DATE	VALUE
Augusta National Golf Club (cont.):		
"The Masters 1993"	1993	$15
"The Masters 1994"	1994	$10
"The Masters 1995"	1995	$10
"The Masters 1996"	1996	$10
"The Masters 1997"	1997	$10
"The Masters: The First Forty-One Years"	1978	$25
"Arnold Palmer's Scrapbook"	1964	$200
"Portraits: Early Members Of		
The Augusta National Golf Club"	1962	$125
Dick Aultman:		
"101 Ways To Win"	1980	$5
"Better Golf In Six Swings"	1982	$5
"Golf Digest's Golf Primer"	1977	$10
"Learn To Play Golf"	1969	$10
"The Square-To-Square Golf Swing"	1970	$15
Dick Aultman And Ken Bowden:		
"Masters Of Golf: Learning From Their Methods"	1976	$15
"The Methods Of The Golf Masters"	1975	$15
Automobile Association:		
"AA Guide To Golf In Great Britain"	1977	$10
Automobile Club Of Southern California:		
"Golf Courses Of California And Nevada"	1962	$20
L.B. Ayton:		
"How To Play Worthing Golf Course"	1951	$15
Laurie Ayton:		
"Golf As Champions Play It"	1928	$15
A.B.:		
"Told At The 19th Hole, Humorous		
St. Andrews Golfing Stories"	1928	$100
C.J.B. and P.S.W.:		
"Horace On The Links"	1903	$500
E.M.B. and G.R.T.:		
"Humors And Emotions Of Golf"	1905	$110
R. De C. B.:		
"Golf Ballistics"	1941	$20
Raymond Baert:		
"Adventures Of Monsieur DuPont,		
Golf Champion"	1913	$120
Baffy:		
"Golf Problems"	1928	$75
Bill Bailey:		
"Executive Golf: How To Win Big"	1985	$10
Charles W. Bailey:		
"The Brain And Golf"	1923	$125
"The Professor On The Golf Links"	1925	$150
John W. Bailey:		
"Enthusiastic Amateur Golfer Wanders The World"	1965	$10

AUTHOR TITLE	PUB. DATE	VALUE
Archie Baird:		
"Golf On Gullane Hill"	1982	$50
Signed by Baird		$95
Frederick R. Baird:		
"Crystal Downs Golf Club"	1981	$10
Arlene Baker And Elaine Lustig:		
"Golf: To Play This Game You Gotta		
Have Balls And Clubs And Trees"	1984	$10
Stephen Baker:		
"How To Play Golf In The Low 120s"	1962	$5
Bald Peak Country Club:		
"Bald Peak Country Club"	1920	$75
J. Stuart Balfour:		
"Spalding's Athletic Library: Golf"	1893	$4,000
James Balfour:		
"Reminiscences Of Golf On St. Andrews Links"	1887	$4,250
Limited Edition reprint	1982	$75
Brian Ball:		
"Death Of A Low Handicapped Man"	1978	$5
R.E. Ballantine:		
"How To Play Ganton Golf Course"	1952	$10
Jimmy Ballard:		
"How To Perfect Your Golf Swing"	1981	$5
Ballater Golf Club:		
"Ballater Golf Club"	1980	$15
Severiano Ballesteros:		
"Seve Tours: Golf Tours Of Spain"	1982	$15
Severiano Ballesteros And Dudley Doust:		
"Seve: The Young Champion"	1982	$15
Ford Banes:		
"Right Down The Fairway"	1947	$15
Miles Bantlock:		
"On Many Greens: A Book Of Golf And Golfers"	1901	$450
Jerry Barber:		
"The Art Of Putting"	1967	$10
Reg Barker:		
"Eighteen Forever"	1959	$5
Roland Barker:		
"The Bass River Golf Club 1900-1974"	1974	$10
Al Barkow:		
"Golf's Golden Grind: The History Of The Tour"	1974	$15
Raymond G. Barlow:		
"Golf For The Beginner And Confused"	1954	$5
J.W. Barnaby:		
"The History Of The Sorrento Golf Club"	1974	$15
James M. Barnes:		
"A Guide to Good Golf"	1925	$75
"Picture Analysis Of Golf Strokes"	1919	$150

AUTHOR TITLE	PUB. DATE	VALUE
Frank H. Barnett:		
"A Brief History Of Claremont Country Club"	1960	$25
Ted Barnett:		
"Golf Is Madness"	1977	$5
Harry Baron:		
"Golf Resorts Of The U.S.A."	1967	$10
"NBC Sports Guide 1967"	1967	$5
Michael Barratt:		
"Golf With Tony Jacklin"	1978	$10
James Barrie:		
"Historical Sketch Of The Hawick Golf Club"	1898	$1075
Smith Barrier:		
"GCO: The First Forty-Four Years"	1982	$5
John Barrington:		
"The U.S. Golfer's Handbook"	1958	$15
Hugh Barry:		
"Elanora, A History Of Elanora Country Club"	1977	$20
Pam Barton:		
"A Stroke A Hole"	1937	$35
Charles Bartlett:		
"Chicago Golf Club Diamond Jubilee 1892-1967"	1967	$25
"The New 1969 Golfer's Almanac"	1969	$10
Michael Bartlett:		
"Bartlett's World Golf Encyclopedia"	1973	$15
"The Golf Book"	1980	$15
Edmond P. Bartnett:		
"Seventy Years Of Wykagyl 1898-1968"	1968	$20
Charles T. Bassler and Nevin H. Gibson:		
"You Can Play Par Golf"	1966	$10
E.A. Batchelor Jr.:		
"Country Club Of Detroit A History 1897-1979"	1978	$20
Graham Bateman:		
"Selkirk Golf Club 1883-1983,		
A Century Of Golf In Selkirk"	1983	$15
Henry M. Bateman:		
"Adventures At Golf"	1923	$375
Reprint	1977	$20
Bath Golf Club:		
"Bath Golf Club Centenary Festival 1880-1980"	1980	$20
Jack Batten:		
"The Toronto Golf Club 1876-1976"	1976	$80
Aleck Bauer:		
"Hazzards"	1913	$1,200
Dave Bauer:		
"Golf Techniques Of The Bauer Sisters"	1951	$10
Ernest A. Baughman:		
"How To Caddie"	1914	$40

AUTHOR TITLE	PUB. DATE	VALUE
John E. Baxter:		
"Locker Room Ballads"	1923	$190
Peter Baxter:		
"Golf In Perth And Perthshire"	1899	$4,500
Dan Bayless:		
"Riviera's Fifty Golden Years"	1976	$35
S.G. Hulme Beaman:		
"The Adventures Of Larry The Lamb"	1935	$125
Peter Beames:		
"Walk Thru To Par"	1984	$5
Frank Beard:		
"Pro: Frank Beard On The Golf Tour"	1970	$15
"Shaving Strokes"	1970	$10
Frank Beard, Harriet Beard, and David Martin:		
"Turfgrass Bibliography From 1672-1972"	1977	$25
John B. Beardwood:		
"History Of The Los Angeles Country Club		
1898-1973"	1973	$40
Chauncey H. Beasley:		
"Golf In Latin"	1954	$5
"The Magnificent Golf Foursome"	1977	$425
"The Most Difficult Golf Course In America"	1966	$10
James Beattie:		
"The Club Toter"	1929	$20
Alfred Beck:		
"Hints On Golf For Everyone"	1925	$10
Fred Beck:		
"89 Years In A Sand Trap"	1965	$5
"To H*!! With Golf"	1956	$20
Fred Beck and O.K. Barnes:		
"73 Years In A Sand Trap"	1949	$15
Harlan A. Becker:		
"The Knack Of Golf"	1952	$175
J.P. Beckwith:		
"The Golf Links Located In Florida And Nassau"	1900	$125
Lew Bedell:		
"Every Golfer Should Have One"	1965	$5
Bedford And County Golf Club:		
"The Bedford And County Golf Club"	1938	$20
Harold Begbie:		
"J. H. Taylor, Or, The Inside Of A Week"	1925	$400
Max J. Behr:		
"What Is Amateurism?"	1917	$20
John Behrend:		
"St. Andrew's Night And Other Golfing Stories"	1992	$20
John Behrend and Graham John:		
"Golf At Holyoake, A Royal Liverpool		
Golf Club Anthology"	1990	$30

AUTHOR TITLE	PUB. DATE	VALUE
George W. Beldam:		
"Golfing Illustrated: Gowans's Practical Picture Book No. 2"	1908	$225
"Great Golfers: Their Methods At A Glance"	1904	$150
"The World's Champion Golfers"	1924	$400
G.W. Beldam & J.H. Taylor:		
"Golf Faults Illustrated"	1905	$145
Joe Belfore:		
"Golfing Aids"	1940	$10
Clarence Bell:		
"Eighty Golfing Years, A History Of North Adelaide Golf Club 1905-1985"	1985	$30
Peggy Kirk Bell:		
"A Woman's Way To Better Golf"	1966	$10
Bend Golf And Country Club:		
"Historical Review Of The Bend Golf And Country Club"	1981	$10
Tom Bendelow:		
"Golf Courses By The American Park Builders"	1926	$150
Josephine Bender:		
"Kent Country Club, When Kent Was Young, An Early History and Reminiscences"	1980	$20
Tommy Bendert:		
"Golf Is My Life"	1983	$10
David Benedictus:		
"Guru And The Golf Club"	1969	$5
L.W. Benham:		
"Golftique: A Price Guide To Old Golf Clubs and Other Golf Memorabilia"	1977	$15
Andrew Bennett:		
"The Book Of St. Andrews Links"	1898	$3,200
1984 Reprint		$250
Andrew Bennett:		
"St. Andrews Golf Club Centenary 1843-1943"	1943	$200
Arthur Bennett:		
"Southern California Golf Directory"	1963	$15
Guy Bennett:		
"Sunningdale Story"	1962	$20
Benson:		
"Keeping An Eye On Your Balls"	1983	$10
E.F. Benson & E.H. Miles:		
"A Book Of Golf"	1903	$300
Frederick S. Benson:		
"The History Of Canoe Brook Country Club From 1964 To 1976"	1976	$25
Frank Beres:		
"Building 18 Holes Miniature Golf"	1948	$10

AUTHOR TITLE	PUB. DATE	VALUE
Frank Beres(cont.):		
"How To Build and The Forty Secrets		
Of A Golf Driving Range"	1948	$10
Patty Berg:		
"Inside Golf For Women"	1977	$15
Patty Berg and Mark Cox:		
"Golf Illustrated"	1950	$15
Patty Berg and Otis Dypwick:		
"Golf"	1941	$20
Earl Of Berkeley:		
"Sound Golf By Applying Principles Of Practice"	1936	$20
Berkhamsted Golf Club:		
"Berkhamsted Golf Club"	1972	$10
Gus Bernardoni:		
"Golf God's Way"	1978	$5
Bob Bernier:		
"Pro-Golf Teaching Manual"	1964	$5
Edith Heal Berrien:		
"Fiftieth Anniversary Women's		
Metropolitan Golf Association"	1950	$15
Paul Bertholy:		
"The Bertholy Bombshell"	1955	$5
C.H. Bertie:		
"History Of The Manly Golf Club"	1946	$100
James Betinis:		
"Hit The Nail On The Head"	1960	$5
BGSR Guide:		
"BGSR Guide To British Golf Courses"	1985	$15
Michael Biddulph:		
"The Golf Shot"	1980	$5
Dale L. Bidwell:		
"A History Of The Texas Association		
Of Left Handed Golfers"	1983	$5
Birdie:		
"Golf The Game Of A lifetime"	1982	$5
Birdie Book:		
"Pointers On Par"	1958	$5
Birkdale Golf Club:		
"The Birkdale Golf Club"	1952	$15
"Birkdale Golf Club Golden Jubilee 1899-1939"	1939	$125
Furman Bisher:		
"Augusta Revisited: An Intimate View"	1976	$55
"The Birth Of A Legend: Arnold Palmer's		
Golden Year 1960"	1972	$45
H.A. Buz Bizell:		
"Sunset Ridge Country Club:		
Our First Fifty Years 1923-1972"	1973	$15

AUTHOR TITLE	PUB. DATE	VALUE
Andrew Black:		
"The Golf Courses Of Scotland"	1974	$15
Kevin Black:		
"Five 9 Hole Perthshire Golf Courses"	1970	$5
"Six 9 Hole Perthshire Golf Courses"	1970	$5
Norman Blackburn:		
"Lakeside Golf Club Of Hollywood,		
50th Anniversary Book"	1974	$20
Blake, McDowall, and Devlen:		
"The 1978 Open Championship At St. Andrews:		
An Economic Impact Study"	1979	$5
Mindy Blake:		
"The Golf Swing Of The Future"	1972	$5
"Golf: The Technique Barrier"	1978	$5
Jane Blalock:		
"The Guts To Win"	1977	$10
William D. Blatch:		
"The Laws Relating To Golf Clubs"	1943	$175
Blos:		
"Fore! Forty Drawings By Mahood"	1959	$20
Blue Mound Golf And Country Club:		
"The Story Of The Blue Mound Golf		
And Country Club"	1976	$35
Robert G. Bluth:		
"Golf"	1979	$10
John A. Board:		
"The Right Way To Become A Golfer"	1948	$15
Tommy Bolt:		
"The Hole Truth: Inside Big-Time Money Golf"	1971	$30
"How To Keep Your Temper		
On The Golf Course"	1969	$5
G.L. Bond:		
"The Dunstable Book"	1931	$10
Michael Bond:		
"Paddington Hits Out"	1977	$5
Barnett Bookatz:		
"Oakwood Club, 75th Anniversary"	1980	$20
Percy Boomer:		
"On Learning Golf"	1942	$60
Michael Borissow:		
"The Naked Fairways"	1984	$5
Julius Boros:		
"The 3 Tenets For Better Golf"	1956	$5
"How To Play Golf With An Effortless Swing"	1964	$10
"How To Play Par Golf"	1953	$15
"How To Win At Weekend Golf"	1965	$5
"Swing Easy Hit Hard"	1965	$10

AUTHOR TITLE	PUB. DATE	VALUE
Larry Bortstein:		
"Who's Who In Golf"	1972	$15
Charles Boswell:		
"Now I See"	1969	$5
James W. Boswell:		
"Golf: From Another Angle"	1983	$5
George McDonald Bottome:		
"Golf For The Middle Aged And Others"	1946	$10
"Modern Golf"	1949	$10
Roger J. Bounds:		
"Municipal Golf Courses"	1930	$175
Kevin Bourke:		
"Cobram-Barooga Golf Club		
Jubilee History 1928-1978"	1978	$45
John L. Bovis:		
"The It Of Golf"	1927	$25
C. Mal Bowden:		
"Golfer's Diary, Where He Keeps Scores		
I Can't Forget, Or Lies Lies Lies"	1962	$5
Ken Bowden:		
"The Golf Gazetter"	1968	$10
Bob Bowen And B. J. Clemence:		
"Golf Everyone"	1984	$5
Maurine Bowling:		
"Tested Ways Of Teaching Golf Classes"	1964	$5
Sydney Box:		
"Alibi In The Rough"	1977	$15
Angelo V. Boy:		
"Psychological Dimensions Of Golf"	1980	$5
Henry Boynton:		
"The Golfer's Rubaiyat"	1901	$525
Leland P. Bradford and Robert A. Hunt:		
"The Tin Whistles 1904-1979"	1979	$20
Bettie Bradley:		
"The Mississauga Golf And Country Club		
1906-1981"	1981	$35
J. Braid, J.A.T. Bramston & H.G. Hutchinson:		
"A Book Of Golf"	1903	$300
James Braid:		
"Advanced Golf"	1908	$475
"Golf Guide and How To Play Golf"	1906	$10
"Ladies' Field Golf Book"	1908	$175
James Braid and Harry Vardon:		
"How To Play Golf"	1907	$150
Bramshaw Golf Club:		
"Bramshaw Golf Club"	1946	$15
Brand Hall Golf Club:		
"Brand Hall Golf Club"	1938	$55

AUTHOR TITLE	PUB. DATE	VALUE
V.M. Branson:		
"Kooyonga 1923-1928		
The Story Of A Golf Club"	1983	$30
Bray Golf Club:		
"Bray Golf Club"	1952	$15
Marshall Breeden:		
"Us Golfers and Our California Links"	1923	$275
Frank Brett:		
"Cutten Club 1931-1981"	1981	$20
Gay Brewer:		
"Gay Brewer Shows You How To		
Score Better Than You Swing"	1968	$10
"Gay Brewer's Golf Guidebook"	1968	$10
Sid Brews:		
"Golf In A Nutshell"	1937	$25
E. Brickman:		
"A Brief Introduction to the Club		
and St. Andrews Courses"	1969	$10
Brickman, Burnett, Lawson, and Loudon:		
"The Royal And Ancient Golf Club Of		
St. Andrews"	1984	$20
Clare Briggs:		
"Golf: The Book Of A Thousand Chuckles"	1916	$250
Alan Brinton:		
"Mr. And Mrs. Golfer ... Cut Their Handicaps"	1954	$10
R.T. Brittenden:		
"Golf In New Zealand"	1979	$20
W.F. Broadbent:		
"Golf: Fundamental Instructions"	1938	$45
Broadstone Golf Club:		
"The Broadstone Golf Club"	1966	$15
Catherine and Loren Broadus Jr.:		
"From Loneliness To Intimacy"	1976	$10
Howard W. Brod:		
"By Golf Possessed"	1972	$5
Sidney S. Brody:		
"How To Break 90 Before You Reach It"	1967	$5
Bromborough Golf Club:		
"Bromborough Golf Club 1904-1979"	1979	$15
Brooklawn Country Club:		
"A Brief History Of Golf At		
The Brooklawn Country Club"	1974	$20
Brookmans Park Golf Club:		
"Brookmans Park Golf Club 1930-1980"	1980	$15
Brooks Brothers:		
"The Links Book"	1900	$200
Dick Brooks:		
"The Offensive Golfer"	1963	$20

AUTHOR TITLE	PUB. DATE	VALUE
James H. Brookuure:		
"Notes On Golf Pertaining To The Art Of Putting And The Short Approach Shots"	1935	$25
J.E. Broome and John A. Ross:		
"Keep Your Eye On The Ball"	1936	$60
Broughty Golf Club:		
"Broughty Golf Club"	1953	$25
Eric C. Brown:		
"Knave Of Clubs"	1961	$15
"Out Of The Bag"	1964	$15
Gene Brown:		
"The Complete Book Of Golf"	1980	$10
George S. Brown:		
"First Steps To Golf"	1913	$150
Horace Brown:		
"Murder In The Rough"	1948	$175
Innis Brown:		
"Getting Out Of Trouble"	1934	$25
"How To Play Golf"	1930	$25
"How To Putt Better"	1933	$25
J. Lewis Brown:		
"Golf At Glens Falls Country Club"	1923	$250
James Brown:		
"Songs Of Golf"	1902	$1,500
John A. Brown:		
"Short History Of Pine Valley"	1963	$75
Kenneth Brown:		
"Putter Perkins"	1923	$100
M. Gillette Brown:		
"Fell's Teen Age Guide To Winning Golf"	1963	$10
Thomas Brown:		
"Golfiana Or A Day At Gullane"	1869	$4,000
Virginia P. Brown:		
"Grand Old Days Of Birmingham Golf"	1984	$5
William Garrott Brown:		
"Golf"	1902	$395
Liam Browne:		
"The Royal Dublin Golf Club 1885-1985"	1985	$150
Thomas Browne:		
"The Game Of Golf"	1902	$245
Robert H.K. Browning:		
"Aberdare Golf Club"	1946	$45
"Aberdovey Golf Club"	1947	$110
"The Aberystwyth Golf Club"	1934	$55
"Addington Golf Club"	1946	$60
"The Alloa Golf Club"	1948	$30
"The Alnmouth Golf Club"	1948	$45
"The Appleby Golf Club"	1946	$40

AUTHOR TITLE	PUB. DATE	VALUE
Robert H.K. Browning(cont.):		
"The Ardeer Golf Club"	1948	$30
"The Arkley Golf Club"	1955	$15
"The Ashford Manor Golf Club"	1947	$50
"The Aspley Guise & Woburn Sands Golf Club"	1947	$40
"Axe Cliff Golf Club"	1939	$40
"The Ayr Corporation Golf Courses"	1933	$40
"Ballater Golf Club"	1947	$45
"Banchory Golf Club"	1938	$35
"Banstead Downs Golf Club"	1951	$20
"The Barrow Golf Club"	1948	$35
"Bath Golf Club"	1931	$60
"Bedfordshire Golf Club"	1947	$40
"Beeston Fields Golf Club"	1947	$40
"The Betchworth Park Golf Club"	1947	$40
"Bexhill Golf And Sports Club"	1938	$35
"Bexley Heath Golf Club"	1947	$45
"Bin Down Golf Club"	1939	$40
"The Birkdale Golf Club"	1934	$85
"The Bishop Auckland Golf Club"	1947	$40
"The Blackburn Golf Club"	1947	$45
"The Blackmoor Golf Club"	1947	$40
"The Blackpool Golf Club"	1939	$55
"The Blackpool North Shore Golf Club"	1947	$40
"Bolton Golf Club"	1947	$40
"The Borth & Ynslas Golf Club"	1934	$40
"The Bramley Golf Club"	1950	$25
"Brampton Golf Club"	1952	$25
"The Bramshaw Golf Club"	1947	$40
"Branford Golf Club"	1938	$35
"The Brighton & Hove Golf Club"	1947	$50
"The Bristol & Clifton Golf Club"	1948	$35
"The Brocton Hall Golf Club"	1948	$35
"The Brokenhurst Manor Golf Club"	1939	$50
"The Brookmans Park Golf Club"	1938	$40
"Bude And North Cornwall Golf Club"	1932	$40
"Burhill Club"	1949	$30
"The Burnham Beeches Golf Club"	1938	$40
"Burton-On-Trent Golf Club"	1953	$20
"The Bury Golf Club"	1947	$40
"The Bush Hill Park Golf Club"	1951	$20
"The Bushey Hall Golf Club"	1951	$20
"Caernarvonshire Golf Club"	1947	$45
"The Calcot Golf Club"	1952	$20
"Callander Golf Club"	1939	$45
"The Calthorpe Golf Club"	1947	$40
"The Camberley Heath Golf Club"	1947	$45
"The Carlisle City Golf Club"	1947	$40

AUTHOR TITLE	PUB. DATE	VALUE
Robert H.K. Browning (cont.):		
"Carmarthen Golf Club"	1939	$45
"The Castletown Golf Club"	1947	$40
"The Cathcart Castle Golf Club"	1939	$40
"The Cavendish Golf Club"	1939	$40
"The Chester Golf Club"	1947	$40
"The Chesterfield Golf Club"	1947	$40
"Chigwell Golf Club"	1951	$20
"The Childwall Golf Club"	1950	$20
"The Chipstead Golf Club"	1938	$35
"Churston Golf Club"	1939	$40
"The Cirencester Golf Club"	1949	$25
"The City Of Newcastle Golf Club"	1952	$20
"The Clacton-On-Sea Golf Club"	1939	$45
"Clevedon Golf Club"	1947	$45
"The Cleveleys Hydro Golf Club"	1947	$35
"The Colchester Gold Club"	1948	$30
"The Cooden Beach Golf Club"	1950	$30
"Coventry Golf Club"	1947	$40
"Crews Hill Golf Club"	1948	$35
"Crichel Park Golf Club"	1938	$35
"Crieff Golf Club"	1938	$55
"The Croham Hurst Golf Club"	1955	$15
"Cuddington Golf Club"	1934	$45
"Dalmahoy Golf Club"	1938	$35
"Dartford Golf Club"	1948	$35
"The Deepdale Golf Club"	1947	$35
"The Deeside Golf Club"	1938	$45
"The Dewsbury District Golf Club"	1948	$30
"The Didsbury Golf Club"	1948	$35
"The Didsley Golf Club"	1948	$35
"The Dinas Powis Golf Club"	1947	$35
"The Doncaster Golf Club"	1950	$25
"Duddington Golf Club"	1948	$40
"The Dulwich And Sydenham Hill Golf Club"	1952	$25
"Dumfries And County Golf Club"	1938	$35
"The Dunscar Golf Club"	1948	$30
"The Dunstable Downs Golf Club"	1948	$40
"The Eaglescliffe & District Golf Club"	1938	$35
"Ealing Golf Club"	1950	$20
"East Berks Golf Club"	1947	$50
"East Brighton Golf Club"	1947	$45
"East Herts Golf Club"	1947	$40
"East Renfrewshire Golf Club"	1939	$40
"The Eastbourne Downs Club"	1949	$25
"Edgbaston Golf Club"	1939	$55
"Effingham Golf Club"	1947	$40
"The Elgin Golf Club"	1947	$30

AUTHOR TITLE	PUB. DATE	VALUE
Robert H.K. Browning(cont.):		
"Enfield Golf Club"	1948	$35
"Epsom Golf Club"	1947	$40
"The Exmouth Golf Club"	1931	$55
"The Fairhaven Golf Club"	1939	$40
"The Farnham Golf Club"	1955	$15
"The Filey Golf Club"	1934	$45
"The Finchley Golf Club"	1938	$35
"The Firbeck Hall Golf Club"	1938	$35
"The Flackwell Heath Golf Club"	1952	$20
"The Fleetwood Club"	1938	$35
"The Folkstone Golf Club"	1932	$50
"The Formby Ladies Golf Club"	1953	$20
"The Freshwater Bay Golf Club"	1948	$30
"The Frinton Golf Club"	1938	$35
"The Fulford Golf Club"	1948	$30
"Fulford Heath Golf Club"	1951	$25
"Fulneck Golf Club"	1948	$35
"Ganton Golf Club"	1939	$75
"The Gerrards Cross Golf Club"	1947	$35
"The Glamorganshire Golf Club"	1955	$15
"The Glen Gorse Golf Club"	1953	$20
"Golf In Cornwall"	1952	$60
"Golf In Devon"	1952	$50
"Golf In Devon And Cornwall"	1970	$15
"Golf In Essex"	1952	$55
"Golf In Gloustershire"	1954	$20
"Golf In Hants & Dorset"	1955	$50
"Golf In Kent"	1952	$55
"Golf In Somerset"	1952	$60
"Golf In Somerset and Gloucestershire"	1975	$15
"Golf In Surrey"	1957	$30
"Golf In Sussex"	1959	$40
"Golf In The Channel Islands"	1953	$40
"Golf In The Isle Of Man"	1955	$20
"Golf On The Lancs Coast"	1957	$40
"Golf With Seven Clubs"	1950	$35
"The Golfer's Catechism"	1935	$185
"Goodwood Golf Club"	1939	$40
"Gosforth Golf Club"	1947	$40
"The Gosport And Stokes Bay Golf Club"	1948	$35
"The Grand Marine Hotel And Barton-On-Sea Golf Club"	1950	$20
"The Grange Park Golf Club"	1948	$35
"The Greenway Hall Golf Club"	1948	$30
"The Guildford Golf Club"	1948	$30
"The Hadley Wood Golf Club"	1948	$30
"Halifax Bradley Hall Golf Club"	1948	$40

AUTHOR TITLE	PUB. DATE	VALUE
Robert H.K. Browning(cont.):		
"Hallamshire Golf Club"	1947	$45
"Harpenden Golf Club"	1946	$40
"The Harrogate Golf Club"	1947	$45
"The Hastings Golf Club"	1934	$40
"The Hawick Golf Club"	1947	$55
"The Hayling Golf Club"	1931	$45
"The Haywards Heath Golf Club"	1955	$20
"Helensburgh Golf Club"	1938	$50
"The Hendon Golf Club"	1950	$25
"Henley Golf Club"	1938	$40
"The Herne Bay Golf Club"	1948	$35
"The Hesketh Golf Club"	1947	$45
"The Hessle Golf Club"	1948	$25
"Highgate Golf Club"	1936	$50
"The Highwoods Bexhill-On-Sea Golf Club"	1949	$35
"The Hillsborough Golf Club"	1952	$20
"The Hindhead Golf Club"	1938	$45
"A History of Golf, The Royal and Ancient Game"	1955	$375
"Hockley Golf Club"	1949	$25
"Holyhead Golf Club"	1947	$45
"The Honiton Golf Club"	1939	$40
"Hornsea Golf Club"	1947	$50
"The Huddersfield Golf Club"	1947	$40
"The Hull Golf Club"	1947	$35
"Hunstanton Golf Club"	1950	$35
"The Huntercombe Golf Club"	1952	$25
"Ilford Golf Club"	1952	$25
"The Ilkley Golf Club"	1939	$75
"The Inverness Golf Club"	1947	$60
"The Irvine Golf Club"	1947	$40
"The Keighley Golf Club"	1946	$40
"The Kettering Golf Club"	1948"	$30
"The King's Lynn Golf Club"	1949	$20
"Kingsthorpe Golf Club"	1946	$40
"Kingswood Golf Club"	1938	$45
"The Kington Golf Club"	1950	$20
"Kirby Muxloe Golf Club"	1949	$20
"Knole Park Golf Club"	1951	$25
"The Knott End & Fleetwood Golf Club"	1949	$25
"Langland Bay Golf Club"	1955	$20
"Lansdown Golf Club"	1932	$45
"The Leatherhead Golf Club"	1939	$60
"Lee-On-The-Solent Golf Club"	1931	$55
"Leek Golf Club"	1947	$40
"The Leighton Buzzard Golf Club"	1948	$25
"The Lewes Golf Club"	1948	$30
"The Lindrick Golf Club"	1955	$15

AUTHOR TITLE	PUB. DATE	VALUE
Robert H.K. Browning(cont.):		
"The Littlehampton Golf Club"	1938	$50
"The Llandrindod Wells Golf Club"	1951	$25
"The Llandudno Golf Club"	1937	$75
"Long Ashton Golf Club"	1948	$35
"Lothianburn Golf Club"	1948	$35
"The Ludlow Golf Club"	1947	$40
"The Lundin Golf Club"	1947	$50
"The Lytham Golf Club"	1948	$40
"Maidenhead Golf Club"	1937	$65
"The Manchester Golf Club"	1953	$25
"The Mannings Heath Golf Club"	1938	$35
"Mere Golf Club And Country Club"	1938	$35
"Mersea Island Golf Club"	1938	$50
"Minehead And West Somerset Golf Club"	1946	$55
"Moments With Golfing Masters"	1932	$130
"The Moray Golf Club"	1947	$40
"The Morecambe Golf Club"	1934	$40
"The Morpeth Golf Club"	1948	$35
"The Mortonhall Golf Club"	1952	$20
"The Mullion Golf Club"	1949	$30
"Murcar Golf Club"	1938	$40
"The Muswell Hill Golf Club"	1951	$20
"The Naze Golf Club"	1939	$40
"Nevin & District Golf Club"	1947	$40
"The New Golf Club, St. Andrews"	1946	$85
"The New Highwood Golf Club"	1947	$35
"The Newbattle Golf Club"	1947	$40
"The Newbury And Crookham Golf Club"	1952	$20
"Newbury District Golf Club"	1933	$35
"Newport Golf Club"	1953	$20
"The Newton Abbot Golf Club"	1932	$40
"The North Manchester Golf Club"	1953	$25
"The North Shore Golf Club"	1938	$40
"Northcliff Golf Club"	1948	$35
"The Oakdale Golf Club"	1947	$35
"The Old Colwyn Golf Club"	1952	$25
"The Old Links Golf Club"	1948	$30
"Olton Golf Club"	1948	$35
"Ormskirk Golf Club"	1938	$45
"Oxley Park Golf Club"	1947	$45
"The Pannal Golf Club"	1946	$55
"The Panure Golf Club"	1949	$45
"The Parkstone Golf Club"	1928	$40
"The Peebles Municipal Golf Course"	1947	$30
"The Penmaenmawr Golf Club"	1955	$15
"The Penwortham Golf Club"	1949	$30
"The Perranporth Golf Club"	1938	$40

AUTHOR TITLE	PUB. DATE	VALUE
Robert H.K. Browning (cont.):		
"The Piltdown Golf Club"	1947	$40
"Ponteland Golf Club"	1939	$40
"The Prenton Golf Club"	1949	$30
"The Preston Golf Club"	1947	$30
"Prestonfield Golf Club"	1948	$35
"Prestwick St. Nicholas Golf Club"	1939	$95
"Purley Downs Golf Club"	1948	$35
"The Pwlheli Golf Club"	1947	$45
"The Queen's Park Golf Club"	1949	$35
"The Ramsey Golf Club"	1948	$30
"The Reading Golf Club"	1953	$20
"The Rhondda Golf Club"	1948	$35
"The Rhyl Golf Club"	1940	$40
"The Ringway Golf Club"	1949	$30
"Robin Hood Golf Club"	1938	$40
"The Rochelle Golf Club"	1948	$30
"The Roehampton Club"	1955	$15
"The Romford Golf Club"	1947	$40
"Rothley Park Golf Club"	1949	$20
"Rowlands Castle Golf Club"	1948	$35
"The Royal Aberdeen Golf Club"	1940	$150
"The Royal County Down Golf Club"	1951	$85
"The Royal Cromer Golf Club"	1938	$145
"The Royal Isle Of Wight Golf Club"	1947	$115
"The Royal Jersey Golf Club"	1939	$150
"The Royal Norwich Golf Club"	1949	$75
"The Royal Porthcawl Golf Club"	1951	$80
"The Royal Portrush Golf Club"	1949	$110
"Royal Winchester Golf Club"	1934	$125
"The Rushcliffe Golf Club"	1953	$20
"The Rushmere Golf Club"	1948	$30
"The Ryde Golf Club"	1949	$25
"The Salisbury And South Wilts Golf Club"	1928	$35
"The Sand Moor Golf Club"	1948	$35
"Sandiway Golf Club"	1939	$40
"The Scarborough South Cliff Golf Club"	1939	$90
"The Seacroft Golf Club"	1939	$40
"The Seaford Golf Club"	1938	$55
"Shaw Hill Golf Club"	1948	$35
"The Sherringham Golf Club"	1938	$50
"The Sherwood Forest Golf Club"	1948	$30
"The Sidmouth Golf Club"	1947	$45
"Shifnal Golf Club"	1948	$35
"Shipley Golf Club"	1948	$40
"Shrewsbury Golf Club"	1939	$40
"Sickleholme Golf Club"	1938	$40
"Sitwell Park Golf Club"	1948	$35

AUTHOR TITLE	PUB. DATE	VALUE
Robert H.K. Browning (cont.):		
"The Sonning Golf Club"	1938	$40
"The South Herts Golf Club"	1932	$75
"The South Shields Golf Club"	1948	$30
"The Southport & Ainsdale Golf Club"	1946	$75
"The Spalding Golf Club"	1951	$20
"The St. Annes Old Links Golf Club"	1946	$60
"St. Enodoc Golf Club"	1934	$60
"St. Georges Hill Golf Club"	1955	$25
"The St. Ives Golf Club"	1949	$30
"St. Leonard's Golf Club"	1938	$45
"The Stanley Park Golf Course"	1949	$20
"The Stanmore Golf Club"	1955	$15
"The Stinchcombe Hill Golf Club"	1948	$35
"The Stoneham Golf Club"	1947	$40
"The Strathpeffer Spa Golf Club"	1947	$35
"The Strawberry Hill Golf Club"	1951	$20
"The Stymie"	1910	$300
"The Sunningdale Golf Club"	1950	$35
"Super Golf"	1919	$145
"Sutton Coldfield Golf Club"	1948	$45
"The Swanage & Studland Golf Club"	1939	$45
"The Swansea Bay Golf Club"	1948	$35
"The Swindon Golf Club"	1934	$50
"The Tavistock Golf Club"	1938	$45
"The Teignmouth Golf Club"	1948	$45
"The Tenby Golf Club"	1938	$55
"Thorndon Park Golf Club"	1948	$25
"The Thrope Hall Golf Club"	1949	$20
"Thurlestone Golf Club"	1939	$50
"The Tiverton Golf Club"	1947	$35
"Torbay Country Club"	1947	$35
"The Trentham Golf Club"	1938	$40
"Trevose Golf Club"	1934	$55
"Troon Golf Club"	1951	$40
"The Truro Golf Club"	1947	$35
"Tyneside Golf Club"	1948	$40
"Tyrrells Wood Golf Club"	1939	$40
"The Ulverston Golf Club"	1939	$40
"The Vale Of Leven Golf Club"	1947	$45
"The Wakefield Golf Club"	1949	$25
"Walsall Golf Club"	1956	$45
"The Wanstead Golf Club"	1947	$40
"The Warren Golf Club"	1947	$35
"The Waterlooville Golf Club"	1948	$30
"The Wentworth Golf Club, Virginia Water"	1953	$65
"The Wentworth Golf Club"	1953	$20
"The West Byfleet Golf Club"	1950	$25

AUTHOR TITLE	PUB. DATE	VALUE
Robert H.K. Browning(cont.):		
"The West Herts Golf Club"	1952	$35
"West Hove Golf Club"	1939	$45
"The West Kent Golf Club"	1939	$45
"The Westgate-On-Sea and		
Birchington Golf Club"	1929	$45
"The Weston-Super-Mare Golf Club"	1949	$40
"When You Are Off Your Game"	1929	$95
"The Whitley Bay Golf Club"	1939	$40
"The Whitsand Bay Golf Club"	1948	$25
"The Windwhistle Golf Club"	1948	$25
"The Winterfield Golf Club"	1938	$45
"The Withington Golf Club"	1948	$30
"Woodbridge Gold Club"	1948	$30
"The Woodcote Park Golf Club"	1952	$20
"The Woolton Golf Club"	1948	$25
"The Worcestershire Golf Club"	1939	$40
"The Workington Golf Club"	1949	$25
"The Worlebury Golf Club"	1938	$40
"The Worthing Golf Club"	1938	$55
"The Wrekin Golf Club"	1938	$40
"The Yelverton Golf Club"	1951	$25
"York Golf Club"	1951	$25
R.C. Brownlee:		
"Dunbar Golf Club, A Short History 1794-1980"	1980	$20
Ben Bruce And Evelyn Davies:		
"Beginning Golf"	1962	$10
George Bruce:		
"Destiny And Other Poems"	1876	$165
Jeremy Bruce-Watt:		
"Gleneagles Hotel Diamond Jubilee		
Souvenir Book 1924-1984"	1984	$10
Nancy Bruff:		
"The Country Club"	1969	$10
Dorothy and Marguerite Bryan:		
"Michael and Patsy On The Golf Links"	1933	$65
R.I. Bryden and D.T. Hood:		
"The Kintansett Club A Brief History 1922-1968"	1968	$30
Walter C. Brzoza:		
"Putting Secrets Of The Old Masters"	1968	$10
Bulawayo Golf Club:		
"The Bulawayo Golf Club 1895-1970"	1970	$15
Bulger:		
"Echos From The Links"	1924	$400
Linda K. Bunker and De De Owens:		
"Golf: Better Practice For Better Play"	1984	$5
Ron Burd:		
"Ron Burd's Basic Principles Of Golf"	1966	$5

AUTHOR TITLE	PUB. DATE	VALUE
E.A.R. Burden:		
"A History Of St. Enodoc Golf Club"	1965	$10
Burke Golf Company:		
"Golf As She Ought To Be Played"	1929	$50
"Making The Clubhead Work"	1931	$20
Jack Burke:		
"The Natural Way To Better Golf"	1954	$10
"Ten Lessons In Golf"	1923	$15
Jack Burke Jr.:		
"The Three Dimensions Of Golf"	1966	$5
Jack Burke Jr. And Others:		
"How To Solve Your Golf Problems"	1963	$5
James Francis Burke:		
"Guard The Game Of Golf Against The Danger Of Becoming A Humdrum, Haphazard, Meaningless Pastime"	1925	$75
John Burke:		
"Southwald Golf Club 1884-1984"	1984	$10
Peter Burles and Geoffrey Piper:		
"Bernard Darwin and Aberdovey"	1996	$45
Bobby Burnette:		
"The St. Andrews Open"	1990	$30
Burnham Ladies Golf Club:		
"Burnham Ladies Golf Club"	1947	$15
Burning Tree Club:		
"Burning Tree Club, The Fifth Decade 1963-1972"	1972	$40
"Burning Tree Club, A History 1922-1962"	1962	$55
Ralph F. Burns:		
"Historical Review Of LaGrange Country Club 1899-1949"	1949	$25
Miles Burton:		
"Tragedy At The Thirteenth Hole"	1933	$75
Percy Burton:		
"To Sweden & Denmark & Back"	1947	$15
Richard Burton:		
"Length With Discretion"	1940	$15
Business Man's Golf Course:		
"Business Man's Golf Course" Six Volumes	1924	$25
Buston & High Peak Golf Club:		
"The Buston & High Peak Golf Club"	1948	$20
William M. Butler:		
"The Golfers Manual"	1907	$525
"The Golfer's Guide"	1907	$375
Butte Country Club:		
"Observing 30 Years With The Present Butte Country Club House"	1945	$20

AUTHOR TITLE	PUB. DATE	VALUE
Mrs. Howard P. Buttress:		
"The History Of Women's Golf In Southern California"	1959	$15
W.K.C.:		
"The History Of The Warrender Golf Club"	1906	$35
Caddie Coloring Book:		
"Caddie Coloring Book"	1950	$15
Caddie Manual:		
"Caddie Manual"	1948	$45
Michael Cady:		
"AA 1986 Guide To Golf Courses In Britain"	1985	$10
Caernarvonshire Golf Club:		
"Caernarvonshire Golf Club"	1937	$25
William Caesar:		
"Carnoustie Golf Links Bazaar"	1892	$3,500
Howard Cain:		
"Briarwood Country Club 1958-1983"	1983	$15
Sylvia Potter Cain:		
"Instruction For Elementary Golfers"	1939	$20
Patrick Cake:		
"The Pro-Am Murders"	1979	$15
Mrs. Guy T. Calafato:		
"Deal Golf and Country Club 1898-1973"	1973	$10
Calgary Golf And Country Club:		
"Calgary Golf And Country Club 1897-1972 75th Anniversary"	1972	$20
Leighton Calkins:		
"A System For Club Handicapping"	1905	$75
Lionel F. Callaway:		
"New And Improved System Of Simplified Handicapping For Golfers"	1952	$10
Came Down Golf Club:		
"The Came Down Golf Club"	1933	$25
Dave Camerer:		
"Golf With The Masters"	1955	$10
"Improve Your Game"	1958	$10
Keith Camp:		
"Leighton Buzzard Golf Club Diamond Jubilee 1925-1985"	1985	$25
Walter Camp and Lillian Brooks:		
"Drives And Putts"	1899	$450
Bailey Campbell:		
"Golf Lessons From Sam Snead"	1964	$10
Duncan C. Campbell:		
"The Royal Montreal Golf Club 1873-1973"	1973	$75
Guy Colin Campbell:		
"Golf For Beginners"	1922	$25
"Golf At Prince's And Deal"	1950	$280

AUTHOR TITLE	PUB. DATE	VALUE
John Campbell:		
"Greenkeeping"	1982	$15
Patrick Campbell:		
"Patrick Campbell's Golfing Book"	1972	$10
"How To Become A Scratch Golfer"	1963	$15
"Round Ireland With A Golf Bag"	1937	$95
F.C. Canausa:		
"How To Win At Golf"	1956	$5
Peter Canham:		
"Introduction To Golf"	1975	$5
Cannington Park Golf Club:		
"Cannington Park Golf Club"	1935	$5
Capper & Capper:		
"Motor Guide To Golf Links About Chicago"	1918	$100
Elmer O. Cappers:		
"Centennial History Of		
The Country Club 1882-1982"	1982	$20
Howard Capps:		
"Take The Wrists Out, A Life In Golf"	1985	$5
Henry M. Carl:		
"Analytical Physical Culture Golf"	1928	$15
Robert D. Carlisle:		
"The Montclair Golf Club,		
A Way Of Life 1893-1983"	1984	$20
George F. Carnegie:		
"Golfiana"	1883	$18,000
Carnoustie Golf Courses:		
"Carnoustie Commentary"	1937	$750
"Carnoustie Commentary,		
Championship Supplement"	1937	$875
"Carnoustie Golf Course"	1933	$675
"Carnoustie The New Championship		
Golf Course"	1931	$600
Ashley Carpenter:		
"In The Rough"	1984	$10
Edward Carpenter:		
"Subjective Golf Strategy"	1979	$5
Joseph Carpenter:		
"Only Golfers Know The Feeling"	1983	$5
Dick Carr:		
"You Too Can Golf In The Eighties"	1977	$5
Hayden Carruth:		
"A Hand Book Of Golf For Bears"	1900	$95
Billy Casper:		
"295 Golf Lessons"	1973	$5
"Chipping And Putting: Golf Around The Greens"	1961	$10
"Golf Shotmaking With Billy Casper"	1966	$10
"The Good Sense Of Golf"	1980	$5

AUTHOR TITLE	PUB. DATE	VALUE
Billy Casper: cont.		
"My Million Dollar Shots"	1970	$10
"Saving Strokes Around The Green"	1973	$10
Cavalcade Of Golf:		
"Cavalcade Of Golf: From		
King James To King Jones"	1935	$60
"Cavalcade Of Golf: From		
King James To Silver King"	1938	$65
Walter Cavanaugh:		
"The Art Of Golf"	1927	$50
William Caw:		
"King James VI Golf Club, Record And Records"	1912	$400
Philip And Florence Chabody:		
"The 86 Proof Pro"	1974	$5
H.H. Chadwick:		
"Golf In Vermont: A Directory Of Courses"	1946	$15
Faustina E. Chamberlain:		
"Charley Emery; Pro: Biography		
Of A Maine Golf Pro"	1982	$5
Peter Chamberlain:		
"Good Golf"	1985	$5
"Winning Golf"	1985	$5
Charles E. S. Chambers:		
"Early Golf At Bruntsfield And Leith"	1932	$850
"Golfing, A Handbook To The Royal And		
Ancient Game With A List Of Clubs, Rules, &		
Also Golfing Sketches And Poems"	1887	$1,200
Robert Chambers:		
"A Few Rambling Remarks On Golf With		
The Rules As Laid Down By The Royal And		
Ancient Club Of St. Andrews."	1862	$7,000
Limited Edition Reprint	1983	$75
"Gymnastics, Golf And Curling"	1866	$1,500
Leonard R. Chandler:		
"A History Of Essex Golf And Country Club		
1902-1983"	1983	$15
Eric Channon:		
"Lewes Golf Club"	1952	$10
T. Chape And W. Ogilvie:		
"Newbiggin GolfCountry Centenary 1884-1984"	1984	$10
H.J. Chapman:		
"The Story Of The Dalhousie Golf Club		
1868-1968"	1968	$20
Hay Chapman:		
"Law Of The Links: Rules, Principles And		
Ettiquette Of Golf"	1922	$200
Richard Chapman And Ledyard Sands:		
"Golf As I Play It"	1940	$35

AUTHOR TITLE	PUB. DATE	VALUE
Bob Charles:		
"The Bob Charles Left Handers Golf Book"	1985	$20
"Left Handed Golf"	1965	$15
"Left Hander From New Zealand"	1965	$20
Charles River Country Club:		
"Life At The Charles River Country Club 1921-1946"	1946	$20
Chattanooga Golf And Country Club:		
"At The End Of The Trolley A History Of The Chattanooga Golf And Country Club 1896-1961"	1961	$25
C.C. Chattell:		
"The Golfers Guide 1908"	1908	$95
Billye Ann Cheatum:		
"Golf"	1969	$5
Ike Cheeves:		
"Play Better Golf"	1966	$5
Edward Cheney:		
"An Eightsome Of Golfing Badgers"	1945	$15
George Cherellia:		
"All About Hitting The Sweet Spot"	1975	$5
"Tempo: The Heart Of A Golf Swing"	1971	$5
Cherry Hills Country Club:		
"Cherry Hills Country Club"	1978	$40
Chevin Golf Club:		
"Chevin Golf Club"	1965	$10
Bob Chieger and Pat Sullivan:		
"Inside Golf: Quotations On The Royal And Ancient Game"	1985	$5
Frank Chinnock:		
"How To Break 90 Consistently"	1976	$5
Chislehurst Golf Club:		
"Chislehurst Golf Club"	1928	$20
Ben Chlevin:		
"Golf For Industry: A Planning Guide"	1962	$10
Maureen Chodosh And Maggie Weiss:		
"The Golfer's Cookbook: Recipes Collected At Pebble Beach"	1984	$10
Agatha Christie:		
"The Murder On The Links"	1923	$500
Joe Chronicles:		
"Uncle Jed, Caddie Master"	1934	$85
Edward Chui:		
"Golf"	1969	$5
Cincinnati Country Club:		
"Cincinnati Country Club 1903-1975"	1975	$25
C.B. Clapcott:		
"The History Of Handicapping"	1924	$1,200

AUTHOR TITLE	PUB. DATE	VALUE

C.B. Clapcott(cont.):
"The Rules Of Golf Of The Ten Oldest Clubs From
   1754 To 1848 Together With The Rules Of Golf
   Of The Royal & Ancient Golf Club Of St. Andrews
   For The Years 1858, 1875, 1888" 1935 $1,500

Charles E. Clark:
"The New Haven Country Club,
   The First Fifty Years 1898-1948" 1949 $20

Robert Clark:
"Golf, A Royal & Ancient Game" First Edition 1875 $2,500
   Second Edition $675
   Third Edition $495
   Reprint 1975 $60
   Reprint 1984 $25
"Poems On Golf" 1867 $2,200

Mrs. A.B. Clarke:
"History Of Elie Golf House Club Jubilee" 1925 $150

Charles Clarke And Mottram Gilbert:
"Commonsense Golf" 1914 $60

Fred C. Clarke Jr.:
"The Woodstock Country Club 1895-1959" 1959 $20

R.N. Clarke:
"A Sudbrook Chronicle, Being a History Of
   Richmond Golf Club 1891-1932" 1976 $25

Richard W. Clarke:
"The Bedford Golf And Tennis Club 1890-1965" 1965 $15

Joe Clement:
"Classic Golf Clubs: A Pictorial Guide" 1980 $95

Charles Blair Cleveland:
"Approach And Putting" 1953 $10

Harold J. Cliffer:
"Planning The Golf Club House" 1956 $10

T.R. Clougher:
"Golf Clubs Of The Empire A Golfing Annual 1926"1926 $150
"Golf Clubs Of The Empire A Golfing Annual 1927" 1927 $150
"Golf Clubs Of The Empire A Golfing Annual 1928" 1928 $150
"Golf Clubs Of The Empire A Golfing Annual 1929" 1929 $150
"Golf Clubs Of The Empire A Golfing Annual 1930" 1930 $175
"Golf Clubs Of The Empire A Golfing Annual 1931" 1931 $125
"Golf Clubs Of The Empire A Golfing Annual 1932" 1932 $125

Clovelly Country Club:
"Clovelly Country Club 1932-1982,
   50th Anniversary" 1982 $10

William E. Clow Jr.:
"Good Golf" 1942 $15

Albert Cobe:
"Great Spirit" 1970 $5

AUTHOR TITLE	PUB. DATE	VALUE
Alistair Cochran and John Stobbs:		
"The Search For The Perfect Swing"	1968	$50
A.S. Cockfield and Herb McNally:		
"The Pro Golf Teacher"	1980	$10
Martin E. Coffey:		
"Golfing In Ireland"	1953	$85
Colchester Golf Club:		
"Colchester Golf Club"	1938	$60
Coldstream Country Club:		
"Coldstream Country Club 25th Anniversary		
1959-1984"	1984	$20
Albert Colebank:		
"A History Of Red Hill Country Club"	1972	$10
Neil Coles:		
"Neil Coles On Golf"	1965	$15
Ben Coll:		
"The Country Club"	1961	$5
"I Love Golf"	1950	$5
Glenna Collett:		
"Golf For Young Players"	1926	$90
Signed By Collett		$475
Reprint	1984	$25
"Ladies In The Rough"	1928	$150
Basil Collier:		
"Local Thunder"	1936	$10
Sargent F. Collier:		
"Green Grows Bar Harbour, Reflections		
From Kebo Valley"	1964	$95
David R. Collins:		
"Super Champ! The Story Of Babe		
Didrickson Zaharias"	1982	$15
Albert W.K. Colmer and Ivor D. Ray:		
"History Of The Ardglas Castle And		
Ardglas Golf Club"	1982	$10
Reggie Colomb:		
"Rutland Country Club"	1985	$10
The Colonel:		
"Golfing By the Numbers"	1927	$95
Harry S. Colt and C.H. Alison:		
"Some Essays On Golf Course Architecture"	1920	$1,100
Reprint	1993	$85
J. Arthur Colver:		
"A History Of Lindrick Golf Club 1891-1979"	1980	$25
George M. Colville:		
"Five Open Champions And		
The Musselburgh Golf Story"	1980	$100
James Colville:		
"The Glasgow Golf Club 1787-1907"	1907	$650

AUTHOR TITLE	PUB. DATE	VALUE
Colwyn Bay Golf Club:		
"Colwyn Bay Golf Club"	1934	$75
John L. Comer:		
"Putting: A New Approach"	1962	$10
Archie Compston and Stanley Anderson:		
"Love On The Fairway: A Romance Of The Open Championship"	1936	$175
Archie Compston and Henry Longhurst:		
"Go Golfing"	1937	$100
C. H. Compton:		
"The Antiquity Of Golf"	1881	$1,800
Harvey Conley:		
"Golf Made Easy The H.A.R.D. Way"	1965	$10
Robert Connolly:		
"How To Become A Golfer And Have No One To Blame But Yourself"	1955	$5
"Carnaby Threep's Golf Class"	1970	$5
Brandon Conron:		
"The London Hunt And Country Club"	1985	$25
William Conroy:		
"Forty Years Of Apawamis"	1940	$200
A. D. Converse:		
"Toy Town Golf Course"	1926	$60
Bernard Cooke:		
"Newnes All Color Golf Guide"	1984	$10
David Cooper:		
"Golfing Resorts On The Glasgow And South-Western Railway"	1901	$5
Jim Cooper:		
"A.G. Spalding & Bros., Pre-1930 Clubs, Trademarks, Sub-Marks And Etc. And Other Spalding Collectibles"	1985	$10
Samuel W. Cooper:		
"The Nineteenth Hole And Other Lyrics Of The Links"	1921	$375
Edwin J. Coopman:		
"The History Of The San Francisco Golf Club"	1978	$35
Copt Heath Golf Club:		
"Copt Heath Golf Club 1907-1977"	1977	$10
"Copt Heath Golf Club 1910-1985"	1985	$10
Fred Corcoran:		
"Unplayable Lies"	1965	$25
Signed By Corcoran		$95
Geoffrey S. Cornish and William G. Robinson:		
"Golf Course Design, An Introduction"	1972	$25
Geoffrey S. Cornish and Ronald W. Whitten:		
"The Golf Course"	1981	$35

AUTHOR TITLE	PUB. DATE	VALUE
Royal Cortissoz:		
"The Ekwanok Country Club"	1937	$50
"Nine Holes Of Golf"	1922	$95
Roaslynde Cossey:		
"Golfing Ladies: Five Centuries Of Golf In		
Great Britain And Ireland"	1984	$40
A.J. Costelloe:		
"Faversham Golf Club 1902-1983"	1983	$10
C.K. Cotton:		
"Porters Park Golf Club"	1971	$10
Henry Cotton:		
"Henry Cotton Says..."	1962	$35
"Henry Cotton's Guide To Golf		
In The British Isles"	1969	$40
"This Game Of Golf"	1948	$65
"Golf: Being A Short Treatise For The Use Of		
Young People Who Aspire To Proficiency		
In The Royal And Ancient Game"	1931	$120
"Golf: A Pictorial History"	1975	$40
"Hints on Playing With Steel Shafts"	1933	$170
"A History Of Golf Illustrated"	1975	$60
"My Golfing Album"	1959	$50
"My Swing"	1952	$25
"The Picture Story Of The Golf Game"	1965	$45
"Play Better Golf"	1973	$35
Signed By Cotton		$175
"Some Golfing Ifs"	1948	$175
"Study The Golf Game With Henry Cotton"	1964	$45
"Thanks For The Game"	1980	$45
Country Club Of Fairfield:		
"The Country Club Of Fairfield 1914-1966"	1966	$20
Country Club Of York:		
"Country Club Of York Yearbook In Which		
The History Of The Club Is Reviewed"	1929	$15
Geoffrey Cousins:		
"Golf In Britain"	1975	$30
"Golfers At Law"	1958	$65
"The Handbook Of Golf"	1969	$20
"Lord Of The Links"	1977	$30
"Manor House Hotel Golf Course"	1965	$15
Geoffrey Cousins And Bill Cox:		
"The State Express: The Book Of Golf"	1962	$20
Geoffrey Cousins and Don Pottinger:		
"An Atlas Of Golf"	1974	$35
Geoffrey Cousins And Tom Scott:		
"A Century Of Opens"	1971	$55
Coventry Hearsall Golf Club:		
"Coventry Hearsall Golf Club"	1937	$75

AUTHOR TITLE	PUB. DATE	VALUE
A.T. Cowell:		
"Kinderminster Golf Club"	1971	$10
A. Bertran Cox:		
"Fairways Of The Mount 1927-1977"	1977	$15
"Out Of The Rough, A History Of The Mount Lofty		
Golf Club 1925-1975"	1975	$15
Paul Cox And Jim Koger:		
"The City That Broke Par"	1971	$5
Wiffy Cox:		
"The Wiffy Cox Story"	1970	$15
"How To Cut Strokes Off Your Score"	1960	$5
William J. Cox:		
"Can I Help You? The Guide To Better Golf"	1954	$75
"W. J. Cox And Golf"	1936	$25
"Improve Your Game"	1963	$10
"Play Better Golf"	1952	$10
William J. Cox and Nicholas Trmayne:		
"Bill Cox's Golf Companion"	1969	$15
John Coyne:		
"Better Golf"	1972	$5
"Golf For Women"	1975	$10
"The New Golf For Women"	1973	$10
Linda Craft And Penny Zavichas:		
"The Craft-Zavichas Golfer's Cookbook"	1979	$5
"The Craft-Zavichas Golfer's Cookbook II"	1983	$5
Brian Crafter:		
"Winning Golf"	1983	$5
Charles E. Crane:		
"Brattleboro Country Club"	1926	$30
Leo Crane:		
"California Golf Directory"	1953	$75
"Putting: The Name Of The Game"	1966	$10
Peter G. Cranford:		
"The Winning Touch In Golf"	1961	$20
Frank Craven:		
"The 19th Hole, A Comedy In Three Acts"	1928	$150
Crawford, MacGregor, and Canby:		
"Golf: The Game Of Games"	1922	$150
"How Boys Can Enjoy Golf"	1920	$95
"Stepping Stones To A Golf Course"	1921	$110
Iain Crawford:		
"The Open Guide To Royal St. George's		
And Sandwich"	1981	$10
"The Open Guide To Royal Troon And Kyle"	1982	$10
"Scottish Brewers Open Guide To		
The Old Course & St. Andrews"	1982	$10
Leonard Crawley:		
"The Golfing Year 1954"	1954	$15

AUTHOR TITLE	PUB. DATE	VALUE
Leonard Crawley (cont.):		
"Playfair Golf Annual 1950"	1950	$25
"Playfair Golf Annual 1951"	1951	$25
"Playfair Golf Annual 1952"	1952	$35
"Playfair Golf Annual 1953"	1953	$35
John Creagh:		
"Golden Years Of Australian Golf"	1977	$20
William Crehan:		
"Who's Who In Golf"	1971	$10
Eric Cremin:		
"Par Golf"	1952	$10
D.D. Crews and J.G. Germuga:		
"Caddie Handbook"	1946	$20
T.M. Cribbin:		
"The Wilmslow Golf Club"	1950	$15
Thomas Cribbin:		
"Correct Caddy Conduct"	1920	$35
Martha O. Crisp And Ruth A. Leffer:		
"Women's Long Island Golf Association, The First Fifty Years 1930-1980"	1980	$10
Corrine Crogen:		
"Golf Fundamentals"	1964	$5
"Golf Fundamentals For Students And Teachers"	1960	$5
Charles Crombie:		
"The Rules Of Golf Illustrated"	1905	$1,200
Reprint	1966	$150
Robert A. Cromie:		
"Golf For Boys And Girls"	1965	$10
"New Angles On Putting And Chipping"	1960	$15
"Par For The Course: A Golfer's Anthology"	1964	$25
A.C.M. Croome:		
"The Camberley Heath Golf Club"	1913	$150
Povan Crosbie:		
"Fairways And Foul"	1964	$20
William H. Crouch:		
"Guide To The Analysis Of Golf Clubs And Country Clubs"	1968	$10
Charles Cruickshank:		
"The Tang Murders"	1976	$25
Frederick D. Cruickshank:		
"The History Of The Weston Golf And Country Club"	1980	$20
George L. Cummings:		
"It Goes Where You Hit It"	1948	$10
James Cundell:		
"Rules of The Thistle Club"	1824	$12,000
Golf House Reprint	1983	$95

AUTHOR TITLE	PUB. DATE	VALUE
Andrew S. Cunningham:		
"The Golf Clubs Round Largo Bay"	1909	$1,850
"Inverkeithing, North Queens Ferry, Limekilns,		
Charlestown, The Ferryhills"	1899	$575
"Lundin Links, Upper And Lower Largo		
And Leven"	1913	$500
Carl Cunningham:		
"Down The Middle"	1952	$10
Calamo Currente:		
"Half Hours With An Old Golfer"	1895	$550
Frederick H. Curtis and John Heard:		
"The Country Club 1882-1932"	1932	$300
Dalbeattie Golf Club:		
"The Book Of Dalbeattie Golf Club"	1912	$2,000
W. Dalrymple:		
"Golfer's Guide To The Game And		
Greens Of Scotland"	1894	$1,825
"The Golfer's Referee"	1897	$750
"Handbook Of Golf"	1895	$500
Fred Daly:		
"Golf As I See It"	1951	$25
"Golfing In Northern Ireland"	1971	$35
Marshall Dann:		
"Golfdom's Greatest Tournaments"	1952	$10
James Dante and Leo Diegel:		
"The Nine Bad Shots In Golf And What		
To Do About Them"	1947	$65
James Dante and Len Elliott:		
"Four Magic Moves To Winning Golf"	1962	$20
"Stop That Slice"	1953	$20
"What's Wrong With Your Golf?"	1978	$10
L. Claughton Darbyshire:		
"Go Golfing In Britain A Hole By Hole		
Survey of 25 Famous Seaside Courses"	1961	$50
Richard Darlington:		
"Aberdovey Golf Club: A Round Of A Hundred		
Years 1886-1986"	1986	$35
Darsie L. Darsie:		
"My Greatest Day In Golf"	1950	$35
Bernard Darwin:		
"About These New Rules"	1954	$200
Signed By Darwin		$575
"Aldeburgh Golf Club"	1939	$195
"Ashridge Golf Club"	1938	$200
"At Odd Moments"	1941	$35
"The Beaconsfield Golf Club"	1947	$40
"Berkhamsted Golf Club"	1946	$110
"The Bogner Golf Club"	1938	$195

AUTHOR　TITLE	PUB. DATE	VALUE
Bernard Darwin (cont.):		
"James Braid"	1952	$90
Signed By Darwin		$495
Reprint	1981	$20
"British Clubs"	1947	$30
"British Golf"	1946	$50
"Burhill Club"	1939	$150
"The Burnham & Berrow Golf Club"	1938	$200
"The Carlisle & Silloth Golf Club"	1946	$75
"Come To Britain For Golf"	1946	$400
"The Crowsborough Beacon Golf Club"	1934	$195
"A Day's Golf At Leeds Castle May 15th 1934"	1934	$875
"The Dorset Golf Club"	1932	$250
"The Downe Golf Club"	1947	$35
"The East Devon Golf Club"	1947	$40
"Every Idle Dream"	1948	$30
"The Farnham Golf Club"	1938	$175
"The Formby Golf Club"	1934	$200
"A Friendly Round"	1922	$1,200
"The Frilford Heath Golf Club"	1938	$175
"Golf Between Two Wars"	1944	$135
Reprint	1985	$20
"The Golf Courses Of The British Isles"	1910	$1,150
"The Golf Courses Of Great Britain"	1925	$425
"Golf From The Times"	1912	$1,500
"Golf In Great Britain And Ireland"	1930	$575
"Golf, Pleasures Of Life Series"	1954	$225
"Golf: Some Hints And Suggestions"	1920	$2,000
"A Golfer's Gallery By Old Masters"	1920	$2,000
"Golfing By-Paths"	1946	$150
"Green Memories"	1928	$475
"Harewood Downs Golf Club"	1948	$20
"The Hayling Golf Club"	1947	$40
"Hints On Golf"	1912	$2,500
"Huntstanton Golf Club"	1928	$225
"Knole Park Golf Club"	1926	$225
"The Ilfield Golf And Country Club"	1947	$35
"The Ilkley Golf Club"	1931	$200
"Life Is Sweet Brother"	1940	$225
"The Liphook Golf Club"	1947	$30
"The Lucifer Golfing Society"	1942	$125
"The New Golf Club St. Andrews"	1923	$275
"North Foreland Golf Club"	1939	$150
"North Hants Golf Club"	1949	$20
"Out Of The Rough"	1932	$150
"Pack Clouds Away"	1941	$50
"Playing The Like"	1934	$95
"Playing The Like"	1952	$50

AUTHOR TITLE	PUB. DATE	VALUE
Bernard Darwin (cont.):		
"Prince's Golf Club"	1938	$225
"The Rochester And Cobham Park Golf Club"	1938	$195
"A Round Of Golf"	1937	$400
"A Round Of Golf On The L. & N.E.R."	1925	$450
"The Royal Ashdown Forest Golf Club"	1938	$275
"The Royal Blackheath Golf Club"	1938	$400
"The Royal Cinque Ports Golf Club"	1935	$300
"The Royal Liverpool Golf Club"	1922	$475
"The Royal North Devon Golf Club"	1921	$475
"The Royal West Norfolk Golf Club"	1923	$375
"The Royal Wimbleton Golf Club"	1922	$450
"Rubs Of The Green"	1936	$450
"The Rye Golf Club"	1939	$200
"The Saunton Golf Club"	1926	$275
"Second Shots: Casual Talks About Golf"	1930	$295
"Six Golfing Shots By Six Famous Players"	1927	$375
"St. Enodoc Golf Club"	1947	$50
"The Sundridge Park Golf Club"	1946	$50
"The Tandridge Golf Club"	1925	$250
"Tee Shots And Others"	1911	$475
Signed By Darwin		$925
USGA Reprint	1984	$145
"The Teignmouth Golf Club"	1925	$250
"The Walton Heath Golf Club"	1937	$225
"West Hill Golf Club"	1946	$50
"West Kent Golf Club"	1951	$25
"The West Lancashire Golf Club"	1934	$195
"The West Surrey Golf Club"	1938	$195
"The West Sussex Golf Club"	1935	$225
"The Willingdon Golf Club"	1947	$25
"The Working Golf Club"	1949	$20
"The World That Fred Made"	1955	$85
Signed By Darwin		$495
"The Worplesdon Golf Club"	1946	$60
Bernard Darwin and Others:		
"A History Of Golf In Britain"	1952	$450
R.E. Davidson:		
"Golfing At Yokine"	1967	$10
J. Davies and G.W Brown:		
"The Royal North Devon Golf Club 1864-1989"	1989	$90
Signed By The Authors		$275
John Davies:		
"Yardley Country Club A Casual History		
1928-1978"	1978	$10
Peter Davies:		
"Davies' Dictionary Of Golf Terms"	1980	$15

AUTHOR TITLE	PUB. DATE	VALUE
Joe Davis:		
"Blue Book Of Chicago Golfers"	1925	$150
Joe G. Davis:		
"Major Golf Trophies"	1928	$35
Robert H. Davis:		
"Do You Know How A Golf Ball Is Made"	1928	$65
"The Way Of A Caddie With A Man"	1926	$150
William Davis:		
"The Punch Book Of Golf"	1973	$15
William H. Davis:		
"100 Great Golf Courses-And Then Some"	1982	$20
"Great Golf Courses Of The World"	1974	$15
Davyhulme Park Golf Club:		
"Davyhulme Park Golf Club 75th Anniversary"	1985	$15
George Dawkins:		
"Keys To The Golf Swing"	1976	$10
DB Golf Annual:		
"The DB Golf Annual 1974"	1974	$45
"The DB Golf Annual 1975"	1975	$25
"The DB Golf Annual 1976"	1976	$25
"The DB Golf Annual 1977"	1977	$20
"The DB Golf Annual 1978"	1978	$20
"The DB Golf Annual 1979"	1979	$15
"The DB Golf Annual 1980"	1980	$10
W. DeAula:		
"St. Andrews: Ancient and Modern"	1870	$850
Betty Debenham:		
"The Carlisle And Silloth Golf Club"	1950	$15
"The Luffenham Heath Golf Club"	1950	$15
Robert Debenham:		
"The Metropolitan Golf Club 1908-1929"	1929	$35
Paul Deegan:		
"Jack Nicklaus: The Golden Bear"	1974	$15
Deeside Golf Club:		
"History Of The Deeside Golf Club 1903-1953"	1953	$25
Louis DeGarmo:		
"Play Golf And Enjoy It"	1954	$10
Christian DeGuerre and Patrick Failliott:		
"Europe's Golf Guide"	1982	$15
Del Monte:		
"Golf At Del Monte California"	1903	$85
"Golf And Other Sports At Del Monte"	1913	$60
Delaware And Hudson Railroad:		
"Golf: A Directory Of Courses In The Summer Paradise On The Delaware And Hudson Line"	1916	$95
G. Delgado:		
"Golf Of All Kinds"	1935	$225

AUTHOR TITLE	PUB. DATE	VALUE
Delgany Golf Club:		
"Delgany Golf Club 75th Anniversary		
1908-1983"	1983	$15
Ralph Dellor:		
"British Golf Courses: A Guide To Courses		
In The British Isles"	1974	$20
James Demaret:		
"My Partner Ben Hogan"	1954	$125
Signed By Demaret		$375
John DeMonte:		
"A Collection And Portfolio Of Golf Humor"	1983	$10
"The Kings James' Version Of		
The Game Of Golfe"	1980	$15
"The Kings James' Version Of The Game		
Of Golfe Book II"	1982	$15
Frank T. Denis:		
"The Kanawaki Golf Club 50th Anniversary Book"	1964	$20
Tom Dentino:		
"The Basic Golf Swing"	1970	$10
George Bernhard Depping:		
"Evenings Entertainments" 2 Volumes	1811	$175
Blaine R. Detrick:		
"Golf And The Gospel: How To Improve Your		
Score In The Game Of Life"	1985	$10
Detroit Country Club:		
"Facts About The Links Of		
The Detroit Country Club"	1916	$110
Detroit Golf Club:		
"Detroit Golf Club A Chronicle Of 40 Years Of		
Substantial Achievement 1899-1939"	1939	$295
Dominic Devine:		
"Three Green Bottles"	1972	$10
Bruce Devlin:		
"Australia's Bruce Devlin Championship Golf"	1970	$10
"Bruce Devlin Flip Book Instructions, Drive		
And Wedge"	1971	$20
"Play Like The Devil"	1967	$15
William O. DeWitt:		
"DeWitt's Golf Year Book"	1953	$20
E.R. Ted Dexter:		
"My Golf"	1982	$10
E.R. Ted Dexter and Clifford Makins:		
"Deadly Putter"	1979	$10
E.R. Ted Dexter and Michael McDonnell:		
"The World Of Golf"	1970	$10
Joseph C. Dey Jr.:		
"Golf"	1977	$10
"Golf Rules In Pictures"	1964	$10

AUTHOR TITLE	PUB. DATE	VALUE
M.E. Deyo:		
"The Easy Way To Stay In Shape For Golf"	1971	$10
Carrol Diaz:		
"Golf: A Beginners Guide"	1974	$5
Patric Dickinson:		
"The Good Minute: An Autobiographical Study"	1965	$55
"A Round Of Golf Courses: A Selection		
Of The Best Eighteen"	1951	$75
Pat Dickson:		
"Short History Of The Covelly Country Club"	1974	$14
Robert W. Diehl and Tom Vardon:		
"The Diehl-Vardon Manual"	1927	$140
Directory Of Amateur Golfers:		
"Directory Of Amateur Golfers, Volume 1		
Arizona, Nevada And Utah"	1976	$15
Direlton Castle Golf Club:		
"Direlton Castle Golf Club, 1854-1954		
First Centenary"	1954	$20
Harold Dix:		
"A Handbook On The Rules Of Golf"	1927	$25
H. Macneile Dixon:		
"Golf-and How"	1949	$15
Peter Dobereiner:		
"The Book Of Golf Disasters"	1983	$25
"Down The Nineteenth Fairway;		
A Golfing Anthology"	1982	$25
"For The Love Of Golf: The Best Of Dobereiner"	1981	$25
"The Game With A Hole In It"	1970	$45
"The Glorious World Of Golf"	1973	$50
"Golf Explained: How To Take Advantage		
Of The Rules"	1977	$25
"The Golfers - The Inside Story"	1982	$25
"Stroke, Hole Or Match"	1976	$50
"The World Of Golf: The Best Of Peter Dobereiner"	1981	$20
Marcus Dods:		
"The Bunker At The Fifth"	1927	$125
Mike Doherty:		
"Golf Classics Price And Identification Guide"	1978	$20
Anne R. Dolan:		
"Congressional Country Club 1924-1984"	1984	$40
Charles Donohue And Paul Care:		
"Guide To Golf In Hampshire"	1977	$15
Richard E. Donovan and Joseph E. Murdoch:		
"The Game Of Golf And		
The Printed Word 1566-1985"	1988	$65
Robert Donovan:		
"GHO '84 - The New Era"	1985	$10

AUTHOR TITLE	PUB. DATE	VALUE
J. H. Douglas And E. R. Wastnedge:		
"The History of Carlisle Golf Club"	1985	$15
James Gordon Dow:		
"The Crail Golfing Society 1786-1936"	1936	$1,600
Rick Doyle:		
"How To Cheat At Golf"	1985	$5
Tom Drury:		
"Blackwell Golf Club, Worcestershire A History"	1953	$15
Alasdair M. Drysdale:		
"The Golf House Club, Elie:		
A Centenary History"	1975	$20
Abel Dubb:		
"Why Golf"	1921	$45
Joe Duffer:		
"The Power Swing"	1949	$10
Will Duke:		
"Fair Prey"	1958	$10
Thomas Dulack:		
"Pork, Or The Day I Lost The Masters"	1968	$10
Dunany Country Club:		
"The Story Of The Dunany Country Club"	1967	$15
Dunbar Golf Club:		
"Dunbar Golf Club"	1955	$20
David Scott Duncan:		
"The Golfing Annual 1892-1893"	1893	$645
"The Golfing Annual 1893-1894"	1894	$500
George Duncan:		
"Golf At The Gallop"	1951	$150
"Golf For Women"	1912	$75
"Present Day Golf"	1922	$85
George Duncan And Bernard Darwin:		
"Present Day Golf"	1921	$100
Dundas Valley Golf And Curling Club:		
"Dundas Valley Golf And Curling Club		
1929-1979 50th Anniversary"	1979	$20
Caddie Dunlop:		
"Leaves From My Diary"	1919	$200
Dunlop Rubber:		
"The Making Of A Maxfli"	1924	$60
Noel Dunlop-Hill:		
"History Of The Scottish Ladies Golfing		
Association 1903-1928"	1929	$85
Sandy Dunlop:		
"The Golfing Bodymind"	1980	$10
Edward T. Dunn:		
"The Park Club Of Buffalo 1903-1978"	1978	$15
J. Dunn:		
"Golf From Rabbit To Tiger"	1955	$10

AUTHOR TITLE	PUB. DATE	VALUE
John D. Dunn:		
"A-B-C Of Golf"	1916	$75
"Elements Of The Golf Swing"	1930	$60
"Golf"	1941	$70
"How To Drive-How To Approach-How To Putt" (3. Vols)	1922	$85
"Intimate Golf Talks"	1920	$60
"Natural Golf"	1931	$165
John D. Dunn & Jessup Elon:		
"Intimate Golf Talks"	1920	$175
Seymour Dunn:		
"The Complete Golf Joke Book"	1953	$20
"Golf Fundamentals"	1922	$250
Reprint	1977	$20
"Standardized Golf Instructions"	1934	$65
Dorothy Dunnett:		
"Match For A Murderer"	1971	$20
Bob Dunning:		
"Green Construction"	1960	$15
Colin Dunsmore:		
"In Celebration Of The Golden Anniversary Of The New South Wales Golf Club 1928-1978"	1978	$15
Ted Durien:		
"The First Fifty Years, 1925-1975; Monterey Penninsula Country Club"	1975	$45
Duties Of A Caddie:		
"The Duties Of A Caddie"	1932	$60
Olin Dutra:		
"All You Need To Know To Start Golf"	1941	$20
"Golf Doctor"	1948	$10
Olin Dutra And Others:		
"Your Guide To Golf In Southern California"	1940	$45
James Dwight:		
"Golf: A Handbook For Beginners"	1895	$375
D.H. Dwyer:		
"Killara Golf Club A History"	1966	$15
East London Golf Club:		
"East London Golf Club 1893-1968"	1968	$15
East Lothian Golf:		
"East Lothian Golf"	1983	$10
Victor J. East:		
"Better Golf In 5 Minutes"	1956	$25
L.F. Easterbrook:		
"Ipswich Golf Club"	1965	$15
Eastern Airlines:		
"Eastern's Guide To Great Golf Courses"	1966	$10
Eaton Golf Club:		
"Eaton Golf Club"	1948	$20

AUTHOR TITLE	PUB. DATE	VALUE
Harry Eaton:		
"Dunmurray Golf Club 75th		
Anniversary 1905-1980"	1980	$20
Bill Ebert:		
"The Invitation"	1983	$10
Jackie Eddy:		
"The Second Slice: Over 250 Delicious, Time Saving		
Recipes For Golfers And People On The Go"	1985	$10
J. Douglas Edgar:		
"The Gate To Golf"	1920	$350
Reprint	1983	$25
Edinburgh Burgess Golfing Society:		
"History Of The Edinburgh Burgess		
Golfing Society"	1906	$1,500
Reprint	1984	$25
Jolee Edmondson:		
"The Woman Golfer's Catalogue"	1980	$10
C.G. Edmonstone:		
"A Study Of Golf From Its Mechanical Aspect"	1954	$15
Leslie Edwards:		
"Golf On Merseyside And District"	1954	$20
"The Royal Liverpool Golf Club 1869-1969; A Short		
History Of The Club And Of Championships Played		
Over The Holyoake Links"	1969	$35
"A Short History Of The Royal Liverpool Golf Club and		
Of Championships Played Over The Links"	1983	$20
"Wallasey Golf Club"	1960	$10
"The West Lancashire Golf Club Centenary		
1873-1973"	1973	$20
R. Stanford Edwards:		
"Wee Burn Country Club"	1949	$45
Russ Edwards:		
"The Golpher: His Origin And His Finish"	1929	$75
John Egan:		
"Castlebar Golf Club 1910-1985"	1985	$15
El Caballero Country Club:		
"El Caballero Country Club, Silver Anniversary		
1957-1982"	1982	$15
Patricia Eldred:		
"Kathy Whitworth"	1975	$10
Ashton G. Eldridge:		
"A History Of The Huntington Country Club		
1910-1980"	1981	$20
Elements Of Golf Course Layout:		
"Elements Of Golf Course Layout And Design"	1968	$25
Charles Elliot:		
"East Lake Country Club History, Home		
Course Of Bobby Jones"	1984	$75

AUTHOR TITLE	PUB. DATE	VALUE
Len Elliott And Barbara Kelly:		
"Who's Who In Golf"	1976	$10
A.D. Ellis:		
"History Of The Royal Melbourne Golf Club.		
Vol. 1 1891-1941"	1941	$200
Wes Ellis Jr.:		
"All Weather Golf"	1967	$25
James Ellroy:		
"Brown's Requiem"	1981	$10
David Emery:		
"The Ryder Cup '85"	1985	$20
"Who's Who In International Golf"	1983	$30
Fred Emery:		
"Colonel Bogey's Coloring Book For Golfer's"	1981	$15
Howard R Endersby:		
"Lessons From Great Golfers"	1924	$65
Erewash Valley Golf Club:		
"The Erewash Valley Golf Club		
75th Aniversary 1905-1980"	1980	$20
Erskine Park Golf Club:		
"Erskine Park Golf Club Silver Anniversary		
1925-1950"	1950	$15
Esquire Magazine:		
"The Name Of The Game Is Golf"	1968	$5
Eurogolf:		
"Eurogolf 1972"	1972	$10
Charles "Chick" Evans Jr.:		
"Caddy Manual"	1928	$120
"Chick Evans Golf Book"	1921	$200
"Chick Evans Golf Book, The Story Of The Sporting		
Battles Of The Greatest Of All Amateur Golfers"	1924	$185
Signed Limited Edition		$750
Reprint	1978	$25
Memorial Tournament Reprint	1985	$25
"Chick Evans Guide To Better Golf"	1924	$65
"Golf For Boys And Girls"	1954	$80
Charles "Chick" Evans Jr. and Barrie Payne:		
"Ida Broke"	1929	$195
Webster Evans:		
"Encyclopedia Of Golf"	1971	$10
"Rub Of The Green: Golf's Triumphs And		
Tragedies"	1969	$15
Webster Evans and Tom Scott:		
"In Praise Of Golf"	1950	$25
H.S.C. Everard:		
"Golf In Theory And Practice"	1896	$350
"A History of The Royal And Ancient Golf Club,		
St. Andrews From 1754-1900"	1907	$1,600

AUTHOR TITLE	PUB. DATE	VALUE
Exmoor Country Club:		
"Exmoor Country Club Semi-Centennial Year 1896-1946"	1946	$60
"Exmoor Country Club Seventy-Fifth Anniversary, 1896-1971"	1972	$40
Fable Of The Lost Golf Ball:		
"The Fable Of The Lost Golf Ball"	1940	$50
Walter Fairbanks:		
"Some Hints On Learning Golf"	1900	$275
Jack Fairlie:		
"Chicagoland Golf Course Guide"	1974	$15
Walter E. Fairlie:		
"The Old Course At St. Andrews"	1908	$350
Fairview Country Club:		
"Fairview Country Club Twenty-Fifth Anniversary 1904-1929"	1929	$60
Fairways:		
"Fairways; A Detailed Graphic Description Of All Los Angeles City And County Operated Golf Courses"	1967	$15
Nick Faldo:		
"Enjoying Golf With Nick Faldo"	1985	$15
"The Rough With The Smooth"	1980	$15
Robert G. Falls:		
"Golfing In South Africa Edition 1958"	1958	$25
"History Of Golf At The Cape"	1918	$975
"A Short History Of The Mowbray Golf Club"	1939	$85
"Southern Africa Golf Annual 1967-68"	1968	$25
Farmington Country Club:		
"Farmington Country Club"	1932	$35
Guy B. Farrar:		
"The Royal Liverpool Golf Club"	1947	$100
"The Royal Liverpool Golf Club, A History1869-1932"	1933	$600
J. Farrell:		
"Golf"	1930	$50
Johnny Farrell:		
"Johnny Farrell On Golf Sportsmanship"	1929	$25
"How To Play Your Golf Course"	1929	$35
"If I Were In Your Golf Shoes"	1951	$15
"Putting To Win"	1929	$25
"The Weekend Golfer"	1952	$10
Fascination Of Golf:		
"The Fascination Of Golf"	1918	$75
Max Faulkner:		
"Golf-Right From The Start"	1965	$20
"Play Championship Golf All Your Life"	1972	$25
Max Faulkner & Louis T. Stanley:		
"The Faulkner Method"	1952	$35

AUTHOR TITLE	PUB. DATE	VALUE
W.H. Faust:		
"The Hectic Game Of Golf"	1930	$45
Dike Faxon:		
"History Of Echo Lake Country Club 1899-1956"	1956	$25
H.B. Fenn:		
"A Box Of Matches"	1922	$60
Ronnie Fenton:		
"The Easy Road To Good Golf"	1962	$10
Len Fereday:		
"The Burbage Common Golf Club"	1951	$15
Fernando, Kadirgamar, and Candappo:		
"Royal Columbo Golf Club 100 Years		
1879-1979"	1979	$65
Ferndown Golf Club:		
"Ferndown Golf Club"	1939	$40
James Ferrier:		
"Golf Shots"	1940	$30
"Low Score Golf"	1948	$15
Fifty Miles Of Golf:		
"Fifty Miles Of Golf Round London"	1938	$120
Benjamin and Howard Fine:		
"The Fine Method Of Golf"	1958	$10
James W. Finegan:		
"The Great Links In Ireland"	1977	$20
Joseph S. Finger:		
"The Business End Of Building Or Rebuilding		
A Golf Course"	1972	$25
Dow Finsterwald:		
"Fundamentals Of Golf"	1961	$20
"The Wedges, Pitching And Sand"	1965	$35
Morris Fishbein:		
"To Golf Or Not To Golf"	1943	$50
Lew Fishman:		
"Golf Magazine's Short Cuts To Better Golf"	1979	$10
George Fitch:		
"Golf For The Beginner"	1908	$80
Hugh Louis Fitzpatrick:		
"Golf Don'ts"	1900	$225
Five Secrets Of Winning Golf:		
"Five Secrets Of Winning Golf"	1945	$20
Thomas Flaherty:		
"The Masters: The Story Of Golf's		
Greatest Tournament"	1961	$20
"The U.S. Open 1895-1965"	1966	$20
H.A. Fleager:		
"History Of The Seattle Golf Club"	1959	$40

AUTHOR TITLE	PUB. DATE	VALUE
Alvin Fleishman:		
"Compend Of Golf Supplemented By		
Atomic Gold Aids"	1946	$35
David Hay Fleming:		
"Historical Notes & Extracts Concerning The Links		
Of St. Andrews 1552-1893"	1893	$3,000
Charles Fletcher:		
"How To Play Bad Golf"	1935	$25
Jim Flick:		
"Square To Square Golf In Pictures"	1974	$15
Violet Flint:		
"A Golfing Idyll Or The Skippers Round With		
The Devil On The Links At St. Andrews"	1892	$1,750
Mrs. Harrison F. Flippin:		
"Golf Is Fun"	1956	$10
Channing Floyd:		
"The Little Golf Teacher"	1925	$65
Frank Harris Floyd:		
"The Mechanics Of The Golf Swing And The Techniques		
Of The Contestants At Oakmont, Pittsburgh Open		
Tournament 1927"	1927	$25
Colleen Fogarty:		
"The Powelton Club The First Hundred Years		
1882-1982"	1982	$20
Follow Through:		
"The Essence Of Golf"	1954	$20
Edwin B. Foote:		
"Oakmont Country Club: The First		
Seventy Five Years"	1980	$95
John D. Forbes:		
"The Mt. Anthony Country Club"	1944	$20
Doug Ford:		
"The Brainy Way To Better Golf"	1961	$10
"Getting Started In Golf"	1964	$10
"Golf"	1960	$10
"How I Play Inside Golf"	1960	$10
"Start Golf Young"	1955	$10
"The Wedge Book"	1963	$15
Forest Lake Club:		
"Forest Lake Club From Its Beginning		
Through 1964"	1965	$15
Forfar Golf Club:		
"Forfar Golf Club"	1923	$60
"Forfar Golf Club 1871-1971"	1971	$15
Robert Forgan:		
"The Golfers Handbook"	1881	$2,500
"The Golfers Manual"	1897	$1,250

AUTHOR TITLE	PUB. DATE	VALUE
James Forrest:		
"The Basics Of The Golf Swing"	1925	$55
"Golf Made Easy"	1933	$40
"The Golf Stroke"	1930	$45
"A Natural Golfer: Hand Action in Games"	1938	$40
Fred Forrester:		
"The Guilford Golf Club A Centenary 1886-1985"	1985	$15
Fort Wayne Country Club:		
"Fort Wayne Country Club Diamond Jubilee 1908-1983"	1983	$15
Fortrose and Rosemarkie Golf Club:		
"Fortrose And Rosemarkie Golf Club"	1948	$20
Bruce Fossum and Mary Dagraedt:		
"Golf"	1969	$10
Cy Foster:		
"Golf Is Easy"	1950	$30
David Foster:		
"Thinking Golf"	1979	$15
N.R. Foster:		
"History Of The Royal Wimbleton Golf Club 1865-1929"	1929	$200
Peter Fowlie:		
"The Science Of Golf"	1922	$40
"The Technique Of The Golf Swing"	1934	$25
G.D. Fox:		
"The Golfer's Pocket Tip Book"	1911	$175
W.F. Fox Jr.:		
"Golf's Guardian Angels"	1954	$10
William P. Fox:		
"Doctor Golf"	1963	$15
Gladys L. Foxley:		
"A History Of Bexley Heath Golf Club 1907-1977"	1977	$15
Oscar Fraley:		
"Golf In Action"	1952	$20
Joseph Francis:		
"Dutch Open Champion 1959 "Papwa" Sewsunker Sewgoolum"	1959	$15
Richard S. Francis:		
"Golf: Its Rules and Decisions"	1937	$75
"Rules Of Golf With Interpretations"	1937	$45
H. Xavier M. Frankenberg:		
"Golf Made Easy"	1948	$10
George Fraser and James Mearns:		
"Royal Aberdeen Golf Club"	1981	$35
Fraserburgh Golf Club:		
"The Fraserburgh Golf Club"	1947	$20
Chick Frasier:		
"Pictorial Golf" 4 Vols.	1922	$125

AUTHOR TITLE	PUB. DATE	VALUE
Frasier's Golf Directory:		
"Frasier's Golf Directory and Year Book 1923"	1923	$220
"Frasier's International Year Book 1924"	1924	$175
"Frasier's International Year Book 1925-26"	1925	$150
"Frasier's International Year Book 1926-27"	1926	$150
"Frasier's International Year Book 1927"	1927	$125
"Frasier's International Year Book 1928"	1928	$125
"Frasier's International Year Book 1929"	1929	$150
"Frasier's International Year Book 1930"	1930	$200
"Frasier's International Year Book 1931"	1931	$125
"Frasier's International Year Book 1932"	1932	$125
"Frasier's International Year Book 1933"	1933	$110
"Frasier's International Year Book 1934"	1934	$95
"Frasier's International Year Book 1935"	1935	$95
"Frasier's International Year Book 1936"	1936	$100
"Frasier's International Year Book 1937"	1937	$95
George M. Frazier:		
"Records And Statistics, Firestone Country Club"	1975	$15
Adrian Frederick:		
"The 1984 South African PGA Golf Annual"	1984	$15
Victor Fredericks:		
"For Golfers Only"	1964	$10
James L. Freeborn:		
"The Edgewood Club 1884-1937"	1937	$20
Adrian French:		
"World Senior Golf International Team Matches And World Senior Championships A History"	1977	$15
Ford Frick:		
"This Is St. Andrews 1888-1973"	1973	$20
Friendly Fairways:		
"Friendly Fairways Of Michigan; A Directory Of Public, Municipal And Semi Private Golf Courses Located Within The State Of Michigan"	1979	$15
David Frome:		
"The Murder On The Sixth Hole"	1931	$150
"The Strange Death Of Martin Green"	1931	$25
John G. Frothingham:		
"The Country Club Of New Canaan 1893-1968"	1968	$20
Robert Fukushima:		
"Kagero Golf Club Fiftieth Anniversary 1925-1975"	1975	$25
Harry Fulford:		
"Golf's Little Ironies"	1919	$125
"Potted Golf"	1910	$95
Neal Fulkerson and John T. Thatcher:		
"The Garden City Golf Club, Seventy-Fifth Anniversary 1899-1974"	1974	$100

AUTHOR TITLE	PUB. DATE	VALUE
J.R. Fullarton:		
"Instructions For Caddies"	1938	$75
Timothy Fuller:		
"Reunion With Murder"	1941	$50
Furness Golf Club:		
"Furness Golf Club, A Centenary Story 1872-1972"	1972	$20
Charlie Gaal and Nate Collier:		
"Your Golf"	1948	$15
Jonothan Gair:		
"The Australian Masters 1972-1982"	1983	$15
William Galbraith:		
"Prestwick St. Nicholas Golf Club"	1950	$275
Saul Galin:		
"Golf In Europe: A Traveler's Guide To 200 Of Europe's Best Golf Courses"	1967	$20
Paul Gallico:		
"Golf Is A Friendly Game"	1942	$55
Don Gallup:		
"Golf Courses Of Colorado"	1984	$15
W. Timothy Gallwey:		
"The Inner Game Of Golf"	1981	$10
Phil Galvano:		
"The Gentle Arts Of Chipping and Putting"	1959	$15
"Seagram's Guide To Strategic Golf"	1960	$10
"Secrets Of Accurate Putting And Chipping"	1957	$15
"The Secrets Of The Perfect Golf Swing"	1961	$10
Joe Gambatese:		
"Golf Guide 1963"	1963	$10
"Pro Am Guide To Golf"	1981	$5
Game Of Golf:		
"The Game Of Golf"	1900	$275
Peter Gammond:		
"Bluff Your Way In Golf"	1985	$10
Garden City:		
"Facts About The Course At Garden City"	1913	$175
Don Gardner:		
"Don Gardners's Golf Book: Three Point Method"	1947	$15
Howard R. Garris:		
"Uncle Butter and Uncle Wiggley Play Golf"	1924	$95
J.T. Garrity:		
"Golfer's Guide To Florida Courses"	1973	$15
Bud Gaskill:		
"Golf At A Glance"	1958	$15
John B. Gates:		
"The First Seventy-Five Years Of The United States Seniors Golf Association 1905-1980"	1980	$15
"Round Hill Golf Club 1972-1979"	1979	$10

AUTHOR TITLE	PUB. DATE	VALUE
J.W. Gaudin:		
"Method In Golf"	1929	$35
William C. Gault:		
"The Long Green"	1965	$15
Michael Gedye:		
"Golf In Portugal"	1975	$10
"Golf In The Sun 1974-75"	1975	$10
"Holiday Golf In Spain & Portugal"	1970	$20
Al Geiberger:		
"Tempo: Golf's Master Key"	1980	$10
General:		
"Golf And How To Play It"	1912	$145
Paul H. Gerrits:		
"The Golfer's Guide"	1947	$15
Walt Gerzin:		
"Eclectic Golf; Featuring The AWH Takeaway"	1976	$10
James Gibbins:		
"Sudden Death"	1983	$15
Nevin H. Gibson:		
"The Encyclopedia Of Golf"	1958	$45
"Great Moments In Golf"	1973	$20
"A Pictorial History Of Golf"	1968	$45
Nevin H. Gibson and Tom Kouzmentoff:		
"Golf's Greatest Shots By The World's Greatest Golfers"	1981	$15
W.H. Gibson:		
"Curragh Golf Club Centenary 1883-1983"	1983	$10
James Gilbert:		
"Boyce Hill Golf Club"	1938	$10
Reg Gilchrist:		
"The Knott End Story, History Of A Golf Club"	1983	$10
Howard Gill:		
"Fun In The Rough From Golf Digest"	1957	$10
Donald J. Gillen:		
"A History Of Wolforts Roost Country Club"	1985	$10
Norman Giller:		
"The Book Of Golf Lists"	1985	$10
Percy J. Gillespie:		
"Putting"	1957	$15
Stair A. Gillon:		
"The Honorable Company Of Edinburgh Golfers At Muirfield 1891-1914"	1946	$975
C.J. L. Gilson:		
"Golf"	1928	$35
"Golf: Warnes Recreation Books"	1928	$35
J.D. Gilruth:		
"Arbroath Golf Course"	1909	$300

AUTHOR TITLE	PUB. DATE	VALUE
Bernard Glacier:		
"Captain At Kiawah"	1991	$25
Glamorganshire Golf Club:		
"Short History Of The Glamorganshire		
Golf Club 1890-1950"	1950	$25
Dan Gleason:		
"The Great, The Grand And The Also-Ran: Rabbits		
and Champions On The Pro Golf Tour"	1976	$45
John F. Gleason Jr.:		
"A Brief History Of The Shaker Heights		
Country Club"	1978	$15
Peter Glenn:		
"The Golfers Guidebook: A Guide To The PGA		
Winter Spring Tour"	1965	$10
Gloucester Golf Club:		
"Gloucester Golf Club"	1938	$65
Thomas Glover:		
"Ladies Open Golf Championship May 1902"	1902	$125
Webster Glynes:		
"The Maiden: A Golfing Epic"	1893	$12,000
Edna Glynn:		
"A Century Of Golf At Lahinch 1892-1992"	1992	$35
Ray Goates:		
"Los Angeles City Bicentennial Honor Of		
Champions"	1981	$20
Doug Godlington:		
"The Un-Golfer"	1974	$15
Austin Goetz:		
"The Golf Champ"	1934	$55
Golf:		
"Golf"	1973	$20
"Golf"	1983	$15
Golf & Club Magazine:		
"Great Golf Cartoons From Golf &		
Club Magazine"	1971	$15
Golf And Ping Pong:		
"Golf And Ping Pong"	1903	$65
Golf Canada:		
"Golf Canada"	1984	$25
Golf Clubs Of Devon:		
"The Golf Clubs Of Devon"	1935	$60
Golf Clubs Of Fife:		
"The Golf Clubs Of Fife"	1933	$65
Golf Course Superintendents:		
"History Of The Northern Ohio Chapter Of The Golf		
Course Superintendents Association Of America		
1923-1976"	1976	$15

AUTHOR TITLE	PUB. DATE	VALUE
Golf Courses California and Nevada:		
"Golf Courses California And Nevada"	1970	$15
Golf Courses in New York State:		
"Golf Courses In New York State"	1968	$15
Golf Courses in Switzerland:		
"Golf Courses In Switzerland"	1928	$75
Golf Courses of New Hampshire:		
"Golf Courses Of New Hampshire"	1929	$35
Golf Courses of Victoria:		
"Golf Courses Of Victoria, A Listing Of Over 300 Golf Courses In The State Of Victoria Australia"	1980	$15
Golf Courses on the G.W.R.:		
"Golf Courses On The G.W.R"	1923	$275
"Golf Courses Served By The G.W.R. and Where To Stay"	1934	$150
"Golf Courses Served By The G.W.R. and Where To Stay"	1937	$150
"Golf Courses Served By The G.W.R. and Where To Stay"	1939	$125
Golf Digest Almanac:		
"The Golf Digest Almanac 1984"	1984	$15
"The Golf Digest Almanac 1985"	1985	$10
Golf Digest Magazine:		
"15 Point Annual Check Up"	1983	$5
"80 5-Minute Golf Lessons"	1968	$10
"All About Putting"	1973	$15
"The Art Of Putting"	1976	$10
"The Best Of Golf Digest: The First 25 Years"	1975	$25
"Better Golf For Boys"	1965	$5
"Better Golf"	1974	$10
"Golf Digest's 20 Ways To Hit It Farther"	1982	$10
"Golf Digest's Pocket Golf Tips"	1977	$10
"Golf: A Golden Pocket Guide"	1968	$10
"How To Break 90 At Golf"	1967	$5
"Instant Golf Lessons"	1978	$10
"Gene Littler Presents 38 Checkpoints To Improve Your Swing"	1962	$15
"Arnold Palmer"	1967	$20
"Rand McNally Golf Course Guide"	1966	$15
"Three Pillars Of Power"	1965	$10
"Tips From The Tour"	1985	$5
"Travelers Guide To Golf"	1976	$10
Golf Fitness Instruction Course:		
"Golf Fitness Instruction Course"	1984	$10
Golf Foundation:		
"Making Room For Golf"	1963	$5
Golf Guidebook:		
"Golf Guidebook"	1965	$10

AUTHOR TITLE	PUB. DATE	VALUE
Golf Illustrated Magazine:		
"Fore! Golf Illustrated Annual"	1912	$275
Golf in Bermuda:		
"Golf In Bermuda"	1957	$15
Golf in Britain:		
"Golf In Britain"	1959	$20
Golf in California:		
"Golf In California"	1900	$350
Golf in Germany:		
"Golf In Germany"	1926	$120
Golf in Italy:		
"Golf In Italy"	1935	$110
Golf in Japan:		
"Golf In Japan"	1934	$200
Golf in Maine:		
"Golf In Maine Annual Guide"	1930	$90
Golf in Scandinavia:		
"Golf In Scandinavia"	1972	$15
Golf in Schools:		
"Golf In Schools"	1939	$15
Golf in Scotland:		
"Golf In Scotland"	1939	$150
Golf in Spain:		
"Golf In Spain"	1971	$15
Golf in The Sun:		
"Golf In The Sun"	1963	$15
Golf n Town and Country:		
"The Golf Courses in Angus and Kincardine"	1932	$35
Golf n Yorkshire:		
"Golf In Yorkshire"	1934	$10
Golf It Up:		
"Golf It Up! Tips For Juniors"	1983	$10
Golf Know How:		
"An Amazing Encyclopedia Of Golf Tips"	1957	$15
Golf Links of France:		
"The Golf Links Of France"	1930	$175
Golf Links on the Grand Rapids & Indiana Railroad:		
"Golf Links On The Grand Rapids & Indiana Railroad"	1900	$100
Golf Made Easy:		
"Golf Made Easy Through Scotch Secrets"	1936	$75
Golf Magazine:		
"America's Golf Book"	1970	$15
"Georgia Guide To Golf"	1970	$10
"Golf Magazine's Handbook Of Putting"	1973	$15
"Golf Magazine's Pro Pointers And Stroke Savers"	1964	$15
"Golf Magazine's Tips From The Teaching Pros"	1969	$15

AUTHOR TITLE	PUB. DATE	VALUE
Golf Magazine (cont.):		
"Golf Magazine's Winning Pointers From The Pros"	1965	$15
"Golf Magazine's Your Long Game"	1964	$15
"Golf Magazine's Your Short Game"	1962	$15
"The Greenbriar's Sam Snead Teaches Golf"	1966	$10
"Kwik Pro"	1963	$10
Golf Masters:		
"A Sure Way To Play Better Golf"	1940	$55
Golf Match Club:		
"Record Of Matches 1897-1908"	1909	$200
Golf Mind Vs. Business Mind:		
"The Neutro-Mental System For The Golfer"	1924	$30
Golf Par Excellence:		
"Golf Par Excellence 1980"	1980	$10
Golf Professional's Handbook:		
"Golf Professional's Handbook Of Business"	1932	$40
Golf Quotes:		
"Golf Quotes"	1984	$10
Golf Service Book:		
"Golf Service Book For Caddies and Members"	1922	$65
Golf Slang:		
"Golf Slang"	1978	$10
Golf Technique And Guide:		
"Golf Technique And Guide Of Southern California"	1940	$35
Golf Twaddle:		
"Golf Twaddle, Containing A Few Hints To Duffers"	1897	$325
Golf Where To Play And Where To Stay:		
"Golf: Where To Play And Where To Stay"	1983	$15
Golf World Magazine:		
"The Picadilly World Of Golf 1972"	1972	$20
"The Picadilly World Of Golf 1973-1974"	1973	$20
"Turf Mirth Compiled From The Pages Of Golf World"	1962	$10
"The World Of Golf 1973"	1973	$15
"The World Of Golf 1974"	1974	$15
"The World Of Golf 1975"	1975	$15
"The World Of Golf 1976"	1976	$15
Golfer's Digest:		
"Golfer's Digest Volume I"	1966	$15
"Golfer's Digest Volume II"	1967	$20
"Golfer's Digest Volume III"	1968	$15
"Golfer's Digest Volume IV"	1969	$15
"Golfer's Digest Volume V"	1970	$15
"Golfer's Digest Volume VI"	1971	$15
"Golfer's Digest Volume VII"	1972	$15

AUTHOR TITLE	PUB. DATE	VALUE
Golfers' Guide:		
"Golfers' Guide And Handbook"	1931	$60
"The Golfers' Guide And Official Handbook		
For Scotland"	1901	$675
"Golfers' Guide For The United Kingdom"	1895	$1,300
"Golfers' Guide To Georgia 1980"	1980	$15
"Golfers' Guide To Happy Holidays"	1924	$60
"Golfers' Guide To The Counties Of Kent,		
Surrey, Sussex"	1967	$20
"Golfers' Guide To The Game And Greens		
Of Scotland"	1894	$1,600
Golfer's Handbook:		
"Golfer's Handbook" First published	1899	$400
Golfers Magazine:		
"The Grip In Golf"	1923	$65
Golfers' Record:		
"Golfers' Record 1903"	1903	$250
Golfer's Trilogy:		
"The Golfer's Trilogy: The Driver Book;		
The Putter Book; The Wedge Book"	1965	$85
Golfers Yearbook:		
"Golfers Yearbook 1938"	1938	$50
"Golfers Yearbook 1939"	1939	$50
Golfing Annual:		
"Golfing Annual" First published	1888	$675
Golfing In Scotland:		
"Golfing In Scotland In 100 Holiday Resorts"	1936	$250
Golfing In Southern England:		
"Golfing In Southern England And On		
The Continent"	1931	$150
Golfing On Long Island:		
"Golfing On Long Island"	1902	$175
J.W.D. Goodban:		
"History Of The English Golf Union 1924-1984"	1984	$30
"Royal North Devon Golf Club, A Centenary		
Anthology 1864-1964"	1964	$295
Edward D. Goodman:		
"Meadowbrook Country Club, A Descriptive History		
From Its Beginnings In 1957 Through 1984"	1984	$15
Ross Goodner:		
"The 75 Year History		
Of Shinnecock Hills Golf Club"	1966	$250
"Golf's Greatest: The Legendary World Golf		
Hall Of Famers"	1978	$20
Richard D. Gordin and Roderick W. Meyers:		
"Golf Fundamentals"	1973	$10
Bob Gordon:		
"Basic Golf"	1972	$10

AUTHOR TITLE	PUB. DATE	VALUE
Charles A. Gordon:		
"The Gordon Caddie Guide"	1921	$75
Hugh H. Gordon:		
"Repair Your Own Golf Clubs"	1959	$20
Jack Gordon:		
"Ten Commandments Of The Golf Stroke"	1929	$75
Reprint	1969	$20
"Understandable Golf"	1926	$115
Gorham Golf Book:		
"The Gorham Golf Book"	1903	$975
Goring & Streatley Golf Club:		
"Goring And Streatley Golf Club"	1938	$60
Bea Gottlieb:		
"Golf For Southpaws"	1953	$15
"I Have The Secret Of Putting"	1965	$10
Stan Graff:		
"So You Want To Play Golf: The Golf Swing Explained Simply And Logically"	1974	$10
Herb Graffis:		
"Easy Cures For Your Ailing Golf"	1959	$15
"Esquire's World Of Golf"	1965	$25
"Fun And Larceny"	1936	$20
"The Golf Club Organizers Handbook"	1931	$35
"Golf Facilities"	1949	$15
"Golfing's Dictionary Of Golf Information"	1960	$15
"Golfing's Digest Of Golf Lessons"	1955	$20
"Golfing's Picture Story Of Good Golf"	1954	$20
"Golfing's Treasury Of Golf Tips"	1963	$15
"More Business For You"	1954	$15
"The PGA: The Official History Of The Professional Golfer's Association Of America"	1975	$15
"Planning The Professionals Shop"	1951	$15
"The Primer Of Good Golf"	1957	$15
"Simply Golf"	1959	$10
"Six Champions Tell You How"	1953	$25
"A Treasury Of Golf Tips"	1940	$40
"TWA And Your Golf Professional Want You To Have This In Flight Golf Lesson"	1971	$15
A.S. Graham:		
"Graham's Golf Club"	1965	$10
David Graham:		
"Your Way To Winning Golf"	1985	$12
Ian R. Graham:		
"The Merchants Of Edinburgh Golf Club 1907-1982"	1982	$15
Lou Graham:		
"Mastering Golf"	1978	$10

AUTHOR TITLE	PUB. DATE	VALUE
Grange-Over-Sands:		
"Grange-Over-Sands New Golf Club"	1951	$25
Arthur Grant:		
"Golf: The Pocket Professional"	1930	$60
Donald Grant:		
"Personal Memories Of Royal Dornoch Golf Club 1900-1925"	1978	$65
"Donald Ross Of Pinehurst and Royal Dornoch"	1973	$65
H.R.J. Grant and John F. Moreton:		
"Aspects Of Collecting Golf Books"	1996	$85
Charles Graves & Henry Longhurst:		
"Candid Caddies"	1935	$90
Robert Muir Graves:		
"A Practice Golf Facility For Athletic Fields"	1961	$15
Harry J. Gray:		
"Last Blast At Wethersfield"	1983	$10
Maxwell Gray:		
"The Great Refusal"	1906	$25
Michael Green:		
"The Art Of Coarse Golf"	1967	$10
Sandy Green:		
"Don'ts For Golfers"	1925	$65
Kell Greene:		
"The Swing Of Bobby Jones"	1931	$250
Wayne Greenhaw:		
"The Golfer"	1967	$15
Greenways:		
"Fifty Golf Hints For Beginners"	1928	$35
George W. Greenwood:		
"Golf Really Explained"	1926	$25
Gregory's Guide:		
"Gregory's Guide For Golfers"	1939	$35
Jim Gregson:		
"Golf Rules"	1984	$10
Gene Gregson:		
"Hogan The Man Who Played For Glory"	1978	$65
Malcolm Gregson:		
"Golf With Gregson"	1968	$15
Ian Greig:		
"The King's Club Murder"	1930	$35
"The Silver King Mystery"	1930	$35
Gren:		
"The Duffer's Guide To Golf"	1984	$10
Peter Gresswell:		
"Weekend Golfer"	1977	$10
Francis Grierson:		
"Boomerang Murder"	1951	$25

AUTHOR TITLE	PUB. DATE	VALUE
James Grierson:		
"Delineations Of Saint Andrews"	1807	$2,250
"Saint Andrews As It Was And It Is, Being The Third		
Edition Of Dr. Grierson's Delineations"	1838	$2,000
Marcus Griffin:		
"A History Of The Concord Golf Club 1899-1939"	1939	$60
E.M. Griffiths:		
"With Club And Caddie"	1909	$650
Bruce E. Griggs:		
"Golfgraphs"	1933	$50
R. Grimsdell:		
"Golf In South Africa"	1928	$275
Will Grimsley:		
"Golf: Its History, People and Events"	1966	$75
James P. Grode:		
"The Full Gospel Golfer As Revealed By		
The Holy Spirit"	1983	$10
Milton Gross:		
"Eighteen Holes In My Head"	1959	$10
Jack Grout:		
"Jack Grout's Golf Clinic"	1985	$10
"Let Me Teach You Golf As I Taught		
Jack Nicklaus"	1975	$15
Guaranteed Golf Lesson:		
"The Guaranteed Golf Lesson"	1968	$10
Guide To Golf Clubs:		
"A Guide To Golf Clubs In And Around London"	1955	$20
Guide To Golf Courses:		
"Guide To Golf Courses In The U.K."	1973	$15
David Guiney:		
"The Dunlop Book Of Golf"	1973	$10
Ralph Guldahl:		
"Grove Your Golf"	1939	$125
Guldahl, Revolta, Sarazen, and Shute:		
"Four Masters"	1937	$55
Signed By Guldahl		$150
Bill Gukkick:		
"The Country Club Caper"	1971	$20
Geoffrey Gullik:		
"History Of Lindrick Golf Club 1891-1951"	1951	$55
Philip Gundelfinger Jr.:		
"Golf's Who's Who: Records Of The Pros"	1958	$15
Harry E. Gunn:		
"How To Play Golf With Your Wife And Survive"	1976	$10
Lealand Gustavson:		
"Enjoy Your Golf"	1954	$15
T.H.:		
"A Barton Ballad"	1918	$50

AUTHOR TITLE	PUB. DATE	VALUE
Harry J. Haas:		
"A Handbook For Caddies And Members"	1922	$125
"Golf Service Book For Caddies And Members"	1938	$50
James Haber:		
"Golf Made Easy: How To Achieve A Consistently		
Effective Golf Swing"	1974	$15
"Mastering The Art Of Winning Golf"	1976	$15
John C. Hackbarth:		
"The Key To Better Golf"	1929	$40
Buddy Hackett:		
"The Truth About Golf And Other Lies"	1968	$10
Bob Hackey:		
"Golf Annual '74: World Golf		
Hall Of Fame Edition"	1974	$20
Stewart Hackney:		
"Carnoustie Links: Courses and Players"	1989	$25
Haddington Municipal:		
"Haddington Municipal Golf Course"	1953	$15
Walter Hagen:		
"Golf Clubs And How To Use Them"	1929	$85
"The Walter Hagen Story"	1956	$50
Signed By Hagen		$750
Memorial Tournament Reprint	1977	$45
"The How And Why Of Golf"	1932	$135
James & Lynn Hahn:		
"Nancy Lopez, Golfing Pioneer"	1979	$15
"Patty! The Sports Career Of Patricia Berg"	1981	$15
Paul Hahn:		
"From The Pen And Camera Of Paul Hahn"	1965	$10
"Paul Hahn Shows You How To Play		
Trouble Shots"	1965	$10
"Links Logic"	1951	$15
Paul Hahn Jr.:		
"No Trick To It"	1975	$10
Thomas Haliburton:		
"Rabbit Into Tiger"	1964	$15
Halifax Golf And Country Club:		
"Programme Commemorating The Official Opening Of The		
New Course, Halifax Golf And Country Club" 1970		$15
Holworthy Hall:		
"Dormie One, And Other Golf Stories"	1917	$375
John H. Hall:		
"The Victoria Club 1903-1978"	1978	$20
Ray Hall:		
"A Golf Plan For Schools"	1952	$15
William Hallberg:		
"The Rub Of The Green"	1988	$15

AUTHOR TITLE	PUB. DATE	VALUE
A.E. Hallem:		
"Straight Road To Golf"	1928	$75
B.C. Hamilton:		
"Golf: A Treatise On The Royal And Ancient Game"	1947	$45
David Hamilton:		
"Early Golf At Edinburgh & Leith: The Account Books Of Sir John Foulis Of Ravelston"	1988	$150
"Early Aberdeen Golf, Golfing Small Talk In 1636"	1985	$95
"Early Golf At St. Andrews"	1986	$95
"Early Golf In Glasgow 1589-1787"	1985	$65
Signed By Hamilton		$275
"The Good Golf Guide To Scotland"	1982	$10
"John Kerr, The Sporting Padre..."	1989	$210
"The South Sea Brithers" Signed By Hamilton	1992	$150
Eddie Hamilton:		
"Golfing Gimmicks"	1958	$10
Edward A. Hamilton and Charles Preston:		
"Golfing America"	1958	$40
Rory Hamilton:		
"A Golfer's Guide To Wee Places: Luffness, Gullane, Muirfield"	1980	$40
J.A. Hammerton:		
"Mr. Punch's Golf Stories Told By His Merry Men"	1909	$95
"Mr. Punch On The Links"	1935	$75
"The Rubaiyat Of A Golfer"	1946	$35
Daryn Hammond:		
"The Golf Swing, The Ernest Jones Method"	1920	$95
Ike S. Handy:		
"How To Hit A Golf Ball Straight"	1967	$10
"It's The Dammed Ball"	1951	$15
Charles Steadman Hanks:		
"Hints To Golfers"	1913	$95
Chris Hannan:		
"Outlands Golf Club Golden Anniversary 1931-1981"	1981	$15
Sebastian Hannay:		
"All Square: A Light Hearted Rhyming Guide To The Rules Of Golf And Other Verses"	1980	$10
George Harbottle:		
"The Northumberland Golf Club Story"	1978	$15
Harburn Golf Club:		
"Harburn Golf Club"	1939	$35
Byron Harcke:		
"Fore: Golf Fundamentals"	1960	$10
Michael Hardcastle:		
"Aim For The Flagg"	1969	$10

AUTHOR TITLE	PUB. DATE	VALUE
Merrill D. Hardy and Eleanor Walsh:		
"Golf"	1980	$10
Burnham Hare:		
"The Golfing Swing Simplified And Its Mechanism		
Correctly Explained"	1913	$65
J.R. Harker:		
"The Finchley Golf Club"	1929	$55
Bob Harlow:		
"Golf State, North Carolina"	1953	$15
"True Golf Facts"	1940	$70
Paul Harney:		
"Golf Is A Simple Game"	1972	$10
"How To Putt A Flip Vision Golf Manual"	1965	$20
Harpenden Golf Club:		
"Harpenden Golf Club, 1894-1954"	1954	$20
Edward Harriman:		
"The Story Of Eastward Ho"	1978	$15
Mark G. Harris:		
"New Angles On Putting And Chip Shots"	1940	$65
Richard Harris:		
"Drive For Show Putt For Dough"	1972	$10
"How To Take The Fun Out Of Golf"	1970	$10
Robert Harris:		
"Proposed New Rules Of Golf A Threat		
To The Game As A Sport"	1949	$45
"Sixty Years Of Golf"	1953	$175
Al Hart:		
"Golfun: A Humorous Approach To		
A Serious Subject"	1966	$10
Ken Hart-Thomast:		
"Minehead And West Somerset Golf Club		
1882-1982"	1982	$15
George Hartley:		
"A History Of St. George's Hill Golf Club		
1913-1983"	1983	$45
John C. Harvey:		
"The Golfer's Repair And Maintenance		
Handbook"	1984	$15
Sam Hasegawa:		
"Johnny Miller"	1975	$10
Peter Haslam:		
"The World Of Scottish Golf"	1985	$15
John Hassall:		
"The Seven Ages Of Golf"	1899	$1,200
H.A. Hattstrom:		
"Golf After Forty"	1946	$20
"The In-Line Method Of Putting and		
Approaching"	1959	$15
"On And Off The Green"	1955	$10

AUTHOR TITLE	PUB. DATE	VALUE
Arnold Haultain:		
"The Mystery Of Golf" A Limited First Edition	1908	$1,250
Second Edition	1914	$225
Reprint	1965	$75
Ken Hawkes:		
"BBC Book Of Golf"	1975	$10
Rodney Hawkins:		
"Golf At Letchworth"	1985	$10
F.W. Hawtree:		
"The Golf Course: Planning, Design,		
Construction, & Maintenance"	1983	$35
Fred Hawtree:		
"Colt & Co; A Biographical Study Of Henry Shapland Colt		
1869-1951 With His Partners C.H. Alison; J.S.F. Morrison		
and Dr. Mackenzie" Signed By Hawtree	1991	$195
"Colt & Co; Golf Course Architects..."	1991	$75
Alex Hay:		
"The Golf Manual"	1980	$10
"The Handbook Of Golf"	1984	$10
"The Mechanics Of Golf"	1979	$10
"Skills & Tactics Of Golf"	1980	$10
Alex Hay and Bill Robertson:		
"Young Golfer"	1980	$10
Hayes, Evans, and Isaac:		
"The Care Of The Golf Course"	1992	$40
Hayling Golf Club:		
"Hayling Golf Club Centenary 1883-1983"	1983	$15
Sandra Haynie:		
"Golf: A Natural Course For Women"	1975	$20
Abel Haywood:		
"The Manchester Golf Club"	1909	$950
John C. Haywood:		
"The Silver Creek"	1908	$35
Ann Hazell:		
"A Slice Of History, Blackwood Golf Club		
1930-1980"	1979	$15
Ronald Heager:		
"Kings Of Club"	1968	$25
Kay Healey:		
"Heritage Of Oakland Hills As Of 1982"	1982	$75
Ian Heath:		
"The Golden Rules Of Golf"	1984	$10
Peter Heath:		
"Towards One Hundred Years: Edgbaston		
Golf Club 1896-1996"	1996	$45
Michael Hebron:		
"See And Feel The Inside Move The Outside"	1984	$10

AUTHOR TITLE	PUB. DATE	VALUE
Phyllis F. Heck:		
"History Of The Dayton Country Club		
1896-1976"	1976	$20
Genevieve Hecker:		
"Golf For Women"	1904	$1,000
Jack G. Heise:		
"How You Can Play Better Golf Using		
Self-Hypnosis"	1961	$15
"Super Golf With Self-Hypnosis"	1962	$20
Eleanor E. Helme:		
"After The Ball"	1931	$125
"The Best Of Golf"	1925	$60
"Family Golf"	1938	$95
"The Lady Golfer's Tip Book"	1923	$175
Myra B. Helmer and Inez L. Klumph:		
"Father Gander Golf Book"	1909	$250
Charles T. Helmes and Kenneth W. Price:		
"Waccabuc Country Club: Seventy Five Years		
Of History"	1983	$35
Henderson's Photographic:		
"Henderson's Photographic Golf Instructor"	1923	$30
Ian T. Henderson and David I. Stirk:		
"The Compleat Golfer: An Illustrated History Of		
The Royal And Ancient Game"	1982	$60
"Golf In The Making"	1979	$150
Special Edition Signed	1982	$550
"The Heritage Of Golf: An Illustrated History"	1985	$60
"Royal Blackheath"	1981	$100
Signed By Both		$275
"Shortspoon-Major F. P. Hopkins 1830-1913		
Golfing Artist and Journalist"	1984	$175
J. Lindsay Henderson:		
"The Records Of The Panmure Golf Club"	1926	$350
L.J. Henderson:		
"Golf By The Masters"	1950	$20
"The P.G.A. Golfer's Guide"	1949	$20
Robert W. Henderson:		
"Line Of Flight, A Manual Of Golf"	1939	$55
J. Hendren:		
"The Knock Golf Club, A History 1895-1982"	1982	$20
W. Garden Hendry:		
"The Dynamic Anatomy Of The Golf Swing, A Scientific		
Approach To Improvement At Golf"	1985	$15
Henly Golf Club:		
"Henly Golf Club"	1916	$175
Harold Henning:		
"Drive Around Southern Africa With		
Harold Henning"	1974	$15

AUTHOR TITLE	PUB. DATE	VALUE
Harold Henning (cont.):		
"Harold Henning's Golfer's Guide Of Southern Africa"	1984	$15
Bill F. Hensley:		
"North Carolina-Golf State U.S.A."	1953	$15
Tom Hepburb and Selwyn Jacobson:		
"America's Most Difficult Golf Holes"	1983	$20
"Australia's Most Difficult Golf Holes"	1982	$25
"Canada's Most Difficult Golf Holes"	1983	$20
"Even More Of Australia's Most Difficult Golf Holes"	1983	$25
"Great Britain And Ireland's Most Difficult Golf Holes"	1983	$20
"Great Golf Holes Of New Zealand"	1981	$20
"Great Golf Holes Of South Africa"	1984	$25
"New Zealand's Toughest Golf Courses Book II"	1983	$25
"South East Asia's Toughest Golf Holes"	1984	$20
"The World's 72 Toughest Golf Holes"	1984	$20
Sandy Herd:		
"My Golfing Life"	1923	$325
Hergenroeder, Wright, and Hillum:		
"The Conduct Compendium Of Golf"	1979	$10
Roger F. Hermanson:		
"The Rules Of Golf In Programmed Form"	1968	$10
Charles Herndon:		
"Golf Made Easier"	1930	$30
Donald Herold:		
"Adventures In Golf"	1965	$10
"Love That Golf"	1952	$10
Frederick W. Hetzel:		
"You Can Improve Your Golf With A Sling-Master"	1956	$10
Karla L. Heuer:		
"Golf Course, A Guide To Analysis and Valuation"	1980	$10
Cyril Hewerston:		
"Walton Heath Golf Club, The Story Of The First 75 Years, 1904-1979"	1979	$25
Paul L. Hexter:		
"You Can Play Golf Forever"	1979	$10
John Heywood:		
"John Heywood's Guide To Lancashire, Cheshire, Derbyshire, Yorkshire And North Wales Golf"	1920	$60
May Hezlet:		
"Ladies Golf"	1904	$675
Angus Hibbard:		
"Golf And The Glen View Club"	1970	$15
Keith C. Hick:		
"The Hesketh Golf Club 1885-1985"	1985	$50

AUTHOR TITLE	PUB. DATE	VALUE
Darrell Hickok:		
"Play Better Golf"	1966	$10
Elizabeth Mary Hicks:		
"Fundamentals Of Golf"	1948	$15
Elizabeth Mary Hicks and Ellen J. Griffin:		
"Golf Manual For Teachers"	1949	$15
Highland Country Club:		
"Highland Country Club 50th Anniversary 1901-1951"	1951	$25
Walter J. Highman:		
"A Heavenly Meeting, A Sequel"	1925	$20
Dave Hill and Nick Seitz:		
"Teed Off"	1977	$15
J.C.H. Hill:		
"The Lyre On The Links And Other Verses"	1935	$250
Hillerich & Bradsby:		
"Grand Slam Of Golf Classics"	1931	$45
Gerald Hillinthorn:		
"Your First Game Of Golf"	1891	$1,500
A.J. Hills:		
"Golf At Jasper Park"	1948	$200
Hilton Park Golf Club:		
"Hilton Park Golf Club Jubilee Year 1927-1977"	1977	$25
Harold H. Hilton:		
"Modern Golf"	1913	$125
"My Golfing Reminiscences"	1907	$475
Harold Hilton & Garden G. Smyth:		
"The Royal And Ancient Game Of Golf"		
Limited Edition Of 100	1912	$2,750
Limited Edition Of 900	1912	$1,250
Maurice Hime:		
"The Unlucky Golfer: His Handbook"	1904	$125
Darce Hindle:		
"Links Of Love, A Story Of The Riviera"	1904	$275
Geneive Hingst and Mary E. McKee:		
"The Game Of Golf; Programmed Instructions Of Playing Procedures"	1968	$15
Ruth Hirst and Jean Lockwood:		
"Meltham Golf Club"	1982	$15
Thomas K. Hitch and Mary I. Kuranote:		
"Ailae Country Club, The First Half Century"	1981	$15
Jimmy Hitchcock:		
"Master Golfer"	1967	$10
Michael Hobbs:		
"50 Masters Of Golf"	1983	$20
"Golf For The Connoisseur: A Golfing Anthology"	1979	$20
"Golf To Remember"	1978	$15

AUTHOR TITLE	PUB. DATE	VALUE
Michael Hobbs(cont.):		
"The Golfer's Companion"	1988	$20
Signed By Hobbs		$35
"Great Opens: Historic British And American		
Championships 1913-1975"	1976	$20
"In Celebration Of Golf"	1982	$15
"The Ryder Cup: The Illustrated History"		
Limited Edition	1989	$250
William G. Hobson:		
"It Ain't Necessarily So"	1959	$10
Howard H. Hoddinott:		
"Kingsknowe Golf Club Limited 1908 -1983"	1983	$15
Bert Hodson:		
"Your Best Way To Play The Chigwell		
Golf Course"	1952	$25
Arthur Hoffman:		
"The Golfer's Catalog"	1984	$10
Bob Hoffman:		
"The Functional Isometrics Contraction For Golf"	1963	$10
Davy Hoffman:		
"America's Greatest Golf Courses"	1987	$25
Ben Hogan:		
"Five Lessons: The Modern Fundamentals		
Of Golf"	1957	$75
Signed By Hogan		$475
"Here's Your Free Golf Lesson"	1940	$65
"Power Golf"	1948	$40
Signed By Hogan		$450
Ben Hogan And Others:		
"The Complete Guide To Golf"	1955	$35
Hollingworth, Birmingham, and Pender:		
"Golf: Par Fore"	1982	$10
Billy Hon:		
"Prominent Golfers In Caricature"	1930	$55
Richard W. Hooper:		
"The Game Of Golf In East Africa"	1953	$900
Brad Hoot:		
"Golf Is An Easy Game"	1983	$10
Bob Hope:		
"Bob Hope's Confessions Of A Hooker"	1985	$5
Anthony Hopkins:		
"Songs For Swinging Golfers"	1981	$5
Frank Hopkins:		
"Golf Holes They Talk About" Signed	1927	$475
John Hopkins:		
"Beacon Golfing Handbook"	1983	$10
"Nick Faldo In Perspective"	1985	$15

AUTHOR TITLE	PUB. DATE	VALUE
Cecil Hopkinson:		
"Collecting Golf Books 1743-1938"	1938	$1,500
Reprint	1980	$375
John Hornabrook:		
"Golden Years Of New Zealand Golf"	1967	$45
D. Hornady:		
"The History Of The Seaton Carew Golf Club 1874-1974"	1974	$40
W.B.J. Horne:		
"The History Of The Royal Wimbleton Golf Club 1865-1949"	1949	$150
Paul Hornung:		
"The Story Of Muirfield Village Golf Club and The Memorial Tournament"	1985	$20
Chester Horton:		
"Better Golf"	1930	$35
"Golf: The Long Game"	1969	$10
"Golf: The Short Game"	1970	$10
"Chester Hortons Golf Lesson"	1925	$45
Howard C. Hosmer:		
"From Little Acorns, The Story Of Oak Hill 1901-1976"	1977	$60
"Through Half A Century"	1945	$60
"The Year Of The Diamond, Being An Account Of The First Seventy-Five Years Of The Country Club Of Rochester"	1971	$125
Horace L. Hotchkiss:		
"Origin And Organization Of The Senior's Tournament"	1922	$50
George Houghton:		
"Addict In Bunkerland"	1962	$20
"An Addicts Guide To British Golf"	1959	$75
"Believe It Or Not-That's Golf"	1974	$15
"Confessions Of A Golf Addict: An Anthology Of Carefree Notes And Drawing"	1959	$35
"Confessions Of A Golf Addict"	1952	$35
"Full Confessions Of A Golf Addict"	1966	$15
"Golf Addict Among The Irish"	1965	$20
"Golf Addict Among The Scots"	1967	$20
"Golf Addict Goes East"	1967	$15
"Golf Addict In Gaucho Land"	1970	$15
"Golf Addict Invades Wales"	1969	$20
"Golf Addict Strike Again"	1963	$15
"Golf Addict Visits The USA"	1956	$20
"Golf Addicts Galore"	1968	$15
"Golf Addicts Omnibus: The Best Of George Houghton"	1966	$45
"Golf Addicts On Parade"	1959	$15
"Golf Addicts Through The Ages"	1956	$20

AUTHOR TITLE	PUB. DATE	VALUE
George Houghton(cont.):		
"Golf Addicts To The Fore"	1985	$15
"Golf On My Pillow"	1958	$15
"Golf Visits"	1955	$25
"Golf With A Whippy Shaft"	1971	$55
"Golfer's ABC"	1953	$25
"Golfers In Orbit"	1968	$15
"Golfers Treasury: A Personal Anthology"	1964	$30
"How To Be A Golf Addict"	1971	$15
"I Am A Golf Widow"	1961	$15
"Just A Friendly ... A Book Of Golf Addict Cartoons"	1973	$20
"More Confessions Of A Golf Addict"	1954	$20
"Portrait Of A Golf Addict"	1960	$15
"Secret Diary Of A Golf Addict's Caddie"	1964	$20
"The Truth About Golf Addicts"	1957	$15
Archie Hovanesian:		
"Golf Is Mental"	1960	$10
How to Be a Good Caddie:		
"How To Be A Good Caddie"	1952	$20
How to Cut Strokes:		
"How To Cut Strokes From Your Score"	1968	$10
How to Improve Your Golf:		
"How To Improve Your Golf: Lessons By British Masters"	1925	$40
How to Play the Old Course:		
"How To Play The Old Course, St. Andrews"	1932	$150
Robert E. Howard:		
"Lessons From Great Golfers"	1924	$75
Audrey Howell:		
"Harry Vardon: The Revealing Story Of A Champion Golfer"	1991	$30
Edmund Hoyle:		
"Hoyles Games Improved"	1790	$1,250
American Edition	1814	$475
Hubbard Trail Country Club:		
"Hubbard Trail Country Club 50 Years 1925-1975"	1975	$15
D.C.N. Hudson:		
"Your Book Of Golf"	1967	$10
Brian Huggett:		
"Better Golf"	1964	$15
Percy Huggins:		
"The Golfer's Miscellany"	1971	$10
"Troon Golf Club"	1972	$15
E.H. Hughes:		
"The History Of The Spokane Country Club, 75th Anniversary"	1973	$35

AUTHOR TITLE	PUB. DATE	VALUE
Henry Hughes:		
"Golf For The Late Beginner"	1911	$40
"Golf Practice For Players Of Limited Leisure"	1913	$40
Margaret Hughes:		
"A Round With Darwin"	1984	$20
W.E. Hughes:		
"Chronicles Of The Blackheath Golfers"	1897	$2,500
Robert H.H. Hugman:		
"Putting Know-How"	1963	$10
Gerald Hulme:		
"Cheadle Golf Club 1885-1985"	1985	$15
Ronald W. Hulse:		
"Dinsdale Spa Golf Club"	1960	$15
"Hexham Golf Club"	1960	$15
Humorist On Golf:		
"The Humorist On Golf"	1930	$65
Eric Humphreys:		
"The Dunlop Golfer's Companion"	1977	$10
Orrin T. Hunt:		
"The Joy Of Golf"	1977	$10
David S. Hunter:		
"Golf Simplified"	1921	$85
Mac Hunter:		
"Golf For Beginners"	1973	$15
N.C. Hunter:		
"The Losing Hazard"	1951	$20
Robert Hunter:		
"The Links"	1926	$650
Robert E. Hunter:		
"Royal & Ancient Game Of Golf, A Golf Diary Of 72 Years"	1966	$15
Willie Hunter:		
"The Easyway To Winning Golf"	1935	$125
Mervyn J. Huston:		
"Golf And Murphy's Law"	1981	$20
"Great Golf Humor, A Collection Of Stories & Articles"	1977	$15
Horace G. Hutchinson:		
"Aspects Of Golf"	1900	$3,200
"The Book Of Golf and Golfers"	1899	$450
Reprint	1900	$275
"British Golf Links, A Short Account Of The Leading Golf Links Of The United Kingdom"	1897	$975
"Bert Edward, The Golf Caddie"	1903	$500
"Famous Golf Links"	1891	$1,500
"Fifty Years Of Golf"	1919	$525
USGA Reprint	1985	$95

AUTHOR TITLE	PUB. DATE	VALUE
Horace G. Hutchinson(cont.):		
"Golf"	1890	$375
Reprint	1892	$275
Limited Edition Large Paper Copy	1892	$1,500
"Golf, A Complete History Of The Game"	1900	$200
"Golf Greens and Greenskeeping"	1906	$750
"Golfing"	1901	$200
"Golfing - The Oval Series Of Games"	1893	$575
"A Golfing Pilgrim On Many Links"	1898	$525
"Hints On The Game Of Golf"	1886	$750
Signed By Hutchinson		$2,800
"The Lost Golfer"	1930	$2,200
"The New Book Of Golf"	1912	$400
Jock Hutchison:		
"Better Golf"	1928	$75
E.J. Hyde:		
"The Story Of The Pennant Hills Golf Club 1922-1959"	1959	$40
Theo B. Hyslop:		
"Mental Handicaps In Golf"	1927	$85
Grace Iarrobino and Elayne Slaughter:		
"The Golfer's Cookbook"	1968	$15
Clete Idoux:		
"Play Better Golf"	1966	$15
Ilfracombe Golf Club:		
"Ilfracombe Golf Club"	1963	$20
Ignotus:		
"Golf In A Nutshell"	1919	$95
James Igoe Jr.:		
"Hooks And Slices"	1950	$20
Betty P. Imhoff:		
"History Of The Country Club Of York 1899-1975"	1975	$15
Indian Valley Country Club:		
"Indian Valley Country Club 1952-1977"	1977	$15
John Ingham:		
"Best Golfing Jokes"	1969	$10
Michael Innes:		
"An Awkward Lie"	1971	$10
Instant Golf:		
"How To Do It In Slow Motion"	1973	$10
Interesting Facts:		
"Interesting Facts For Every Golfer"	1932	$45
Inverness Club:		
"Inverness Club"	1979	$15
Inverness Golf Club:		
"Inverness Golf Club 1883-1983"	1983	$15
Ireland:		
"Ireland: A Golfer's Paradise"	1968	$20

AUTHOR TITLE	PUB. DATE	VALUE
Irish Golf Courses:		
"Irish Golf Courses 1983/84"	1984	$10
Hale Irwin:		
"Play Better Golf"	1980	$10
J.F. Irwin:		
"Golf Sketches"	1892	$1,250
N.L. Irwin:		
"St. Georges Golf And Country Club 50 Years		
1929-1979"	1979	$10
Kenneth Isenogle:		
"Anatomy Of Right Handed Golf"	1980	$10
Isle Of Purbeck:		
"Isle Of Purbeck Golf Club"	1984	$10
Isles Of Scilly Golf Club:		
"Isles Of Scilly Golf Club"	1950	$20
Cho Ito:		
"Golfers Treasures"	1925	$1,275
Signed By Ito		$1,650
J.A.C.K.:		
"Golf In The Year 2000"	1892	$2,500
Reprint	1984	$65
Tony Jacklin:		
"100 Jacklin Golf Strips From The Daily Express"	1970	$20
"Golf Step By Step"	1969	$15
"Golf With Tony Jacklin"	1969	$10
"Jacklin: The Champion's Own Story"	1970	$15
"Tony Jacklin, The First Forty Years"	1985	$15
"Tony Jacklin's Guide To Professional Golf"	1970	$10
"The Ryder Cup '85"	1985	$25
Tony Jacklin and Peter Dobereiner:		
"Jacklin's Golf Secrets"	1983	$15
Allan Jackson:		
"The British Professional Golfers 1887-1930		
A Register"	1994	$45
Barney Jackson:		
"History Of The Canadian Open At Glenn Abbey"	1984	$15
David Jackson:		
"Golf Songs And Recitations"	1886	$6,000
Robert B. Jackson:		
"Supermex: The Lee Trevino Story"	1973	$20
John Jacobs:		
"Another Consultation With Doctor Golf"	1965	$10
"Golf"	1963	$10
"Golf Doctor"	1979	$10
"John Jacobs Analyses Golf's Superstars"	1974	$15
"Play Better Golf"	1972	$15
"Play Better Golf With John Jacobs"	1969	$15
"Practical Golf"	1972	$15
"Quick Cures For Weekend Golfers"	1979	$10

AUTHOR TITLE	PUB. DATE	VALUE
Linda Jacobs:		
"Laura Baugh: Golf's Golden Girl"	1975	$10
"Lee Elder, The Daring Dream"	1976	$15
"Ellen The Expert"	1974	$10
James River Country Club:		
"James River Country Club Commemorating		
The Fiftieth Anniversary"	1982	$15
"James River Country Club		
Twenty-Fifth Anniversary"	1957	$20
Francis James:		
"Brancepeth Castle Golf Club"	1949	$20
"The Hesketh Golf Club"	1951	$20
"Llandudo Golf Club"	1960	$20
"The Okehampton Golf Club"	1951	$15
"Warren Golf Club"	1960	$15
Joseph James:		
"How To Give Up Golf"	1970	$10
"Kill It Before It Moves"	1961	$10
"Quiet On The Tee"	1963	$10
"So You're Taking Up Golf?"	1969	$10
"What It Is, Is Golf"	1965	$10
Sid James:		
"From Tee To Cup"	1955	$15
Don January and Al Carrell:		
"Golf Is A Funny Game"	1967	$10
T.G. Jarrett:		
"A History Of The New Club, St. Andrews"	1982	$20
Dan Jenkins:		
"Dead Solid Perfect"	1974	$45
"The Dogged Victims Of Inexorable Fate"	1970	$55
"Sports Illustrated's: The Best 18 Golf Holes		
In America"	1966	$40
L.C. Jenkins:		
"Parkstone: A History Of Its Golf Club"	1987	$40
Albert Jenny:		
"The Royal Game: Stories Around A Little		
White Ball"	1962	$10
Owen Fox Jerome:		
"The Golf Club Murder"	1929	$85
J.C. Jessop:		
"Teach Yourself Golf"	1950	$20
Carol C. Johnson and Ann C. Johnstone:		
"Golf: A Positive Approach"	1975	$10
Johnson, Oliver and Shields:		
"Golf"	1979	$10
Hank Johnson:		
"End Your Fear Of Sand Forever"	1981	$10

AUTHOR TITLE	PUB. DATE	VALUE
J.W. Johnson:		
"A Wonderful Golf Score"	1920	$75
Owen Johnson:		
"Even Threes"	1930	$60
William O. Johnson and Nancy P. Williams:		
"Whatta Gal: The Babe Didrickson Story"	1977	$20
Willis Johnson Jr.:		
"Peachtree Golf Club"	1978	$120
Alastair J. Johnston:		
"The Clapcott Papers"	1985	$150
Aistair J. Johnston and Joseph Murdock:		
"C.B. Clapcott and His Golf Library"	1988	$85
A.C. Jones:		
"The Royal Country Down Golf Club"	1970	$40
Ernest Jones:		
"Swing The Clubhead"	1952	$40
Signed By Jones		$145
"Swing's The Thing In Golf"	1940	$25
Ernest Jones And Innes Brown:		
"Swinging Into Golf"	1937	$35
Molly S. Jones:		
"Golden Jubilee"	1958	$15
Rees L. Jones & Guy L. Rando:		
"Golf Course Development"	1974	$20
Robert Jones:		
"British Golf Odyssey"	1977	$25
"Gulls On The Golf Course"	1975	$20
"Sherlock Holmes, The Golfer"	1981	$15
Robert E. Jones:		
"A History Of The Missoula Country Club"	1979	$15
Robert Trent Jones:		
"Description Of The Golden Horseshoe Golf Course		
At Williamsburg Inn"	1965	$20
"Golf Course Architecture"	1938	$875
"Great Golf Stories"	1982	$20
Robert Tyre Jones Jr.:		
"Golf Bobby Jones-Out Of The Rough And Putt"	1930	$325
"Golf Is My Game"	1960	$75
"Golf Shots By Bobby Jones-Brassie And		
Iron Shots"	1930	$325
"Golf Shots By Bobby Jones-Driver And		
Mashie Shots"	1930	$325
"How A College Or School Should Publicize The Showing		
Of A Motion Picture On Golf"	1936	$250
"How To Organize Golfers In A Municipality"	1936	$250
"How To Play Golf"	1929	$375
"How To Run A Golf Tournament"	1936	$375
"Bobby Jones On The Basic Golf Swing"	1969	$60

AUTHOR TITLE	PUB. DATE	VALUE
Robert Tyre Jones Jr. (cont.):		
"Bobby Jones On Golf"	1930	$375
"My Twelve Most Difficult Shots"	1929	$375
"Rights And Wrongs Of Golf"	1935	$150
"A Short Love Story: The People Of St. Andrews And Robert T. (Bobby) Jones Jr."	1973	$75
"Some Tips From Bobby Jones"	1935	$375
"Suggestions How To See The Masters Tournament"	1949	$250
Robert Tyre Jones Jr. & O.B. Keeler:		
"Down The Fairway"	1927	$250
Signed By Jones		$3,500
Robert Tyre Jones Jr. and Harold Lowe:		
"Group Instructions In Golf"	1939	$200
Robert Tyre Jones and Clifford Roberts:		
"The Masters Tournament"	1952	$150
Tony Jones:		
"A Brief History Of Abergele And Pensarn Golf Club 75th Anniversary Year 1910-1985"	1985	$20
G. Gunby Jordan:		
"Caddies"	1987	$20
Harry H. Jordan:		
"Ye Golf Booke"	1928	$275
Alex Josey:		
"Golf In Singapore"	1969	$20
H. Stanley Judd:		
"How To Play Golf The Easy Way"	1980	$10
John Junkermeier:		
"The Glorious Past Of Stockdale Country Club"	1978	$15
Nancy Jupp:		
"Nairn Golf Club"	1957	$20
Liz Kahn:		
"Tony Jacklin: The Price Of Success"	1979	$15
Marilyn M. Kahn:		
"Inwood Country Club Seventy-Fifth Anniversary 1901-1976"	1976	$25
Kane, Kane Jr., and MacDonald:		
"Tedesco Country Club 1903-1978"	1978	$25
Jim Kaplan:		
"Hillerich & Bradsby: History - Catalogs"	1982	$15
"MacGregor Golf: History - Catalogs"	1980	$15
"Wilson Golf: History - Catalogs"	1981	$15
Karen Country Club:		
"Karen Country Club, Past and Future"	1978	$10
Peter V. Karpovich:		
"A Study Of Some Physiological Effects Of Golf"	1928	$35
Shirli Kaskie:		
"A Woman's Golf Game"	1982	$10

AUTHOR TITLE	PUB. DATE	VALUE
James E. Kavanagh:		
"Golf Made Easy"	1953	$15
L.V. Kavanaugh:		
"The History Of Golf In Canada"	1973	$40
Thomas Kay:		
"The Prestwick St. Nicholas Golf Club"	1947	$85
Christopher Keane:		
"The Tour"	1974	$15
Tom Kearney:		
"A Funny Thing Happened"	1985	$10
Kebo Valley Club:		
"The Kebo Valley Sixtieth Anniversary Year 1888-1948"	1948	$75
O.B. Keeler:		
"The Autobiography Of The Average Golfer"	1925	$250
"The Boy's Life Of Bobby Jones"	1931	$300
"Golf In North Carolina"	1938	$150
Francis B. Keene:		
"Lyrics Of The Links"	1923	$375
Nicholas Keith:		
"Golf: Sportsviewers Guide"	1984	$15
Homer Kelley:		
"The Golfing Machine: The Star System Of Golf"	1969	$40
James E. Kelley:		
"Minnesota Golf: 75 Years Of Tournament History"	1976	$20
G.M. Kelly:		
"Golf In New Zealand; A Centennial History"	1971	$45
Kelso Golf Club:		
"Kelso Golf Club Bazaar Cookery Book"	1914	$475
Charles F. Kemp:		
"Smart Golf: A Study Of The Mental And Emotional Side Of Golf"	1974	$10
"The World Of Golf & The Game Of Life"	1978	$10
Kenilworth Golf Club:		
"Kenilworth Golf Club"	1951	$15
Mrs. Edward Kennard:		
"The Golf Lunatic And His Cycling Wife"	1902	$500
"The Sorrows Of A Golfers Wife"	1896	$650
Daniel E. Kennedy:		
"Golf In Sapphira's Days"	1910	$80
Des Kennedy and Harry Georgiades:		
"A Slice Of Fun"	1965	$10
Patrick Kennedy:		
"Golf Clubs Trademarks: American 1898-1930"	1984	$20
Don Kennington:		
"The Source Book Of Golf"	1981	$40

AUTHOR TITLE	PUB. DATE	VALUE
John H. Kent:		
"Rhythm Golf"	1958	$10
Kenwood Golf And Country Club:		
"Kenwood 50 Years 1928-1978"	1978	$15
Michael Kenyon:		
"The Shooting Of Dan McGrew"	1972	$10
Barbara K. Keogh and Carol E. Smith:		
"Personal Par: A Psychological System Of Golf		
For Women"	1985	$15
Shirley K. Kerns:		
"Fifty Years Of Brae Burn 1897-1947"	1947	$95
John Kerr:		
"The Golf Book Of East Lothian"	1896	$1,500
"The Golf Song Book"	1903	$1,200
Kaye W. Kessler:		
"The Golf Club"	1982	$10
Bob Kiehl:		
"Duffer Golf Or How To Break 100"	1979	$10
Thomas Kiernan:		
"Wood - Irons"	1981	$15
Killarney Golf And Fishing Club:		
"Killarney Golf And Fishing Club"	1951	$80
Albert E. Killeen:		
"The Ten Million Dollar Golf Ball"	1983	$15
J.B. King:		
"St. Austell Golf Club"	1924	$60
Leslie King:		
"Master Key To Good Golf"	1976	$10
"The Master Key To Success At Golf"	1962	$10
W.R. King:		
"Mohawk Golf Club, Three Quarters Of		
A Century"	1973	$20
H.A. Kinney:		
"Brighton And Hove Golf Club, 1887-1973"	1973	$15
Charles Kip:		
"The Amateur Championship Golf Competition		
At Morris County Golf Club"	1898	$275
Andra Kirkaldy:		
"Fifty Years Of Golf, My Memories"	1921	$375
Joe Kirkwood:		
"The Links Of Life"	1973	$50
John Kissling:		
"Seventy Years: A History Of The Metropolitan		
Golf Club, Oakleigh Victoria"	1973	$55
Ernie Klappenbach:		
"A Forty-Two Year History 1935-1971		
Southern Hills Country Club"	1977	$30

AUTHOR TITLE	PUB. DATE	VALUE
Dave Klein:		
"Golf's Big Three"	1973	$10
"Great Moments In Golf"	1971	$10
Jerry Kloppenburg:		
"Cure The Yips"	1985	$5
Elizabeth And James Klugness:		
"The Nongolfers Cookbook"	1982	$10
Mary C. Klute:		
"Golfers Always Say"	1984	$10
Knaresborough Golf Club:		
"Knaresborough Golf Club"	1929	$40
Bob Kneedler:		
"Golfitis: Golf It Is"	1965	$5
Reg Knight:		
"Golf For Beginners"	1970	$10
"Learn Golf Backwards"	1965	$10
William A. Knight & T.T. Oliphant:		
"Stories On Golf"	1894	$800
Knollwood Country Club:		
"Knollwood Country Club 1894-1969, 75 Years Of Golf"	1969	$10
Edmund G.V. Knox:		
"Mr. Punch On The Links"	1929	$75
Ronald A. Knox:		
"The Viaduct Murder"	1926	$120
Lee Kocsis:		
"Kinks On The Links: With Spiked Footnotes"	1982	$5
Albert E. Koehl:		
"Ardsley Country Club"	1955	$50
Elaine B. Koehl:		
"Ponte Vedra Club 1927-1982 The First Fifty-Five Years"	1982	$20
Aileen P. Koehler:		
"Wawashkame Golf Club"	1982	$20
Peter Kostis:		
"The Inside Path To Better Golf"	1982	$10
Ruben Kraetz:		
"Golf In Ten Lessons"	1938	$25
John B. Kritzer:		
"Butterfield Country Club 1920-1970"	1970	$15
Jared Jay Kullman:		
"101 Winning Golf Tips"	1980	$5
"How To Play Winning Golf"	1980	$5
Shela and Joel Kushell:		
"Golf Resorts"	1983	$15
Bob Labbance:		
"The Centennial History Of The Woodstock Country Club"	1994	$30

AUTHOR TITLE	PUB. DATE	VALUE
Bob Labbace and David Cornwell:		
"The Golf Courses Of New Hampshire"	1989	$15
"The Maine Golf Guide"	1991	$15
Rudy Lachenmeir:		
"Are You A Gope Or A Golfer"	1952	$15
Ladies Championship:		
"Ladies Championship Golf 1893-1932 In Aid Of The Golfers Cot"	1932	$100
Renton Laidlaw:		
"Wentworth: A Host Of Happy Memories"	1993	$150
Lake Placid:		
"Lake Placid Club Golf Courses"	1910	$95
Ivan Lake:		
"Falmouth Golf Club"	1974	$10
Roy Lalande:		
"Inverness Golf Club 1926-1974"	1974	$15
Lamberhurst Golf Club:		
"Lamberhurst Golf Club"	1951	$20
Harry J. Lambeth:		
"A Directory Of The Leading Builders Of The Nation's Golf Courses"	1974	$15
Lancaster Golf Club:		
"Lancaster Golf Club"	1933	$60
"Lancaster Golf Club 50th Anniversary"	1983	$20
"Lancaster Golf Club Souvenir Booklet"	1933	$40
H. Boswell Lancaster:		
"Ridiculous Golf, In Story And In Verse"	1938	$75
Andrew Lang:		
"A Batch Of Golfing Papers"	1892	$275
"Echoes Re-Echoed: An Anthology Of St. Andrews Verse"	1934	$60
"Old Friends: Essays in Epistolary Parody"	1890	$125
David Langdon:		
"How To Play Golf And Stay Happy"	1964	$10
"How To Talk Golf: A Glossary Of Golf Terms"	1975	$15
William B. Langford:		
"Golf Course Architecture In The Chicago District"	1915	$125
Lansdown Golf Club:		
"Lansdown Golf Club"	1939	$45
Robert Lapham:		
"Twenty Years Of Life Begins At Forty"	1972	$10
George E. Lardner:		
"Cut Your Score"	1933	$20
"Golf Technique Simplified"	1933	$25
"How To Play Golf"	1927	$25
Rex Lardner:		
"Downhill Lies And Other Falsehoods Or How To Play Dirty Golf"	1973	$10

AUTHOR TITLE	PUB. DATE	VALUE
Rex Lardner (cont.):		
"The Great Golfers"	1970	$15
"Out Of The Bunker And Into The Trees Or		
The Secret Of High Tension Golf"	1960	$10
Lawrence Lariar:		
"Golf And Be Damned"	1954	$15
"You've Got Me In A Hole"	1955	$10
Mary Liz Larmore:		
"The Resort Book For Swingers, A Golfer's		
Vacation Guide"	1981	$10
Herbert Larsen:		
"Women's Metropolitan Golf Association		
1899-1974"	1975	$20
Lucy Larson:		
"Garden State Women's Golf Association		
1953-1978"	1978	$15
Mario Laureti:		
"All Putts Should Count 1/2 Stroke"	1981	$10
Janice Law:		
"Death Under Par"	1981	$20
Peter Lawless:		
"The Golfer's Campanion"	1937	$100
Stewart Lawson:		
"The Original Rules Of Golf"	1981	$15
A.P. Layer:		
"The Simplicity Of The Golf Swing"	1911	$125
Joe Lazaro:		
"The Right Touch"	1978	$10
Henry Leach:		
"Great Golfers In The Making"	1907	$225
"The Happy Golfer"	1914	$525
"Letters Of A Modern Golfer To His Grandfather"	1910	$550
"The Spirit Of The Links"	1907	$650
Brendan D. Leahey:		
"One Hundred Years At Vesper Country Club"	1979	$20
Leamington Golf Club:		
"Leamington Golf Club"	1937	$40
James P. Lee:		
"Golf And Golfing: A Practical Manual"	1895	$950
"Golf In America"	1895	$1,350
Stan Lee:		
"Golfers Anonymous"	1961	$10
Lee-On-The-Solent Golf Club:		
"Lee-On-The-Solent Golf Club The First 75 Years		
A Brief History"	1980	$15
Leicestershire Golf Club:		
"Leicestershire Golf Club"	1938	$45

AUTHOR TITLE	PUB. DATE	VALUE
Dell Leigh:		
"Golf At Its Best On The L.M.S."	1925	$450
"Twelve Of The Best On The L.M.S."	1930	$375
Ernest P. Leigh-Bennett:		
"An Errant Golfer"	1929	$65
"Some Friendly Fairways"	1930	$75
"Southern Golf"	1935	$75
Cecil Leitch:		
"Golf"	1922	$75
"Golf For Girls"	1914	$175
"Golf Simplified"	1924	$60
Tony Lema:		
"Champagne Tony's Golf Tips"	1966	$30
"Golfer's Gold: An Inside View Of The Pro Tour"	1964	$45
"How To Break 100/90/80"	1965	$35
G.E. Leman:		
"A Short History Of The Origins Of Golf At Northam And The Foundation Of The Present Royal North Devon Golf Club"	1926	$375
George J. Lemmon:		
"About Golf"	1941	$25
John Leng:		
"Leng's Golfer's Manual"	1907	$100
Mark Lerner:		
"Golf Is For Me"	1982	$10
Bill Leslie and Gene O'Brien:		
"Aim and Hang Loose"	1976	$10
Letchworth Golf Club:		
"Letchworth Golf Club"	1938	$75
Let's Play Golf:		
"Let's Play Golf"	1933	$35
Jack Level:		
"St. George's Golf And Country Club Thirtieth Anniversary"	1945	$50
Stephen M. Levine:		
"Woodcrest Country Club - A History"	1985	$20
John G. Levison:		
"A Short History Of The Presidio Golf Club"	1964	$25
Don Lewis:		
"After Dinner Golf"	1976	$10
I.G. Lewis:		
"Turf: A Book About Golf Greens, Tennis Courts, Bowling Greens, And Playing Pitches Etc."	1948	$35
Robert Lewis:		
"Win Those Saturday Games"	1979	$10
Life Magazine:		
"Fore! Life's Book For Golfers"	1900	$650

AUTHOR TITLE	PUB. DATE	VALUE
John A. Lillie:		
"Ninety Years A Golfer"	1981	$10
Lindy Lindberg:		
"Lindy Lindberg's Spot System Of Chipping"	1977	$10
R.C. Lindholm:		
"Lindy's Golf Course Guide For The Washington-Baltimore Area"	1983	$10
Walter C. Lindley:		
"Oahu Country Club Seventy-Five Years"	1981	$15
Lo Linkert:		
"Around The Course In 19 Holes"	1983	$10
"Duffers, Hackers, and Other Golfers"	1981	$10
"Golftoons"	1977	$10
W.T. Linskill:		
"Golf"	1889	$650
Liphook Golf Club:		
"The Liphook Golf Club"	1925	$40
Horace M. Lippincott:		
"A History Of The Philadelphia Cricket Club 1854 To 1954"	1954	$45
Howard Liss:		
"The Masters Tournament"	1974	$35
Listen To This One:		
"Listen To This One"	1933	$20
David Lister:		
"I'd Like To Help The World To Swing"	1977	$10
"The Ultimate Simplification"	1981	$10
Little Ashton Golf Club:		
"Little Ashton Golf Club 1908-1983"	1983	$15
Gene Littler:		
"How to Master The Irons"	1962	$35
"Iron Tactics, My Secrets To Winning Golf"	1962	$10
"The Long And Medium Irons"	1965	$15
"The Real Score"	1976	$15
"Stroke Minder: The Long Irons: The Driver: Sandwedge: The Pitch Shot: The Short Irons" 5 Vols.	1978	$85
Littlestone Golf Club:		
"Littlestone Golf Club"	1951	$35
John Littlewood:		
"Oxford & Cambridge Golfing Society The President's Putter, 50 Putters; 1920-1976"	1976	$40
Llandrindod Golf Club:		
"The Llandrindod Golf Club"	1948	$20
F.B. Lloyd:		
"The Seniors: Being The Story Of Senior Golf"	1975	$10
Bobby Locke:		
"The Basis Of My Game"	1950	$50
"Golf Hints"	1955	$75

AUTHOR TITLE	PUB. DATE	VALUE
Bobby Locke(cont.):		
"How To Improve Your Putting"	1949	$40
"Bobby Locke On Golf"	1953	$75
Tony Locke:		
"Golf Is My Mistress: Memoirs Of A Club		
Proffesional"	1981	$15
Joseph N. Lockyer and W. Rutherford:		
"The Rules Of Golf"	1896	$650
Robert L. Loeffelbein:		
"How To Goof-Proof Your Golf Game"	1971	$10
John Logue:		
"Follow The Leader"	1979	$30
Carl Lohren:		
"One Move To Better Golf"	1975	$15
London, Midland Scottish Railway Services:		
"Gleneagles Hotel"	1924	$750
Long Ashton Golf Club:		
"Long Ashton Golf Club"	1939	$15
Long Ball:		
"The Long Ball, Add 50 Yards Or More To		
Your Drive"	1978	$10
Gordon Long:		
"The Geelong Golf Club 1892-1967"	1967	$40
Longcliffe Golf Club:		
"Longcliffe Golf Club"	1938	$35
Henry Longhurst:		
"Addington Golf Club"	1953	$40
"The Best Of Henry Longhurst: On Golf And Life"	1979	$30
"Golf In Ireland"	1953	$175
"Golf Mixture"	1952	$75
"Golf"	1937	$70
"How To Get Started In Golf"	1967	$20
"It Was Good While It Lasted"	1941	$150
"John O'Gaunt Golf Club"	1950	$35
"Mere Golf And Country Club"	1947	$40
"My Life and Soft Times"	1971	$45
"Never On Weekdays"	1968	$50
"Only On Sundays"	1964	$50
"Round In Sixty-Eight"	1953	$70
"Southport: Golf Centre Of Europe"	1969	$35
"Talking About Golf"	1966	$50
"Turnberry Hotel And Its Golf Courses"	1958	$100
"Turnberry Hotel And The Ailsa Golf Course"	1953	$150
"Unwritten Golf Contract"	1952	$75
"West Sussex Golf Club"	1960	$40
"The Wilderness Country Club"	1937	$60
Henry Longhurst and Geoffrey Cousins:		
"The Old Course At St. Andrews"	1961	$150

AUTHOR TITLE	PUB. DATE	VALUE
Henry Longhurst and Geoffrey Cousins(cont.):		
"Ryder Cup 1965"	1965	$45
Peter Longo:		
"Simplified Golf: There's No Trick To It"	1980	$10
Doreen Longrigg:		
"Ladies On The Fairway"	1981	$10
Longue Vue Club:		
"Longue Vue Club Fiftieth Anniversary 1920-1970"	1970	$20
Samuel L. Looker:		
"On The Green: An Anthology For Golfers"	1922	$225
Nacy Lopez:		
"The Education Of A Woman Golfer"	1979	$15
LeRoy B. Lorenz:		
"The Science Of Golf"	1955	$15
Phillip Q. Loring:		
"Rhymes Of A Duffer"	1915	$250
Los Angeles Country Club:		
"Golden Anniversary Of The Clubhouse 1911-1961"	1961	$60
"The History Of The Los Angeles Country Club"	1936	$75
Dic Loscalzo:		
"On The Links"	1926	$250
George Low:		
"The Master Of Putting"	1983	$20
John L. Low:		
"Concerning Golf"	1903	$245
"F. G. Tait, A Record Being His Life, Letters, And Golfing Diary"	1900	$275
W.W. Lowe:		
"Bedrock Principles Of Golf"	1937	$35
Laddie Lucas:		
"The Sport Of Prince's, Reflections Of A Golfer"	1980	$25
Ted Lucock:		
"Golf Mad"	1981	$10
"Golfing With Lu"	1980	$10
Luffness Golf Club:		
"A Brief Histroy Of Luffness Golf Club And Kilspinde Golf Club"	1967	$20
Evelyn Lunemann:		
"Fairway Danger"	1969	$15
Norman Lupovich:		
"Elm Ridge Country Club 1924-1974"	1974	$20
Douglas Lutz:		
"Metropolitan Golf Guide: New York Edition"	1973	$15
Theodore Luxton:		
"The Dynamics Golf Correspondence Course"	1973	$10
"The Real Truth About The Golf Swing"	1985	$15

AUTHOR TITLE	PUB. DATE	VALUE

Sandy Lyle:

"The Championship Courses Of Scotland"	1982	$20
"Dunlop Golf Guide - Carnoustie"	1982	$20
"Dunlop Golf Guide - Muirfield"	1982	$20
"Dunlop Golf Guide - Royal Troon"	1982	$20
"Dunlop Golf Guide - Turnberry"	1982	$20

Lyme Regis Golf Club:

"Lyme Regis Golf Club"	1951	$40

John M. Lynham:

"The Chevy Chase Club: A History 1885-1957"	1958	$45

Harry Lyons and Dick Johnson:

"The Hazards Of Golf: A Complete How-Not-To Book"	1979	$10

R.H. Lyttleton:

"Out-Door Games: Cricket And Golf"	1901	$295
150 Limited Edition	1901	$725

P.J.M.:

"Golfing Trifles"	1985	$10

J.C. Macabe:

"The First Eighty Years, Douglas Park Golf Club"	1982	$20

Charles MacArthur:

"The Golfer's Annual for 1869-1870"	1870	$3,500

Charles C. MacBeth:

"Modern Golfing Methods By British And American Experts"	1933	$75

Eddie MacCabe:

"The Ottowa Hunt Club, 75 Years Of History 1908-1983"	1983	$40

Maccauvlei Golf Club:

"Maccauvlei Golf Club"	1948	$20

Charles B. MacDonald:

"National Golf Links Of America"	1912	$1,000
"Scotland's Gift: Golf"	1928	$475
Signed Limited Edtion	1928	$2,200
Reprint	1985	$50

John MacDonald:

"Crail Golfing Society, A Short History"	1983	$35

John S. MacDonald:

"Deck And Home Golf"	1905	$125

Robert G. MacDonald:

"Golf"	1927	$250
"Golf At A Glance"	1931	$95

Robert G. MacDonald and Leo Bolstad:

"Golf"	1961	$15

C.A. Macey:

"Golf Through Rhythm"	1957	$10

Machrihanish Golf Club:

"Machrihanish Golf Club"	1919	$375

AUTHOR TITLE	PUB. DATE	VALUE
Elizabeth MacKay:		
"Royal Dornoch Golf Club 1877-1977"	1977	$55
Thomas Mackay:		
"A Histroy Of The Liverpool Golf Club"	1972	$20
Alistair J. Mackenzie:		
"Golf Architecture: Economy In Course		
Contruction And Green Keeping"	1920	$950
Alistair J. Mackenzie and L.A. & P.J.A. Berkmans:		
"Desription Of The Bobby Jones Golf Course With		
An Historical Sketch Of Fruitlands"	1924	$1,250
David A. MacKenzie:		
"A History Of The Melrose Golf Club"	1979	$20
Dr. Mackenzie's Golf Architecture:		
"Dr. Mackenzie's Golf Architecture"	1982	$225
Mrs. Louie Mackern and M Boys:		
"Our Lady Of The Green"	1899	$600
Richard T. Mackey:		
"Golf"	1962	$10
"Golf: Learn Through Auditory And Visual Cues"	1978	$10
Keith Mackie and Iain Crawford:		
"Capital Golf: A Colour Guide To More Than 35		
Courses In And Around Edinburgh"	1984	$15
Ian M. Mackintosh:		
"Troon Golf Club Its History From 1878"	1974	$65
Muir Maclaren:		
"The Australian Golfer's Handbook"	1957	$25
"The Golfer's Bedside Book"	1976	$15
G.A. MacLean:		
"Golf Through The Ages"	1923	$75
R.J. MacLennon:		
"Golf At Gleneagles"	1921	$800
John MacLeod:		
"The Golfer's Dictionary"	1935	$150
Ray MacMillan:		
"Masterminding Golf"	1960	$10
T.J. Macnamara:		
"The Gentile Golfer"	1905	$450
Duncan MacPherson:		
"Golf Simplified"	1936	$75
Angus MacVicar:		
"Golf In My Gallowses, Confessions Of A		
Fairway Fanatic"	1983	$20
"Murder At The Open"	1965	$20
David Magowan:		
"The Scarsdale Golf Club 1898-1948"	1948	$30
James J. Mahon:		
"Baltusrol, 90 Years In The Mainstream Of		
American Golf"	1985	$85

AUTHOR TITLE	PUB. DATE	VALUE
Jack Mahoney:		
"The Golf History Of New England"	1973	$40
Mahopac Golf Club:		
"Mahopac Golf Club 1898-1980"	1980	$20
Stewart Maiden:		
"Ten Lessons In Golf"	1930	$375
Lewine Mair:		
"The Dunlop Lady Golfer's Companion"	1980	$10
Norman Mair:		
"Muirfield, Home Of The Honorable Company		
1744-1994"	1994	$95
Signed Limited Edition	1994	$575
Ralph Maltby:		
"Golf Club Assembly Manual"	1981	$15
"Golf Club Design, Fitting, Alteration And Repair"	1974	$20
"Golf Club Repair In Pictures"	1978	$15
Manchester Country Club:		
"Manchester Country Club 1923-1973"	1973	$35
Manchester Courier:		
"Manchester Courier Guide To Lancashire, Cheshire,		
Derbyshire And North Wales Golf"	1914	$95
Manchester Golf Club:		
"The Manchester Golf Club"	1936	$350
Manchester Guardian:		
"Golf In 1938"	1938	$175
"Golf In 1939"	1939	$150
Lloyd Mangrum:		
"Golf: A New Approach"	1949	$25
"How To Break 90 At Golf"	1952	$15
"How To Drive A Golf Ball"	1955	$20
"How To Play Better Golf"	1954	$20
James S. Manion:		
"Culbertson's Contract Golf"	1932	$75
Manito Golf And Country Club:		
"Manito Golf And Country Club 50 Years		
1922-1972"	1972	$20
Frederick G. Mann:		
"Lord Rutherford On The Golf Course"	1976	$35
Reg Manning:		
"From Tee To Cup"	1954	$15
Mannings Heath Golf Club:		
"Mannings Heath Golf Club"	1955	$10
Manual For Caddies:		
"Manual For Caddies"	1937	$75
G.E. Mappin:		
"The Golfing You"	1948	$15
Major G.F. Mappin:		
"The Haunted Major"	1937	$25

AUTHOR TITLE	PUB. DATE	VALUE
David Marchuk:		
"The Golf Log Book"	1989	$10
Marietta:		
"Six Golfing Stories"	1905	$300
Sara W. Marks:		
"Fore! ... Women Only; An Anatomy Of		
A Woman's Golf Club"	1966	$15
John P. Marquand:		
"Life At Happy Knoll"	1957	$25
Dave Marr:		
"Woods From The Tee And Fairway, A Flip Vision		
Golf Manual"	1965	$20
Thomas Marsh:		
"Blackheath Golfing Lays"	1873	$7,000
Harry Marshall:		
"Sixty Years And More A History Of Low Laithes		
Golf Club"	1985	$20
Keith Marshall:		
"Golf Galore"	1960	$15
Robert Marshall:		
"The Haunted Major"	1902	$450
1951 Edition	1951	$50
1960 Edition	1960	$35
1973 Edition	1973	$20
"The Enchanted Golf Clubs"	1920	$125
Harry B. Martin:		
"Fifty Years Of American Golf"	1936	$475
Limited First Edition Of 355 Copies Signed By Martin		$750
"The Garden City Golf Club 1899-1949"	1949	$150
"Golf For Beginners"	1930	$45
"Golf Made Easy"	1932	$65
"Golf Yarns"	1913	$85
"Great Golfers In The Making"	1932	$95
"How To Play Golf"	1936	$125
"The Making Of A Champion"	1928	$75
"Pictorial Golf"	1928	$40
"Sketches Made At The Winter League Of Advertising Interests,		
At Pinehurst, North Carolina, January 1915"	1915	$175
"St. Andrews Golf Club 1888-1963"	1963	$250
"What's Wrong With Your Golf Game"	1930	$45
Harry B. Martin & A.B. Halliday:		
"Saint Andrews (New York) Golf Club 1888-1938"		
Signed By Halliday	1938	$375
John S. Martin:		
"The Curious History Of The Golf Ball"	1968	$300
Maryland Interclub Seniors:		
"A History Of MISGA 1976-1985"	1985	$20

AUTHOR TITLE	PUB. DATE	VALUE
Gard Mason:		
"Durand Eastman Golf Club Member Information Package"	1978	$10
J.T. Mason:		
"Build Yourself A Golf Swing By The Seven Steps Of The Mason Methods"	1974	$10
Massachusetts Golf Association:		
"Caddie Instruction Manual"	1946	$45
S.M. Masse:		
"Caddy Savvy"	1947	$60
Massereene Golf Club:		
"Massereene Golf Club 1895-1974"	1975	$10
Arnaud Massy:		
"Golf"	1914	$75
Master Golf:		
"Learn Golf With The Stars, The Neil Coles Way"	1977	$15
Donald Mackay Mathieson:		
"The Golfer's Handbook"	1898	$750
Thomas Mathison:		
"The Goff"	1743	$27,000
Second Edition	1763	$22,000
Third Edition	1793	$20,000
USGA Reprint	1981	$95
Geoffrey J. Matson:		
"Off The Tee: Favourite Golfing Stories and Anecdotes Of The Famous"	1963	$15
D.B. Matthew:		
"Broughty Golf Club History 1878-1978"	1978	$15
William Charles Maughan:		
"Picturesque Musselburgh And Its Golf Links"	1906	$1,200
George S. May:		
"Highlights Of George S. May's Tam O'Shanter Golf Tournaments 1941-1956"	1956	$15
John Allan May:		
"Bedside Duffer"	1969	$10
"Duffer's A.B.C."	1970	$10
"Duffer's Discoveries"	1972	$10
"Duffer's Guide"	1967	$15
"Duffer's Progress"	1968	$15
Julian May:		
"The Masters"	1975	$15
"The PGA Championship Tournament"	1976	$15
"Lee Trevino, The Golf Explosion"	1974	$15
"The U.S. Open Championship"	1975	$15
Dick Mayer:		
"How To Think And Swing Like A Golf Champion"	1958	$10

AUTHOR TITLE	PUB. DATE	VALUE
John F. Mayhew:		
"Par Excellence, Highlights Of Sixty-Five Years At		
Barton Hills Country Club 1917-1982"	1983	$10
Cliff McAdam:		
"Golf Illustrated Presents Arnie"	1976	$15
"How To Break 90/80/Par"	1973	$10
Alexander J. McAlister:		
"The Eternal Verities Of Golf"	1911	$300
Evelyn Ditton McAllister:		
"Golf For Beginners. A Golfing Handbook"	1969	$15
Bert McAndrew and T. McClurg:		
"Basic Principles And Practice Of Golf"	1975	$10
J. McAndrew:		
"Golfing Step By Step"	1910	$250
J. McBain and W. Fernie:		
"Golf: Dean's Champion Handbooks"	1899	$475
J.C. McBeth:		
"Golf From A-Z"	1935	$45
"Golf: Professional Methods British		
And American"	1930	$60
"Methods Of The Golf Masters"	1934	$60
"Modern Golfing Methods By British And		
American Experts"	1933	$60
"One Way Golf, The Secret And Simplicity Of		
The Perfect Swing"	1935	$40
George McCallister:		
"Golfercises"	1960	$10
Colman McCarthy:		
"The Pleasures Of The Game: The Theory		
Free Guide To Golf"	1977	$10
Harry McCaw and Brum Henderson:		
"Royal County Down Golf Club:		
The First Century"	1989	$40
R.M. McClaren:		
"The Honorable Company Of Edinburgh Golfers		
1744-1944"	1944	$900
Peter McCleery:		
"More Instant Golf Lessons"	1985	$10
James McConnaughey:		
"Just Swing The Clubhead"	1946	$20
Mark H. McCormack:		
"Arnie: The Evolution Of A Legend"	1967	$20
"Dunhill Golf Yearbook 1979"	1979	$20
"Dunhill Golf Yearbook 1980"	1980	$15
"Dunhill World Of Professional Golf 1981"	1981	$15
"Dunhill World Of Professional Golf 1982"	1982	$15
"Dunhill World Of Professional Golf 1983"	1983	$15
"Ebel World Of Professional Golf 1984"	1984	$15

AUTHOR TITLE	PUB. DATE	VALUE
Mark H. McCormack (cont.):		
"Ebel World Of Professional Golf 1985"	1985	$15
"Golf '67: World Professional Golf:		
The Facts And Figures"	1968	$25
"The Wonderful World Of Professional Golf"	1973	$35
"The World Of Professional Golf 1968"	1968	$25
"The World Of Professional Golf:		
Golf Annual 1969"	1969	$25
"The World Of Professional Golf:		
Mark H. McCormack's Golf Annual 1970"	1970	$25
"The World Of Professional Golf:		
Mark H. McCormack's Golf Annual 1971"	1971	$20
"The World Of Professional Golf Annual 1972"	1972	$20
"The World Of Professional Golf:		
Mark H. McCormack's Golf Annual 1973"	1973	$25
"The World Of Professional Golf:		
Mark H. McCormack's Golf Annual 1974"	1974	$25
"The World Of Professional Golf:		
Mark H. McCormack's Golf Annual 1975"	1975	$25
"The World Of Professional Golf:		
Mark H. McCormack's Golf Annual 1976"	1976	$20
"The World Of Professional Golf:		
Mark H. McCormack's Golf Annual 1977"	1977	$20
"The World Of Professional Golf:		
Mark H. McCormack's Golf Annual 1978"	1978	$20
Bill McCormick:		
"The Complete Beginner's Guide To Golf"	1974	$15
J. McCormick:		
"Fore: How To Play Good Golf"	1932	$150
Carol McCue:		
"How To Conduct Golf Club Championships"	1964	$10
J. McCullough:		
"Golf: Containing Practical Hints With Rules		
Of The Game"	1899	$400
D.J. McDiardmid:		
"100 Years Of Golf At Machrihanish 1876-1976"	1976	$55
H. Spencer McDonald:		
"Pacific Coast Golf And Outdoor Sports"	1913	$200
Michael McDonnell:		
"The Complete Book Of Golf"	1985	$20
"Golf: The Great Ones"	1971	$15
"Great Moments In Sport: Golf"	1974	$20
"The World Of Golf 1971-1972"	1972	$20
Bill McDonough:		
"Common Sense Golf"	1975	$10
Stan McDougal:		
"101 Great Golf Jokes and Stories"	1968	$10
"The World's Greatest Golf Jokes"	1980	$10

AUTHOR TITLE	PUB. DATE	VALUE
Donald McDougall:		
"Davie"	1977	$20
Roy L. McFrederick:		
"The Golfer's Handbook, A Manual On Golf As It Is		
Played And Taught By The Old Masters"	1926	$95
Charles McGehee:		
"History Of The Southern Seniors Golf Association		
Fifty Years On 1930-1980"	1980	$15
Donald McGraw:		
"The Full Bag, Or The Golf Duffer's Golf Book:		
How To Keep From Breaking 100"	1962	$15
George F. McGregor:		
"Open Reflections"	1948	$20
"Open Reflections"	1949	$15
"Open Reflections"	1950	$15
"Open Reflections"	1952	$15
Robert McGurn and S.A. Williams:		
"Golf Power In Motion"	1967	$10
John C. McHose:		
"The Wilshire Country Club 1919-1979"	1979	$20
Ralph McInerny:		
"Lying Three: A Father Dowling Mystery"	1979	$15
Jan McIntosh:		
"Hooked On Golf"	1982	$10
David McKay:		
"Leith And The Origins Of Golf"	1984	$15
S.L. McKinlay:		
"Gleneagles Hotel Golf Courses Scotland"	1969	$10
"The Millport Golf Club"	1948	$20
"Western Gailes 1897-1947"	1947	$25
Richmond McKinney:		
"The Honourable Company Of Edinburgh Golfers		
1744-1944"	1944	$600
Iaen McLachlan:		
"Attack The Flag"	1977	$10
"One Hundred Golf Tips By Leading Australian		
And New Zealand Golfers"	1973	$20
"Putting Tips From The Top"	1980	$10
Iaen McLachlan: cont.		
"Swing To Win, The Story And Techniques Of		
Leading Proette, Judy Perkins"	1975	$10
Jack McLean:		
"One Knuckle Grip"	1939	$35
"Why Not Beat Bogey"	1937	$75
Terry McLean:		
"A Simpler Place In Time, Golfing		
In New Zealand"	1980	$20

AUTHOR TITLE	PUB. DATE	VALUE
Rod McLeod:		
"St. Andrews Old"	1970	$20
Thomas G. McMahon:		
"What Price Uniformity? The Golf Handicap Situation"	1966	$10
Valarie McMahan:		
"Bumps: The Golf Ball Kid And The Little Caddies"	1929	$60
P. McMaugh:		
"Golf Green Construction"	1955	$25
John McMurtie:		
"The Golfers' Guide And Official Handbook For Scotland 1901-1902"	1902	$675
Rand McNally:		
"All About Golf"	1975	$20
J. Gordon McPherson:		
"Golf And Golfers, Past And Present"	1891	$1,650
Eoin McQuillan:		
"The Fred Daly Story"	1978	$55
D.G. McRae:		
"The Principle Of Human Automation As Applied To Golf"	1945	$20
Joseph W. McSpadden:		
"How To Play Golf"	1907	$100
Michael McTeigue:		
"The Keys To The Effortless Golf Swing"	1985	$15
Paul McWeeney:		
"Milltown Golf Club Golden Jubilee"	1981	$10
James A. G. Mearns:		
"200 Years Of Golf 1780-1980 Royal Aberdeen Golf Club"	1980	$40
Standish F. Medina:		
"A History Of The Westhampton Club 1890-1955"	1955	$20
Ross Mehalski and John Skinner:		
"The Christchurch Golf Club 1873-1973, A Century Of Golf In Christchurch"	1973	$50
Bill Mehlhorn:		
"Golf Secrets Exposed"	1984	$35
Joseph G. Mele and Charles R. Wayne Jr.:		
"A Golfer's Guide To Public Golf Courses In New Jersey Vol. 1 North Jersey"	1985	$15
Gordon Menzies:		
"The World Of Golf"	1982	$10
Merion Course:		
"Facts About The Merion Course At Ardmore PA"	1916	$175
Merion Cricket Club:		
"The Merion Cricket Club 1865-1965"	1965	$125

AUTHOR TITLE	PUB. DATE	VALUE
Merion Golf Club:		
"Golf At Merion 1896-1976"	1977	$35
Anthony F. Merrill:		
"The Golf Course Guide"	1950	$35
Eddie Merrins:		
"Golf For The Young"	1983	$10
"Swing The Handle-Not The Clubhead"	1973	$15
Ben Merwin:		
"Idylwylde, First Fifty Years 1922-1972"	1972	$15
Leigh Metcalfe and Ted Mertz:		
"Today's Humor, The Golf Number"	1927	$60
Metropolitan Golf Association:		
"Caddie Management Manual"	1956	$20
"Electric Golf Survey In The Metropolitan New York Area"	1956	$15
"Golf Car Usage And Control In The Metropolitan New York Area"	1960	$15
"Manual Caddie Management"	1932	$75
Dick Metz:		
"The Secret To Par Golf"	1940	$45
"Short Cuts To Improve Your Golf"	1940	$15
Richard Metz:		
"The Graduated Swing Method"	1981	$10
Sol Metzger:		
"Putting Analyzed"	1929	$75
D. Swing Meyer:		
"The Method: A Golf Success Strategy"	1981	$10
Fred Meyer:		
"The Golf Special, A Musical Foozle, A Musical Comedy In Three Acts"	1909	$225
Meyrick & Queens Park Golf Club:		
"The Meyrick & Queens Park Golf Club"	1938	$75
Thomas Michael:		
"Golf's Winning Stroke: Putting"	1967	$15
Cliff Michaelmore:		
"The Businessman's Book Of Golf"	1981	$15
Edward C. Michener:		
"The Everglades Club, A Retrospective 1919-1985"	1985	$15
G.H. Micklem:		
"Help In The Interpretation Of The Rules Of Golf"	1979	$15
Mickleover Golf Club:		
"Mickleover Golf Club"	1938	$10
Cary Middlecoff:		
"Advanced Golf"	1957	$15
"Golf Doctor"	1950	$15
"The Golf Swing"	1974	$15
"Cary Middlecoff's Master Guide To Golf"	1960	$15

AUTHOR TITLE	PUB. DATE	VALUE
Cary Middlecoff and Tom Michael:		
"14 Classic Tips For The Year From The CBS Classic At Firestone C.C."	1967	$15
Ralph Middleton:		
"Alwoodley Golf Club 1907-1983"	1985	$15
Alfred H. Miles:		
"Golfer's Calendar"	1913	$75
Mill Creek Park Golf Course:		
"Mill Creek Park Golf Course 50th Anniversary 1927-1977"	1977	$15
Beryl Buck Miller:		
"Play A Round With Beryl Buck Miller"	1979	$10
Dick Miller:		
"America's Greatest Golfing Resorts"	1977	$20
"Triumphant Journey"	1980	$40
Douglass B. Miller:		
"So You Want To Play Golf"	1947	$15
Hack Miller:		
"The New Billy Casper: More Important Things In Life Than Golf"	1968	$15
Helen M. Miller:		
"So You Want To Be A Champion: Babe Didrickson Zaharias"	1961	$25
Johnny Miller:		
"Pure Golf"	1976	$35
Robert V. Miller:		
"Golf, The Ageless Game"	1985	$10
T.D. Miller:		
"Famous Scottish Links And Other Golfing Papers"	1911	$1,250
"The History Of The Royal Perth Golfing Society"	1935	$1,100
Theodore T. Miller:		
"Essex Country Club, Its History, Its Traditions"	1954	$20
Donald Millus:		
"On The Southern Greens"	1983	$15
John Milton:		
"A History Of Royal Eastbourne Golf Club 1887-1987"	1987	$45
H. Craig Miner:		
"A History Of The Wichita Country Club 1900-1975"	1975	$15
Charles Miron:		
"Murder On The 18th Hole"	1978	$20
Abe Mitchell:		
"Down To Scratch"	1933	$50
"Essentials Of Golf"	1927	$55
"Length On The Links"	1935	$50

AUTHOR TITLE	PUB. DATE	VALUE
William F. Mitchell:		
"Cochrane Castle Golf Club, Its History From 1895"	1980	$15
George Mobbs:		
"Northamptonshire Country Club, History Of The Course"	1969	$15
F.C. Moffatt:		
"Seventy-Five Years Of Golf, Morpeth Golf Club 1906-1981"	1981	$15
Hilario C. Moncado:		
"360 Power Swing"	1951	$10
Sil Monday:		
"Golf In The Ohio Sun"	1970	$10
Monifeith Golf Links:		
"Monifeith Golf Links Bazaar Book"	1899	$2,000
William K. Montague:		
"The Golf Of Our Fathers"	1952	$250
Signed By Montague		$345
"Rule Changes"	1961	$15
Monte Carlo Country Club:		
"Monte Carlo Country Club Presents The Lighter Side Of Golf"	1982	$15
Orville Moody:		
"Golf By Orville Who?"	1972	$10
Theodore Moone:		
"Golf From A New Angle"	1934	$75
Moore Park Golf Club:		
"Moore Park Golf Club"	1968	$20
Bertha Moore:		
"Bunkered: A Duologue For Two Women"	1922	$250
Charles Moore:		
"The Mental Side Of Golf"	1929	$50
Frank W. Moran:		
"Book Of Scottish Courses"	1939	$75
"Golfers' Gallery"	1946	$40
"Gullane Golf Club"	1955	$35
"Scotland For Golf"	1962	$25
"Westlinks Golf Course New Club, North Berwick"	1954	$25
Sharron Moran:		
"Golf Is A Womans Game Or How To Be A Swinger On The Fairway"	1971	$10
Albert A. Morey:		
"Tee Time, Enjoy It And Live"	1952	$10
Jerome E. Morgan:		
"Golf Analysis Log"	1979	$10
John Morgan:		
"Golf"	1976	$10

AUTHOR TITLE	PUB. DATE	VALUE
David C. Morley:		
"The Missing Links: Golf And The Mind"	1976	$15
Michael E. Morley:		
"The Art and Science Of Putting"	1982	$15
H. Messon Morris:		
"Church Stetton Golf Club"	1967	$15
John Morris and Leonard Cobb:		
"Great Golf Holes Of Hawaii"	1977	$60
"Great Golf Holes Of New Zealand"	1971	$35
Warren E. Morris:		
"The Totec Twist, Or My Dad's Notebook on Golf"	1955	$10
Alex J. Morrison:		
"A New Way To Better Golf"	1932	$60
"Better Golf Without Practice"	1940	$55
"Pocket Guide To Better Golf"	1934	$35
Erwin G. Morrison:		
"Here's How In Golf"	1949	$20
"Here's How To Play Money Golf"	1953	$15
"Life With Par"	1958	$10
J.S.F Morrison:		
"Around Golf"	1939	$250
Stuart Morrison:		
"Golf Faults: How To Improve Your Game Fifty Percent"	1912	$65
Charles and Ann Morse:		
"Lee Trevino"	1974	$15
Charles Mortimer & Fred Pignon:		
"The Story Of The Open Championship 1860-1950"	1952	$75
Cecil W Morton:		
"Golf: The Confessions Of A Golf Club Secretary"	1963	$15
Jerry Mosca:		
"Experiencing Golf In Scotland: A Guide To Scottish Courses"	1984	$15
Moseley Golf Club:		
"Moseley Golf Club"	1939	$45
R.J.H. Moses:		
"Fore"	1937	$175
Most Convenient Setting Forth:		
"A Most Convenient Setting Forth Of Much Interesting Information Regarding Golf"	1900	$120
Mountain Ash Golf Club:		
"Mountain Ash Golf Club 1908-1983"	1983	$15
Mountain View Country Club:		
"Early Days Of The Mountain View Country Club 1898-1927"	1927	$15
Mowbray Golf Club:		
"Mowbray Golf Club"	1932	$125

AUTHOR TITLE	PUB. DATE	VALUE
Steve Mucha:		
"How To Break 100: Golfing Shortcuts The Pros Don't Teach You"	1982	$10
Graham Muir:		
"Dumfries and Galloway Golf Club 1880-1980"	1980	$15
Muirfield Village Golf Club:		
"Muirfield Village Golf Club"	1977	$15
Richard Mullins:		
"The Phoenix Open - A 50 Year History"	1984	$15
Mark Mulvoy:		
"Sports Illustrated Golf"	1983	$20
Mark Mulvoy and Art Spander:		
"Golf: The Passion And The Challenge"	1977	$20
Thomas F. Mulvoy Jr.:		
"Wollaston Golf Club"	1970	$15
Joseph Murdoch:		
"The Library Of Golf 1743-1966"	1968	$475
Signed		$550
"The Library Of Golf 1743-1977"	1978	$200
"The Murdoch Golf Library"	1991	$65
Joseph Murdoch and Janet Seagle:		
"Golf: A Guide To Information Sources"	1979	$75
Michael Murphy:		
"Golf In The Kingdom" First Edition	1972	$125
Thomas J. Murphy:		
"Woodland Golf Club, A 75 Year History 1902-1977"	1977	$20
Tom Murphy:		
"Official Used Glub Guide 1965"	1964	$15
Henry A. Murray:		
"The Golf Secret"	1953	$20
"More Golf Secrets"	1954	$15
J.P. Murray:		
"Golfing In Ireland" Two Vols.	1952	$750
Robinson Murray:		
"Are Golfers Human?"	1951	$15
Burton H. Musser:		
"Turf Management"	1950	$195
Bill Mutter:		
"Golf On Ayrshire Coast"	1981	$15
Charles Mutter:		
"The Story Of The Piltdown Golf Course 1904-1974"	1974	$20
Edward L. Myers:		
"Experiences Of A Caddy"	1927	$150
Kent Myers:		
"Golf In Oregon"	1977	$20

AUTHOR TITLE	PUB. DATE	VALUE
D.T. Mylrea:		
"Sale Golf Club, Twenty-First Anniversary		
1913-1934"	1934	$15
C.J. Naden:		
"Golf"	1970	$10
Charles S. Naftal:		
"Games That Golfer's Play"	1984	$10
Kel Nagle and Others:		
"The Secrets Of Australia's Golfing Success"	1961	$20
Ted Naismith:		
"Golf"	1948	$55
Virginia L. Nance and Craig D. Elwood:		
"Golf"	1966	$15
George C. Nash:		
"General Forecursue And Co.; More Letters To		
The Secretary Of A Golf Club"	1936	$75
"Golfing In Northern Ireland"	1955	$275
"Golfing In Ulster"	1949	$200
"Letters To The Secretary Of A Golf Club"	1936	$75
"Whelks Postbag"	1937	$85
National Golf Foundation:		
"Beginning Golf, The Game"	1948	$20
"Golf Coach's Guide"	1975	$10
"Golf Fundamentals"	1949	$15
"Golf In Physical Education"	1941	$20
"Golf Instructor's Guide"	1972	$10
"Golf Lessons"	1950	$15
"Golf Operations Handbook And Golf Facility		
Development Guide"	1985	$15
"Golf Operator's Handbook"	1956	$15
"Golf Range Operator's Handbook"	1947	$20
"How To Improve Your Golf"	1952	$15
"Minature Golf Courses"	1949	$15
"Miniature Putting Course And Golf Driving		
Range Manual"	1971	$15
"Organizing And Operating Public Golf Courses"	1971	$15
"Par 3 And Executive Golf Course, Planning And		
Operation Manual"	1974	$15
"Planning And Building The Golf Course"	1958	$25
"Planning And Building The Par-3 Or		
Executive Golf Course Manual"	1960	$15
"Planning And Conducting Competitive		
Golf Events"	1973	$10
"Planning Information For Private And Daily		
Fee Golf Clubs"	1978	$10
"Planning Information For Private Golf Clubs"	1965	$20
"Public Opinion Survey"	1955	$10
"Speedy Golf"	1969	$10

AUTHOR TITLE	PUB. DATE	VALUE
National Golf Foundation (cont.):		
"Suggestions For Conducting Intramural Golf Tournaments"	1950	$15
Neath Golf Club:		
"Neath Golf Club"	1951	$15
Sylvia K. Neff:		
"Know Your Golf"	1940	$15
Nefyn & District Golf Club:		
"Nefyn & District Golf Club 1907-1982"	1982	$15
Mark Neil:		
"The Awful Golfer's Book"	1957	$10
A.S. Neill:		
"The Booming Of A Bunkie"	1925	$150
Jim Nelford:		
"Seasons In A Golfer's Life"	1984	$10
Byron Nelson:		
"How I Played The Game" Signed By Nelson	1993	$65
"How To Score Better Than You Swing"	1955	$25
"Shape Your Swing The Modern Way"	1976	$20
Signed By Nelson		$100
"Winning Golf"	1946	$25
Limited Edition Signed By Nelson		$150
Dwayne Netland:		
"The Crosby: Greatest Show In Golf"	1975	$15
New Yorker Magazine:		
"Fore!"	1967	$10
T. Palmer Newbould:		
"The Dieppe Golf Club"	1912	$175
Newbury And Crookham Golf Club:		
"Newbury And Crookham Golf Club 1873-1973"	1973	$15
Joseph Newman:		
"The Official Golf Guide Of America For 1900"	1900	$900
Josiah Newman:		
"The Official Golf Guide Of The United States And Canada"	1899	$975
M.H. Newmark:		
"Something About Golf"	1922	$35
Newton Abbot Golf Club:		
"Newton Abbot Golf Club"	1954	$25
Niblick:		
"Hints To Golfers"	1902	$130
"Introduction To Golf"	1932	$45
"Par Golf"	1926	$50
Niblick Club:		
"The Niblick Club 1922-1947"	1947	$40
Bobby Nichols:		
"Never Say Never: The Psychology Of Winning Golf"	1965	$15

AUTHOR TITLE	PUB. DATE	VALUE
Lois Nichols:		
"Green Hills Country Club 1930-1980"	1980	$10
Jack Nicklaus:		
"18 Holes: The Master Professional Describes His Tee To Green Technique To You"	1970	$15
"All About The Grip"	1965	$15
"The Best Way To Better Golf"	1966	$15
"The Best Way To Better Golf Number 2"	1968	$10
"The Best Way To Better Golf Number 3"	1969	$10
"The Full Swing"	1984	$15
"Golf My Way"	1974	$15
"The Greatest Game Of All: My Life In Golf"	1969	$45
"My 55 Ways To Lower Your Golf Score"	1964	$15
"Jack Nicklaus Golf Handbook: 25 Self Contained Lessons By The World's Greatest Golfer"	1973	$15
"Jack Nicklaus Plays The NCR South"	1969	$10
"Jack Nicklaus, Profile Of A Champion"	1968	$20
"Jack Nicklaus' Lesson Tee: Back To Basics"	1977	$15
"Jack Nicklaus' Lesson Tee"	1977	$15
"Jack Nicklaus' Playing Lessons"	1981	$15
"On And Off The Fairway: A Pictorial Autobiography"	1978	$25
"Play Better Golf, The Swing From A-Z"	1980	$15
"Play Better Golf, Volume II The Short Game and Scoring"	1981	$15
"Play Better Golf Volume III Short Cuts To Lower Scores"	1983	$15
"Power Plus"	1966	$15
"Practice Tips"	1965	$15
"Reading And Controlling Putts"	1965	$15
"Take A Tip From Me"	1968	$15
"Total Golf Techniques"	1977	$15
"Winning Golf"	1969	$15
E. A. Nickson:		
"The Lytham Century, A History Of The Roayal Lytham And St. Annes Golf Club 1886-1986"	1986	$85
Eric Nicol and Dave More:		
"The Agony & The Ecstacy"	1982	$10
Tom Nieporte and Don Sauers:		
"Mind Over Golf: What 50 Top Pros Can Teach You About The Mysterious Mental Side Of Golf"	1968	$10
Nisbet's Yearbook:		
"Nisbet's Golf Yearbook 1905"	1905	$475
"Nisbet's Golf Yearbook 1906"	1906	$400
"Nisbet's Golf Yearbook 1907"	1907	$400
"Nisbet's Golf Yearbook 1908"	1908	$400
"Nisbet's Golf Yearbook 1909"	1909	$375
"Nisbet's Golf Yearbook 1910"	1910	$400

AUTHOR TITLE	PUB. DATE	VALUE
Nisbet's Yearbook(cont.):		
"Nisbet's Golf Yearbook 1911"	1911	$350
"Nisbet's Golf Yearbook 1912"	1912	$375
"Nisbet's Golf Yearbook 1913"	1913	$350
"Nisbet's Golf Yearbook 1914"	1914	$350
John Noble:		
"The Official Duffer's Rules Of Golf"	1981	$10
James Nolan:		
"Golf Antiques"	1962	$45
"Of Golf And Dukes And Princes:		
Early Golf In France"	1982	$25
William H. Nolan:		
"Caddie Routine"	1951	$25
Jim Norland:		
"Fifty Years Of Mostly Fun: The History Of		
Cherry Hills Country Club 1922-1972"	1972	$65
Greg Norman:		
"Greg Norman: My Story"	1983	$40
North Carolina, Golf State USA:		
"North Carolina, Golf State USA"	1974	$15
North Foreland Golf Club:		
"The North Foreland Golf Club"	1951	$20
North Manchester Golf Club:		
"North Manchester Golf Club"	1938	$150
Northbourne Golf Club:		
"Northbourne Golf Club"	1951	$35
Ronald Norval:		
"Gone To The Golf"	1965	$10
"King Of The Links"	1951	$15
Joe Norwood:		
"Help Yourself To Joe Norwood's Swing"	1941	$10
"Joe Norwood's Golf-O-Metrics"	1978	$10
Joe Novak:		
"Golf Can Be An Easy Game"	1962	$10
"How To Put Power And Direction In Your Golf"	1954	$15
"The Novak System Of Mastering Golf"	1969	$10
"Par Golf In 8 Steps"	1950	$15
Nuneville:		
"Illustrated Lessons In Golf"	1924	$95
Eddy Nunn:		
"Mechanics Of Golf"	1962	$15
Oahu Country Club:		
"Oahu Country Club"	1956	$25
Oak Bluff Country Club:		
"Oak Bluff Country Club"	1914	$60
Oak Park Country Club:		
"Oak Park Country Club Fifth Anniversary		
1914-1919"	1919	$75

AUTHOR TITLE	PUB. DATE	VALUE
Oakley Country Club:		
"Oakley Country Club 1898-1948"	1948	$30
"Oakley Country Club 1898-1973: Notes On		
Seventy-Five Happy Years"	1973	$30
Oakwood Club:		
"Oakwood Club 1905-1955,		
Fiftieth Anniversary"	1955	$40
Oban Golf Club:		
"Oban Golf Club"	1915	$60
Harry Obitz and Dick Farley:		
"Six Days To Better Golf: The Secrets Of Learning		
The Golf Swing"	1977	$15
Gene O'Brien:		
"Aim And Hang Loose"	1985	$10
Robert O'Byrne:		
"Senior Golf"	1977	$15
Anthony O'Connor:		
"Golfing In The Green"	1977	$15
Christy O'Connor:		
"Christy O'Connor, His Autobiography"	1985	$30
C.F. Odell:		
"History Of The Pretoria Country Club 1909-1975"	1977	$60
Paddy O'Donnell:		
"South Africa's Wonderful World Of Golf"	1973	$30
Official Golf Guide:		
"Official Golf Guide 1947"	1947	$20
"Official Golf Guide 1948"	1948	$20
"Official Golf Guide 1949"	1949	$20
Willie Ogg:		
"Golf As I Know It"	1961	$15
Old Golfer:		
"Golf On A New Principle: Iron Clubs		
Superseded"	1897	$475
Old Link Golf Club:		
"The Old Link Golf Club"	1938	$60
Old Player:		
"Golf And How To Play It"	1905	$275
Old Warson Country Club:		
"Old Warson Country Club, 10th Anniversary"	1964	$25
Oldest Member:		
"The Etiquette And Traditions Of Golf"	1920	$150
Jake Olgiati:		
"Pocket Golf Book Illustrated"	1924	$85
John M. Olman:		
"The Squire: The Legendary Golfing Life		
Of Gene Sarazen" Signed By Sarazen	1987	$150
John M. and Morton W. Olman:		
"The Encyclopedia Of Golf Collectibles"	1985	$35
"Olman's Guide To Golf Antiques"	1992	$25

AUTHOR TITLE	PUB. DATE	VALUE
Morton W. Olman:		
"The Byron Nelson Story" Signed By Nelson	1980	$150
James T. Olsen:		
"Arnold Palmer: The King On The Course"	1974	$20
Bill Olson And Lo Linkert:		
"Beat The Links"	1979	$10
George W. Olson:		
"Bamboozled And Hornswogled"	1962	$10
Olympia Fields Country Club:		
"Olympia Fields Country Club"	1923	$150
Bill O'Malley:		
"Fore And Aft"	1969	$10
"Golf Fore Fun"	1953	$15
Mark Oman:		
"Portrait Of A Golfaholic"	1984	$10
"The Sensuous Golfer"	1976	$10
Currey O'Neil:		
"The Age Pro Golf Tips"	1984	$75
The Open Championship:		
"The Open Championship 1984"	1984	$60
"The Open Championship 1985"	1985	$35
E. Philips Oppenheim:		
"A Lost Leader"	1907	$65
Nan O'Reilly:		
"Bobby Jones Had To Defeat Himself"	1927	$15
Orchard Ridge Country Club:		
"Orchard Ridge Country Club 1924-1984		
60th Anniversary"	1984	$10
Original Golf Facts:		
"The Original Golf Facts 1971"	1971	$20
Ormskirk Golf Club:		
"Ormskirk Golf Club Golden Jubilee		
1899-1949"	1949	$10
Randall M. O'Rourke:		
"To Golf Here's How To Teach It"	1960	$10
"The Truth About Golf"	1955	$10
Robert Osborn:		
"How To Play Golf"	1949	$10
Gil O'Shaughnessy:		
"New Zealand Golf Guide"	1968	$20
Mary Jo O'Shea:		
"Laura Baugh"	1976	$10
H.T. Ostermann:		
"Golf In Europe 1961"	1961	$20
"Golf In Europe 1962"	1962	$20
"Golf In Europe 1963"	1963	$20
"Golf In Europe 1964"	1964	$20
"Golf In Europe 1965"	1965	$20

AUTHOR TITLE	PUB. DATE	VALUE
H.T. Ostermann(cont.):		
"Golf In Europe 1966"	1966	$20
"Golf In Europe 1967"	1967	$20
"Golf In Europe 1968"	1968	$20
"Golf In Europe 1969"	1969	$15
"Golf In Europe 1970"	1970	$15
"Golf In Europe 1971"	1971	$15
"Golf In Europe 1972"	1972	$15
Neville C. Oswald:		
"Thurlestone Golf Club, A Short History 1897-1983"	1983	$20
Francis Ouimet:		
"A Game Of Golf, A Book Of Reminiscence"	1932	$275
Limited First Edition Signed By Ouimet		$1,500
Reprint	1963	$95
Memorial Tournament Reprint	1978	$35
"Golf Facts For Young People"	1921	$450
"The Rules Of Golf"	1948	$40
De De Owens:		
"Teaching Golf To Special Popualtions"	1984	$10
Oxford And Cambridge Golfing Society:		
"Oxford And Cambridge Golfing		
Society American Tour 1978"	1978	$20
T.H. Oyler:		
"The Golfers Glossary"	1920	$75
Ozone Club:		
"Down The Fairway And In The Rough With		
The Ozone Club 1901-1927"	1927	$50
Pa Golf:		
"Fore"	1934	$85
Lee Pace:		
"Pinehurst Stories: A Celebration Of Great Golf		
And Good Times"	1992	$90
Al Pach:		
"Artists And Writers Golf Association"	1948	$15
John Pacini:		
"It's Your Honour: An Account Of The First Fifty Years		
Of The Penisula Golf Club"	1975	$20
Alfred H. Padgham:		
"The Par Golf Swing"	1936	$25
Luis Palangue:		
"Portugal 1984, The Golfer's Paradise"	1984	$15
Arnold Palmer:		
"495 Golf Lessons"	1973	$15
"Go For Broke: My Philosophy Of Winning Golf"	1973	$40
"Golf Tactics"	1970	$15
"Graph-Check System For Golf"	1963	$15
"How To Improve Your Putting"	1964	$35
"My Game And Yours"	1965	$15

AUTHOR TITLE	PUB. DATE	VALUE
Arnold Palmer (cont.):		
"Arnold Palmer The Man And The Golfer"	1966	$15
"The Arnold Palmer Method"	1968	$15
"Arnold Palmer Plays Merion"	1971	$15
"Arnold Palmer's Best 54 Golf Holes"	1977	$25
"Arnold Palmer's Golf Book: Hit It Hard"	1961	$45
"Portrait Of A Professional Golfer"	1964	$15
"The Rolex Book Of Golf"	1975	$15
"Situation Golf"	1970	$15
Norman Palmer and William V. Levy:		
"Five Star Golf"	1964	$10
John Panton:		
"My Way Of Golf"	1951	$15
Charles Papp:		
"Swing It Like A Pendulum"	1965	$10
Par Excellance Magazine:		
"Par Excellance Guide To Wisconsin"	1984	$10
William Park Jr.:		
"The Game Of Golf"	1896	$575
Second Edition		$300
Willie Park Jr.:		
"The Art Of Putting"	1920	$950
Samuel L. Parrish:		
"Some Facts, Reflections And Personal Reminiscences, Connected With The Introduction Of The Game Of Golf Into The United States, More Especially As Associated With The Foundation Of The Shinnecock Hill Golf Club"	1923	$1,200
R. Parsons:		
"Golfing Thinking"	1983	$10
H.M. Paskow:		
"Instant Golf"	1965	$10
Bob Patey:		
"Welcome To The Club"	1981	$10
G.Z. Pattem:		
"Birth Of Greatness: The Story Of The Honors Course"	1984	$15
A. Willing Patterson:		
"The Story Of Gulf Mills Golf Club 1916-1976"	1976	$25
H. Pattison & Co:		
"Golf Course And Sports Ground Equipment"	1962	$65
Carol S. Patton:		
"Memories And Golf Stories"	1977	$10
Pau Golf Club:		
"Statutes"	1927	$65
Carl F. Paul:		
"Club Making And Repair"	1984	$15
"Golf Club Design And Repair"	1978	$15

AUTHOR TITLE	PUB. DATE	VALUE

Edward F. Pazdur:
"Golf And Country Club Directory"	1976	$10
"Golf And Country Club Guest Policy Directory"	1977	$10
"Private Country Club Guest Policy Directory"	1980	$10

V.J. Pazzetti Jr.:
| "Saucon Valley Country Club" | 1951 | $45 |

Leonard Pearl:
| "The Big Secret Of Golf" | 1962 | $10 |

T.F. Pearson:
| "Hohne Station Golf Club" | 1974 | $15 |

Samuel M. Peck:
| "The Golf Girl" | 1899 | $450 |

J.D. Peden:
| "Uplands Golf Club 1922-1982, 60th Aniversary" | 1982 | $15 |

Michael W. Peers:
| "A History Of The Manchester Golf Club 1882-1982" | 1982 | $55 |

Paul D. Peery:
| "Billy Casper: Winner" | 1969 | $15 |

William F. Peet:
| "The Beginnings Of Golf In St. Paul And The Early History Of The Town And Country Club" | 1930 | $65 |
| "The Story Of Town And Country Club 1888-1948" | 1948 | $45 |

Pentland Peille:
| "Clanbrae: A Golfing Idyll" | 1908 | $250 |

Alexander Pendleton:
| "Better Golf With Brains" | 1941 | $15 |

Toney Penna:
| "My Wonderful World Of Golf" | 1965 | $30 |

Pennard Golf Club:
| "Pennard Golf Club" | 1941 | $50 |

Harvey Pennick & Bud Shrake:
| "Harvey Pennick's Little Red Book" Signed | 1992 | $75 |

Frank Pennink:
"Golfer's Companion"	1962	$45
"Homes Of Sport: Golf"	1952	$45
"Frank Pennink's Choice Of Golf Courses"	1976	$20
"Royal Ashdown Forest Golf Club The Old And The New Courses"	1965	$55

Penzance Golf Club:
| "Penzance Golf Club" | 1914 | $275 |

George Peper:
| "Golf's Supershots: How The Pros Played Them - How You Can Play Them" | 1982 | $25 |
| "Scrambling Golf: How To Get Out Of Trouble And Into The Cup" | 1977 | $10 |

AUTHOR TITLE	PUB. DATE	VALUE
Helen B. and Roy F. Perkins:		
"Wannamoisett Country Club 1898-1948"	1948	$60
Reprint	1985	$15
W.F. Perkins:		
"Golfer's Guide To Emotional Management"	1981	$10
Louis J. Perrottet:		
"A History Of Canoe Brook Country Club		
1901-1965"	1965	$25
Phyllis Perry:		
"From Green To Gold: The First Fifty Years		
Of The Australian Ladies Golf Union"	1976	$20
Gordon Petch:		
"Ashdown Over The Years"	1973	$20
H. Thomas Peter:		
"Reminiscences Of Golf And Golfers"	1899	$5,000
Peterhead Golf Club:		
"Peterhead And The Peterhead Golf Club"	1939	$45
Andrew Petnuch:		
"Turn To Golf"	1969	$10
Roy A. Pettitt:		
"The Straight-Line Golf Swing"	1946	$15
PGA:		
"The Book On Golf: On The Occasion Of The Ninth		
Biennial Ryder Cup Matches Pinehurst N.C.		
Nov 2nd and 4th 1951"	1951	$225
"Education And Teaching Clinics And Seminars"	1956	$20
"European Tournament Players' Division		
Tournament Guide 1977"	1977	$20
"European Tournament Players' Division		
Tournament Guide 1978"	1978	$20
"European Tournament Players' Division		
Tournament Guide 1979"	1979	$20
"European Tournament Players' Division		
Tournament Guide 1980"	1980	$20
"European Tournament Players' Division		
Tournament Guide 1981"	1981	$20
"European Tournament Players' Division		
Tournament Guide 1982"	1982	$15
"The Golf Professional At A Military Course"	1981	$10
"The Golf Professional At A Public Course"	1983	$15
"Golf's Professional Man"	1943	$35
"Greener Pastures At Dunedin Isles"	1946	$35
"Ideas To Assist Golf Clubs And Courses Make		
Money To Reduce Costs"	1981	$15
"Official Record Book 1936-37"	1937	$75
"Official Record Book 1938-39"	1939	$70
"Official Tournament Guide 1972"	1972	$20
"Official Tournament Guide 1973"	1973	$20

AUTHOR TITLE	PUB. DATE	VALUE
PGA(cont.):		
"Official Tournament Guide 1974"	1974	$20
"Official Tournament Guide 1975"	1975	$20
"Official Tournament Guide 1976"	1976	$20
"Official Tournament Record Book 1940-41"	1941	$75
"Official Tournament Record Book 1941-49"	1949	$45
"Official Tournament Record Book 1950-58"	1958	$25
"Official Tournament Record Book 1959-64"	1965	$25
"PGA Book Of Golf 1968"	1968	$25
"PGA Book Of Golf 1969"	1969	$25
"PGA Book Of Golf 1970"	1970	$25
"PGA Book Of Golf 1973"	1973	$25
"PGA Book Of Golf 1974"	1974	$25
"PGA Book Of Golf 1975"	1975	$25
"PGA Book Of Golf 1976"	1976	$20
"PGA Book Of Golf 1977"	1977	$20
"PGA Book Of Golf 1978"	1978	$20
"PGA Book Of Golf 1979"	1979	$25
"PGA Book Of Golf 1980"	1980	$25
"PGA Caddie Manual"	1964	$20
"PGA European Tour Official Guide 1983"	1983	$15
"PGA European Tour Official Guide 1984"	1984	$15
"PGA European Tour Official Guide 1985"	1985	$15
"PGA Golf Professionals Guide"	1963	$20
"PGA Teachers Guide"	1951	$20
"Success Stories In The Golf Business"	1978	$20
"Teaching Manual"	1950	$20
"Tour 1980"	1980	$20
"Tour 1981"	1981	$20
"Tour 1982"	1982	$15
"Tour 1983"	1983	$15
"Tour 1984"	1984	$15
"Tour 1985"	1985	$15
"Tournament And Player Record Book For 1934"	1935	$75
"Tournament And Player Record Book For 1935"	1936	$75
Betty Lou Phillips:		
"Picture Story Of Nancy Lopez"	1980	$15
Michael J. Phillips:		
"How To Play Miniature Golf"	1930	$10
Philmont Country Club:		
"Since The Spring Of 1906"	1946	$20
George A. Philpot:		
"The Birstall Golf Club"	1938	$35
"The Bournemouth Golf Club"	1936	$40
"The Bridport & West Dorset Golf Club"	1946	$40
"The Chigwell Golf Club"	1939	$40
"The Cleethorpes Golf Club"	1937	$35
"The Grimsley Golf Club"	1938	$35

AUTHOR TITLE	PUB. DATE	VALUE
George A. Philpot (cont.):		
"The North Wales Golf Club"	1947	$50
"The Reading Golf Club"	1947	$25
Photographic Study Of Pebble Beach:		
"Photographic Study Of Pebble Beach Golf Links		
Stroke By Sroke"	1952	$200
Arthur E. Pickens Jr.:		
"The Golf Bum"	1970	$15
H.O. Pickworth:		
"Golf The Pickworth Way"	1949	$10
Fred J.C. Pignon:		
"Spalding Golfer's Year Book"	1960	$25
Phil Pilley:		
"Golfing Art"	1988	$50
Charles V. Piper & Russell A. Oakley:		
"Turf For Golf Courses"	1929	$200
Kin Platt:		
"The Kissing Gourami"	1970	$10
Jules Platte:		
"Better Golf Through Better Practice"	1958	$10
Michael Platts:		
"Illustrated History Of Golf"	1988	$35
Play It Pro:		
"Golf From Beginner To Winner"	1960	$20
Gary Player:		
"124 Golf Lessons"	1968	$15
"395 Golf Lessons"	1972	$15
"Golfing S.A."	1980	$25
"Good Test For The U.S. Open, Haziltine		
National Golf Club"	1970	$20
"Grand Slam Golf"	1966	$15
"Improve Your Golf"	1962	$15
"The Medium Iron To The Green"	1971	$15
"More Tips From Gary Player"	1968	$15
"Play Better Golf With Gary Player"	1970	$15
"Play Golf With Player"	1962	$20
"Gary Player On Fitness And Success"	1979	$10
"Gary Player Tells You All About The Shakespeare Fiberglass		
Wondershaft And What It Can Do For You"	1964	$15
"Gary Player World Golf Pro"	1974	$20
"Gary Player's Golf Book For Young People"	1980	$10
"Gary Player's Golf Class Book 1 100 Lessons"	1967	$20
"Gary Player's Golf Class Book II 100 Lessons"	1969	$15
"Gary Player's Golf Class Book III 162 Lessons"	1975	$15
"Gary Player's Golf Class Book IV 170 Lessons"	1980	$15
"Gary Player's Golf Clinic"	1981	$15
"Gary Player's Golf Guide"	1974	$20
"Gary Player's Golf Secrets"	1962	$25
Signed By Player		$65

AUTHOR TITLE	PUB. DATE	VALUE
Gary Player (cont.):		
"Positive Golf: Understanding And Applying		
The Fundamentals Of The Game"	1967	$15
"The Tee Shot"	1971	$15
"Weathering The Sand And Storm"	1971	$20
George Plimpton:		
"The Bogey Man"	1968	$10
Chris Plumridge:		
"The Book Of Golf Disasters & Bizarre Records"	1985	$20
"How To Play Golf"	1979	$15
Pocket Pro:		
"Pocket Pro"	1948	$25
P. Byron Polakoff:		
"Arnold Palmer And The Golfin' Dolphin"	1984	$60
Frank B. Pollard:		
"Golf On The Peninsula: An Illustrated Guide To		
The World Famous Courses On The Monterey		
Peninsula"	1973	$60
Jack Pollard:		
"Golf: The Australian Way"	1970	$20
"Gregory's Australian Guide To Golf"	1964	$25
William H. Pollock:		
"You The Golfer"	1937	$55
Harold M. Pond:		
"Guide To 1,870 North American Golf Courses"	1954	$20
Pontypridd Golf Club:		
"Pontypridd Golf Club"	1924	$55
Kelly Pool:		
"Selected Drawing Of Clare Briggs"	1930	$175
William Poole:		
"The History Of Onwentsia 1895-1945"	1985	$15
Nicholas Popa:		
"Caddy Tip$"	1953	$10
Mary Kay Poppenberg and Marlene Parrish:		
"I'd Rather Play Golf Than Cook"	1976	$10
Portmarnock Golf Club:		
"Portmarnock Golf Club"	1939	$200
Portsea Golf Club:		
"Portsea Golf Club History 1925-1975		
50th Anniversary Souvenir"	1975	$15
Mitchell P. Postel:		
"History Of The Burlingame Country Club"	1983	$30
E.C. Potter:		
"Midlothian Melodies, Mnemonic Maunderings		
Of The Merry Muse"	1900	$500
Stephen Potter:		
"The Complete Golf Gamesmanship"	1968	$20
"Golfmanship"	1968	$15

AUTHOR TITLE	PUB. DATE	VALUE
Potters Bar Golf Club:		
"The Potters Bar Golf Club"	1926	$60
George Pottinger:		
"Muirfield And The Honorable Company"	1972	$55
M. Powersland:		
"Great Yarmouth & Caister Golf 1882-1982"	1982	$15
Eric M. Prain:		
"Live Hands: A Key To Better Golf"	1946	$45
"The Oxford And Cambridge Golfing Society		
1898-1948"	1949	$250
William Pratt and Keith Jennison:		
"Year-Round Conditioning For		
Part Time Golfers"	1979	$10
Arthur Preedy:		
"Home Park Golf Club"	1950	$20
Prestatyn Golf Club:		
"Prestatyn Golf Club"	1951	$25
Prestbury & Upton Golf Club:		
"The Prestbury & Upton Golf Club"	1950	$35
Charles Preston:		
"Fore: Golf Cartoons From		
The Wall Street Journal"	1962	$15
Charles Price:		
"The American Golfer"	1964	$75
"Black's Picture Sports: Golf"	1976	$20
"Esquire's Golfer's Guide"	1972	$35
"Golf Magazine's Pro Pointers And		
Stroke Savers"	1960	$20
"Golfer-At-Large: New Slants On		
The Ancient Game"	1982	$35
"Shell's Wonderful World Of Golf 1963"	1963	$60
"Sports Illustrated Book Of Golf"	1970	$40
"Sports Illustrated Golf"	1972	$30
"The World Of Golf: A Panorama Of Six Centuries		
Of The Games' History"	1962	$75
Charles Price and George C. Rogers Jr.:		
"The Carolina Low Country, Birthplace Of		
American Golf 1786"	1980	$75
Prince's Golf Club:		
"Prince's Golf Club"	1932	$200
Pro Am Guide To Golf:		
"Pro Am Guide To Golf"	1982	$15
Pro's Handbook Of Golf:		
"Pro's Handbook Of Golf"	1967	$15
Robert D. Pryde:		
"The Early History Of Golf In		
New Haven Connecticut"	1952	$40

AUTHOR TITLE	PUB. DATE	VALUE
Punch Magazine:		
"The Funny Side Of Golf"	1909	$400
"Mr. Punch On The Links"	1935	$100
"Mr. Punch's Golf Stories Told By His Merry Men"	1909	$150
"That Game Of Golf And Some Other Sketches"	1902	$400
Puttenham Golf Club:		
"Puttenham Golf Club"	1951	$25
A.Q.:		
"The Swing In Golf And How To Learn It"	1919	$35
Nancy Quantz:		
"Tee Party"	1969	$10
Joseph Quinzi:		
"Back To The Basics In Golf"	1980	$10
Joseph Quinzi and Catherine McKenzie Shane:		
"The Women's World Of Golf"	1980	$15
Qvist:		
"Golfermania"	1985	$10
Claude Radcliffe:		
"Holed Out In One"	1919	$175
Radyr Golf Club:		
"Radyr Golf Club 1902-1977"	1977	$15
Tony Rafty:		
"Tony Rafty's Golfing Greats"	1983	$25
Martin A. Ragaway:		
"Golfer's Dictionary"	1984	$20
"Sex Before Golf"	1982	$10
"The Worlds Worst Golf Jokes"	1974	$10
William Ralston:		
"North Again, Golfing This Time"	1894	$275
Neil Ramsay:		
"Scotland's Golfing Heritage"	1984	$20
Allan Ramsey:		
"West Sussex Golf Club Golden Jubilee 1931-1981"	1981	$20
Lon W. Ramsey:		
"Secrets Of Winning Golf Matches"	1960	$10
Tom Ramsey:		
"25 Great Australian Golf Courses"	1981	$40
"Golfer's Gift Book"	1983	$10
"How To Cheat And Hustle At Golf"	1983	$10
"Tom Ramsey's World Of Golf"	1977	$15
Richard C. Randolph:		
"You Will Win Betting On The Golf Course-I'll Betcha"	1983	$10
Judy Rankin:		
"A Natural Way To Golf Power"	1976	$15
Milton Rappaport:		
"Oh No!, A Golf Duffer's Handbook"	1956	$15

AUTHOR TITLE	PUB. DATE	VALUE
Bertil Rarald:		
"Get Fit For Golf"	1985	$10
Roy And Betty Rasmussen:		
"1981 Michigan Golfers Map And Guide"	1981	$10
Wally Rasmussem:		
"The Preaching Pro"	1979	$10
Ratho Park Golf Club:		
"Ratho Park Golf Club"	1948	$20
Jeanette E. Rattray:		
"Fifty Years Of The Maidstone Club 1891-1941"	1941	$65
Anthony Ravielli:		
"What Is Golf"	1976	$15
Edward Ray:		
"Driving, Approaching, Putting"	1926	$65
"Golf Clubs And How To Use Them"	1922	$95
"Inland Golf"	1914	$185
Ted Ray:		
"Golf: My Slice Of Life"	1972	$25
Milton Reach:		
"Night Golf"	1955	$10
Opie P. Read:		
"Opie Read On Golf"	1925	$65
Rebar, Jaske, And Doran:		
"Cross Word Golf: A Game For Two Players"	1933	$25
Redditch Golf Club:		
"Redditch Golf Club"	1936	$65
Ken Redford and Nick Tremayne:		
"Success In Golf"	1977	$10
Jack Redmond:		
"Golf Training"	1930	$55
John Reece:		
"Golf Of Course"	1983	$15
Betty Jane Reed:		
"Golfin With A Dolphin"	1968	$20
Dai Rees:		
"Golf My Way"	1951	$25
"Golf Today"	1962	$15
"The Key To Golf"	1961	$25
"Dai Rees On Golf"	1959	$25
"Thirty Years Of Championship Golf"	1968	$65
Dean Refram and Arthur Burgone:		
"Golf-O-Genics"	1978	$15
Conrad H. Rehling:		
"Golf For The Physical Education Teacher and Coach"	1954	$15
Hastings C. Reid:		
"The Key To The Rules Of Golf And Definitions"	1946	$25

AUTHOR TITLE	PUB. DATE	VALUE
Steven Reid:		
"Get To The Point At The County Sligo Golf Club"	1991	$45
William Reid:		
"Golfing Reminiscences: The Growth Of The		
Game 1887-1925"	1925	$1,350
Signed By Reid		$1,800
"Seventy-Five Years Of Golf At Cathkin Braes		
1888-1963"	1963	$40
Marion Renick:		
"Champion Caddy"	1943	$75
John Ressich:		
"Thir Braw Days"	1933	$150
Alexander H. Revell:		
"The Pro And Con Of Golf"	1915	$165
Ralph H. Reville:		
"Golf In Canada"	1926	$150
Johnny Revolta:		
"6 Lessons From Johnny Revolta"	1954	$15
Johnny Revolta And Charles Cleveland:		
"Johnny Revolta's Short Cuts To Better Golf"	1949	$20
Frank Reynolds:		
"Hamish McDuff"	1937	$300
"The Frank Reynolds Golf Book: Drawing		
From Punch"	1932	$375
"The Frank Reynolds Golf Collection"	1970	$25
Morgan B. Reynolds:		
"Seventy Years Of Belle Meade Country Club		
1901-1971"	1971	$35
Rhode Island Country Club:		
"Rhode Island Country Club 1911-1951"	1952	$35
Hal Rhodes:		
"Fundamental Principles Of Golf"	1952	$15
Louis Rhodes:		
"Stop Action Golf: The Driver"	1971	$10
W.H. Ricardo:		
"Golfing Parodies"	1930	$175
"Out Of Bounds No. 1"	1927	$60
"Out Of Bounds No. 2"	1927	$60
Grantland Rice:		
"Fore-With A Glance Aft"	1929	$150
"The Bobby Jones Story"	1953	$75
Reprint	1980	$15
"Sam Snead, Mystery Man Of Golf"	1949	$25
Grantland Rice & Clare Briggs:		
"The Duffers Handbook Of Golf"	1926	$120
Limited Edition Signed By Both Rice And Briggs		$800
Endicott Rich And Foley Johnson:		
"You Can Think Ten Strokes Off		
Your Game, We Did"	1931	$45

AUTHOR TITLE	PUB. DATE	VALUE
Bruce Richardson:		
"Richardson's Common Sense Golf"	1984	$10
Donald H. Richardson:		
"World Wide Golf Directory"	1973	$20
Forest B. Richardson:		
"Broadmoor Castle Club"	1983	$25
William D. Richardson:		
"The Eastern Golfer"	1939	$40
William D. Richardson and Lincoln A. Werden:		
"Annual Golf Review 1931"	1932	$50
"Annual Golf Review 1933"	1934	$45
"Annual Golf Review 1934"	1935	$45
"Golfer's Yearbook 1930"	1930	$60
"Golfer's Yearbook 1931"	1931	$35
"Golfer's Yearbook 1932"	1932	$30
"Golfer's Yearbook 1933"	1933	$50
Richmond Country Club:		
"Historical Souvenir Book Of The Fiftieth Anniversary Of The Richmond Country Club 1888-1938"	1938	$60
Bill Rickard:		
"Army Golf Club 1883-1983"	1983	$15
C.A.P. Ricornus:		
"The Goat Club Golf Book"	1911	$80
Gervase C. Riddell:		
"Practical Golf Course Design And Construction"	1973	$60
Ridgewood Country Club:		
"The Ridgewood Country Club History 1890-1940"	1940	$75
John Riley:		
"Royal Salisbury Golf Club Commemorative Brochure"	1968	$25
Norman H. Rimmer:		
"Mere Golf And Country Club Golden Jubilee 1934-1984"	1985	$15
Ringway Golf Club:		
"Ringway Golf Club 75th Anniversary 1909-1984"	1984	$20
Robert K. Risk:		
"Songs Of The Links"	1904	$225
George Robb:		
"Historical Gossip About Golf And Golfers"	1863	$9,000
James Robb:		
"Murrayfield Golf Club, The Story Of Fifty Years"	1947	$125
J. Cameron Robbie:		
"The Chronicle Of The Burgess Golfing Society Of Edinburgh 1735-1935"	1936	$300
Reprint	1983	$45
Arthur E. Roberts:		
"Handbook For Caddies"	1914	$125

AUTHOR TITLE	PUB. DATE	VALUE
Clifford Roberts:		
"The Story Of The Augusta National Golf Club"	1976	$65
Henry Ed Roberts:		
"The Green Book Of Golf 1923-1924"	1923	$350
"The Green Book Of Golf 1925-26"	1925	$250
Palmer W. Roberts:		
"Fore: The Golfer's International Cookbook"	1978	$15
A.J. Robertson:		
"The A.B.C. Of Golf"	1904	$90
Frank N. Robertson:		
"Golf Gleanings Old And New And The History Of		
The Maritime Seniors' Golf Association"	1953	$250
G.S. Robertson:		
"A History Of The Stromness Golf Courses, With Notes		
On The Kirkwall And Isles Courses"	1974	$20
James K. Robertson:		
"St. Andrews: Home Of Golf"	1967	$25
Kolin Robertson:		
"Some Yorkshire Golf Courses"	1935	$375
Maud Gordon Robertson:		
"Hints To Lady Golfers"	1909	$300
Heath W. Robinson:		
"Humors Of Golf"	1923	$400
Larry Robinson:		
"Golf Secrets Of The Pros"	1956	$10
Lawrence Robinson:		
"History Of The Blind Brook Club"	1947	$25
Robby Robinson:		
"Golf Guide To The Caribbean, Including		
The Bahamas & Bermuda"	1983	$20
Nancy Robison:		
"Nancy Lopez: Wonder Woman Of Golf"	1979	$15
Rock Island Arsenal Golf Club:		
"Rock Island Arsenal Golf Club"	1982	$15
Phillip H. Rodgers:		
"How To Play St. Andrews Old Links Course"	1951	$35
Robert Rodrigo:		
"The Birdie Book"	1967	$35
Chi Chi Rodriguez:		
"Chi Chi's Secret Of Power Golf"	1967	$15
"Everybody's Golf Book"	1975	$10
Chi Chi Rodriguez and Harry Stroiman:		
"Chi Chi's Golf Secret"	1964	$10
O.B. Rominger:		
"The Desert Valley Country Club"	1975	$15
Romsey Golf Club:		
"Romsey Golf Club"	1951	$20

AUTHOR TITLE	PUB. DATE	VALUE
J.P. Rooney:		
"Play Good Golf"	1939	$35
Bob Rosburg:		
"The Putter Book"	1963	$20
William G. Rose & Charles M. Newcomb:		
"Cut Down That Score: The Psychology Of Golf"	1925	$250
A.C. Gordon Ross:		
"A Mixed Bag Of Golfing Verse"	1977	$10
Campbell Ross:		
"The Fun On The Fairway"	1943	$195
"More Fun On The Fairway"	1945	$250
Charles Ross:		
"The Haunted Seventh"	1922	$200
Donald J. Ross:		
"The Partial List Of Prominent Golf Courses Designed By Donald J. Ross"	1930	$575
John M. Ross:		
"Golf Businessman's Almanac 1968"	1968	$10
"Golf Businessman's Almanac 1969"	1969	$10
"The Golfer's Coloring Book"	1962	$15
"Liberty Mutual's 18 Tips From 18 Legends Of Golf"	1986	$10
Robert J. Rotella and Linda Bunker:		
"Mind Mastery For Winning Golf"	1981	$10
Rother Golf Club:		
"The Rother Golf Club"	1924	$75
John Rotherfield:		
"The Official Handbook Of Golf In Somerset 1938-1939"	1939	$125
J.H. Rothwell and F. Purchas:		
"Brighton And Hove Golf Club Jubilee 1887-1937"	1937	$150
Ralph Rowland:		
"The Humors Of Golf"	1903	$175
Royal And Ancient Game Of Goff:		
"The Royal And Ancient Game Of Goff"	1950	$25
Royal And Ancient Golf Club Of St. Andrews:		
"Decisions By The Rules of Golf Committee Of The Royal And Ancient Golf Club 1909-1910"	1911	$175
"Decisions By The Rules of Golf Committee Of The Royal And Ancient Golf Club 1909-1913"	1914	$125
"Decisions By The Rules of Golf Committee Of The Royal And Ancient Golf Club 1909-1919"	1920	$90
"Decisions By The Rules of Golf Committee Of The Royal And Ancient Golf Club 1909-1924"	1925	$90
"Decisions By The Rules of Golf Committee Of The Royal And Ancient Golf Club 1909-1928"	1929	$90
"Decisions By The Rules of Golf Committee Of The Royal And Ancient Golf Club 1934"	1935	$60

AUTHOR TITLE	PUB. DATE	VALUE
Royal And Ancient Golf Club Of St. Andrews (cont.):		
"Golf Rules Illustrated"	1969	$20
"Royal And Ancient Golf Club Of St. Andrews Reports For 1948"	1949	$150
Royal Blackheath Golf Club:		
"Royal Blackheath Golf Club"	1970	$100
Royal Bombay Golf Club:		
"Centenary Souvenir Handbook Of The Royal Bombay Golf Club 1842-1942"	1942	$200
Royal Burgess Golfing Society:		
"Royal Burgess Golfing Society Of Edinburgh 1735-1985 250th Anniversary Celebration"	1985	$35
Royal Canberra Golf Club;		
"Royal Canberra Golf Club Jubilee History 1926-1976"	1976	$65
Royal Cape Golf Club:		
"Royal Cape Golf Club Centennary Year 1885-1985"	1985	$65
Royal Cinque Ports Golf Club:		
"Royal Cinque Ports Golf Club"	1921	$150
Royal Dublin Golf Club:		
"Royal Dublin Golf Club 1885-1963"	1963	$95
Royal Eastbourne Golf Club:		
"Royal Eastbourne Golf Club"	1938	$90
Royal Jersey Golf Club:		
"The Royal Jersey Golf Club"	1950	$45
Royal Lytham And St. Annes:		
"Royal Lytham And St. Annes Golf Club"	1938	$150
"Royal Lytham And St. Annes Golf Club Diamond Jubilee 1898-1958"	1958	$60
Royal Montreal Golf Club:		
"The Royal Montreal Golf Club 1873-1923"	1923	$475
Royal Musselburgh Golf Club:		
"Royal Musselburgh Golf Club 1774-1974"	1974	$150
Royal Portrush Golf Club:		
"Royal Portrush Golf Club"	1980	$60
Royal Salisbury Golf Club:		
"Royal Salisbury Golf Club, 75th Anniversary 1898-1973"	1973	$85
Royal Sydney Golf Club:		
"Short History Of The Royal Sydney Golf Club"	1949	$175
Royal Worlington And Newmarket Golf Club:		
"The Royal Worlington And Newmarket Golf Club"	1950	$85
Lorne Rubenstein and J. Briggs:		
"Brantford Golf And Country Club 1879-1979"	1979	$15
Earl Ruby:		
"The Caddy-Cism: A Manual For Caddies"	1937	$65

AUTHOR TITLE	PUB. DATE	VALUE
Mason Rudolph:		
"The Short Irons"	1965	$20
Rugby Golf Club:		
"Rugby Golf Club"	1951	$15
Bob Rule:		
"Champions Golf Club 1957-1976"	1976	$60
Paul Runyan:		
"Golf Is A Game"	1939	$35
"Paul Runyan's Book For Senior Golfers"	1962	$10
"Short Way To Lower Scoring"	1979	$10
Benjamin Rush:		
"Sermons To Gentlemen Upon Temperance And Exercise"	1772	$2,000
Lorraine Rush:		
"Golf Lessons"	1981	$10
Edwin F. Russell:		
"Siwanoy Country Club 1901-1976 75th Anniversary"	1976	$40
George C. Russell:		
"The Williamwood Golf Club 1906-1981 Three Over Fours"	1981	$25
Joseph E. G. Ryan:		
"Golfers' Green Book 1902"	1902	$375
William Ryan:		
"The History Of Innes Arden 1899-1973"	1973	$15
"The History Of Innes Arden 1899-1980"	1980	$15
Peter Ryde:		
"Halford Hewitt: A Festival Of Foursomes"	1984	$15
"Mostly Golf: A Bernard Darwin Anthology"	1976	$55
"Royal And Ancient Championship Records 1860-1980"	1981	$60
"Strokesaver The Official Course Guide, The Royal St. George's Golf Club"	1981	$15
G.S.:		
"Northern Golf Club, Abridged History 1896-1946"	1946	$25
Ernie Sabayrac:		
"Professionalizing The Golf Pro Shop"	1975	$15
Edwin L. Sabin:		
"The Magic Mashie And Other Golfish Stories"	1902	$475
Allan Sadler:		
"The Magic Move Of Golf"	1974	$15
Harold Sagar:		
"A History Of Purley Downs Golf Club"	1983	$25
Salisbury and South Wilts Golf Club:		
"Salisbury And South Wilts Golf Club"	1939	$75
Ross Salmon:		
"Devon Golf Clubs"	1984	$10
"Golf Clubs Of Cornwall, Isles Of Scilly, and Jersey"	1985	$10

AUTHOR TITLE	PUB. DATE	VALUE
J.B. Salmond:		
"The Story Of The R&A"	1956	$145
Saltburn-By-The-Sea Golf Club:		
"Saltburn-By-The-Sea Golf Club"	1949	$40
Victor Salvatore Jr.:		
"The Otsego Golf Club"	1994	$10
Harold A. Sampson:		
"Golf Instruction Simplified"	1950	$20
"Primer Of Golf Instruction"	1932	$35
Doug Sanders:		
"Come Swing With Me"	1974	$10
"Compact Golf"	1964	$15
Amelia Sands:		
"Indian Hill Club 1914-1964"	1964	$15
Sandy Lodge Golf Club:		
"Sandy Lodge Golf Club"	1965	$15
"Sandy Lodge Golf Club 1910-1960"	1960	$15
Sante Fe Railroad:		
"Come And Golf In California"	1931	$150
Ross Santee:		
"The Bar X Golf Course"	1933	$65
Reprint	1971	$35
Sapper:		
"Uncle James' Golf Match"	1932	$150
Reprint	1942	$50
Gene Sarazen:		
"Better Golf After Fifty"	1967	$20
"Golf: New Horizons, Pan Am's Guide To		
Golf Courses Round The World"	1966	$25
"Gene Sarazen's Commonsense Golf Tips"	1924	$60
"Gene Sarazen's World Golf Directory"	1977	$25
"Thirty Years Of Championship Golf"	1950	$60
Signed By Sarazan	1953	$375
"Want To Be A Golf Champion?"	1945	$60
Gene Sarazen and Others		
"From Tee To Cup"	1937	$50
Signed By Sarazen		$150
"The Golf Clinic"	1949	$25
George Sargent:		
"Golf, The Proper Way"	1912	$75
Howard A. Sasse:		
"Putting Facts And Fallacies"	1972	$15
Vivien Saunders:		
"The Complete Woman Golfer"	1975	$15
"The Golfing Mind"	1984	$10
"Successful Golf"	1980	$10
Vivien Saunders and Clive Clark:		
"The Young Golfer"	1977	$10

AUTHOR TITLE	PUB. DATE	VALUE
Saunton Golf Club:		
"Saunton Golf Club"	1984	$35
E.J. Savage:		
"The Story Of Felixstowe Ferry Golf Club		
1880-1980"	1980	$20
Savannah Golf Club:		
"Brief History Of The Savannah Golf Club"	1975	$20
John G. Saxe:		
"The Jones' Golf Swing And Other Suggestions"	1948	$225
"The Jones' Golf Swing, With Practical		
Suggestions By Many Experts"	1951	$125
Arthur C. Scarlett:		
"Index And Representitive Price Guide		
To Golf Books 1743-1970"	1979	$20
Charles Scatchard:		
"The Pannal Golf Club"	1960	$15
Dick Schapp:		
"Massacre At Winged Foot: The U.S. Open,		
Minute By Minute"	1974	$20
"The Masters"	1970	$30
Robert Scharff:		
"The Collier Quick And Easy Guide To Golf"	1963	$10
"Golf: Collier Quick And Easy Series"	1966	$10
"Golf Magazine's Encyclopedia Of Golf"	1970	$25
"Golf Magazine's Great Golf Courses		
You Can Play"	1973	$15
"Golf Magazine's Handbook Of Golf Strategy"	1971	$10
Helen B. Schleman:		
"Group Golf Instruction"	1934	$75
Leslie Schon:		
"The Psychology Of Golf"	1922	$85
Chuck Schmitt:		
"My Golf Clinic"	1967	$10
Jackson Scholz:		
"Fairway Challenge"	1964	$10
J. Ellsworth Schrite:		
"Divots For Dubs"	1934	$100
Reg Schroeter:		
"Rivermead Golf Club 1910-1985"	1985	$15
Charles M. Schultz:		
"Snoopy's Grand Slam"	1972	$25
Craig Schumacher:		
"Nancy Lopez"	1979	$15
Clinton Scollard:		
"The Epic Of Golf"	1923	$175
Scot:		
"Consistent Golf, Or, How To Become A		
Champion"	1934	$125

AUTHOR TITLE	PUB. DATE	VALUE
Scotland For Golf:		
"Scotland For Golf"	1961	$60
Scotland Home Of Golf:		
"Scotland Home Of Golf"	1960	$50
"Scotland Home Of Golf"	1978	$30
"Scotland Home Of Golf"	1981	$25
Garnet Scott:		
"A Centenary History Of The Worcestershire Golf Club"	1979	$35
Lewis Scott:		
"Par Golf: With 1934 Rule Changes"	1934	$30
Mike Scott:		
"The Crazy World Of Golf"	1985	$10
O.M. Scott and Sons:		
"The Seeding And Care Of Golf Courses"	1922	$275
Tom Scott:		
"A Century Of Golf 1860-1960"	1960	$95
"Adleburgh Golf Club"	1957	$15
"Ashridge Golf Club"	1955	$20
"Axe Cliff Golf Club"	1962	$15
"Barton-On-Sea Golf Club"	1958	$15
"The Bedford And Country Golf Club"	1948	$35
"The Berkshire Golf Club"	1955	$20
"The Bigbury Golf Club"	1957	$10
"Burnham & Berrow Golf Club"	1957	$15
"Camberley Heath Golf Club"	1950	$25
"Chipstead Golf Club"	1960	$15
"Club Golfer's Handbook"	1972	$15
"The Concise Dictionary Of Golf"	1978	$35
"Dartford Golf Club"	1955	$20
"Ealing Golf Club"	1960	$15
"Fifty Miles Of Golf Round London"	1952	$40
"Filey Golf Club"	1957	$15
"Formby Golf Club"	1958	$20
"Golf At Brighton: Hollingsbury Park, Dyke And Waterhall Courses"	1951	$35
"Golf With The Experts"	1959	$15
"Golf-Begin The Right Way"	1974	$15
"Golfing Technique In Pictures"	1957	$10
"The Ferndown Golf Club"	1957	$15
"Hayling Golf Club"	1955	$20
"Hillside Golf Club"	1958	$15
"Hornsea Golf Club"	1960	$15
"Hull Golf Club"	1960	$15
"Hythe & Dibden Golf Club"	1951	$35
"King's Lynn Golf Club"	1960	$15
"Knole Park Golf Club"	1955	$20
"Moor Park Golf Club"	1960	$15

AUTHOR TITLE	PUB. DATE	VALUE
Tom Scott(cont.):		
"More Golf With The Experts"	1965	$15
"Notts Golf Club"	1955	$20
"The Observer's Book Of Golf"	1975	$15
"Prince's Sandwich"	1960	$25
"The Royal Birkdale Golf Club"	1955	$35
"The Royal Cinque Ports Club"	1951	$45
"The Royal Cinque Ports Golf Club"	1968	$35
"Royal Cromers Golf Club"	1960	$25
"The Royal Eastbourne Golf Club"	1951	$40
"The Royal Norwich Golf Club"	1960	$25
"Royal Porthcawl Golf Club"	1960	$35
"Saunton Golf Club"	1960	$20
"Scarborough South Cliff Golf Club"	1951	$35
"Seacroft Golf Club"	1960	$20
"The Seaford Golf Club And Dormy House Club"	1960	$15
"Secrets Of The Golfing Greats"	1965	$25
"Sixty Miles Of Golf Around London"	1975	$15
"Sonning Golf Club"	1965	$15
"The South Herts Golf Club"	1955	$35
"The Story Of Golf"	1972	$45
"Sunningdale Ladies Golf Club"	1960	$15
"The Swanage And Studland Golf Club"	1964	$15
"Teignmouth Golf Club"	1960	$15
"Thurlestone Golf Club"	1960	$15
"Tyrrells Wood Golf Club"	1955	$15
"The Western-Super-Mare Golf Club"	1955	$25
"Westgate And Birchington Golf Club"	1951	$20
"The Wilderness Golf Club"	1960	$15
"Wimbledon Park Golf Club"	1951	$20
"Woodhall Spa Golf Club"	1960	$15
"Worcestershire Golf Club"	1967	$15
"Yelverton Golf Club"	1960	$15
Tom Scott and Geoffrey Cousins:		
"Golf Begins At 45"	1960	$25
"Golf For The Not So Young"	1960	$15
"The Golf Immortals"	1969	$45
"Golf Secrets Of The Masters"	1968	$25
"The Ind Coope Book Of Golf"	1965	$30
"The Wit Of Golf"	1972	$15
Tom Scott and Webster Evans:		
"The Golfer's Year"	1950	$25
"The Golfer's Year Volume II"	1951	$25
Scottish Golfer:		
"Swing Minded"	1932	$75
Scrabo Golf Club:		
"Scrabo Golf Club 1907-1982 75th Anniversary Souvenir Brochure"	1983	$20

AUTHOR TITLE	PUB. DATE	VALUE
Scriba:		
"Tour Round Scottish Golf Links"	1888	$1,500
Romeyn B. Scribner:		
"Senior Golf, Golf Is More Fun After Fifty-Five"	1960	$45
Signed By Chick Evans		$150
Edward Scudmore:		
"Royal Wimbleton Golf Club Centenary 1965"	1965	$60
Janet Seagle:		
"The Club Makers"	1980	$25
Alice D. Seagrave:		
"Golf Retold: The Story Of Golf In Cleveland"	1940	$65
Henry Seaton-Karr:		
"Golf: Greenings Useful Handbook Series"	1907	$475
Seattle Golf Club:		
"Seattle Golf Club 1900-1950"	1950	$35
Secrets To The Short Game:		
"Secrets To The Short Game: Pitching, Chipping, Putting"	1976	$20
Secrets Of Winning Golf Matches:		
"Secrets Of Winning Golf Matches With A Total Concept For Winning Golf And 12 Winning Golf Discoveries"	1959	$15
H.A. Seifert:		
"The First 75 Years Of The Manawatu Golf Club 1895-1970"	1979	$40
Nick Seitz:		
"Quick Tips From The CBS Golf Spot"	1982	$10
"Super Stars Of Golf"	1978	$15
Selangor Golf Club:		
"Twelve Under Fours: An Informal History Of The Selangor Golf Club; Diamond Jubilee 1953"	1953	$200
Don Selby:		
"Examiner Golf Foto Lessons"	1955	$15
Jack Selleck and Art Bernard:		
"Golf Is A Trap"	1968	$10
Eric Sen:		
"The Lodhi-Delhi Golf Club"	1977	$15
Prosper L. Senat:		
"Through The Greens And Golfers Year Book"	1898	$295
Tom Serpell:		
"Golf On Old Picture Postcards"	1988	$25
Lancelot C. Servos:		
"Practical Instruction In Golf"	1905	$100
Burt Seymour:		
"All About Golf: How To Improve Your Game"	1924	$75
Craig Shankland:		
"The Golfer's Stroke-Saving Handbook"	1978	$15
"Stroke-Saving For The Handicap Golfer"	1979	$10

AUTHOR TITLE	PUB. DATE	VALUE
Shanklin & Sandown Golf Club:		
"The Shanklin & Sandown Golf Club"	1939	$60
Harold Shapiro:		
"Get Golf Straight"	1972	$15
Sharon Country Club:		
"The Sharon Country Club Sixtieth Anniversary 1895-1955"	1955	$15
James E. Shaw:		
"Prestwick Golf Club, A History And Some Records"	1938	$875
Signed By Shaw		$2,000
Joseph T. Shaw:		
"Out Of The Rough"	1934	$85
Arthur Shay:		
"40 Common Errors In Golf And How To Correct Them"	1978	$10
Joseph M. Sheehan:		
"How Maureen Orcutt Won 10 Metropolitan Golf Championships"	1969	$25
Larry Sheehan:		
"Best Golf Humor From Golf Digest"	1972	$20
"Great Golf Humor From Golf Digest"	1979	$15
"The Whole Golf Catalog"	1979	$15
Alan Sheldon:		
"Rhode Island Country Club 1911-1961 Fiftieth Anniversary"	1962	$20
Colin Sheldon:		
"Reigate Heath And Its Golf Club"	1982	$15
Shell Oil Co.:		
"Shell's Wonderful World Of Golf 1966"	1966	$45
"Shell's Wonderful World Of Golf 1967"	1967	$25
"Shell's Wonderful World Of Golf 1968"	1968	$20
"Shell's Wonderful World Of Golf 1969"	1969	$20
"Shell's Wonderful World Of Golf 1970"	1970	$20
Warner Shelly:		
"Pine Valley Golf Club, A Chronicle"	1982	$35
F.S. Shenstone:		
"Golf Rules Of Golf Decisions, Tables Of Penalties And General Index"	1927	$85
James Shepherd Jr.:		
"Golf Shots"	1924	$125
James Sheridan:		
"Sheridan Of Sunnydale: My Fifty Six Years As A Caddie Master"	1967	$55
John D. Sheridan:		
"It Stands To Reason"	1947	$20
James W. Sherman:		
"Joey Gets The Golf Bug"	1961	$10

AUTHOR TITLE	PUB. DATE	VALUE
Sherwood Forest Golf Club:		
"Sherwood Forest Golf Club"	1924	$75
Robert L. Shinnie:		
"The Book Of Kingussie"	1911	$200
Shirley Park Golf Club:		
"The Shirley Park Golf Club"	1955	$15
R.K. Shone:		
"Bedford Golf Club 1892-1967"	1967	$15
Josselyn M. Shore:		
"The Story Of The Fresh Meadow Country Club"	1985	$20
Julian Shore:		
"Rattle His Bones"	1941	$25
Cleeke Shotte:		
"The Golf Craze: Sketches and Rhymes"	1905	$450
I. Robert M. Shultz:		
"Directory Of Municipal And Tax Supported		
Golf Courses"	1959	$15
Sidcup Golf Club:		
"Sidcup Golf Club"	1911	$65
"The Sidmouth Golf Club"	1931	$60
Silver Niblick:		
"The Silver Niblick: A Fond Remembrance		
And Good Times"	1972	$15
Jim Silvey:		
"Golf As I See It"	1969	$15
"How To Learn The Total Game"	1982	$10
Richard Simek and Richard O'Brien:		
"Total Golf: A Behavioral Approach"	1981	$15
Marlin L. Simmons:		
"Golf And The Subconscious Mind"	1984	$10
George Simms:		
"John Player Golf Yearbook 1973"	1973	$15
"John Player Golf Yearbook 1974"	1974	$15
"John Player Golf Yearbook 1975"	1975	$15
"John Player Golf Yearbook 1976"	1976	$15
"The World Of Golf 1977"	1977	$15
"The World Of Golf 1978"	1978	$15
"The World Of Golf 1979"	1979	$15
"The World Of Golf 1980"	1980	$15
Leonard Simons:		
"The Royal & Ancient Beginning Of Franklin Hills		
Country Club"	1985	$20
Harold Simpson:		
"The Seven Stages Of Golf, and Other Golf		
Stories In Picture And Verse"	1909	$1,500
S. Raleigh Simpson:		
"A Green Crop"	1937	$400
"The Lyre Of The Links"	1920	$475

AUTHOR TITLE	PUB. DATE	VALUE
Sir Walter Grindley Simpson:		
"The Art Of Golf"	1887	$1,250
USGA Reprint	1982	$275
Mrs. James Singleton and Eliot Thorpe:		
"Sara Bay Country Club 1926-1976"	1976	$15
Sirrah:		
"Slaves Of The Links"	1914	$275
Sitwell Park Golf Club:		
"Sitwell Park Golf Club"	1937	$40
Billy Sixty:		
"Golfax"	1946	$25
Billy Sixty Sr. And Billy Sixty Jr.:		
"Have Fun Golfing In The 60's"	1960	$15
Skerries Golf Club:		
"Skerries Golf Club"	1977	$15
Dick Skuse:		
"One Hundred Years, The Olympic Club Centennial 1860-1960"	1960	$45
Ann Slack:		
"The Mountain View Country Club 1898-1976"	1976	$15
L. Ert Slack:		
"Golf Putting"	1936	$40
Sleepy Hollow Country Club:		
"The Sleepy Hollow Country Club"	1919	$45
"The Sleepy Hollow Of Today"	1931	$35
Patrick Smartt:		
"Golf Grave And Gay"	1964	$15
"If You Must Play Golf"	1963	$20
"Sussex Golf, The 19th Century Club"	1977	$15
Allan E. Smith:		
"History Of The Seattle Golf Club 1960-1972"	1972	$35
Alex Smith:		
"Lessons In Golf"	1907	$200
Banjo Smith:		
"Columbia Country Club 1948-1952"	1952	$35
Charles Smith:		
"Aberdeen Golfers: Record and Reminiscences"	1909	$1,800
Don Smith:		
"The Young Sportsman's Guide To Golf"	1961	$10
Douglas Larue Smith:		
"Winged Foot Story: The Golf, The People, The Friendly Trees"	1984	$75
Emil Smith:		
"Golf Laffs: 150 Cartoons To Suit You To A Tee"	1964	$10
Everett M. Smith:		
"Synonym Golf: A New Indoor Game"	1931	$75
Frank S. Smith:		
"How You Can Become A Good Putter"	1925	$110

AUTHOR TITLE	PUB. DATE	VALUE
Frederick W. Smith:		
"Skytop-An Adventure"	1963	$15
Garden C. Smith:		
"Golf"	1897	$475
"Side Lights On Golf"	1907	$450
"The World Of Golf: The Isthmian Library"	1898	$750
George F. Smith:		
"Hints To Golfers"	1929	$75
Horton Smith and Marian Benton:		
"The Velvet Touch"	1965	$35
Horton Smith and Dawson Taylor:		
"The Master's Secrets Of Holing Putts"	1982	$15
"The Secret Of Holing Putts"	1965	$35
"The Secret Of Perfect Putting"	1963	$35
James Greig Smith:		
"Woodspring"	1898	$2,000
Jim Smith:		
"Acton Golf Club, A History"	1981	$20
Joseph S.K. Smith and B.S. Weastell:		
"The Foundations Of Golf"	1925	$35
Kenneth Smith:		
"Golf Club Alterations And Repairs"	1965	$15
Larry Smith:		
"Golf Pix: A Pictorial Guide To Golfing, Palm Beach County Including Tequesta"	1984	$15
Mel Smith:		
"Golf Mel's Way"	1975	$10
Parker Smith:		
"Golf Techniques: How To Improve Your Game"	1973	$10
R. Boyd Smith:		
"The History Of The Sylvania Country Club"	1959	$15
R. Craig Smith:		
"Enjoy Golf And Win"	1981	$10
Robert Howie Smith:		
"The Golfer's Yearbook For 1866"	1867	$2,800
Seamus Smith:		
"Grange Golf Club"	1977	$15
Shirlee H. Smith:		
"The Tacoma Country And Golf Club"	1980	$30
Terry Smith:		
"Aussie Golf Trivia"	1985	$10
"Australian Golf, The First 100 Years"	1982	$30
"The Complete Book Of Australian Golf"	1975	$35
"Tony Rafty's Golfers: A Treasury Of Stars in Caricature"	1975	$15
Bryan Smyth:		
"Wetherby Golf Club, A Short History"	1985	$15

AUTHOR TITLE	PUB. DATE	VALUE
J.C. Snaith:		
"Lord Cobbleigh Disappears"	1936	$40
"Curiouser And Curiouser"	1935	$45
Myrene Snarr and Patricia Corn:		
"An Illustrated Guide To Northern California		
Golf Courses"	1978	$20
Sam Snead:		
"Correcting Common Golf Faults"	1952	$20
"The Driver Book"	1963	$25
"The Education Of A Golfer"	1962	$20
"Golf Begins At Forty"	1978	$15
"How To Hit A Golf Ball From Any Sort Of Lie"	1950	$25
"How To Play Golf, And Professional Tips		
On Improving Your Score"	1946	$30
"Natural Golf"	1953	$20
"Short Cuts To Long Drives"	1965	$15
"Sam Snead On Golf"	1961	$15
"Sam Snead Teaches You His Simple Key		
Approach To Golf"	1975	$40
"Sam Snead's Basic Guide To Good Golf"	1968	$15
"Sam Snead's Celebrity Golf Tips"	1960	$15
"Sam Snead's Quick Way To Better Golf"	1938	$35
"Sam Snead's Secrets Of Golf"	1960	$15
"Stop-Action Golf Book, 2-4 Iron"	1960	$25
Sam Snead and Bob Considine:		
"How To Cut Strokes Off Your Game"	1945	$40
Richard Sneddon:		
"The Golf Stream"	1941	$65
George P. Snell:		
"Golf At Hotel Del Monte"	1904	$200
Franklin B. Snyder:		
"Early Days of the Mountain View		
Country Club 1898-1927"	1927	$125
Clyne Soley:		
"How Well Should You Putt? A Search For A		
Putting Standard"	1977	$15
Somerset and Its Golf:		
"Somerset And Its Golf"	1932	$95
John Sommerville:		
"A Foursome At Rye"	1898	$1,500
Gary L. Sorensen:		
"The Architecture Of Golf"	1976	$125
Souchak, Middlecoff, and Snead:		
"Improve Your Golf"	1959	$15
Daniel C. Soutar:		
"The Australian Golfer"	1906	$300
Southhampton Golf Club:		
"Southhampton Golf Club 1925-1975"	1975	$20

AUTHOR TITLE	PUB. DATE	VALUE
Southern California Golf Association:		
"History Of Golf In Southern California"	1925	$275
Southern Hills Country Club:		
"Brief History And Guide To The Golf Course		
Of Southern Hills Country Club"	1977	$35
Southport Municipal Golf Links:		
"The Southport Municipal Golf Links"	1933	$125
A.G. Spalding:		
"Golf Reporters Almanac"	1958	$20
"Kro-Flite Kronicles Or Grey Matter For Golfers"	1935	$60
Anthony Spalding:		
"Golf For Beginners"	1935	$20
Spalding's Official Golf Guide:		
"Spalding's Official Golf Guide" First Published	1895	$2,700
Spectator's Guide To Golf:		
"A Spectator's Guide To Golf"	1969	$15
Johnny Spence:		
"Golf Pro For God"	1965	$10
"How To Lose At Golf"	1971	$10
Sydney Spicer:		
"Boomerang Golf"	1968	$10
John Spooner:		
"Golf Facts: Product Knowledge-Basic Information		
On The Art Of Selling Golf Equipment"	1973	$15
Sports Illustrated:		
"Golf Lessons From The Pros"	1961	$15
"Sports Illustrated Golf Tips From The		
Top Professionals"	1961	$15
"Ten Top Tips"	1958	$10
"Tips On Top Performance: With Golf Tips From		
Sam Snead And Mickey Wright"	1955	$15
Jack Springman:		
"The Beauty Of Pebble Beach"	1964	$375
"The Many Faces Of The American Golf Course"	1963	$400
St. Andrews Golf Club:		
"St. Andrews Golf Club"	1934	$125
"St. Andrews Golf Club 1888-1963"	1963	$40
St. Augustine's Golf Club:		
"The St. Augustine's Golf Club"	1951	$35
St. Charles Country Club:		
"St. Charles Country Club 1905-1965"	1966	$20
St. Cloud Country Club:		
"The St. Cloud Country Club"	1927	$45
St. Joseph Country Club:		
"Fore: St. Joseph Country Club Yearbook"	1953	$25
Alicia St. Ledger:		
"Monkstown Golf Club 1908-1983"	1983	$15

AUTHOR TITLE	PUB. DATE	VALUE
J.H. Stainton:		
"The Golf Courses Of Yorkshire"	1912	$375
Stambaugh Golf Course:		
"Henry Stambaugh Golf Course		
50th Anniversary 1923-1973"	1973	$35
Stancliffe:		
"An Astounding Golf Match"	1914	$350
"The Autobiography Of A Caddy-Bag"	1924	$375
"Golf Do's And Don't's"	1902	$125
"Quick Cuts To Good Golf"	1920	$95
Stanley Golf Club:		
"Stanley Golf Club House"	1933	$60
Dave Stanley:		
"A Treasury Of Golf Humor"	1949	$15
Dave Stanley And George C. Ross:		
"The Golfer's Own Book"	1957	$25
Louis T. Stanley:		
"The Book Of Golf"	1960	$20
"Fontana Golf Book"	1957	$15
"Fresh Fairways"	1949	$45
"Golf With Your Hands"	1966	$20
"The Golfer's Bedside Book"	1955	$40
"Green Fairways"	1947	$35
"How To Be A Better Woman Golfer"	1952	$20
"Master Golf In Action"	1950	$20
"Pelham Golf Year"	1981	$35
"St. Andrews"	1986	$45
"Style Analysis"	1951	$25
"Swing To Better Golf"	1957	$15
"This Is Golf"	1954	$25
"This Is Putting"	1957	$35
"The Woman Golfer"	1952	$20
Stanwich Club:		
"The Stanwich Club"	1972	$15
A. Stark:		
"Physical Training For Golfers"	1937	$85
Allan D. Starr:		
"The Easy Way To Lower Your Golf Score"	1975	$10
Donald Steel:		
"The Golfer's Bedside Book"	1971	$30
"Guiness Book Of Golf Facts And Feats"	1980	$25
Donald Steel and Peter Ryde:		
"The Encyclopedia Of Golf"	1975	$25
"The Shell International Encyclopedia Of Golf"	1975	$65
Chester K. Steele:		
"The Golf Course Mystery"	1919	$75
Eldon P. Steeves:		
"Nineteenth & Twentieth Century Golf Literature		
And Memorabilia"	1996	$150

AUTHOR TITLE	PUB. DATE	VALUE
Jennette A. Stein and Emma F. Waterman:		
"Golf For Beginning Players"	1934	$45
Harris B. Steinberg:		
"The Hackers: Twelve Golf Drawings"	1956	$30
H.G. Stephenson:		
"A History Of Todmorden Golf Club"	1983	$15
Leonard Stern and Ed Powers:		
"The World's Greatest And Funniest Golf Awards"	1985	$10
Elizabeth S. Stevenson:		
"The Belvedere Club, Memoirs Of Members 1878-1968"	1969	$15
Earl Stewart Jr. and Dr. Harry E. Gunn:		
"Golf Begins At Forty"	1977	$10
"Left Hander's Golf Book"	1976	$10
Hal D. Stewart:		
"The Nineteenth Hole A Play In One Act"	1933	$295
James L. Stewart:		
"Golfiana Miscellanea, Being A Collection Of Interesting Monographs On The Royal And Ancient Game Of Golf"	1887	$900
T. Ross Stewart:		
"Lays Of The Links: A Score Of Parodies"	1895	$450
Fred Stibbons:		
"Norfolk's Caddie Poet"	1923	$175
Leo Stillings:		
"Golf Fundamentals And Helpful Hints"	1935	$40
Charley Stine:		
"1983 Golf Directory"	1983	$15
Frank M. Stipe:		
"The Australian"	1980	$15
David Stirk:		
"Carry Your Bag Sir?"	1989	$45
"Golf: The Great Clubmakers"	1991	$65
"Golf: The History Of An Obsession"	1987	$40
Stirling Golf Club:		
"Stirling Golf Club Centenary 1869-1969"	1969	$15
John Stirling:		
"Fit For Golf"	1984	$10
"Golf: The Skills Of The Game"	1985	$15
M.A. Stobart:		
"Won At The Last Hole: A Golfing Romance"	1893	$2,200
John Stobbs:		
"An A.B.C. Of Golf"	1964	$20
"The Anatomy Of Golf: Technique And Tactic"	1962	$20
"At Random Through The Green"	1966	$15
"Camberley Heath Golf Club"	1955	$15
"Tackle Golf This Way"	1961	$10

AUTHOR TITLE	PUB. DATE	VALUE
William L. Stoddard:		
"The New Golfer's Almanac"	1909	$350
Sydney Stokes:		
"A History Of Ekwanok"	1974	$75
Story Of The Open:		
"The Story Of The Open 1860-1960"	1960	$40
Carlton Stowers:		
"The Unsinkable Titanic Thompson"	1982	$20
Lewis Strang:		
"Golf And Business"	1925	$65
Stratford-On-Avon Golf Club:		
"The Stratford-On-Avon Golf Club"	1946	$55
John Strawn:		
"Driving The Green: The Making Of A Golf Course"	1991	$20
Frank Strazza:		
"Golf's Inside Secrets"	1955	$15
Mabel A. Stringer:		
"Golfing Reminiscences"	1924	$1,000
Horace D. Strong:		
"Thru The Years At The Brooklawn Country Club 1895-1945 50th Anniversary"	1945	$50
Joseph Strutt:		
"The Sports And Pastimes Of The People Of England"	1801	$875
Ian Stuart:		
"Golf In Hertfordshire"	1972	$15
Don Sturgess:		
"Basic Golf"	1954	$10
J. Hamilton Stutt:		
"The Reclamation Of The Derelict Lands For Golf"	1980	$35
Louise Suggs:		
"Par Golf For Women"	1953	$25
Louise Suggs And Others:		
"Golf For Women"	1960	$15
Des Sullivan:		
"Essex Falls Country Club 1896-1950"	1950	$20
George Sullivan:		
"The Champions Guide To Golf"	1966	$10
Sunset Magazine:		
"Golf Course Directory For California"	1964	$15
Pearson Surita:		
"The Royal Calcutta Golf Club 150th Anniversary 1829-1979"	1979	$95
Eddie Sussalla:		
"Tournament Players Magazine"	1979	$15
Susie Takes Up Golf:		
"Susie Takes Up Golf"	1940	$60

AUTHOR TITLE	PUB. DATE	VALUE
Helen G. Sutin and Beatrice Quinn:		
"Chips And Putts"	1969	$10
Martin A.F. Sutton:		
"The Book Of The Links: A Symposium On Golf"	1912	$600
"Golf Courses, Design, Construction		
And Upkeep"	1933	$875
"Laying Out And Upkeeping Of Golf Courses And		
Putting Greens"	1906	$1,750
Brian Swarbick:		
"The Duffer's Guide To Bogey Golf"	1973	$15
Henry E. Swanson:		
"Fifty Years Of Woodland Golf Club 1902-1952"	1952	$40
Swanston Golf Club:		
"Swanston Golf Club"	1948	$35
O.F.T.:		
"Aldeburgh Golf Club The First 100 Years		
1884-1984"	1984	$15
S. Takahata:		
"The Story Of The Kobe Golf Club"	1966	$40
Jimmy Tarbuck:		
"Tarbuck On Golf"	1983	$15
Jerry Tarde:		
"How To Hit Crisp Iron Shots"	1980	$10
Tavistock Country Club:		
"Tavistock Country Club 1921-1971"	1971	$25
Arthur V. Taylor:		
"Origines Golfianae: The Birth Of Golf And Its Early		
Childhood As Revealed In A Chance Discovered		
Manusript From A Scottish Monastery"		
Special Edition Of 500	1912	$800
Bert L. Taylor:		
"A Line O'Gowf Or Two"	1923	$125
Chip Taylor:		
"What You Should Know To Putt For Bread"	1976	$10
Dawson Taylor:		
"Inside Golf"	1978	$15
"The Masters"	1973	$55
Deluxe Edition		$125
"The Masters: An Illustrated History"	1981	$45
"St. Andrews Cradle Of Golf"	1976	$40
Hugh Taylor:		
"Golf Dictionary"	1970	$15
J. Fred Taylor and W.D. Kerr:		
"The Beaconsfield Golf Club 1904-1979		
Seventy-Fifth Anniversary"	1979	$40
J.H. Taylor:		
"Golf: My Life's Work"	1943	$450
Second Edition	1943	$150

AUTHOR TITLE	PUB. DATE	VALUE
J.H. Taylor (cont.):		
"Southampton Public Golf Courses"	1935	$60
"Taylor On Golf, Impressions,		
Comments, And Hints"	1902	$575
Signed First Edition		$1,250
James Taylor:		
"Formby Golf Club 1884-1984"	1984	$30
John L. Taylor:		
"Golf Collectors Price Guide"	1983	$45
Joshua Taylor:		
"The Art Of Golf"	1913	$200
Signed By Taylor	1913	$275
"The Lure Of The Links"	1920	$375
Paula Taylor:		
"Golf's Greatest Winner: Jack Nicklaus"	1977	$20
William D. Taylor:		
"Wallasey Golf Club 1891-1953"	1953	$25
Tea Time At The Masters:		
"Tea Time At The Masters:		
A Collection Of Recipies"	1977	$15
Tedesco Country Club:		
"Tedesco Country 1903-1953"	1953	$35
Tee Party On The Green:		
"Tee Party On The Green"	1925	$125
Tee Up:		
"Tee Up"	1962	$15
Lawrence Teeman:		
"Consumer Guide Complete Guide To Golf"	1975	$10
David Shea Teeple:		
"How To Beat At Golf"	1958	$10
Tehidy Park Golf Club:		
"Tehidy Park Golf Club"	1947	$40
H.A. Templeton:		
"Vector Putting: The Art And Science Of		
Reading Greens and Computing Break"	1984	$15
This Golf From Tee To Green:		
"This Golf From Tee To Green"	1936	$150
M.D. Thom:		
"Instructions To Young Golfers"	1959	$15
"It's A Golf Rule"	1951	$35
"Tricky Golf Rules"	1952	$125
David Thomas:		
"Modern Golf"	1967	$15
George C. Thomas Jr.:		
"Golf Architecture In America, Its Strategy		
And Construction"	1927	$600
Signed By Thomas		$2,250

AUTHOR TITLE	PUB. DATE	VALUE
Ivor S. Thomas:		
"Formby Golf 1884-1972"	1972	$35
P. Richard Thomas:		
"The Country Club Of Meadville 1905-1976"	1977	$15
Peter H. Thomas:		
"Golf Reminiscences By An Old Hand"	1985	$65
James K. Thompson Golden Anniversary:		
"James K. Thompson Golden Anniversary"	1968	$15
John Thompson:		
"Golfing And Other Poems And Songs"	1893	$925
Kenneth R. Thompson:		
"The Mental Side Of Golf"	1947	$40
M.B. Thompson:		
"Miniature Golf: A Treatise On The Subject		
Containing Business Building Ideas"	1930	$90
P.M. Thompson:		
"The Experience Of A Dub Golfer"	1925	$275
Phillips B. Thompson:		
"Simplifying The Golf Stroke"	1929	$125
W.J. Thompson:		
"Commonsense Golf"	1923	$75
Bernard Thomson:		
"How To Play Golf"	1939	$40
Dave Thomson:		
"Practical Golf"	1923	$60
George A. Thomson:		
"The Story Of The Yarra Yarra Golf Club"	1972	$45
Jimmy Thomson:		
"Hit Em A Mile! How To Drive A Golf Ball"	1940	$50
Peter Thomson and Desmond Zwar:		
"This Wonderful World Of Golf"	1969	$20
Will J.A. Thomson:		
"Golfing Memories, Including A Short History Of		
The Titirangi Golf Club And Excerpts From		
Golf Lies And Otherwise"	1951	$75
Arthur W. Tillinghast:		
"Cobble Valley Golf Yarns And Other Sketches"	1915	$675
"The Mutt And Other Golf Yarns"	1925	$500
Signed Copy		$1,000
"Planning A Golf Course"	1917	$1,200
Bud Timbrook:		
"Golf Mystic Solved"	1982	$15
W.A. Timpson:		
"Hale Golf Club Seventy Five Years 1903-1978"	1978	$15
Desmond Tolhurst:		
"Golf At Merion"	1989	$65
"St. Andrews Golf Club: The Birthplace		
Of American Golf"	1989	$250

AUTHOR TITLE	PUB. DATE	VALUE
Cyril J.H. Tolley:		
"Drive And Iron"	1930	$175
"The Modern Golfer"	1924	$95
Torquay Golf Club:		
"The Torquay Golf Club"	1932	$90
Bob Toski:		
"12 Short Cuts To Better Golf"	1975	$15
"A Beginners Guide To Golf"	1955	$15
"Golf For A Lifetime"	1981	$15
"How To Cure Golf's Six Most Common Faults"	1974	$15
"Bob Toski's Complete Guide To Better Golf"	1977	$15
"Bob Toski's Guide To Better Golf"	1975	$15
"The Touch System For Better Golf"	1971	$15
Bob Toski and Jim Flick:		
"How To Become A Complete Golfer"	1978	$15
Tournament Player Golf Annual:		
"The Tournament Player Golf Annual 1978"	1977	$10
Tournament Player's Championship:		
"Tournament Player's Championship 1982"	1982	$10
Kristen Tow:		
"International Golf Directory: Resorts, Clubs, Courses Around The World"	1974	$20
Peter Townsend:		
"Golf: 100 Ways To Improve Your Game"	1977	$10
Richard B. Townshend:		
"Inspired Golf"	1921	$95
Ann Trabue:		
"History Of The Los Angeles Country Club"	1936	$60
Jerome D. Travers:		
"Travers Golf Book"	1913	$250
Jerome D. Travers & James R. Crowell:		
"The Fifth Estate"	1926	$125
Jerome D. Travers & Grantland Rice:		
"The Winning Shot"	1915	$200
Walter J. Travis:		
"Practical Golf"	1902	$325
Walter J. Travis and Jack White:		
"The Art Of Putting"	1904	$175
Archibald Treat:		
"Golf And Lawyers"	1932	$150
Nicholas Tremayne:		
"Golf How To Become A Champion"	1975	$10
Phil Tresidder:		
"The Golfer Who Laughed"	1981	$15
Paul Trevillion:		
"Dead Heat: The '69 Ryder Cup Classic"	1969	$40
"Tony Jacklin In Play"	1970	$15
"The Perfect Putting Method"	1971	$15
"Save Strokes Like The Stars"	1970	$10

AUTHOR TITLE	PUB. DATE	VALUE
Lee Trevino:		
"Can I Help Your Game?"	1972	$15
"Groove Your Golf Swing My Way"	1976	$10
"I Can Help Your Game"	1971	$15
"Lee's Secret: The Fascinating Success Story		
Of Lee Trevino"	1969	$15
"Swing My Way"	1976	$10
"They Call Me Super Mex"	1982	$15
Lee Trevino and Sam Blair:		
"The Snake In The Sandtrap"	1985	$10
George Trevor:		
"A Blind Man Breaks 80"	1957	$10
Trevose Golf Club:		
"Trevose Golf Club"	1985	$15
Paul Triefus:		
"The Most Excellent Historie Of MacHamlet"	1922	$300
Eldon H. Trimingham:		
"Golf In Bermuda"	1952	$35
William A. Tripp:		
"The Geometry Of Golf"	1960	$15
Pette C. Triscott:		
"Golf In Six Lessons"	1924	$195
John F. Trump:		
"From A Hundred And Two To Eighty-Two		
In A Month Or Two"	1934	$20
Cecil F. Tucker:		
"Nineteenth Hole Romances And The Devious		
Methods Of Joseph Blotchford"	1927	$175
William H. Tucker:		
"A Golf Course For Your Community"	1925	$70
Walter R. Tuckerman:		
"The History Of The Burning Tree Club"	1948	$55
Richard S. Tufts:		
"The Principles Behind The Rules Of Golf"	1960	$125
"The Scottish Invasion"	1962	$60
W.W. Tulloch:		
"The Life Of Tom Morris, With Glimpses Of		
St. Andrews And Its Golfing Celebrities"	1908	$1,200
Reprint	1982	$350
Turnberry Story:		
"The Turnberry Story"	1985	$15
Rupert Turner:		
"Novelty Golf Match"	1942	$60
Jim Turnesa:		
"12 Lessons To Better Golf"	1953	$20
"Driver: A Swing Analysis In Slow Motion"	1950	$50
"Low Score Golf"	1953	$15

AUTHOR TITLE	PUB. DATE	VALUE

Turning Point:
"Turning Point-The 54th Amateur Championship Of
   The United States Golf Association-1954 Winner
     Arnold Palmer"   1983 $20
Gary Turnquist:
   "Golf: Solving A Puzzle"   1985 $10
Mex Tuthill:
   "Golf Without Gall"   1940 $10
Anthony Tuttle:
   "Drive For The Green"   1969 $15
Two Counties Golf Guide:
   "Two Counties Golf Guide: Being The Itinerary Of
     The Golf Courses In Lancashire and Cheshire" 1939 $90
Two Hundred Funny Golf Stories:
   "200 Funny Golf Stories As Told At The 19th" 1932 $125
Two Of His Kind:
   "The Six Handicap Golfer's Companion"   1909 $175
Martin Tyler:
   "Sportsman's World Of Golf"   1976 $10
Ralph G. Tyler:
   "The Golf Oracle Or Golf Made Easy For
     The Vest Pocket"   1913 $100
   "A Handbook For Golf Beginners"   1914 $125
Frederick D. Tyner:
   "The Golfer's Dream"   1936 $150
Tyrrells Wood Golf Club:
   "The Tyrrells Wood Golf Club"   1951 $20
Uitenhage Golf Club:
   "Uitenhage Golf Club 75th Anniversary
     1891-1966"   1966 $15
UK & Eire 1983 Golf Guide:
   "UK & Eire 1983 Golf Guide"   1983 $15
Ulen Country Club:
   "The Ulen Country Club Silver Anniversary
     1924-1949"   1949 $20
Joe Ungvary:
   "How To Be A Good Caddy"   1961 $10
United Services Golf Club:
   "United Services Golf Club"   1951 $15
U. S. Open Official Annual:
   "85th U.S. Open Official Annual-Oakland Hills" 1985 $15
United States Golf Association:
   "Calkin System Of Calculating Handicap"   1927 $20
   "Decisions On The Rules Of Golf"   1971 $15
   "Golf Committee Manual And USGA
     Handicap Systems"   1965 $15
   "Record Book Of The USGA Championships
     1895-1953"   1953 $35

AUTHOR TITLE	PUB. DATE	VALUE
United States Golf Association(cont.):		
"Record Book Of The USGA Championships 1895-1980" Two Vols.	1980	$15
"Record Book Of The USGA Championships And International Events"	1947	$45
"Record Book Of The USGA Championships"	1972	$15
"The Conduct Of Womens Golf"	1945	$20
"USGA Course Rating System"	1985	$10
"USGA GHIN: Golf Handicap And Information Operations Manual"	1984	$10
"USGA Handicap System With USGA Course Rating Systems For Men And Women And Golf Committe Manual"	1984	$15
"USGA Women's Golf Course Rating System"	1985	$10
United States Government Printing Office:		
"Hickory Golf Shafts"	1930	$60
United States Junior Chamber Of Commerce:		
"Jaycee Junior Golf Instructional Handbook"	1962	$15
United States Senior's Golf Association:		
"The First Seventy-Five Years of USSGA 1905-1980"	1980	$45
"A Record Of Fifty Years USSGA 1904-1954"	1954	$65
"Senior Golf In The United States, Canada, And Great Britain"	1936	$60
J.M. Urry:		
"To St. Andrews For The Open Championship 1946"	1946	$40
Thomas H. Uzzell:		
"Golf In The World's Oldest Mountains"	1926	$800
H.A. Vachell:		
"The New Forest Golf Club"	1925	$45
Pembroke A. Vaile:		
"Golf On The Green"	1915	$100
"How To Approach"	1919	$60
"How To Drive"	1919	$60
"How To Learn Golf: Spalding Primer Series"	1919	$55
"How To Putt And Training For Golf"	1919	$50
"Illustrated Rules Of Golf"	1919	$65
"Modern Golf"	1909	$250
"The New Golf"	1916	$95
"The New Golf"	1917	$75
"Putting Made Easy: The Mark G. Harris Method"	1935	$95
"Scientific Putting"	1927	$85
"The Short Game"	1928	$95
"The Soul Of Golf"	1912	$335
"Swerve Or Flight Of The Gull"	1905	$75
Jessie Valentine:		
"Better Golf Definitely"	1967	$10

AUTHOR TITLE	PUB. DATE	VALUE
Jim Valli:		
"Golf Guide: Central Otago-Southland"	1979	$35
Nicholas Van Daalen:		
"International Golf Guide"	1976	$20
Maxine Van Evera:		
"Building Your Swing For Better Golf		
With Amy Alcott"	1981	$10
Steven J. H. Van Hengel:		
"Early Golf"	1982	$50
"Early Golf: History And Development"	1972	$75
Charles E. Van Loan:		
"Fore"	1918	$95
W.G. Van T. Sutphen:		
"The Golfer's Alphabet"	1899	$975
Reprint	1967	$35
"The Golficide and Other Tales Of		
The Fair Green"	1898	$400
"Harper's Official Golf Guide 1901"	1901	$1,200
"The Nineteenth Hole"	1901	$275
"The Official Golf Guide 1902"	1902	$1,000
"The Peripatetic Hazard"	1921	$200
Guernsey Van Riper Jr.:		
"Golfing Greats: Two Top Pros"	1975	$10
Cicely Van Straten:		
"Caddie For A Crook"	1985	$15
John M. Vander Meulen:		
"Getting Out Of The Rough"	1926	$80
Alfred Vardon And E.W.J. Wilson:		
"Golfing Hints"	1912	$175
Facsimile	1996	$25
Harry Vardon:		
"The Complete Golfer"	1907	$400
Signed By Vardon		$1,250
"The Gist Of Golf"	1922	$100
"Golf Club Selection"	1916	$275
"How To Play Golf"	1912	$110
"My Golfing Life"	1933	$600
Memorial Tournament Reprint	1981	$100
Reprint	1985	$125
Reprint	1992	$35
"Progressive Golf"	1920	$200
Harry Vardon And Others:		
"Success At Golf"	1914	$125
E.C. Vare:		
"Hip Pocket Golf Coach"	1983	$15
Bill Ventreska:		
"Play Better Golf"	1966	$10

AUTHOR TITLE	PUB. DATE	VALUE
Ken Venturi:		
"Comeback: The Ken Venturi Story"	1966	$25
"Let's Analyze Your Golf Swing"	1960	$10
"Venturi Analysis: Learning Better Golf From Champions"	1981	$15
"The Venturi System With Special Material On Shotmaking For The Advanced Golfer"	1983	$15
Verulam Golf Club:		
"The Verulam Golf Club"	1934	$40
Veteran:		
"The Secret Of Golf For Occasional Players"	1922	$95
Victim:		
"An ABC Of Golf"	1898	$800
Al Victor:		
"Arnie And His Army"	1964	$15
Dennis Vidler:		
"Rye Golf Club, The First 90 Years"	1984	$65
Dean Vietor:		
"Your Golf Game's In Big Trouble When"	1984	$10
Lawrence Viney:		
"Ashridge Golf Club 1932-1982"	1982	$15
V.S. Viscellette:		
"Golf Club Reconditioning"	1964	$10
Norman Von Nida:		
"Golf Is My Business"	1956	$20
"Golf Isn't Hard"	1949	$10
Clifton L. Voorhies:		
"The Mental Game Of Golf"	1950	$15
Jerry Vroom:		
"So You Want To Be A Golfer"	1973	$15
E.W.:		
"The Yorkshire Union Of Golf Clubs, First County Championship"	1894	$375
G.B.W.:		
"The Phraseology Of Golf 3"	1893	$1,200
James Wagenvoord:		
"Golf Diary"	1981	$10
Corydon Wagner:		
"Pacific Northwest Golf Comes Of Age 1892-1926"	1973	$10
"Tacoma Country And Golf Club 1894-1969 Seventy-Fifth Anniversary"	1969	$30
Susan F. Wagner:		
"History Of Flossmoor Country Club 1899-1979"	1979	$15
Wales, A Golfing Guide:		
"Wales: A Golfing Guide For The Business Traveller"	1980	$20
David G. Walker:		
"Rick Tees Off"	1985	$10

AUTHOR TITLE	PUB. DATE	VALUE
Oscar W. Walker:		
"Practical Golf Lessons From A New Angle"	1949	$20
Robert Walker:		
"Fairhaven Golf Glub"	1965	$10
"Ham Manor Residential Golf Club"	1951	$20
"The Newquay Golf Club"	1951	$20
"The Southerndown Golf Club"	1955	$15
"The Verulam Golf Club"	1957	$10
Lillian Wallcock:		
"With A Song In My Cart"	1970	$10
Brian Wallis:		
"Echoes From An Old Fairway"	1986	$20
"A History Of Horbury And		
District Golf Club 1907-1965"	1965	$10
Walmer And Kingsdown Golf Club:		
"Walmer And Kingsdown Golf Club"	1937	$75
Walsall Golf Club:		
"Walsall Golf Club"	1938	$60
John H. Walsh:		
"Seaford Golf Club: A History"	1986	$45
Leigh Walsh:		
"How To Teach Yourself The Expert Golf Swing"	1956	$10
Tom Walsh:		
"The Picture Way To Better Golf"	1956	$10
Charles Ward:		
"How To Play Little Aston Golf Course"	1965	$10
Hugh Ward:		
"Effortless Golf"	1956	$10
Peter Ward:		
"Came Down To Golf"	1984	$35
P.A. Ward-Thomas:		
"The Long Green Fairway"	1966	$15
"Masters Of Golf"	1961	$20
"Not Only Golf: An Autobiography"	1981	$35
"The Royal And Ancient"	1980	$25
"Shell Golfers' Atlas Of England, Scotland		
And Wales"	1968	$25
Pat Ward-Thomas and Others:		
"The World Atlas Of Golf"	1976	$45
G. Waring:		
"Golf: A Scientific Approach, The Mechanics		
Of The Game"	1958	$15
Washington Golf and Country Club:		
"History Of The Washington Golf And		
Country Club"	1947	$60
E.R. Wason:		
"Golf Without Tears"	1951	$35

AUTHOR TITLE	PUB. DATE	VALUE
T.F.R. Waters:		
"A History Of The Royal Hong Kong Golf Club"	1960	$100
A. Campbell Watson:		
"Podson's Golfing Year"	1930	$175
Alan S. Watson:		
"The First 100 Years, A History Of The Royal Belfast Golf Club 1881-1981"	1981	$90
Gilbert Watson:		
"A Caddie Of St. Andrews"	1907	$650
"Skipper"	1906	$575
Gilbert Watson:		
"A Short History Of Craigmillar Park Golf Club1895-1974"	1974	$15
J.W. Watson:		
"Little Lessons In Golf"	1921	$40
Tom Watson:		
"Getting Up And Down"	1983	$15
"The New Rules Of Golf"	1984	$15
Signed By Watson		$50
"The Rules Of Golf"	1980	$10
"Tom Watson's Key Swing Thoughts"	1978	$15
Alick A. Watt:		
"Collecting Old Golf Clubs" Signed	1985	$75
"Collecting Old Golf Clubs"	1990	$40
Wyn Weaver:		
"Golf Clubs, An Eccentric Sketch"	1925	$110
Warren H. Webb:		
"Lessons On Golf"	1907	$95
Louis Webber and Dennis Kennedy:		
"Golf Manners"	1968	$15
Walter H. Webling:		
"Fore: A Few More Golf Shots"	1908	$275
"Fore: The Call Of The Links"	1909	$375
"Golf: In Verse And Reverse"	1924	$375
"An Interrupted Golf Match and Other Stories"	1910	$300
"Locker Room Ballards"	1925	$200
"On And Off The Links"	1921	$275
Wee Burn Country Club:		
"Wee Burn Country Club, A History"	1979	$20
Bob Weeks:		
"The World's Greatest Golf Courses"	1992	$15
Edward Weeks:		
"Myopia, A Centennial Chronicle 1875-1975"	1975	$50
Harry Weetman:		
"Add To Your Golf Power"	1963	$15
"Golf Drive And 7-Iron Shot"	1960	$100
"The Way To Golf"	1953	$15

AUTHOR TITLE	PUB. DATE	VALUE
Ralph Weidemnkopf:		
"The Science Of Controlled Relaxation In Golf"	1936	$35
Tom Weiskopf:		
"Go For The Flag"	1969	$15
Mike Weiss:		
"100 Handy Hints On How To Break 100"	1951	$10
Jane F. Welch, Wade M. Welch, and Richard F. Radford:		
"1000 Questions: The Golfer's Book Of Trivia"	1985	$10
Stanley Weld:		
"A History Of The Great Chebeague Golf Club"	1962	$15
Charles W. Welsh:		
"Seventy-Five Years Of Golf At		
The Royal Eastbourne Golf Club 1887-1962"	1962	$60
Clifford C. Wendehack:		
"Golf And Country Clubs"	1929	$375
William P. Wendt:		
"The Distance Builder"	1982	$10
Wentworth Club:		
"Wentworth Club"	1959	$15
D.N. Werner:		
"Great Golfers Of The Twentieth Century"	1971	$20
"Lower Your Golf Score"	1972	$10
Nick Weslock:		
"Your Golf Bag Pro: Nick Westlock's Little		
Black Book Of Key Golf Secrets"	1985	$10
Douglas B. Wesson:		
"I'll Never Be Cured And I Don't Much Care"	1928	$80
West Wilts Golf Club:		
"West Wilts Golf Club"	1938	$45
Henry L. West:		
"The Columbia Country Club As It Was		
In The Beginning"	1938	$40
"Lyrics Of The Links"	1921	$225
Western Golf Association:		
"Caddie Committee Manual"	1947	$20
"Caddie Master Manual"	1955	$25
"Caddie Operations Manual"	1969	$10
"Camera Tour Of Caddieville"	1955	$10
"Case For Caddies"	1965	$15
"New Caddie Committee Guide And		
Electric Cart Survey"	1955	$10
"Pin Pointers"	1948	$15
"Recruiting And Retaining Your Caddies"	1951	$25
Westgate-On-Sea And Birchington Golf Club:		
"The Westgate-On-Sea And Birchington		
Golf Club"	1926	$75
Westmount Golf And Country Club:		
"Westmount Golf And Country Club 1931-1981"	1981	$15

AUTHOR TITLE	PUB. DATE	VALUE
John W. Weston:		
"A History Of Coombe Wood Golf Club		
1904-1970"	1985	$15
Weston-Super Mare Golf Club:		
"The Weston-Super Mare Golf Club"	1955	$20
H.N. Wethered:		
"The Perfect Golfer"	1931	$125
H.N. Wethered and T. Simpson:		
"The Architectural Side Of Golf"	1929	$2,200
Signed Limited Edition		$12,000
"Design For Golf"	1952	$200
Joyce Wethered:		
"Golfing Memories and Methods"	1933	$100
Reprint	1954	$20
Joyce Wethered and Others:		
"The Game Of Golf, The Lonsdale Library"	1931	$125
Roger Wethered:		
"The Temple Golf Club"	1938	$35
Roger and Joyce Wethered:		
"Golf From Two Sides"	1925	$75
Weymouth Golf Club:		
"The Weymouth Golf Club"	1951	$20
Vera Wheatley:		
"Mixed Foursomes: A Saga Of Golf"	1936	$125
Where To Golf In Kansas City:		
"Where To Golf In Kansas City"	1982	$10
H.J. Whigham:		
"Athletic Sports The Outdoor Library"	1897	$145
"How To Play Golf"	1897	$200
Charles A. Whitcombe:		
"Charles Whitcombe On Golf"	1931	$30
"Golf"	1949	$20
"Golf Shots: The Drive, Fairway Hazard Pocket		
Pro Series No. 1"	1933	$50
"Golf Shots: The Iron, Fairway Hazard Pocket		
Pro Series No. 2"	1933	$45
"Golf Shots: The Mashie Niblick, Fairway Pocket		
Pro Series No. 3"	1933	$45
"Golf Shots: Niblick And Putter, Fairway & Hazard		
Pocket Pro Series No. 4"	1933	$45
Ernest R. Whitcombe:		
"The Golf I Teach"	1947	$20
"How To Play Meyrick Park Golf Course"	1951	$15
Reginald A. Whitcombe:		
"Golf's No Mystery"	1938	$20
Fairmount R. White:		
"Golf In The Seventies For Those		
In The Sixties"	1962	$10

AUTHOR TITLE	PUB. DATE	VALUE
Jack White:		
"Easier Golf"	1924	$75
"Putting"	1921	$225
Ronald J. White:		
"Golf As I Play It"	1953	$35
Signed By White		$125
Stewart E. White:		
"The Shepper-Newfounder"	1931	$65
James F. Whiteford:		
"Tam At Golf Or The Nineteenth Hole"	1939	$60
Eric Whitehead:		
"Hathstauwk: The Story Of Capilano Golf		
And Country Club"	1981	$45
Whiteleaf Golf Club:		
"Whiteleaf Golf Club"	1967	$20
Marshall Whitlatch:		
"Golf For Beginners And Others"	1910	$35
Caspar W. Whitney:		
"A Sporting Pilgrimage"	1895	$125
Don E. Whitney:		
"Golf From A-Z"	1982	$10
Howard F. Whitney:		
"Decisions On The Rules Of Golf"	1927	$40
Irvo H Whitton:		
"Golf"	1947	$30
Who's Who:		
"Who's Who In Golf And Directory Of Golf Clubs		
And Members"	1909	$600
Price Wickersham And Frank Lauder:		
"The K.C.G.A. Caddie Book"	1921	$95
Verne Wickham:		
"The Municipal Golf Course: Organizing And		
Operating Guide"	1955	$20
Lawrence A. Wien:		
"The Golf Club At Astetuck"	1974	$15
H.J. Wigham:		
"How To Play Golf"	1897	$275
Morton Wild:		
"Inwood Country Club Fiftieth Anniversary		
1901-1951"	1951	$40
Payson S. Wild And Bert L. Taylor:		
"The Links Of Ancient Rome"	1912	$375
Roland Wild:		
"The Loneliest Game"	1969	$15
Larry Wilde:		
"The Official Golfer's Joke Book"	1977	$10
Wilderness Country Club:		
"Wilderness Country Club And Golf Course"	1930	$40

AUTHOR TITLE	PUB. DATE	VALUE
Elizabeth D. Wilkinson:		
"History Of The Toledo Women's		
District Golf Association"	1931	$35
George Will:		
"Golf The Modern Way"	1968	$10
Ambrose Williams:		
"The Principles Of The Golf Swing"	1965	$10
Arthur C. Williams:		
"Brooklawn Country Club 1895-1970		
75th Anniversary"	1970	$25
David Williams:		
"How To Coach And Play Championship Golf"	1962	$10
"The Science Of The Golf Swing"	1969	$15
Eddie Williams:		
"How To Improve Your Golf With The Developar"	1958	$10
Evan "Big Cat" Williams:		
"You Can Hit The Golf Ball Farther"	1979	$10
Gwen Williams:		
"Unique Golf Resorts Of The World"	1983	$20
Lewis Williams:		
"Golf Without Tears"	1940	$35
Michael Williams:		
"Daily Telegraph Pocket Sports Facts: Golf"	1984	$10
"History Of Golf"	1985	$20
J.E. Willmott:		
"Sutton Coldfield Golf Club Jubilee 1899-1939"	1939	$85
Wilson Sporting Goods:		
"For The Esquire Of The Golf Links"	1938	$45
"From Tee To Cup"	1955	$30
"The Gateway To Golf 1953"	1953	$65
"Presenting The 7-Up Golf Tips By The Experts"	1957	$15
Enid Wilson:		
"A Gallery Of Women Golfers"	1961	$55
"Golf For Women"	1964	$20
Enid Wilson And Robert A. Lewis:		
"So That's What I Do"	1935	$30
Harry L. Wilson:		
"So This Is Golf"	1923	$80
J.H. Wilson:		
"The Golfers A Past Era"	1977	$10
Kenneth Wilson:		
"It's All In The Swing"	1947	$15
"To Better Golf In Two Strides"	1938	$30
Mark Wilson:		
"The Best Of Henry Longhurst"	1978	$15
Winchester Golf Club:		
"Rules For Caddies"	1926	$40

AUTHOR TITLE	PUB. DATE	VALUE
Herbert Warren Wind:		
"The Complete Golfer"	1954	$40
"Following Through"	1985	$35
"The Gilded Age Of Sports"	1961	$40
"Golf Quiz"	1980	$20
"Golf Tips From The Top Professionals"	1958	$20
"The Lure Of Golf"	1971	$40
"On The Tour With Harry Sprague"	1960	$75
"The Open's Fourth Visit To Winged Foot"	1984	$60
"Shell's Wonderful World Of Golf 1962"	1962	$90
"The Story Of American Golf: Its Champions		
And Its Championships"	1948	$400
"Thorny Lea Golf Club 1900-1950		
50th Anniversary"	1950	$60
"Tips From The Top"	1955	$20"
"Tips From The Top Book 2"	1956	$20
"Herbert Warren Wind's Golf Book"	1971	$40
Windemere Golf Club:		
"The Windemere Golf Club"	1949	$20
Frank Wing:		
"Fore! Eighty-Two Sketches Of The Same		
Number Of Minneapolis Golfers"	1929	$75
Roland Wingate:		
"12 Money Shots In Golf"	1935	$35
"Saving Strokes"	1934	$50
Ed Winter:		
"Simplified Golf Instructions"	1950	$10
Gary Wiren:		
"Golf"	1971	$10
"Planning And Conducting Junior Golf Programs"	1973	$10
"Super Power Golf: Techniques For		
Increasing Distance"	1984	$10
Dr. Gary Wiren and Dr. Richard Coop:		
"The New Golf Mind"	1978	$10
Kris M. Wise:		
"The Answers To Par Golf"	1978	$10
Sidney L. Wise:		
"Carolina Golfer Directory 1976"	1976	$10
J.R. Wishart:		
"Golf Course Guide To Southern Africa"	1983	$15
Tom W. Wishon:		
"The Golf Club Identification And Price Guide"	1985	$20
Harry Woan:		
"Swing Secrets Analysed, Explained		
and Simplified"	1934	$25
P.G. Wodehouse:		
"The Clicking Of Cuthbert"	1922	$110
"Divots"	1927	$90

AUTHOR TITLE	PUB. DATE	VALUE
P.G. Wodehouse (cont.):		
"Fore: The Best Of Wodehouse On Golf"	1983	$20
"The Golf Omnibus"	1973	$125
Reprint	1991	$25
"Golf Without Tears"	1924	$95
"The Heart Of Golf"	1926	$90
"Wodehouse On Golf"	1940	$195
Wollaston Golf Club:		
"Wollaston Golf Club: The Story Of The Old Club, Fiftieth Anniversary 1895-1945"	1945	$60
Woman Golfer:		
"Golf For Women"	1916	$175
A.G. Wood:		
"Royal Jersey Golf Club"	1965	$20
B. Britten Wood:		
"Piqua Country Club History"	1975	$15
Craig Wood:		
"How To Play Golf"	1935	$75
Harry B. Wood:		
"Golfing Curios And The Like"	1910	$1,500
Signed By Wood		$1,995
Reprint	1980	$60
Roy F. Woodbury and Charlotte I. Claflin:		
"The Woodhall Spa Golf Club"	1951	$20
Arthur L. Woodhead:		
"A History Of Huddersfield Golf Club From 1891-1949"	1949	$40
Alan Woodison:		
"Ayershire Golf Guide"	1983	$15
E.J. Woodward:		
"Golf Greens Of England, Ireland And Wales"	1897	$1,700
Worthing Golf Club:		
"Worthing Golf Club 1905-1980"	1980	$15
Gene Worthington:		
"How To Acquire The Perfect Golf Swing"	1973	$10
Bucky Woy:		
"Sign 'Em Up Bucky: The Adventures Of A Sport Agent"	1975	$10
Wrexham Golf Club:		
"The Wrexham Golf Club"	1937	$60
Wright And Ditson:		
"Wright And Ditson Golf Guide" First Published	1900	$175
Harry Wright:		
"A Short History Of Golf In Mexico And The Mexico City Country Club"	1938	$475
Signed By Wright		$650
Jack W. Wright:		
"Guide To Vancouver Island Courses"	1977	$15

AUTHOR TITLE	PUB. DATE	VALUE
Mickey Wright:		
"Play Golf The Wright Way"	1962	$15
Joyce Wrinch-Schulz:		
"The First Sixty Years, A History Of The Durban Country Club From 1922-1982"	1982	$125
Josephine Wunsch:		
"Girl In The Rough"	1981	$10
Stevan Wygant:		
"What's Your Golf I.Q.?"	1962	$10
Wyke Green Golf Club:		
"Wyke Green Golf Club"	1935	$40
Anthony Wynne:		
"Death Of A Golfer"	1937	$275
Wyoming Valley Country Club:		
"Wyoming Valley Country Club 1896-1984, A History"	1984	$20
Mr. X:		
"Beginners Guide To Golf"	1973	$15
"Golf Lessons With Mr. X"	1969	$15
"Golf Monthly's Lessons"	1968	$15
"More Golf Lessons With Mr. X"	1971	$15
Yakima Country Club:		
"Yakima Country Club, Dedication Of The New Club House"	1949	$10
George A. Yeager:		
"The First Seventy-Five Years- Orange County Club 1899-1974"	1974	$20
Yelverton Golf Club:		
"The Yelverton Golf Club"	1938	$45
Count Yogi:		
"Five Simple Steps To Perfect Golf"	1973	$10
Commodore William Yorgey:		
"The Commodore Yorgey Scientific Stance And Swing"	1972	$15
You and Your Golf Course:		
"You And Your Golf Course"	1955	$10
You Can Break 80:		
"You Can Break 80"	1930	$25
Charley Young:		
"Tips From Western New York Golf Pros"	1955	$10
Douglas Young:		
"St. Andrews: Town And Gown, Royal And Ancient"	1969	$35
Jerome A. Young:		
"Documentary Proof That Insanity Is Hereditary"	1951	$10
Tom McFarlane Young:		
"The Open Championship In Scotland: Prints And History"	1985	$15

AUTHOR TITLE	PUB. DATE	VALUE
Your Golf Clubs:		
"Your Golf Clubs And How To Care For Them"	1955	$10
Your Guide To The Open:		
"Your Guide To The Open, St. Andrews 1970"	1970	$15
Bertha D. Zadnik:		
"The Connecticut Women's Golf Association History 1919-1969"	1969	$10
Babe Didrickson Zaharias:		
"Championship Golf"	1949	$45
"This Life I've Led"	1955	$45
Signed First Edition		$900
Jack Zanger:		
"Excersises For Better Golf"	1965	$10
Bob Zender and Charles B. Cleveland:		
"Winning Golf, The Professional Way"	1985	$10
Charles T. Zimmerman:		
"Sixty Years Of Hartford Golf Club 1896-1955"	1955	$20
Zodiac Home Golf Ball Booklet:		
"Golf And How To Play It"	1910	$125
Joseph M. Zogbie:		
"Golf Club Directory Of 1947"	1947	$30
Desond Zwar:		
"Golf: The Dictionary"	1984	$15

The Masters

by Byron Eder

B yron Eder is a classic club collector who indulges his
passion in Masters Memorabilia. Byron is the PGA
Tour Representative for Bobby Grace Putters. This has
enabled him to develop contacts all over the United States,
Europe, and Japan. His contacts with past and present Tour
players led him to having a greater sense of awareness as to
what is important. Although his input was on the Masters
badges his knowledge of golf memorabilia is both eclectic
and envied.

He can be reached at (352) 683-7590

BADGES

Master badges are highly sought after by the collector.
(The terms "badges" and "tickets" are interchangeable.) Badges
are issued for weekly or daily spectator admission, press, staff,
photographer, club house, trophy room, and many others.
Value is based on the year of issue and not to whom it was
issued.

A price on a spectator badge indicates that it was probably
issued to a season ticket holder. If it has no price, it was probably
issued to a club member. The 1966 through 1972 badges have
a folded paper backing with a message about course etiquette
by Robert T. Jones including a facsimile signature. From 1973
until 1976, the facsimile signature on the paper changed to
that of Clifford Roberts. 1977 saw the back printed for the first

time with course etiquette and facsimile signature. The 1991 through 1994 badges had holograms.

Popularity of the winning player often affects the value of a particular badge. These values are reflected in the listing. A 1985 badge is worth $50 while a 1986 badge is worth $150 as it was the year Nicklaus won his sixth Masters. The 1949 badge is important as that was the year of Snead's first Masters win, and the year they first issued a green jacket to the winner. The 1951 badge is most desirable as that was Hogan's first Masters win. The 1953 badge is desirable because Hogan won all three of the Majors he entered that year. 1963 was Nicklaus' first win at Augusta.

All are very collectible. The plastic badges tend to be brittle so you may find them with pieces broken off. Hologram badges may also be damaged. A badge must be well centered and in great condition for it to be worth the listed prices.

1937 Masters' Badge

1941 Masters' Badge

1942 Masters' Badge

1946 Masters' Badge

1947 Masters' Badge

Year	Winner	Value
Badges:		
1934	Horton Smith	$10,000
1935	Gene Sarazen	$5,000
1936	Horton Smith	$4,000
1937	Byron Nelson	$3,000
1938	Henry Picard	$2,000
1939	Ralph Guldahl	$950
1940	Jimmy Demaret	$900
1941	Craig Wood	$850
1942	Byron Nelson	$800
1943	Not Held	
1944	Not Held	
1945	Not Held	
1946	Herman Keiser	$750
1947	Jimmy Demaret	$700
1948	Claude Harmon	$650
1949	Sam Snead	$750
1950	Jimmy Demaret	$550
1951	Ben Hogan	$750
1952	Sam Snead	$550
1953	Ben Hogan	$750
1954	Sam Snead	$550
1955	Cary Middlecoff	$500
1956	Jack Burke Jr.	$500
1957	Doug Ford	$500
1958	Arnold Palmer	$750
1959	Art Wall Jr.	$500
1960	Arnold Palmer	$650
1961	Gary Player	$500
1962	Arnold Palmer	$500
1963	Jack Nicklaus	$500
1964	Arnold Palmer	$500
1965	Jack Nicklaus	$700
1966	Jack Nicklaus	$300
1967	Gay Brewer	$175
1968	Bob Goalby	$175
1969	George Archer	$175
1970	Billy Casper	$150
1971	Charles Coody	$150
1972	Jack Nicklaus	$200
1973	Tommy Aaron	$125
1974	Gary Player	$125
1975	Jack Nicklaus	$200
1976	Raymond Floyd	$150
1977	Tom Watson	$100
1978	Gary Player	$100
1979	Fuzzy Zoeller	$100

1947 Masters' Badge

1948 Masters' Badge

1953 Masters' Badge

1952 Masters' Badge

1954 Masters' Badge

1956 Masters' Badge

1956 Masters' Badge

1957 Masters' Badge

1960 Masters' Badge

Year	Winner	Value
Badges:		
1980	Seve Ballesteros	$75
1981	Tom Watson	$50
1982	Craig Stadler	$50
1983	Seve Ballesteros	$50
1984	Ben Crenshaw	$75
1985	Bernhard Langer	$50
1986	Jack Nicklaus	$150
1987	Larry Mize	$50
1988	Sandy Lyle	$50
1989	Nick Faldo	$40
1990	Nick Faldo	$40
1991	Ian Woosnam	$40
1992	Fred Couples	$40
1993	Bernhard Langer	r$40
1994	Jose Maria Olazabal	$40
1995	Ben Crenshaw	$40
1996	Nick Faldo	$50
1997	Tiger Woods	$125

1960 Masters' Badge

1963 Masters' Badge

1965 Masters' Badge

1966 Masters' Badge

1972 Masters' Badge

1973 Masters' Badge

1983 Masters' Badge   1987 Masters' Badge

1961 Masters' Badge

1963 Masters' Badge   1964 Masters' Badge

1965 Masters' Badge

1968 Masters' Badge   1969 Masters' Badge

1970 Masters' Badge   1971 Masters' Badge

1973 Masters' Badge

1974 Masters' Badge

1975 Masters' Badge

1976 Masters' Badge

1977 Masters' Badge

1978 Masters' Badge

1979 Masters' Badge

1980 Masters' Badge

1981 Masters' Badge

1982 Masters' Badge

1983 Masters' Badge

1984 Masters' Badge

1985 Masters' Badge

1987 Masters' Badge

1988 Masters' Badge

1989 Masters' Badge

1990 Masters' Badge

1991 Masters' Badge   1992 Masters' Badge   1994 Masters' Badge

1993 Masters' Badge

1995 Masters' Badge   1996 Masters' Badge

1997 Masters' Badge

1946 Masters' Badge

1950 Masters' Badge

1954 Masters' Badge

1954 Masters' Badge

1956 Masters' Badge

1956 Masters' Badge

1959 Masters' Badge

Left 1958 Masters' Badge

1960 Masters' Badge

1961 Masters' Badge

1962 Masters' Badge

1963 Masters' Badge

1963 Masters' Badge

1964 Masters' Badge

1964 Masters' Badge

1965 Masters' Badge

1966 Masters' Badge

1966 Masters' Badge

1967 Masters' Badge

Left 1967 Masters' Badge

1967 Masters' Badge

1968 Masters' Badge

1968 Masters' Badge

1969 Masters' Badge

1970 Masters' Badge

Right 1972 Masters' Badge

1972 Masters' Badge

1973 Masters' Badge

1974 Masters' Badge

1975 Masters' Badge

1976 Masters' Badge

1976 Masters' Badge

1977 Masters' Badge

1977 Masters' Badge

1978 Master's Badge

1980 Master's Badge

1985 Master's Badge

Left 1982 Master's Badge

1983 Master's Badge

Right 1984 Master's Badge

1985 Master's Badge

1985 Master's Badge

PHOTOGRAPHER badge

1987 Master's Badge

GOLF SHOP badge

1989 Master's Badge

1989 Master's Badge

1990 Master's Badge

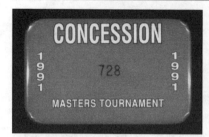

1991 Master's Badge

1991 Master's Badge

1993 Master's Badge

1993 Master's Badge

1993 Master's Badge

1994 Master's Badge

1995 Master's Badge

1996 Master's Badge

Programs:

Only two programs were issued for The Masters.

Year	Winner	Value
1934	Horton Smith	$10,000
1935	Gene Sarazen	$5,000

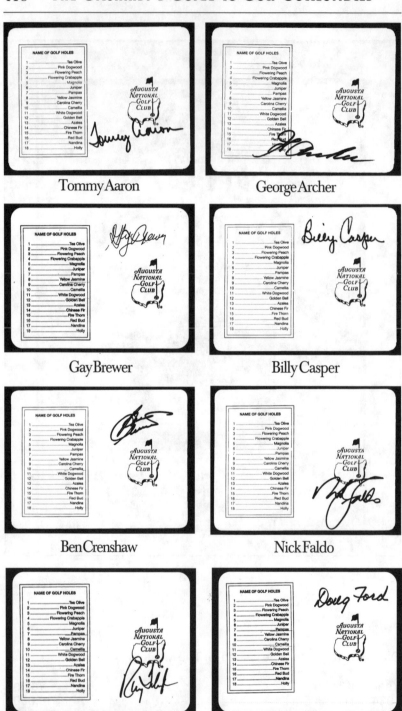

Tommy Aaron

George Archer

Gay Brewer

Billy Casper

Ben Crenshaw

Nick Faldo

Ray Floyd

Doug Ford

Scorecards

The following are prices for the Augusta National Members scorecards signed on the front. Not all winners are included as the very early champions are seldom seen in this form. Two different cards are often seen, the earlier card has the names of the holes on the back while the later card has a plain back. Most cards are signed on the front. Only Masters winners are listed below although Augusta National Scorecards are signed by other players also.

MASTERS WINNERS	VALUE OF SIGNATURE ON SCORECARD
Tommy Aaron	$50
George Archer	$50
Seve Ballesteros	$125
Gay Brewer	$50
Jack Burke	$50
Billy Casper	$50
Charles Coody	$50
Fred Couples	$50
Ben Crenshaw	$75
Nick Faldo	$100
Ray Floyd	$75
Doug Ford	$50
Bob Goalby	$50
Ralph Guldahl	$175
Ben Hogan	$325
Herman Keiser	$125
Bernard Langer	$75
Sandy Lyle	$50
Cary Middlecoff	$50
Larry Mize	$50
Byron Nelson	$75
Jack Nicklaus	$175
Jose Maria Olazabal	$50
Arnold Palmer	$125
Henry G. Picard	$125
Gary Player	$75
Gene Sarazen	$50
Sam Snead	$75
Craig Stadler	$50
Art Wall	$50
Tom Watson	$100
Tiger Woods	$350
Ian Woosnam	$50
Fuzzy Zoeller	$50

Bob Goalby

Ben Hogan

Herman Keiser

Larry Mize

Byron Nelson

Jack Nicklaus

Arnold Palmer

H.G. Picard

Sam Snead   Gene Sarazen

Craig Stadler   Art Wall

Ian Woosnam   Fuzzy Zoeller

Ryder Cup

by Mark Emerson

Programs

R yder Cup programs provide a unique look at the history of the matches. The first known Ryder Cup program is the 1931 match at Scioto Country Club in Columbus Ohio. That rare cover is illustrated here. The programs are assumed to be in good condition with the cover solid and intact and all the interior pages present. As with other collectibles condition is everything.

1931 Ryder Cup Program

1933 Ryder Cup Program

1935 Ryder Cup Program

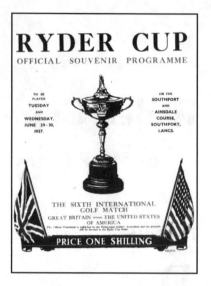

1937 Ryder Cup Program

1947 Ryder Cup Program

1949 Ryder Cup Program

Programs

Year	Winning Team	Where Held	Value
1927	United States9½-2½	Worcester C. C.	none known
1929	Great Britain7-5	Moortown	none known
1931	United States9-3	Scioto	$1,750
1933	Great Britain 6½-5½	Southport & Ainsdale G. C.	$1,000
1935	United States 9-3	Ridgewood C. C.	$1,250
1937	United States 8-4	Southport & Ainsdale G. C.	$850
1939	Not Held		
1941	Not Held		
1943	Not Held		
1945	Not Held		
1947	United States 11-1	Portland G. C.	$750
1949	United States 7-5	Ganton G. C	$600
1951	United States 9½-2½	Pinehurst C. C.	
		Soft Cover	$125
		Hard Cover	$295
1953	United States 6½-5½	Wentworth	$275
1955	United States 8-4	Thunderbird C. C.	$275
1957	Great Britain 7½-4½	Lindrick C. C.	$275
1959	United States 8½-3½	Eldorado C. C.	$500
1961	United States 14½-9½	Royal Lytham & St. Annes	$350
1963	United States 23-9	East Lake C. C.	$200
1965	United States 19½-12½	Royal Birkdale	$250
1967	United States 23½-8½	Champions G. C.	$250
1969	United States 16-16	Royal Birkdale G. C.	$200
1971	United States 18½-13½	Old Warson C. C.	$175
1973	United States 19-13	Muirfield	$175
1975	United States 21-11	Laurel Valley C. C.	$175
1977	United States 12½-7½	Royal Lytham & St. Annes	$150
1979	United States17-11	The Greenbrier	$150
1981	United States 18½-9½	Walton Heath G. C.	$100

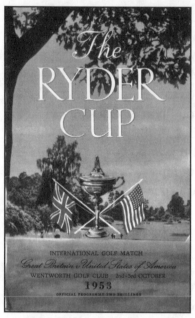

1953 Ryder Cup Program

1955 Ryder Cup Program

1957 Ryder Cup Program

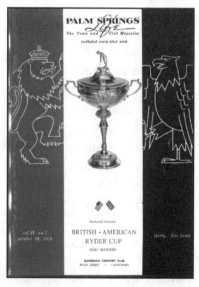

1959 Ryder Cup Program

Programs

Year	Winning Team	Where Held	Value
1983	United States 14½-13½	PGA National	$100
1985	Europe 16½-11½	The Belfry G. C.	$75
1987	Europe 15-13	Muirfield Village G. C.	$75
1989	Europe 14-14	The Belfry G. C.	$75
1991	United States 14½-13½	Kiawah	$75
1993	United States 15-13	The Belfry G. C.	$75
1995	Europe 14½-13½	Oak Hill	$75
1997	Europe 14½-13½	Valderrama	$75

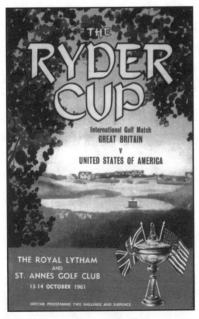

1961 Ryder Cup Program

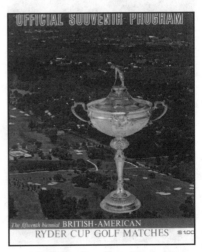

1963 Ryder Cup Program

1965 Ryder Cup Program

1967 Ryder Cup Program

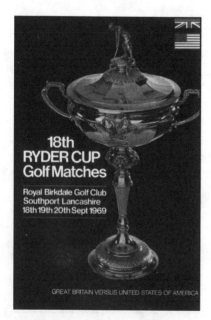

1969 Ryder Cup Program

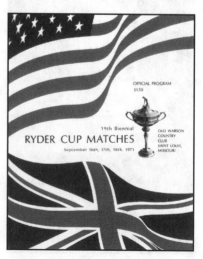

1971 Ryder Cup Program

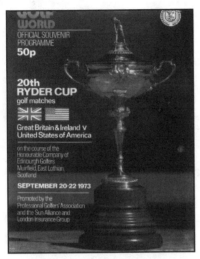

1973 Ryder Cup Program

1975 Ryder Cup Program

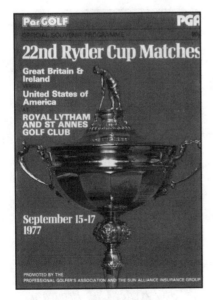

1977 Ryder Cup Program

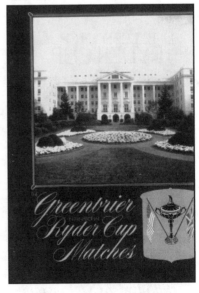

1979 Ryder Cup Program

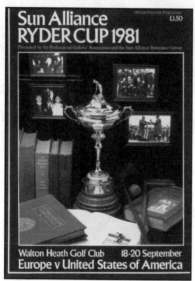

1981 Ryder Cup Program

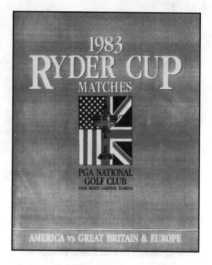

1983 Ryder Cup Program

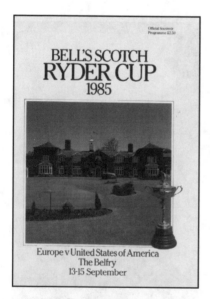

1985 Ryder Cup Program

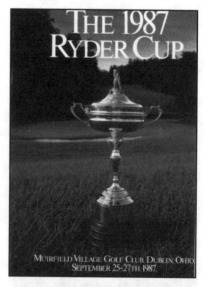

1987 Ryder Cup Program

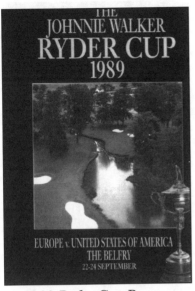

1989 Ryder Cup Program

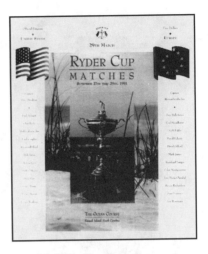

1991 Ryder Cup Program

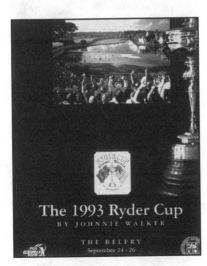

1993 Ryder Cup Program

1995 Ryder Cup Program

1967 Ryder Cup Ticket

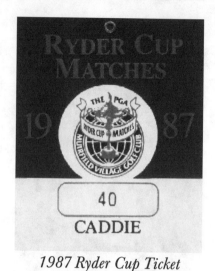

1987 Ryder Cup Ticket

1971 Ryder Cup Ticket

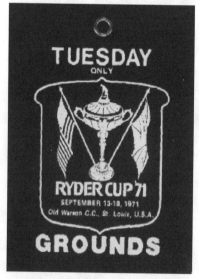

1971 Ryder Cup Ticket

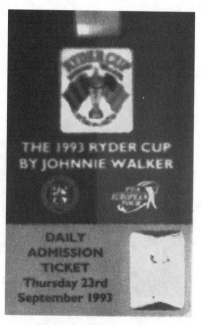

1993 Ryder Cup Ticket

Ryder Cup Tickets
by Mark Emerson

R yder Cup tickets generally are plastic for the series ticket and paper for the daily ticket. They are not readily available and are a desirable collectible.

Tickets

YEAR	WHERE HELD	VALUE
1927	Worcester C. C.	None Known
1929	Moortown	None Known
1931	Scioto	$950
1933	Southport & Ainsdale G. C.	$750
1935	Ridgewood C. C.	$750
1937	Southport & Ainsdale G. C.	$600
1939	Not Held	
1941	Not Held	
1943	Not Held	
1945	Not Held	
1947	Portland G. C.	$500
1949	Ganton G. C.	$400
1951	Pinehurst C. C.	$400
1953	Wentworth	$300
1955	Thunderbird C. C.	$500
1957	Lindrick C. C.	$300
1959	Eldorado C. C.	$500
1961	Royal Lytham & St. Annes	$250
1963	East Lake C. C.	$200
1965	Royal Birkdale	$150
1967	Champions G. C.	$150

Tickets

Year	Where Held	Value
1969	Royal Birkdale G.C.	$150
1971	Old Warson C.C.	$75
1973	Muirfield	$75
1975	Larel Valley C.C.	$75
1977	Royal Lytham & St. Annes	$75
1979	The Greenbrier	$75
1981	Walton Heath G.C.	$50
1983	PGA National	$50
1985	The Belfry G.C.	$50
1987	Muirfield Village G.C.	$50
1989	The Belfry G.C.	$50
1991	Kiawah	$50
1993	The Belfry G.C.	$40
1995	Oak Hill	$30
1997	Valderrama	$30

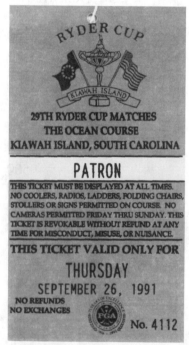

1991 Ryder Cup Ticket

1995 Ryder Cup Ticket

Tickets
by Mark Emerson

The tickets for the United States Open Championship have been printed in many shapes and sizes. The predominant shape is the rectangular shape. For the 39th and 40th Championships, the tickets were round. During 1973-1978 the tickets were star shaped, due to Texaco's involvement. Included are tickets illustrated from the 1926 championship at Scioto Country Club.

Condition is everything. Many tickets had string ties at the top. Torn tops are common but less desirable. Remember the last day for the earlier tournaments was Saturday when they played 36 holes.

1926

1927

1930

1933

1935

1937

1939

1941

1946

1947

U.S. Open

Year	Winner	Where Held	Value
1895	Horace Rawlins	Newport G. C.	None known
1896	James Foulis	Shinnecock Hills G. C.	None known
1897	Joe Lloyd	Chicago G. C.	None known
1898	Fred Herd	Myopia Hunt Club	None known
1899	Willie Smith	Baltimore G. C.	None known
1900	Harry Vardon	Chicago G. C.	None known
1901	Willie Anderson	Myopia Hunt Club	None known
1902	Laurie Auchterlonie	Garden City G. C.	None known
1903	Willie Anderson	Baltusrol	None known
1904	Willie Anderson	Glen View	None known
1905	Willie Anderson	Myopia Hunt Club	None known
1906	Alex Smith	Onwentsia	None known
1907	Alex Ross	Philadelphia Cricket Club	None known
1908	Fred McLeod	Myopia Hunt Club	None known
1909	George Sargent	Englewood G. C.	None known
1910	Alex Smith	Philadelphia Cricket Club	None known
1911	John McDermott	Chicago G. C.	None known
1912	John McDermott	C. C. Of Buffalo	None known
1913	Francis Ouimet	The Country Club	None known
1914	Walter Hagen	Midlothian C. C.	None known
1915	Jerry Travers	Baltusrol	None known
1916	Chick Evans	Minikahda	None known
1917	Not Held		
1918	Not Held		
1919	Walter Hagen	Brae Burn C. C.	None known
1920	Edward Ray	Inverness	None known
1921	Jim Barnes	Columbia C. C.	None known
1922	Gene Sarazen	Skokie C. C.	None known
1923	Robert T. Jones	Inwood C. C.	None known
1924	Cyril Walker	Oakland Hills	None known
1925	Willie MacFarlane	Worcester C. C.	None Known
1926	Robert T. Jones	Scioto C. C.	$1,000
1927	Tommy Armour	Oakmont C. C.	$750
1928	Johnny Farrell	Olympic Fields C. C.	$750
1929	Robert T. Jones	Winged Foot	$850
1930	Robert T. Jones	Interlachen C. C.	$850
1931	Billy Burke	Inverness	$750
1932	Gene Sarazen	Fresh Meadow C. C.	$600
1933	Johnny Goodman	North Shore C. C.	$500
1934	Olin Dutra	Merion	$500
1935	Sam Parks Jr.	Oakmont C. C.	$500
1936	Tony Manero	Baltusrol	$400
1937	Ralph Guldahl	Oakland Hills	$350
1938	Ralph Guldahl	Cherry Hills C. C.	$350
1939	Byron Nelson	Philadelphia C. C.	$325
1940	Lawson Little	Canterbury G. C.	$300
1941	Craig Wood	Colonial C. C.	$300

1949

1950

1951

1954

1953

1955

1956

U.S. Open

Year	Winner	Where Held	Value
1942	Ben Hogan *CALLED* The Hale America Tournament		
		Ridgemoor C. C.	None Known
1943	Not Held		
1944	Not Held		
1945	Not Held		
1946	Lloyd Mangrum	Canterbury C. C.	$250
1947	Lew Worsham	St. Louis C. C.	$250
1948	Ben Hogan	Riviera C. C.	$350
1949	Cary Middlecoff	Medinah	$300
1950	Ben Hogan	Merion	$400
1951	Ben Hogan	Oakland Hills	$400
1952	Julius Boros	Northwood C. C.	$200
1953	Ben Hogan	Oakmont	$250
1954	Ed Furgol	Baltusrol	$200
1955	Jack Fleck	Olympic	$175
1956	Cary Middlecoff	Oak Hill	$150
1957	Dick Mayer	Inverness	$125
1958	Tommy Bolt	Southern Hills C. C.	$100
1959	Billy Casper	Winged Foot	$100
1960	Arnold Palmer	Cherry Hills	$175
1961	Gene Littler	Oakland Hills	$100
1962	Jack Nicklaus	Oakmont	$200
1963	Julius Boros	The Country Club	$85
1964	Ken Venturi	Congressional	$85
1965	Gary Player	Bellerive	$85
1966	Billy Casper	Olympic	$85
1967	Jack Nicklaus	Baltusrol	$150
1968	Lee Trevino	Oak Hill	$75
1969	Orville Moody	Champions G. C.	$75
1970	Tony Jacklin	Hazeltine National G. C.	$75
1971	Lee Trevino	Merion	$65
1972	Jack Nicklaus	Pebble Beach	$75
1973	Johnny Miller	Oakmont	$65
1974	Hale Irwin	Winged Foot	$50
1975	Lou Graham	Medinah	$50
1976	Jerry Pate	Atlanta A. C.	$50
1977	Hubert Green	Southern Hills	$50
1978	Andy North	Cherry Hills	$50
1979	Hale Irwin	Inverness	$50
1980	Jack Nicklaus	Baltusrol	$50
1981	David Graham	Merion	$50
1982	Tom Watson	Pebble Beach	$50
1983	Larry Nelson	Oakmont	$50
1984	Fuzzy Zoeller	Winged Foot	$50
1985	Andy North	Oakland Hills	$50
1986	Raymond Floyd	Shinnecock Hills	$50
1987	Scott Simpson	Olympic	$50

1956

1962

1963

1964

1967

1968

1970

1971

1972

U.S. Open

YEAR	WINNER	WHERE HELD	VALUE
1988	Curtis Strange	The Country Club	$50
1989	Curtis Strange	Oak Hill	$45
1990	Hale Irwin	Medinah	$45
1991	Payne Stewart	Hazeltine National	$45
1992	Tom Kite	Pebble Beach	$45
1993	Lee Janzen	Baltusrol	$35
1994	Ernie Els	Oakmont	$35
1995	Corey Pavin	Shinnecock Hills	$35
1996	Steve Jones	Oakland Hills	$25
1997	Ernie Els	Congressional	$25

1971

1972

1973

1974

1975

1976

1978

1979

1980

1981

1983

1984

1986

1988

1989

1990

1991

1992

1993

1994

1995

1996

1914

1920

1921

1922

1933

1938

1939

1940

1946

1949

1953

1953

1955

1956

1957

1958

1959

1960

1961

1962

1963

1964

1965

1966

1967

1968

1969

1971

1972

1973

1974

1975

1976

1977

1978

1979

1980

1981

1982

1983

1984

1985

1986

1987

1988

1990

1989

1991

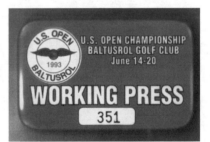

1993

1994

1995

1996

Programs

by Mark Emerson

Mark Emerson is recognized as the ultimate collector, autographs, programs, badges, tickets, and art. He started by collecting the signatures of those who had won four majors or more during their careers but found that too limiting. His help on programs, badges, autographs, and tickets cannot be measured. He can be reached at:

Mark Emerson
4040 Poste Lane Rd
Columbus OH 43221

Programs are an incredible source of history. As well as listing the participants, they often have articles and features on both the host course and the prominent participants. Many of the first programs were small booklets issued in advance of the occasion. They should not be confused by the daily pairing sheets or the Almanacs often issued after the tournament.

The values given are for programs in good condition. The cover should be complete, without tears, stains, or creases, the spine solid, and all the pages present and intact. A mint condition program is of greater value, whereas a grubby torn program of lesser value.

Identification of programs is easy because the event and date are readily found, generally on the cover. Some covers are very ornate while others are plain. The British Open program covers generally have the previous years champion on the cover. The U.S. Open programs generally have the host course featured on the cover. Each cover is unique its own way.

1926 Britsh Open

1929 Britsh Open

1930 Britsh Open

1933 British Open

1935 British Open

1937 British Open

British Open Championship:

Year	Winner	Where Held	Value
1860	Willie Park	Prestwick	None known
1861	Tom Morris	Prestwick	None known
1862	Tom Morris	Prestwick	None known
1863	Willie Park	Prestwick	None known
1864	Tom Morris	Prestwick	None known
1865	Andrew Strath	Prestwick	None known
1866	Willie Park	Prestwick	None known
1867	Tom Morris	Prestwick	None known
1868	Tom Morris Jr.	Prestwick	None known
1869	Tom Morris Jr.	Prestwick	None known
1870	Tom Morris Jr.	Prestwick	None known
1871	Not Held		
1872	Tom Morris Jr.	Prestwick	None known
1873	Tom Kidd	St. Andrews	None known
1874	Mungo Park	Musselburgh Links	None known
1875	Willie Park	Prestwick	None known
1876	Bob Martin	St. Andrews	None known
1877	Jamie Anderson	Musselburgh Links	None known
1878	Jamie Anderson	Prestwick	None known
1879	Jamie Anderson	St. Andrews	None known
1880	Bob Ferguson	MusselburghLinks	None known
1881	Bob Ferguson	Prestwick	None known
1882	Bob Ferguson	St. Andrews	None known
1883	Willie Fernie	Musselburgh Links	None known
1884	Jack Simpson	Prestwick	None known
1885	Bob Martin	St. Andrews	None known
1886	David Brown	Musselburgh Links	None known
1887	Willie Park Jr.	Prestwick	None known
1888	Jack Burns	St. Andrews	None known
1889	Willie Park Jr.	Musselburgh Links	None known
1890	John Ball	Prestwick	None known
1891	Hugh Kirkaldy	St. Andrews	None known
1892	Harold Hilton	Muirfield	None known
1893	William Auchterlonie	Prestwick	None known
1894	J.H. Taylor	Royal St. George's	None known
1895	J.H. Taylor	St. Andrews	None known
1896	Harry Vardon	Muirfield	None known
1897	Harold Hilton	Hoylake	None known
1898	Harry Vardon	Prestwick	None known
1899	Harry Vardon	Royal St. George's	None known
1900	J.H. Taylor	St. Andrews	None known
1901	James Braid	Muirfield	None known
1902	Alex Herd	Hoylake	None known
1903	Harry Vardon	Prestwick	None known
1904	Jack White	Royal St. George's	None known
1905	James Braid	St. Andrews	None known
1906	James Braid	Muirfield	None known

1946 British Open

1947 British Open

1948 British Open

1949 British Open

1950 British Open

1951 British Open

1952 British Open

1953 British Open

1954 British Open

British Open Championship cont.:

YEAR	WINNER	WHERE HELD	VALUE
1907	Arnaud Massy	Hoylake	None known
1908	James Braid	Prestwick	None known
1909	J.H. Taylor	Deal	None known
1910	James Braid	St. Andrews	None known
1911	Harry Vardon	Royal St.Georges	None known
1912	Ted Ray	Muirfield	None known
1913	J. H. Taylor	Hoylake	None known
1914	Harry Vardon	Prestwick	None known
1915	Not Held		
1916	Not Held		
1917	Not Held		
1918	Not Held		
1919	Not Held		
1920	George Duncan	Deal	None known
1921	Jock Hutchison	St. Andrews	None known
1922	Walter Hagen	Royal St. George's	None known
1923	Arthur Havers	Troon	None known
1924	Walter Hagen	Hoylake	None known
1925	Jim Barnes	Prestwick	$2,000
1926	Robert T. Jones	Royal Lytham	$2,500
1927	Robert T. Jones	St. Andrews	$2,000
1928	Walter Hagen	Royal St. George's	s$2,000
1929	Walter Hagen	Muirfield	$1,750
1930	Robert T. Jones	Hoylake	$3,000
1931	Tommy Armour	Carnoustie	$1,500
1932	Gene Sarazen	Prince's	$1,500
1933	Denny Shute	St. Andrews	$1,500
1934	Henry Cotton	Royal St. George's	$1,500
1935	Alf Perry	Muirfield	$1,250
1936	Alf Padgham	Hoylake	$1,000
1937	Henry Cotton	Carnoustie	$1,000
1938	Reg Whitcombe	Royal St. George's	$1,000
1939	Dick Burton	St. Andrews	$1,000
1940	Not Held		
1941	Not Held		
1942	Not Held		
1943	Not Held		
1944	Not Held		
1945	Not Held		
1946	Sam Snead	St. Andrews	$600
1947	Fred Daly	Hoylake	$500
1948	Henry Cotton	Muirfield	$500
1949	Bobby Locke	Royal St. George's	$450
1950	Bobby Locke	Troon	$450
1951	Max Faulkner	Portrush	$500
1952	Bobby Locke	Royal Lytham	$400
1953	Ben Hogan	Carnoustie	$750

1955 British Open

1956 British Open

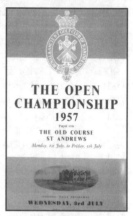

1957 British Open

1958 British Open

1959 British Open

1960 British Open

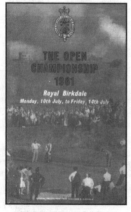

1961 British Open

1962 British Open

1963 British Open

British Open Championship cont.:

Year	Winner	Where Held	Value
1954	Peter Thomson	Royal Birkdale	$350
1955	Peter Thomson	St. Andrews	$300
1956	Peter Thomson	Hoylake	$250
1957	Bobby Locke	St. Andrews	$200
1958	Peter Thomson	Royal Lytham	$175
1959	Gary Player	Muirfield	$175
1960	Kel Nagle	St. Andrews	$175
1961	Arnold Palmer	Royal Birkdale	$275
1962	Arnold Palmer	Troon	$275
1963	Bob Charles	Royal Lytham	$150
1964	Tony Lema	St. Andrews	$150
1965	Peter Thomson	Royal Birkdale	$125
1966	Jack Nicklaus	Muirfield	$350
1967	Roberto di Vicenzo	Hoylake	$125
1968	Gary Player	Carnoustie	$125
1969	Tony Jacklin	Royal Lytham	$125
1970	Jack Nicklaus	St. Andrews	$250
1971	Lee Trevino	Royal Birkdale	$150
1972	Lee Trevino	Muirfield	$125
1973	Tom Weiskopf	Troon	$125
1974	Gary Player	Royal Lytham	$100
1975	Tom Watson	Carnoustie	$125
1976	Johnny Miller	Royal Birkdale	$100
1977	Tom Watson	Turnberry	$100
1978	Jack Nicklaus	St. Andrews	$175
1979	Seve Ballesteros	Royal Lytham	$100
1980	Tom Watson	Muirfield	$85
1981	Bill Rogers	Royal St. George's	$75
1982	Tom Watson	Royal Troon	$85
1983	Tom Watson	Royal Birkdale	$85
1984	Seve Ballesteros	St. Andrews	$85
1985	Sandy Lyle	Royal St. George's	$75
1986	Greg Norman	Turnberry	$65
1987	Nick Faldo	Muirfield	$50
1988	Seve Ballesteros	Royal Lytham	$50
1989	Mark Calcavechia	Royal Troon	$50
1990	Nick Faldo	St. Andrews	$50
1991	Ian Baker Finch	Royal Birkdale	$40
1992	Nick Faldo	Muirfield	$35
1993	Greg Norman	Royal St. George's	$35
1994	Nick Price	Turnberry	$25
1995	John Daly	St. Andrews	$25
1996	Tom Lehman	Royal St. Lytham	$20
1997	Justin Leonard	Troon	$20

1964 British Open

1965 British Open

1966 British Open

1967 British Open

1968 British Open

1969 British Open

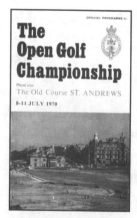

1970 British Open

1971 British Open

1972 British Open

1973 British Open

1974 British Open

1975 British Open

1976 British Open

1977 British Open

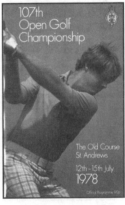

1978 British Open

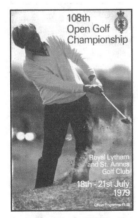

1979 British Open

1980 British Open

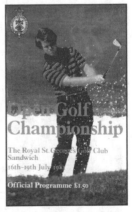

1981 British Open

1982 British Open

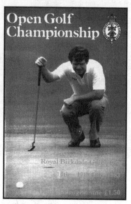

1983 British Open

1984 British Open

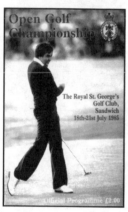

1985 British Open

1986 British Open

1987 British Open

1988 British Open

1989 British Open

1990 British Open

1991 British Open

1992 British Open

1993 British Open

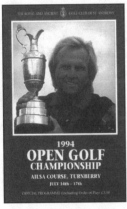

1994 British Open

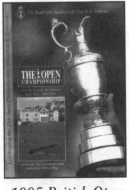

1995 British Open

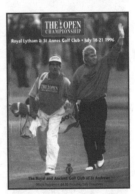

1996 British Open

1926 U.S. Open

1934 U.S. Open

1941 U.S. Open

1942 U.S. Open

1946 U.S. Open

1948 U.S. Open

1949U.S. Open

1951 U.S. Open

1952 U.S. Open

United States Open Championship:

Year	Winner	Where Held	Value
1895	Horace Rawlins	Newport G. C.	None known
1896	James Foulis	Shinnecock Hills G. C.	None known
1897	Joe Lloyd	Chicago G. C.	None known
1898	Fred Herd	Myopia Hunt Club	None known
1899	Willie Smith	Baltimore G. C.	None known
1900	Harry Vardon	Chicago G. C.	None known
1901	Willie Anderson	Myopia Hunt Club	None known
1902	Laurie Auchterlonie	Garden City G. C.	None known
1903	Willie Anderson	Baltusrol	None known
1904	Willie Anderson	Glen View	None known
1905	Willie Anderson	Myopia Hunt Club	None known
1906	Alex Smith	Onwentsia	None known
1907	Alex Ross	Philadelphia Cricket Club	None known
1908	Fred McLeod	Myopia Hunt Club	None known
1909	George Sargent	Englewood G. C.	None known
1910	Alex Smith	Philadelphia Cricket Club	None known
1911	John McDermott	Chicago G. C.	None known
1912	John McDermott	C. C. Of Buffalo	None known
1913	Francis Ouimet	The Country Club	None known
1914	Walter Hagen	Midlothian C. C.	None known
1915	Jerry Travers	Baltusrol	None known
1916	Chick Evans	Minikahda	None known
1917	Not Held		
1918	Not Held		
1919	Walter Hagen	Brae Burn C. C.	None known
1920	Edward Ray	Inverness	None known
1921	Jim Barnes	Columbia C. C.	None known
1922	Gene Sarazen	Skokie C. C.	None known
1923	Robert T. Jones	Inwood C. C.	None known
1924	Cyril Walker	Oakland Hills	None known
1925	Willie MacFarlane	Worcester C. C.	$3,000
1926	Robert T. Jones	Scioto C. C.	$2,500
1927	Tommy Armour	Oakmont C. C.	$1,500
1928	Johnny Farrell	Olympic Fields C. C.	$2,000
1929	Robert T. Jones	Winged Foot	$2,500
1930	Robert T. Jones	Interlachen C. C.	$3,000
1931	Billy Burke	Inverness	$1,500
1932	Gene Sarazen	Fresh Meadow C. C.	$1,500
1933	Johnny Goodman	North Shore C. C.	$1,500
1934	Olin Dutra	Merion	$1,500
1935	Sam Parks Jr.	Oakmont C. C.	$1,250
1936	Tony Manero	Baltusrol	$1,250
1937	Ralph Guldahl	Oakland Hills	$1,000
1938	Ralph Guldahl	Cherry Hills C. C.	$1,000
1939	Byron Nelson	Philadelphia C. C.	$1,000
1940	Lawson Little	Canterbury G. C.	$750

1953 U.S. Open

1954 U.S. Open

1955 U.S. Open

1956 U.S. Open

1957 U.S. Open

1958 U.S. Open

1959 U.S. Open

1960 U.S. Open

1961 U.S. Open

United States Open Championship cont.:

YEAR	WINNER	WHERE HELD	VALUE
1941	Craig Wood	Colonial C. C.	$750
1942	Ben Hogan (Hale America Tournament) Ridgemoor C.C.		$1,500
1943	Not Held		
1944	Not Held		
1945	Not Held		
1946	Lloyd Mangrum	Canterbury C. C.	$400
1947	Lew Worsham	St. Louis C. C.	$750
1948	Ben Hogan	Riviera C. C.	$550
1949	Cary Middlecoff	Medinah	$400
1950	Ben Hogan	Merion	$500
1951	Ben Hogan	Oakland Hills	$550
1952	Julius Boros	Northwood C. C.	$325
1953	Ben Hogan	Oakmont	$550
1954	Ed Furgol	Baltusrol	$300
1955	Jack Fleck	Olympic	$300
1956	Cary Middlecoff	Oak Hill	$275
1957	Dick Mayer	Inverness	$250
1958	Tommy Bolt	Southern Hills C. C.	$225
1959	Billy Casper	Winged Foot	$175
1960	Arnold Palmer	Cherry Hills	$250
1961	Gene Littler	Oakland Hills	$150
1962	Jack Nicklaus	Oakmont	$225
1963	Julius Boros	The Country Club	$150
1964	Ken Venturi	Congressional	$150
1965	Gary Player	Bellerive	$150
1966	Billy Casper	Olympic	$150
1967	Jack Nicklaus	Baltusrol	$200
1968	Lee Trevino	Oak Hill	$150
1969	Orville Moody	Champions G. C.	$150
1970	Tony Jacklin	Hazeltine National G. C.	$125
1971	Lee Trevino	Merion	$100
1972	Jack Nicklaus	Pebble Beach	$175
1973	Johnny Miller	Oakmont	$125
1974	Hale Irwin	Winged Foot	$100
1975	Lou Graham	Medinah	$75
1976	Jerry Pate	Atlanta A. C.	$100
1977	Hubert Green	Southern Hills	$85
1978	Andy North	Cherry Hills	$85
1979	Hale Irwin	Inverness	$85
1980	Jack Nicklaus	Baltusrol	$125
1981	David Graham	Merion	$75
1982	Tom Watson	Pebble Beach	$75
1983	Larry Nelson	Oakmont	$75
1984	Fuzzy Zoeller	Winged Foot	$65
1985	Andy North	Oakland Hills	$65
1986	Raymond Floyd	Shinnecock Hills	$50

1962 U.S. Open   *1963 U.S. Open*   *1964 U.S. Open*

1965 U.S. Open   *1966 U.S. Open*   *1967 U.S. Open*

1968 U.S. Open   *1969 U.S. Open*   *1970 U.S. Open*

United States Open Championship cont.:

Year	Winner	Where Held	Value
1987	Scott Simpson	Olympic	$50
1988	Curtis Strange	The Country Club	$40
1989	Curtis Strange	Oak Hill	$40
1990	Hale Irwin	Medinah	$35
1991	Payne Stewart	Hazeltine National	$35
1992	Tom Kite	Pebble Beach	$30
1993	Lee Janzen	Baltusrol	$30
1994	Ernie Els	Oakmont	$25
1995	Corey Pavin	Shinnecock Hills	$25
1996	Steve Jones	Oakland Hills	$20
1997	Ernie Els	Congressional	$20

1971 U.S. Open

1972 U.S. Open

1973 U.S. Open

1974 U.S. Open

1975 U.S. Open

1976 U.S. Open

1977 U.S. Open   *1978 U.S. Open*   *1979 U.S. Open*

1980 U.S. Open   *1981 U.S. Open*   *1982 U.S. Open*

1983 U.S. Open   *1984 U.S. Open*

1985 U.S. Open

1986 U.S. Open   *1987 U.S. Open*   *1988 U.S. Open*

1989 U.S. Open   *1990 U.S. Open*   *1991 U.S. Open*

1992 U.S. Open   *1993 U.S. Open*   *1994 U.S. Open*

1995 U.S. Open

United States Amateur Championship:

YEAR	WINNER	WHERE HELD	VALUE
1895	Charles Macdonald	Newport G. C.	None Known
1896	H.J. Whigham	Shinnecock Hills G. C.	None Known
1897	H.J. Whigham	Chicago G. C.	None Known
1898	Findlay S. Douglas	Morris County G. C.	None Known
1899	H.M. Harriman	Onwentsia	None Known
1900	Walter J. Travis	Garden City G. C.	None Known
1901	Walter J. Travis	C. C. Of Atlantic City	None Known
1902	Louis N. James	Glen View	None Known
1903	Walter J. Travis	Nassau C. C.	None Known
1904	H. Chandler Egan	Baltusrol	None Known
1905	H .Chandler Egan	Chicago G. C.	None Known
1906	Eben M. Byers	Englewood	None Known
1907	Jerome D. Travers	Euclid	None Known
1908	Jerome D. Travers	Garden City G. C.	None Known
1909	Robert A. Gardner	Chicago G. C.	None Known
1910	William C. Fownes Jr.	The Country Club	None Known
1911	Harold H. Hilton	The Apawamis	None Known
1912	Jerome D. Travers	Chicago G. C.	None Known
1913	Jerome D. Travers	Garden City G. C.	None Known
1914	Francis Ouimet	Ekwanok	None Known
1915	Robert A. Gardner	C. C. Of Detroit	None Known
1916	Charles Evans Jr.	Merion	None Known
1917	Not Held		
1918	Not Held		
1919	S. Davidson Herron	Oakmont	None Known
1920	Charles Evans Jr.	Engineers	None Known
1921	Jesse P. Gullford	St. Louis C. C.	None Known
1922	Jess W. Swester	The Country Club	None Known
1923	Max R. Marston	Flossmoor	None Known
1924	Robert T. Jones Jr.	Merion	3,500
1925	Robert T. Jones Jr.	Oakmont	$2,500
1926	George Von Elm	Baltusrol	$2,000
1927	Robert T. Jones Jr.	Minikahda	$2,500
1928	Robert T. Jones Jr.	Brae Burn C. C.	$2,500
1929	Harrison R. Johnston	Del Monte G. C. C.	$2,000
1930	Robert T. Jones Jr.	Merion	$3,000
1931	Francis Ouimet	Beverly C. C.	$1,000
1932	C. Ross Sommerville	Baltimore C. C.	$850
1933	George Dunlap Jr.	Kenwood C. C.	$750
1934	Lawson Little Jr.	The Country Club	$750
1935	Lawson Little Jr.	The Country Club	$650
1936	John W. Fischer	Garden City G. C.	$600
1937	John Goodman	Alderwood C. C.	$500
1938	William P. Turnesa	Oakmont	$500
1939	Marvin H. Ward	North Shore C. C.	$500
1940	Richard D. Chapman	Winged Foot	$500

1924 U.S. Amateur

1926 U.S. Amateur

1927 U.S. Amateur

1929 U.S. Amateur

1930 U.S. Amateur

1931 U.S. Amateur

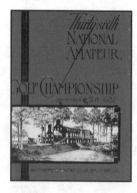

1932 U.S. Amateur

1935 U.S. Amateur

1936 U.S. Amateur

1937 U.S. Amateur

1939 U.S. Amateur

1940 U.S. Amateur

1941 U.S. Amateur

1946 U.S. Amateur

1947 U.S. Amateur

1948 U.S. Amateur

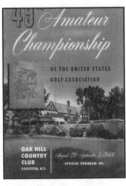

1949 U.S. Amateur

1950 U.S. Amateur

United States Amateur Championship:

Year	Winner	Where Held	Value
1941	Marvin H. Ward	Omaha Field	$500
1942	Not Held		
1943	Not Held		
1944	Not Held		
1945	Not Held		
1946	Stanley E. Bishop	Baltusrol	$300
1947	Robert H. Riegel	Del Monte G. & C. C.	$250
1948	William P. Turnesa	Memphis	$200
1949	Charles R. Coe	Oak Hill	$200
1950	Sam Urzetta	Minneapolis G. C.	$200
1951	Billy Maxwell	Saucon Valley C. C.	$175
1952	Jack Westland	Seattle G. C.	$175
1953	Gene A. Littler	Oklahoma City G. & C. C.	$150
1954	Arnold Palmer	C. C. Of Detroit	$300
1955	E. Harvie Ward Jr.	C. C. Of Virginia	$150
1956	E. Harvie Ward Jr.	Knollwood	$150
1957	Hillman Robbins Jr.	The Country Club	$125
1958	Charles R. Coe	Olympic	$100
1959	Jack W. Nicklaus	Broadmoor	$350
1960	Deane Beman	St. Louis C. C.	$100
1961	Jack W. Nicklaus	Pebble Beach	$250
1962	Labron Harris Jr.	Pinehurst #2	$200
1963	Deane R. Beman	Wakonda	$100
1964	William C. Campbell	Canterbury G. C.	$85
1965	Robert J. Murray Jr.	Southern Hills C. C.	$85
1966	Gary Cowan	Merion	$85
1967	Robert B. Dickson	Broadmoor	$85
1968	Bruce Fleisher	Scioto C. C.	$75
1969	Steve Melnyk	Oakmont C. C.	$75
1970	Lanny Wadkins	Waverley C. C.	$75
1971	Gary Cowan	Wilmington C. C.	$75
1972	Marvin Giles	Oakdale C. C.	$75
1973	Craig Stadler	Inverness C. C.	$75
1974	Jerry Pate	Ridgewood C. C.	$65
1975	Fred Ridley	C. C. Of Virginia	$65
1976	Bill Sander	Bel-Air C. C.	$50
1977	John Fought	Aronimink G. C.	$50
1978	John Cook	Plainfield C. C.	$50
1979	Mark O'Meara	Canterbury G. C.	$50
1980	Hal Sutton	C. C. Of North Carolina	$50
1981	Nathaniel Crosby	Olympic	$50
1982	Jay Sigel	The Country Club	$50
1983	Jay Sigel	North Shore C. C.	$50
1984	Scott Verplank	Oak Tree G. C.	$50
1985	Sam Randolph	Montclair G. C.	$40
1986	Stewart Alexander	Shoal Creek G. C.	$40

1951 U.S. Amateur   *1952 U.S. Amateur*   *1953 U.S. Amateur*

1954 U.S. Amateur   *1955 U.S. Amateur*   *1956 U.S. Amateur*

1957 U.S. Amateur   *1958 U.S. Amateur*   *1959 U.S. Amateur*

United States Amateur Championship:

Year	Winner	Where Held	Value
1987	Billy Mayfair	Jupiter Hills	$30
1988	Eric Meeks	The Holmestead	$30
1989	Chris Patton	Merion	$30
1990	Phil Mickelson	Cherry Hills	$100
1991	Mitch Voges	Honors Course	$20
1992	Justin Leonard	Muirfield Village G. C.	$20
1993	John Harris	Champions G. C.	$20
1994	Tiger Woods	TPC At Sawgrass	$100
1995	Tiger Woods	Newport C. C.	$75
1996	Tiger Woods	Pumpkin Ridge G. C.	$50

1960 U.S. Amateur

1961 U.S. Amateur

1963 U.S. Amateur

1964 U.S. Amateur

1965 U.S. Amateur

1966 U.S. Amateur

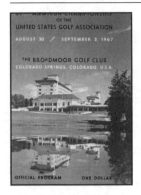
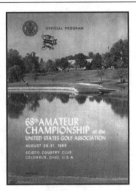

1967 U.S. Amateur   *1968 U.S. Amateur*   *1969 U.S. Amateur*

1970 U.S. Amateur   *1971 U.S. Amateur*   *1972 U.S. Amateur*

1973 U.S. Amateur   *1974 U.S. Amateur*   *1975 U.S. Amateur*

1976 U.S. Amateur

1977 U.S. Amateur

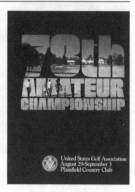

1978 U.S. Amateur

1979 U.S. Amateur

1980 U.S. Amateur

1981 U.S. Amateur

1982 U.S. Amateur

1983 U.S. Amateur

1984 U.S. Amateur

1985 U.S. Amateur

1986 U.S. Amateur

1987 U.S. Amateur

1988 U.S. Amateur

1989 U.S. Amateur

1991 U.S. Amateur

1992 U.S. Amateur

1993 U.S. Amateur

1994 U.S. Amateur

1995 U.S. Amateur   1996 U.S. Amateur

Professional Golf Association Championship:

YEAR	WINNER	WHERE HELD	VALUE
1916	Jim Barnes	Siwanoy C. C.	None known
1917	Not Held		
1918	Not Held		
1919	Jim Barnes	Engineers C. C.	None known
1920	Jock Hutchison	Flossmoor C. C.	None known
1921	Walter Hagen	Inwood C. C.	None known
1922	Gene Sarazen	Oakmont C. C.	None known
1923	Gene Sarazen	Pelham C. C.	None known
1924	Walter Hagen	Frenk Lick C. C.	None known
1925	Walter Hagen	Olympia Fields C. C.	None known
1926	Walter Hagen	Salisbury G. C.	None known
1927	Walter Hagen	Cedar Crest C. C.	None known
1928	Leo Diegel	Five Farms C. C.	None known
1929	Leo Diegel	Hillcrest C. C.	None known
1930	Tommy Armour	Fresh Meadow C. C.	$750
1931	Tom Creavy	Wannamoisett C. C.	$650
1932	Olin Dutra	Keller G. C.	$750
1933	Gene Sarazen	Blue Mound C. C.	$650
1934	Paul Runyan	Park C. C.	$600
1935	Johnny Revolta	Twin Hills C. C.	$500
1936	Denny Shute	Pinehurst C. C.	$500
1937	Denny Shute	Pittsburgh F. C.	$500
1938	Paul Runyan	Shawnee C. C.	$400
1939	Henry Picard	Pomonok C. C.	$350
1940	Byron Nelson	Hershey C. C.	$400
1941	Vic Ghezzi	Cherry Hills C. C.	$400
1942	Sam Snead	Seaview C. C.	$500
1943	Not Held		
1944	Bob Hamilton	Manito G. & C. C.	$400
1945	Byron Nelson	Morraine C. C.	$350
1946	Ben Hogan	Portland C. C.	$450
1947	Jim Ferrier	Plum Hollow	$200
1948	Ben Hogan	Norwood Hills	$450
1949	Sam Snead	Hermitage C. C.	$250
1950	Chandler Harper	Scioto C. C.	$500
1951	Sam Snead	Oakmont	$300
1952	Jim Turnesa	Big Spring C. C.	$250
1953	Walter Burkemo	Birmingham C. C.	$200
1954	Chick Harbert	Keller C. C.	$200
1955	Doug Ford	Meadowbrook C. C.	$175
1956	Jack Burke Jr.	Blue Hill C. C.	$200
1957	Lionel Herbert	Miami Valley C. C.	$150
1958	Dow Finsterwald	Llanerch C. C.	$125
1959	Bob Rosburg	Minneapolis G. C.	$125
1960	Jay Hebert	Firestone C. C.	$100
1961	Dow Finsterwald	Olympia Fields C. C.	$100

1930 PGA   *1931 PGA*   *1932 PGA*

1933 PGA   *1935 PGA*   *1936 PGA*

1938 PGA   *1939 PGA*   *1941 PGA*

1945 PGA

1947 PGA

1950 PGA

1951 PGA

1952 PGA

1953 PGA

1954 PGA

1955 PGA

1957 PGA

1958 PGA

1959 PGA

1960 PGA

1961 PGA

1962 PGA

1963 PGA

Professional Golf Association Championship cont.:

Year	Winner	Where Held	Value
1962	Gary Player	Aronimink G. C.	$100
1963	Jack Nicklaus	Dallas A. C.	$275
1964	Bobby Nichols	Columbus C. C.	$200
1965	Dave Marr	Laurel Valley C. C.	$75
1966	Al Geiberger	Firestone C. C.	$75
1967	Don January	Columbine C. C.	$100
1968	Julius Boros	Pecan Valley C. C.	$100
1969	Raymond Floyd	NCR C. C.	$75
1970	Dave Stockton	Southern Hills	$75
1971	Jack Nicklaus	PGA National C. C.	$150
1972	Gary Player	Oakland Hills C. C.	$75
1973	Jack Nicklaus	Canterbury G. C.	$125
1974	Lee Trevino	Tanglewood G. C.	$75
1975	Jack Nicklaus	Firestone G. C.	$100
1976	Dave Stockton	Congressional C. C.	$100
1977	Lanny Wadkins	Pebble Beach G. L.	$100
1978	John Mahaffey	Oakmont C. C.	$50
1979	David Graham	Oakland Hills C. C.	$50
1980	Jack Nicklaus	Oak Hill C. C.	$75
1981	Larry Nelson	Atlanta A. C.	$50
1982	Ray Floyd	Southern Hills C. C.	$50
1983	Hal Sutton	Riviera C. C.	$50
1984	Lee Trevino	Shoal Creek G. C.	$50
1985	Hubert Green	Cherry Hills C. C.	$40
1986	Bob Tway	Inverness	$40
1987	Larry Nelson	PGA National	$40
1988	Jeff Sluman	Oak Tree G. C.	$30
1989	Payne Stewart	Kemper Lakes G. C.	$30
1990	Wayne Grady	Shoal Creek G. C.	$30
1991	John Daly	Crooked Stick G. C.	$30
1992	Nick Price	Bellerive C. C.	$20
1993	Paul Azinger	Inverness	$30
1994	Nick Price	Southern Hills C. C.	$15
1995	Steve Elkington	Riviera	$15
1996	Mark Brooks	Valhalla	$15
1997	Davis Love III	Winged Foot	$20

1964 PGA   *1965 PGA*   *1966 PGA*

1967 PGA   *1968 PGA*   *1969 PGA*

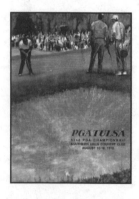

1970 PGA   *1971 PGA*   *1972 PGA*

1973 PGA   *1974 PGA*   *1975 PGA*

1976 PGA   *1977 PGA*   *1978 PGA*

1979 PGA   *1980 PGA*   *1981 PGA*

1982 PGA

1983 PGA

1984 PGA

1985 PGA

1986 PGA

1987 PGA

1988 PGA

1989 PGA

1990 PGA

1991 PGA   *1992 PGA*   *1993 PGA*

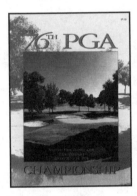 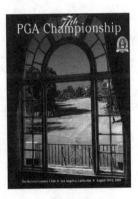 

1994 PGA   *1995 PGA*   *1996 PGA*

Art

by Timothy J. Thorn

Timothy J. Thorn is a golfer who shows his passion for golf through his custom framing. The Ted Williams Mu-seum saw his talent and immediately put him to work on many of their displays. Timothy is renowned in the Clearwater area for his beautiful matting and framing of items for the clubhouse and prizes. He can be reached at:

Timothy J. Thorn
1230 Everglades Ave.
Clearwater, Florida 34624

The first reference to the sport of Golf was in 1457 when James II of Scotland outlawed golf and soccer to encourage archery to protect their country, as stated in the Official Acts of Scottish Parliament. The first published golf print has been recorded as November 22, 1790, when less than fifty black and white mezzotint engravings were done by Valentine Green from an original oil painting by Lemuel Abbott titled "The Blackheath Golfer" picturing William Innes as the Captain of the Society of Golfers at Blackheath England in 1778. The detail of this print is impressive from the clubs to the caddie even the bottle of scotch in his pocket. This print has been reproduced many times in color.

Being a sport for Royalty and the Aristocracy, all artwork before this time was commissioned and portraits in elaborate settings were the fashion of the day. Royal documents show that James IV of Scotland bought golf clubs and played in 1503. Queen Catherine of Aragon, a wife of Henry VIII, wrote to Cardinal Wolsey in 1513 with a reference to her being "busy with the golfe." Mary Queen of Scots played in 1567. Charles II, in 1650-1651, played golf around Perth, Scotland while awaiting his Coronation. In 1740 Bonnie Prince Charles, in exile, played golf in Italy. Golf, and the demand for art work, spread rapidly around the world.

In 1895, the United States staged its first Open in Newport, Rhode Island. Golf and its art were growing as more took up the game, but the turning point was the 1913 U.S. Open when a twenty year old American amateur with his thirteen year old caddie defeated the formidable British contingent. His name was Francis Ouimet.

Statistics show that in 1913 350,000 Americans played golf. In just ten years, by 1923, over two million had taken up the game. Golf became a game for everyone and its art flourished in every aspect from advertising to new found heroes of the sport, beautiful landscape scenes to clubhouse renderings. Today, it is estimated that in excess of one hundred million people play golf.

Framing of artwork, scorecards, clubs, balls, limited edition prints, posters, photographs, pencils, ballmarkers, whatever you can imagine is not undertaken lightly. A custom framer is part engineer, part artist, choosing mats and frames to accent the piece; and part decorator, choosing colors and materials that will tastefully preserve the piece in its original condition to stand the test of time against fashion trends and deterioration. A word of advice here, choose mats and a frame that fits the piece not the couch or the curtains. Do not let the framer intimidate you. Ask lots of questions, become an educated consumer. Good framers have nothing to hide. Unfortunately a multitude of sins can be hidden behind a piece of brown paper backing. Make sure the framer you choose understands your concern for preservation of the piece. Use no masking tape or cardboard as these contain high amounts of acid which will eventually rot your piece. On the other end of the scale materials which are totally acid free are very expensive. 100% cotton fiber (Rag) mats or totally acid free foam core should be used if you have a very valuable piece. In an increasingly competitive industry newer materials giving museum quality protection are becoming more available.

A little imagination and flair will provide you with a very attractive piece, no matter its size or shape. When correctly done it ensures both beauty and longevity.

Autographs

Autographs are probably the most personal contact with the players that many collectors enjoy. Players are hounded from the practice range to the first tee, and beyond. Photos, 3x5 cards, Proset cards, first day covers, major championship sheets, in fact anything that can be signed, is sent through the mail to home addresses, management companies, and tournament sites, in the hope that it will be signed and returned. The more popular the player, the heavier his mail. It has been reported that Arnold Palmer receives and signs in excess of 40,000 pieces of mail per year. Some players are very gracious signers, while others do not respond with any warmth whatsoever, whether through the mail or in person.

The value of an autograph depends so much on its condition and what it is on. 3x5 cards or 8x10 color or black and white photographs are the most desirable collectibles to some. The price is driven by demand. Many players refuse to sign anything that can obviously be resold.

Some players sign agreements with companies whose sole interest is to market their autographed material. There are many reputable autograph dealers who provide autographs, both historical and of current players, at a fair market price.

If a category is blank for an individual's signature, that form is rarely seen.

A special thanks to George and Helen Sanders, authors of **The Sanders Price Guide to Autographs** and **The Sanders Price Guide to Sports Autographs** (both references also published by Alexander Books) for their kind assistance in obtaining many of the following autograph facsimiles.

Tommy Aaron

Percy Alliss

John Adams

Danielle Ammaccapane

Mitch Adcock

Billy Andrade

Kathy Ahern

Donna Andrews

Kristi Albers

George Archer

Amy Alcott

Tommy Armour III

Fulton Allem

Tommy Armour

The first column is the name of the golfer. The second column, Sig., is the price of the golfer's signature. The third column, 1st. Day, is the price for a First Day Cover, an envelope which has a postmark of interest and a commemorative stamp, which has been autographed by the golfer. The fourth column, Ball, is a golf ball which has been signed. The fifth column, M.C.S., is a Major Championship Sheet signed by the winner. The last column, Photo, is a signed photograph.

Name	Sig.	1st. Day	Ball	M. C. S.	Photo
Tommy Aaron	15	35	35	25	25
Rick Acton	5	25	20		20
Rona Adair	75				195
Jimmy Adams	25		50		65
John Adams	5	20	20		20
Lynn Adams	5	20	20		20
Mitch Adcock	5	20	20		20
Pauline Betz Addie	10		45		35
Kathy Ahern	5	20	25		20
Kristi Albers	5	20	20		20
Jim Albus	5	20	25		20
Amy Alcott	5	30	25	20	20
Buddy Alexander	5	20	20		20
Skip Alexander	10	30	35		30
Helen Alfredsson	5	20	25		20
Fulton Allem	5	25	25		20
Jack Allen	350				995
Michael Allen	5	20	25		20
Bud Allin	5	20	20		20
Percy Alliss	50	75			125
Peter Alliss	5	25	25		20
Danielle Ammaccapane	5	20	25		20
Jamie Anderson	750				1,500
Jessie Anderson	50				125
John G. Anderson	35				95
Peter Anderson	695				1,295
Willie Anderson	750				1,950
Billy Andrade	5	25	25		25
Donna Andrews	5	25	25	20	25
Jody Anschutz	5	20	20		20
Bessie Anthony	75				195
Isao Aoki	5	20	25		25
Stuart Appleby	5	20	20		15
George Archer	10	30	25	20	25
Tommy Armour	450				850
Tommy Armour III	5	20	25		20

Emlyn Aubery

Seve Ballesteros

Debbie Austin

Jerry Barber

Tommy Aycock

Miller Barber

Jim Barnes

Paul Azinger

Dave Barr

Butch Baird

Tina Barrett

Ian Baker-Finch

Herman Barron

Kathy Baker

Laura Baugh

Name	Sig.	1st. Day	Ball	M. C. S.	Photo
Wally Armstrong	5	20	25		20
Jean Ashley	5	20	20		20
Emlyn Aubrey	5	20	20		20
Harry Auchterlonie	35				95
William Auchterlonie	475				1,125
Debbie Austin	5	20	25		25
Woody Austin	5	20	20		20
Tommy Aycock	5	20	20		20
Laurie Ayton	35				125
Paul Azinger	10	25	30		30
Douglas Bachli	10				35
Butch Baird	5	20	25		25
Kathy Baker	5	20	25		20
Ian Baker-Finch	10	20	25		25
Al Balding	10		50		40
Leslie Balfour	450				1,295
John Ball	950				1,750
Jimmy Ballard	5	20	20		20
Seve Ballesteros	15	30	50	75	30
Jerry Barber	10	30	45	25	25
Miller Barber	10	30	30	25	25
Brian Barnes	5	20	25		25
Jim Barnes	325				750
John Barnum	10	35	40		25
Dave Barr	5	20	25		25
Tina Barrett	5	20	25		25
Herman Barron	35				75
Arthur Barry	395				950
Pam Barton	50				125
Harry Bassler	10				35
Alice Bauer	10	30	35		25
Dave Bauer	5	20	25		20
Laura Baugh	5	20	25		20
Rex Baxter	5	20	25		20
George Bayer	10	30	35		35
Andy Bean	5	20	25		20
Frank Beard	5	20	25		20
Chip Beck	5	20	25		20
Lillian Behan	5	20	25		20
Art Bell	5	20	25		20
Brad Bell	5	20	25		20
Peggy Kirk Bell	10	35	35		35
Deane Beman	5	25	30		20
Maurice Bembridge	10	20	35		20
Amy Benz	5	20	25		20
Patty Berg	10	35	35	75	25
David Berganio Jr.	5	20	25		25
Suzie Maxwell Berning	5	25	30	30	25

Andy Bean

Frank Beard

Chip Beck

Brad Bell

Deane Beman

Amy Benz

Patty Berg

Susie M. Berning

Missie Berteotti

Al Besselink

Don Bies

Ted Bishop

Phil Blackmar

Ronnie Black

Jay Don Blake

Homero Blancas

Name	Sig.	1st. Day	Ball	M. C. S.	Photo
Missie Berteotti	5	20	25		20
Al Besselink	10	25	35		35
Leo Biagetto	10	25	35		40
Don Bies	5	20	25		20
Georgianna Bishop	75				275
Ted Bishop	45				125
Dave Black	10	25	35		30
John L. Black	25				60
Ronnie Black	5	20	25		20
Woody Blackbum	5	20	25		20
Phil Blackmar	5	20	25		20
Myra Blackwelder	5	20	25		20
Jay Don Blake	5	20	25		20
Jane Blalock	5	20	25		20
Homero Blancas	5	20	25		20
John Bland	5	20	25		20
Chris Blocker	10	30	40		30
Ralph Blomquist	10	30	40		30
P. J. Boatwright Jr.	45				90
Tommy Bolt	15	35	50	35	40
Michael Bonallack	10	20	35		30
Paul Bondeson	10	25	30		35
Julius Boros	15	35	50		35
Elliott Boult	5	20	25		20
Ken Bousfield	5	20	25		20
George Bowden	50				195
Tom Boyd	45				195
Frank Boynton	5	20	25		20
Michael Bradley	5	20	25		20
Pat Bradley	10	25	35		25
Harry Bradshaw	20	45	75		50
Mike Brady	75				225
James Braid	395				895
Gay Brewer	10	25	35		25
J. Briles-Hinton	5	20	25		20
Mike Brisky	5	20	25		20
Bill Britton	5	20	25		20
Jerilyn Britz	5	20	25		20
Paul Broadhurst	5	20	25		20
John Brodie	5	20	25		20
Mark Brooks	5	20	25		20
Al Brosch	10				35
Billy Ray Brown	5	20	25		20
Mrs. C. S. Brown	125				295
David Brown	450				950
Eric Brown	15				45
Pete Brown	5	20	25		20
Olin Browne	5	20	25		20

Tommy Bolt

John Brodie

Michael Bonallack

Mark Brooks

Julius Boros

Billy Ray Brown

Pat Bradley

Bob Brue

Harry Bradshaw

Johnny Bulla

James Braid

Jack Burke

Gay Brewer

Walter Burkemo

Bill Britton

Brandie Burton

Jerilyn Britz

Richard Burton

Name	Sig.	1st. Day	Ball	M. C. S.	Photo
Bob Brue	5	20	25		20
James Bruen	45				125
Bart Bryant	5	20	25		20
Brad Bryant	5	20	25		20
Mary Budke	5	20	25		20
Johnny Bulla	45	75	75		125
Barb Bunkowsky	5	20	25		20
Billy Burke	150				350
Jack Burke	75				195
Jack Burke Jr.	10	25	35	25	30
Patrick Burke	5	20	25		20
Walter Burkemo	95				225
George Burns	5	20	25		20
Jack Burns	450				1,250
Brandie Burton	5	20	25		20
Dick Burton	65				260
Kyle Burton	5	20	25		20
Richard Burton	75				185
Jack Busson	65				145
Bill Buttner	5	20	25		20
Eban Byers	175				475
Sam Byrd	50				125
Curt Byrum	5	20	25		20
Tom Byrum	5	20	25		20
George Cadle	20				45
John Paul Cain	5	20	25		20
Mark Calcavecchia	10	25	30		25
Rex Caldwell	5	20	25		20
Ely Calloway	15	30			40
Scotty Cameron	10	25	30		25
Bill Campbell	20				50
Joe Campbell	20				45
Michael Campbell	5	20	25		20
Paul Canipe	5	20	25		20
Donna Caponi	5	20	25	25	20
Jo Anne Carner	10	20	25	35	25
Joe Carr	25	35	50		50
Billy Casper	10	25	25		25
Jim Cater	5	20	25		20
Alexander Cejka	5	20	25		20
Ron Cerrudo	5	20	25		20
Elizabeth Chadwick	5	20	25		20
Jon Chaffee	5	20	25		20
Doris Chambers	85				225
Brandel Chamblee	5	20	25		20
Richard Chapman	50				125
Bob Charles	10	25	30	20	25

Bill Buttner

Jo Anne Carner

Curt Byrum

Joe Carr

Tom Byrum

Billy Casper

John Paul Cain

Jon Chaffee

Mark Calcavecchia

Brandel Chamblee

Scotty Cameron

Richard Chapman

Bill Campbell

Bob Charles

Paul Canipe

Brian Claar

Donna Caponi

Keith Clearwater

Name	Sig.	1st. Day	Ball	M. C. S.	Photo
Tze-Chung Chen	10	30	40		35
George Christ	40				95
Neil Christian	75				175
Michael Christie	5	20	25		25
Stewart Cink	5	20	25		20
Henri Ciuci	95				225
Brian Claar	5	20	25		20
Bobby Clampett	5	20	25		20
Clarence Clark	65				195
Frank Clark	35				95
Gordon Clark	5	20	25		20
Howard Clark	5	20	25		20
Jimmy Clark	25				55
Keith Clearwater	5	20	25		20
Lennie Clements	5	20	25		20
Russ Cochran	5	20	25		20
Kay Cockerill	5	20	25		20
Charles Coe	55				125
Dawn Coe-Jones	5	20	25		20
Jim Colbert	5	20	25		20
Bobby Cole	5	20	25		20
Neil Coles	10	25	35		30
Glenna Collett Vare	175				395
Janet Collingham	5	20	25		20
Bill Collins	25				50
Archie Compston	65				195
Charles Congdon	35				85
Lynn Connelly	5	20	25		20
Frank Conner	5	20	25		20
Joe Conrad	20				55
Charles Coody	10	25	35		25
John Cook	5	20	25		20
Harry Cooper	10	25	30		25
Pete Cooper	25				75
Fred Corcoran	50				125
Kathy Cornelius	10	25	30		45
Henry Cotton	75				225
Fred Couples	15	30	35	20	30
Chuck Courtney	15				40
Gary Cowan	5	20	25		20
John Cowan	45				195
Wiffy Cox	50				150
William J. Cox	50				150
Jane Crafter	5	20	25		20
Bruce Crampton	5	20	25		25
Richard Crawford	15				40
Tom Creavy	45				150
William Creavy	25				75

Russ Cochran

Henry Cotton

Charles Coe

Fred Couples

Dawn Coe-Jones

Glenna Collett Vare

Gary Cowan

Arch Compston

Bill Cox

Charles Coody

Wiffy Cox

John Cook

Jane Crafter

Harry Cooper

Bruce Crampton

Ben Crenshaw

Fred Corcoran

Diana Critchley

Name	Sig.	1st. Day	Ball	M. C. S.	Photo
Ben Crenshaw	15	25	35		25
Otey Crisman	35				75
Diana Critchley	75				250
Stefania Croce	5	20	25		20
Faye Crocker	15	25	30		35
Bing Crosby	60				150
Elaine Crosby	5	20	25		20
Nathanial Crosby	5	20	25		20
Bobby Cruickshank	195				495
Edith Cummings	95				175
Michael Cunning	5	20	25		20
Buster Cupit	5	20	25		20
Jacky Cupit	10	30	45		30
Rod Curl	5	20	25		20
David Curry	5	20	25		20
Harriot Curtis	195				395
Margaret Curtis	225				450
Fred Daly	50				125
John Daly	10	25	30	30	30
Doug Dalziel	5	20	25		20
Beth Daniel	5	20	25	20	20
Eamonn Darcy	10	20	25		30
Bernard Darwin					
Karen Davies	5	20	25		20
Laura Davies	10	20	30	25	25
Richard Davies	5	20	25		20
William Davies	35				95
Rodger Davis	5	20	25		20
John Dawson	25				75
Marco Dawson	5	20	25		20
Glen Day	5	20	25		20
Simon Thion					
de la Chaume	85				225
Florence Decampe	10	25	30		30
Lally de St. Sauveur	10				35
Roberto De Vicenzo	10	25	35	20	25
John deForest	65				150
Jay Delsing	4	20	25		20
Arthur DeMane	85				225
Jimmy Demaret	125				425
Rolf Deming	5	20	25		20
Jim Dent	5	20	25		20
Helen Dettweiler	35				95
Bruce Devlin	5	20	25		20
Joseph Dey Jr.	30	45			125
Gardner Dickinson	5	20	25		20
Judy Dickinson	5	20	25		20
Bob Dickson	5	20	25		20

Elaine Crosby

Bobby Cruickshank

Rod Curl

Margaret Curtis

Fred Daly

John Daly

Beth Daniel

Bernard Darwin

Laura Davies

Rodger Davis

John Dawson

Marco Dawson

Leo Diegel

Jay Delsing

Jimmy Demaret

Jim Dent

Florence Decampe

Name	Sig.	1st. Day	Ball	M. C. S.	Photo
Leo Diegel	150				350
Terry Diehl	5	20	25		20
Mary Lou Dill	5	20	25		20
Terrance Dill	5	20	25		20
Helen Dobson	5	20	25		20
Lottie Dod	85				175
Stephen Dodd	5	20	25		20
Leonard Dodson	35				95
Art Doering	10				45
Mike Donald	5	20	25		20
Clarence Doser	45				125
Ed Dougherty	5	20	25		20
Dale Douglas	5	20	25		20
Dave Douglas	15				40
Findlay Douglas	95				195
Katrina Douglas	5	20	25		20
Bob Douglass	10	25	25		25
Jack Dowling	65				195
Alan Doyle	5	20	25		20
Patrick Doyle	25				60
Norman Drew	5	20	25		20
Bob Duden	10				45
Ed Dudley	75				175
George Duncan	150				395
George Dunlap, Jr.	75				195
Scott Dunlap	5	20	25		20
Joe Durant	5	20	25		20
Mortie Dutra	50				125
Olin Dutra	95				225
David Duval	5	20	25		20
Pete Dye	5	20	25		20
H. Chandler Eagan	125				375
Syd Easterbrook	45				95
Bob Eastwood	5	20	25		20
Zell Eaton	25				75
J.D. Edgar	45				125
Mitzi Edge	5	20	25		20
John Edmundson	45				125
Danny Edwards	5	20	25		20
David Edwards	5	20	25		20
Joel Edwards	5	20	25		20
Dale Eggeling	5	20	25		20
Dave Eichelberger	5	20	25		20
Lee Elder	10	25	30		30
Steve Elkington	10	25	25		25
Wes Ellis	10				45
Ernie Els	10	25	35	25	25
Bob Erickson	5	20	25		20

Helen Dettweiler

Roberto De Vicenzo

Bruce Devlin

Joseph Dey, Jr.

Gardner Dickinson

Judy Dickinson

Mike Donald

Ed Dougherty

Dale Douglas

Ed Dudley

George Duncan

Olin Dutra

Pete Dye

Danny Edwards

David Edwards

Joel Edwards

Lee Elder

Steve Elkington

Name	Sig.	1st. Day	Ball	M. C. S.	Photo
Sue Ertl	5	20	25		20
Abe Espinosa	25				75
Al Espinosa	35				90
Bob Estes	5	20	25		20
Michelle Estill	5	20	25		20
Chick Evans	5	20	25		20
Chick Evans Jr.	95				295
Duncan Evans	5	20	25		20
Max Evans	10				35
Jack Ewing	10				35
Brad Fabel	5	20	25		20
Don Fairfield	10				35
Nick Faldo	10	25	35	75	30
Johnny Farrell	95				195
Mary Lena Faulk	10	25	30		30
Max Faulkner	35				125
Brad Faxon	5	25	35		25
George Fazio	85				195
Tom Fazio	10	35			35
David Feherty	5	20	25		20
Rick Fehr	5	20	25		20
Vicki Fergon	5	20	25		20
Keith Fergus	5	20	25		20
Bob Ferguson	795				1,750
Vincente Fernandez	5	20	25		20
Willie Fernie	795				1,750
Jim Ferree	5	20	25		20
Jim Ferrier	95				200
Mike Fetchick	5	20	25		25
Forrest Fezler	5	20	25		20
Cindy Figg-Currier	5	20	25		20
Marta Figueras-Dotti	5	20	25		20
Allison Finney	5	20	25		20
Dow Finsterwald	10	30	35		25
Ed Fiori	5	20	25		20
John Fischer	45				95
Dianna Fishwick	50				125
Pat Fitzsimons	5	20	25		20
Jack Fleck	10	30	35	25	30
Marty Fleckman	5	20	25		20
Bruce Fleisher	5	20	25		20
Ray Floyd	10	25	35	35	30
Bob Flynt	5	20	25		20
Doug Ford	10	25	35	20	25
Jack Forrester	45				125
Anders Forsbrand	5	20	25		20
Dan Forsman	5	20	25		20
Martin Foster	10				25

Ernie Els

Bob Erickson

Al Espinosa

Bob Estes

Michelle Estill

Chick Evans

Brad Fabel

Nick Faldo

Johnny Farrell

Mary Lena Faulk

Max Faulkner

Brad Faxon

Rick Fehr

Vicki Fergon

Jim Ferree

Jim Ferrier

Mike Fetchick

Marta Figueras-Dotti

Name	Sig.	1st. Day	Ball	M. C. S.	Photo
George Fotheringhan	65				175
John Fought	5	20	25		20
James Foulis	525				1,250
Jim Foulis	35				95
W.C. Fownes Jr.	150				395
Alexa Sterling Frazer	65				135
Robin Freeman	5	20	25		20
Emmet French	45				125
David Frost	5	20	25		20
Amy Fruhwirth	5	20	25		20
Mark Fry	15				45
Fred Funk	5	20	25		20
Rod Funseth	5	20	25		20
Joanne Furby	5	20	25		20
Ed Furgol	20	35	50	30	45
Marty Furgol	10	25	30		30
Jim Furyk	5	20	25		20
Bernard Gallacher	10	25	30		30
Jim Gallagher Jr.	5	20	25		20
Francis Gallett	45				95
Leonard Gallett	45				95
Robert Gamez	5	20	25		20
Robert Gaona	5	20	25		20
Lori Garbacz	5	20	25		20
Buddy Gardner	5	20	25		20
Robert Gardner	125				275
Philomena Garvey	10	25	35		30
Jim Gauntt	15				50
Jane Geddes	5	20	25		25
Al Geiberger	10	25	35		25
Dorothy Germain	25				75
Cathy Gerring	5	25	25		25
Vic Ghezzi	125				225
Kelly Gibson	5	20	25		20
Leland Gibson	15				45
Gibby Gilbert	5	20	25		20
Bob Gilder	5	20	25		20
Vinny Giles	5	20	25		20
David Gilford	5	20	25		20
Bill Glasson	5	20	25		20
Randy Glover	15				35
Bob Goalby	10	25	35	20	30
W.R. Goebel	45				195
Bob Goetz	10	25	30		25
Dick Goetz	5	20	25		20
Vicki Goetze	5	20	25		20
Willie Goggin	30				90

Dow Finsterwald

Ed Fiori

John Fischer

Jack Fleck

Bruce Fleisher

Ray Floyd

Bob Flynt

Doug Ford

Dan Forsman

Robin Lee Freeman

David Frost

Fred Funk

Ed Furgol

Marty Furgol

Jim Gallagher, Jr.

Bernard Gallacher

Bob Gaona

Jane Geddes

Name	Sig.	1st. Day	Ball	M. C. S.	Photo
John Golden	125				250
Kate Golden	5	20	25		20
John Goodman	165				350
J.C. Goosie	5	20	25		20
Jack Gordon	55				125
Caroline Gowan	5	20	25		20
Paul Goydos	5	20	25		20
Bobby Grace	10	25	35		25
Wayne Grady	10	25	35		30
Herb Graffis	45				95
David Graham	5	20	30		26
Gail Graham	5	20	25		20
Lou Graham	5	25	25		25
Mary Graham	125				250
Elsie Grant-Suttie	95				175
Jack Grant	30				75
Hubert Green	5	25	25	20	25
Ken Green	5	20	25		20
Tammie Green	5	20	25		20
Bert Greene	15				45
Malcolm Gregson	5	20	25		20
Otto Greiner	10				35
Francis Griscon	125				225
Jack Grout	35				75
Charles Guest	10				35
Jesse Guilford	75				225
Ralph Guldahl	125				275
Scott Gump	5	20	25		220
Watts Gunn	50				125
Jon Gustin	15				45
Fred Haas Jr.	20	30	45		65
Jay Haas	5	20	25		20
Otto Hackbarth	35				125
Clarence Hackney	35				125
Dave Hackney	25				60
Walter Hagen	450				1,500
Marlene Hagge	10	25	35		35
Paul Hahn	20				45
Thomas Haliburton	5	20	25		20
Julie Wade Hall	5	20	25		20
Gary Hallberg	5	20	25		20
Dan Halldorson	5	20	25		20
Jim Hallet	5	20	25		20
Bob Hamilton	45				195
Shelley Hamlin	5	20	25		20
Penny Hammel	5	20	25		20
Donnie Hammond	5	20	25		20

Al Geiberger

Cathy Gerring

Vic Ghezzi

Gibby Gilbert

Bob Gilder

Bill Glasson

Bob Goalby

Dick Goetz

John Golden

Johnny Goodman

Lori Garbacz

Bobby Grace

Wayne Grady

Herb Graffis

David Graham

Lou Graham

Hubert Green

Ken Green

Name	Sig.	1st. Day	Ball	M. C. S.	Photo
Harry Hampton	35				95
Phil Hancock	15				35
Beverly Hanson	35				60
Tracy Hanson	5	20	25		20
Chick Harbert	10	25	35		35
Christian Hardin	5	20	25		20
Katherine Harley	85				175
Claude Harmon	175				550
Tom Harmon	25				65
Paul Harney	15	30	45		45
Chandler Harper	15	25	40		30
H.M. Harriman	150				295
Bob Harris	15				45
Labron Harris Jr.	35				95
Robert Harris	45				125
E.J. "Dutch" Harrison	50				130
Dudley Hart	5	20	25		20
Steve Hart	5	20	25		20
Mike Harwood	5	20	25		20
Coburn Haskell	75				175
Morris Hatalshy	5	20	25		20
Michiko Hattori	5	25	30		25
Arthur Havers	125				275
Fred Hawkins	25				45
J.P. Hayes	5	10	20		25
Mark Hayes	5	20	25		20
Clayton Heafner	50				145
Vance Heafner	10	25	30		25
Jerry Heard	5	20	25		30
Jay Hebert	20	35	50	35	40
Lionel Hebert	10	25	30	20	25
Genevieve Hecker	125				250
Dick Hendrickson	5	20	25		20
Nolan Henke	5	20	25		20
Harold Henning	5	20	25		20
Brian Henninger	5	20	25		20
Alex Herd	250				650
Fred Herd	150				350
Davidson Herron	150				375
Tim Herron	5	20	25		20
Jean Hetherington	45				95
May Hezlet	100				250
Greg Hickman	5	20	25		20
Betty Hicks	50				95
Helen Hicks	45				95
Carolyn Hill	5	20	25		20
Cynthia Hill	5	20	25		20

Tammie Green

Ralph Guldahl

Scott Gump

Watts Gunn

Jay Haas

Fred Haas, Jr.

Walter Hagen

Paul Hahn

Jim Hallet

Bob Hamilton

Shelley Hamlin

Donnie Hammond

Beverly Hanson

Chick Harbert

Claude Harmon

Chandler Harper

Dutch Harrison

Dudley Hart

Mike Harwood

Name	Sig.	1st. Day	Ball	M. C. S.	Photo
Dave Hill	5	20	25		20
Mike Hill	5	20	25		25
Opal Hill	50				100
Harold Hilton	550				1,495
Jimmy Hines	45				95
Lon Hinkle	5	20	25		20
Larry Hinson	5	20	25		20
Mayumi Hirase	5	20	25		20
Babe Hiskey	5	20	25		20
Paul Hoad	5	20	25		20
Simon Hobday	5	25	30		25
Jack Hobens	50				125
Scott Hoch	5	20	25		20
Charles Hoffner	75				195
Ben Hogan	125	195	350	350	350
Ernest Holderness	75				145
Marion Hollins	75				175
Helen Holm	75				165
Bud Holscher	15				45
Trevor Homer	5	20	25		20
Bob Hope	35				75
P.H. Horgan III	5	20	25		20
Miriam Burns Horn	95				175
Stanley Horne	10				35
Donna Horton	5	20	25		20
Tommy Horton	5	20	25		25
Beatrix Hoyt	175				350
Bob Hudson Jr	5	20	25		20
Brian Huggett	5	20	25		30
Kate Hughes	5	20	25		25
Jim Hulbert					
Mike Hulbert	5	20	25		20
Gina Hull	5	20	25		20
Ed Humenik	5	20	25		20
Bernard Hunt	10	30	35		30
Guy Hunt	5	20	25		20
Willie Hunter	75				225
Dorothy Campbell Hurd	150				395
Pat Hurst	5	20	25		20
John Huston	5	20	25		20
Charles Hutchings	450				950
Horace Hutchinson	500				1,250
Jock Hutchison Jr.	150				275
Charles Hymers	50				145
Juli Inkster	5	20	25	25	20
Joe Inman	5	20	25		20
John Inman	5	20	25		20
Ann Irvin	5	20	25		20

Arthur Havers

Fred Hawkins

J.P. Hayes

Mark Hayes

Clayton Heafner

Jay Hebert

Lionel Hebert

Dick Hendrickson

Nolan Henke

Harold Henning

Alex Herd

Dave Hill

Mike Hill

Opal Hill

Jimmy Hines

Lon Hinkle

Babe Hiskey

Simon Hobday

Name	Sig.	1st. Day	Ball	M. C. S.	Photo
Hale Irwin	10	25	35	35	30
David Ishi	5	10	25		20
Don Iverson	15				35
Tony Jacklin	10	25	30	25	30
John Jacobs	5	20	25		20
Tommy Jacobs	5	20	25		20
Peter Jacobsen	5	20	25		25
George Jacobus	50				125
Barry Jaeckel	5	20	25		20
Mark James	5	20	25		20
Betty Jameson	25	35	50		75
Jim Jamieson	5	20	25		20
Don January	10	25	30	20	25
Lee Janzen	5	20	25	20	25
J.L.C. Jenkins	175				495
Tom Jenkins	10	25	35		30
Joe Jimenez	5	20	25		20
Brandt Jobe	5	20	25		20
Chris Johnson	5	20	25		20
George Johnson	15				35
Howie Johnson	15				35
Ron Johnston	5	20	25		20
Teri Johnson	10				30
Trish Johnson	5	20	25		20
Bill Johnston	35				75
Cathy Johnston	10				25
Harrison Johnston	65				145
Brain Jones	5	20	25		20
Greer Jones	5	20	25		20
Rees Jones	5	20	25		20
Robert Trent Jones	25	35	45		75
Robert Tyre Jones Jr.					
Vintage	1,750				3,500
40's & 50's	1,450				2,500
Later	650				2,000
As Bob Jones	550				1,650
Rosie Jones	5	20	25		20
Steve Jones	10	25	35		25
Stuart Jones	5				20
Pete Jordan	5	20	25		20
Mike Joyce	5	20	25		20
Tom Joyce	5	20	25		20
Bill Kaiser	50				95
Brian Kamm	5	20	25		20
Yoshinori Kaneko	5	20	25		20
Laurel Kean	5	20	25		20
O.B. Keeler	50				125
Karl Keffer	65				195

Ben Hogan

Ben Hogan (vintage)

Ben Hogan (early)

Mike Hulbert

Ed Humenik

Willie Hunter

John Huston

Jock Hutchison

Juli Inkster

Hale Irwin

David Ishi

Tony Jacklin

Peter Jacobsen

John Jacobs

James Jamieson

Don January

Jim Jimenez

Name	Sig.	1st. Day	Ball	M. C. S.	Photo
Caroline Keggi	5	20	25		20
Herman Keiser	75	100	100	125	150
Al Kelley	5	20	25		20
Jerry Kelly	5	20	25		20
Edwina Kennedy	5	20	25		20
Mrs. W. Kennion	95				175
Tracy Kerdyk	5	20	25		20
George Kerrigan	50				125
Tom Kerrigan	50				125
Tom Kidd	450				950
Jack Kiefer	5	20	25		20
Judy Kimball	10	25	25		25
John Kinder	65				175
Betsy King	5	25	35	35	25
Sam King	35				75
Dorothy Kirby	20				50
Hugh Kirkaldy	825				1,750
Oswald Kirkby	50				125
Joe Kirkwood	45				150
Joe Kirkwood Jr.	10	25	35		45
Tom Kite	10	25	35		30
Emilee Klein	5	20	25		20
Willie Klein	45				150
Harold Kneece	35				70
Kenny Knox	5	20	25		20
George Knudson	10	25	35		35
Hiromi Kobayashi	5	20	25		25
Carin Hj Koch	5	20	25		20
Gary Koch	5	20	25		20
Walter Kozak	45				125
Greg Kraft	5	20	25		20
Bill Kratzert	5	20	25		20
Ted Kroll	10	25	35		30
Al Krueger	35				85
Ok-Hee Ku	5	20	25		20
Gene Kunes	35				95
Alexander Kyle	35				85
Arthur Lacey	75				175
Charles Lacey	55				150
Catherine Lacoste	20	35	50	35	35
Ky Laffoon	50				125
Herbert Lagerblade	75				195
Johnny Laidlay	595				1,195
Tom Lally	65				150
Steve Lamontagne	5	20	25		20
Neal Lancaster	5	20	25		20
Bernard Langer	15	30	40	30	30
Eddie Langert	5	20	25		20

Brandt Jobe

Chris Johnson

Cathy Johnston

Harrison Johnston

Ron Johnston

Robert T. Jones (1928)

Robert T. Jones (1930)

Robert T. Jones (1958)

Robert T. Jones ("Bob")

Robert T. Jones

Robert T. Jones

Robert Trent Jones

Rosie Jones

Steven Jones

Stuart Jones

Mike Joyce

Tom Joyce

Brian Kamm

Name	Sig.	1st. Day	Ball	M. C. S.	Photo
Larry Laoretti	5	20	25		20
E.A. Lassen	475				1,125
Bonnie Lauer	5	20	25		20
David Leadbetter	5	20	25		20
Nanette le Blan	70				150
Art Lees	45				95
Tom Lehman	10	30	40	25	30
Cecil Leitch	95				175
Tony Lema	295				595
Grace Lenczyk	45				95
Justin Leonard	10	20	25		25
Stan Leonard	15				45
Patricia Lesser	10				35
Wayne Levi	5	20	25		20
Frank Lickliter	5	20	25		20
Bruce Lietzke	5	20	25		25
Murle Lindstrom	10	30			30
John Lister	10				35
Lawson Little	85				165
Sally Little	5	25	25		25
Gene Littler	10	25	30	20	25
Joe Lloyd	625				1,250
Bobby Locke	150				375
Emil Loeffler	75				175
Dana Lofland	5	20	25		20
Bob Lohr	5	20	25		20
Michael Long	5	20	25		20
Henry Longhurst	50	75			135
Eddie Loos	75				195
Nancy Lopez	10	25	35	35	35
Lyn Lott	10				35
Dick Lotz	10				35
Davis Love	25				50
Davis Love III	5	20	30		25
Steve Lowery	5	20	25		20
Bob Lunn	10				35
Michael Lunt	5	20	25		20
Ted Luther	50				95
Mark Lye	5	20	25		20
Sandy Lyle	10	25	35	30	25
Catherine MacCann	10				35
C.B. MacDonald	325				775
Robert MacDonald	85				195
Willie MacFarlane	450				995
Allen MacFie	525				1,250
Michelle Mackall	5	20	25		20
Pauline Mackay	95				195
Alister Mackenzie	750				1,500

Caroline Keggi

Jack Kiefer

Herman Keiser

Al Kelley

Judy Kimball

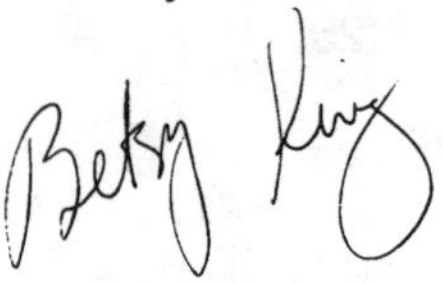

Betsy King

Joe Kirkwood

Tom Kite

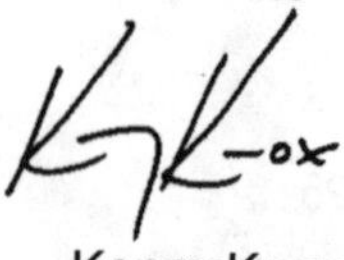

Kenny Knox

Hiromi Kobayashi

Gary Koch

Greg Kraft

Bill Kratzert

Ted Kroll

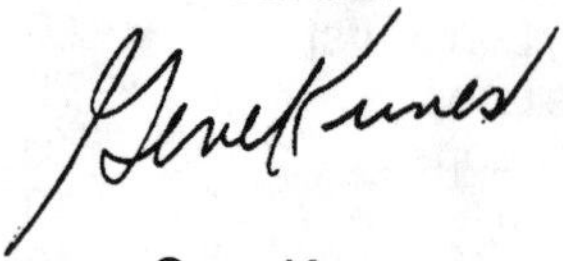

Gene Kunes

Arthur Lacey

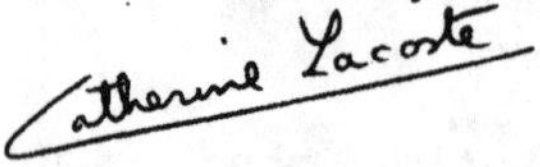

Catherine Lacoste

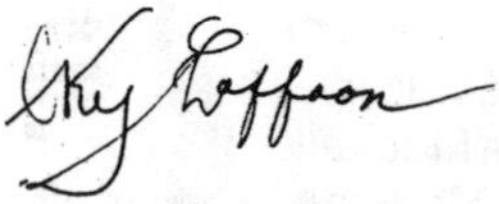

Ky Laffoon

Name	Sig.	1st. Day	Ball	M. C. S.	Photo
Cindy Mackey	5	20	25		20
Issac Mackie	35				75
Maureen Madill	5	20	25		20
Andrew Magee	5	20	25		20
Jeff Maggert	5	20	25		20
John Maginnes	5	20	25		20
John Mahaffey	5	25	35	20	25
Meg Mallon	5	25	35	20	25
Roger Maltbie	5	20	25		20
Tony Manero	225				475
Lloyd Mangrum	95				225
Ray Mangrum	45				90
Carol Mann	10	25	35	30	30
Ellis Maples	10	30			30
Dave Marr	5	20	25	20	25
Graham Marsh	5	20	25		25
Tex Marston	125				250
Fred Marti	10				35
Bob Martin	465				950
Doug Martin	5	20	25		20
Hutt Martin	10				35
Bill Martindale	10				35
Don Massengale	5	20	25		20
Rick Massengale	5	20	25		20
Debbie Massey	5	20	25		20
Arnaud Massy	175				350
Dick Mast	5				20
Len Mattiace	5	20	25		20
Billy Maxwell	10	25	35		35
Norman Maxwell	55				125
Robert Maxwell	495				1,395
George May	65				125
Dick Mayer	10				35
Billy Mayfair	5	20	25		20
Shelley Mayfield	10				35
Charles Mayo Jr.	35				85
Paul Mayo	5	20	25		20
Rives McBee	5	20	25		20
Blaine McCallister	5	20	25		20
Bob McCallister	10				35
Scott McCarron	5	20	25		20
Gary McCord	10	20	25		20
Mark McCormack	10	20	25		25
Samuel McCready	25				65
Mike McCullough	5	20	25		20
Mark McCumber	5	20	25		20
John McDermott	495				975
Bill McDonough	5	20	25		20

Steve Lamontagne

Bernard Langer

Larry Laoretti

David Leadbetter

Art Lees

Tom Lehman

Cecil Leitch

Tony Lema

Wayne Levi

Bruce Lietzke

Lawson Little

Gene Littler

Sally Little

Bobby Locke

Dana Lofland

Bob Lohr

Henry Longhurst

Nancy Lopez

Name	Sig.	1st. Day	Ball	M. C. S.	Photo
Peter McEvoy	5	20	25		20
Michelle McGann	5	25	35		25
Jerry McGee	5	20	25		25
Missy McGeorge	5	20	25		20
Garth McGimpsey	5	20	25		20
Jim McGovern	5	20	25		20
Jack McGowan	10				35
Pat McGowan	5	20	25		20
Marnie McGuire	5	20	25		20
Deborah McHaffie	5	20	25		20
Barbara McIntire	10	25	35		35
George McLean	75				150
Mac McLendon	5				20
Fred McLeod	125				295
John McMullen	10				35
Kathy McMullen	5	15	20		20
Frank McNamara	65				195
Melissa McNamara	5	20	25		20
Tom McNamara	65				195
Mark McNulty	5	20	25		25
Harold McSpaden	75	95			225
Rocco Mediate	5	20	25		20
Eric Meeks	5	20	25		20
Bill Melhorn	75	95	95		225
Meg Mellon	10	25	30		25
Steve Melnyk	5	20	25		20
Lauri Merten	5	20	25	20	25
Dick Metz	45	50	65		95
Phil Mickelson	10	25	35		30
Cary Middlecoff	15	25	35		30
Marion Miley	50				125
Peter Mill	5	20	25		20
Alice Miller	5	20	25		25
Allen Miller	10				30
Johnny Miller	10	30	35	30	30
Mary Mills	5	20	25		20
Abe Mitchell	200				450
Bobby Mitchell	10				35
Jeff Mitchell	10				35
Larry Mize	10	20	25	20	25
Dottie Mochrie	10	25	35	30	30
Robert Moffitt	5	20	25		20
Colin Montgomerie	10	20	35		25
Jack Montgomery	10				35
Eric Monti	15				45
Orville Moody	5	20	25		25
Frank Moore	25				65
Tad Moore	10	25			25

Davis Love III

Steve Lowery

Sandy Lyle

Willie MacFarlane

Andrew Magee

Jeff Maggert

John Mahaffey

Roger Maltbie

Tony Manero

Lloyd Mangrum

Ray Mangrum

Carol Mann

Dave Marr

Don Massengale

Arnaud Massey

Debbie Massey

Dick Mast

Billy Maxwell

Dick Mayer

Name	Sig.	1st. Day	Ball	M. C. S.	Photo
Grant Moorehead	5	20	25		20
Gil Morgan	5	20	25		20
Walter Morgan	5	20	25		20
Wanda Morgan	75				150
Mike Morley	5	20	25		20
Marianne Morris	5	20	25		20
Tom Morris	1,500				3,500
Tom Morris Jr.	2,250				5,500
Jay Morrish	5	20	25		20
Fred Morrison	15				45
John Morse	5	20	25		20
Charles Mothersel	75				195
Larry Mowry	5	20	25		20
Barb Mucha	5	20	25		20
Jodie Mudd	5	25	25		25
Edith Munson	75				150
Rolf Muntz	5	20	25		20
Bob Murphy	5	20	25		20
Ross Murray	5	20	25		20
Larry Nabholtz	75				195
Kel Nagle	10	25	35		35
Bill Nary	15				40
Martha Nause	5	20	25		20
Jim Nelford	5	20	25		20
Byron Nelson	20	35	45	75	35
Larry Nelson	10	25	35	35	30
Liselotte Neumann	5	20	25	20	25
Dwight Nevil	10				35
Jack Neville	75				165
Jack Newton	10				30
Alison Nicholas	5	20	25		20
Bobby Nichols	10	25	35	20	25
Gil Nichols	75				225
Gary Nicklaus	5	20	25		20
Jack Nicklaus	75	100	125	225	150
Jack Nicklaus Jr.	5	20	25		25
Mike Nicolette	5	20	25		20
Tom Nieporte	10				35
Catrin Nilsmark	5	20	25		20
Frank Nobillo	5	20	25		20
Karen Noble	5	20	25		20
Augie Nordone	20				50
Greg Norman	20	35	45	30	45
Tim Norris	10				35
Andy North	10	25	35	30	35
J. J. O'Brien	75				195
Christy O'Connor	20	35	45		35
Christy O'Connor Jr.	5	20	25		20

Billy Mayfair

Blaine McCallister

Gary McCord

Mark McCumber

John McDermott

Michelle McGann

Jerry McGee

Jimmy McGovern

Deborah McHaffie

Fred McLeod

Melissa McNamara

Mark McNulty

Harold McSpaden

Rocco Mediate

Bill Melhorn

Meg Mellon

Lauri Merten

Dick Metz

Name	Sig.	1st. Day	Ball	M. C. S.	Photo
John O'Connor	15				45
Mac O'Grady	5	20	25		20
Patrick O'Hara	75				195
Peter O'Hara	75				195
Jim O'Hern	5	20	25		20
John O'Leary	5	20	25		20
Paul O'Leary	10				35
Martin O'Loughlin	45				125
Mark O'Meara	5	20	25		25
Willie Ogg	75				195
David Ogrin	5	20	25		20
Ayako Okamoto	10	20	25		25
Jose Maria Olazabal	10	25	45		30
Ed Oliver	125				275
Peter Oosterhuis	5	20	25		25
Steve Oppemman	10				35
Edith Orr	150				275
Francis Ouimet	350				750
Charlie Owens	10	25	35		30
Dinak Oxley	5	20	25		20
Joe Ozaki	5	20	25		20
Jumbo Ozaki	10	25	35		35
Roy Pace	10				35
Joanne Pacillo	5	20	25		20
Alf Padgham	95				225
Estelle Lawson Page	45				95
Anne Marie Palli	5	20	25		20
Arnold Palmer	25	35	50	75	75
Johnny Palmer	35				95
Sandra Palmer	5	20	25		25
Catherine Panton	5	20	25		20
John Panton	15				45
Mungo Park	450				950
Willie Park	495				950
Willie Park Jr.	350				795
Philip Parkin	5	20	25		20
Sam Parks Jr.	50				125
Jesper Parnevik	10	25	35		30
Craig Parry	5	20	25		20
Amy Pascoe	125				250
Jerry Pate	5	20	25	20	25
Steve Pate	5	20	25		20
Moira Paterson	10				35
Billy Joe Patton	10	20	25		30
Chris Patton	5	20	25		20
Corey Pavin	10	25	35	20	25
George Payton	30				60
Eddie Pearce	10				35

Phil Mickelson

Cary Middlecoff

Alice Miller

Johnny Miller

Abe Mitchell

Larry Mize

Dottie Mochrie

Colin Montgomerie

Orville Moody

Tad Moore

Gil Morgan

Larry Mowry

Barb Mucha

Jodie Mudd

Ross Murray

Bob Murphy

Kel Nagle

Byron Nelson

Name	Sig.	1st. Day	Ball	M. C. S.	Photo
Becky Pearson	5	20	25		20
Bob Peebles	75				150
Calvin Peete	5	20	25		20
Harvey Penick	35	55	75		75
Toney Penna	40				95
David Peoples	5	20	25		20
Dottie Pepper	5	20	25		20
John Perelli	10				35
Phil Perkins	15				45
Thomas Perkins	45				95
Alf Perry	125				250
Kenny Perry	5	20	25		20
Peter Persons	5	20	25		20
Mark Pfeil	5	20	25		20
Henry Picard	100	150	200	150	225
Caroline Pierce	5	20	25		20
Julie Piers	5	20	25		20
Joan Pitcock	5	20	25		20
Jerry Pittman	10				35
Gary Player	15	30	50	75	40
Phillipe Ploujoux	5	20	25		20
Dan Pohl	5	20	25		20
Don Pooley	5	20	25		20
Sandra Post	10	20	25		25
Lee Porter	5	20	25		20
Kathy Postlewait	5	20	25		20
Jimmy Pott	20				45
Jimmy Powell	5	20	25		25
Greg Powers	5	20	25		20
Elizabeth Price	10				35
Nick Price	10	30	45	35	35
Dicky Pride	5	20	25		20
Dillard Pruitt	5	20	25		20
Jackie Pung	20	35	45		45
Walter Pursey	65				150
Tom Purtzer	5	20	25		25
Fred Pye	75				150
Anne Quast	10				35
Smiley Quick	10				35
Brett Quigley	5	20	25		20
Ronan Rafferty	5	20	25		25
Dave Ragan	10				35
Nancy Ramsbottom	5	20	25		20
Mason Randolph	5	20	25		25
Sam Randolph	5	20	25		20
Judy Rankin	10	25	30		25
Henry Ransom	50				95

Larry Nelson

Liselotte Neumann

Bobby Nichols

Jack Nicklaus

Greg Norman

Andy North

Christy O'Connor

Christy O'Connor, Jr.

David Ogrin

Ayako Okamoto

Jose Maria Olazabal

Ed Oliver

Mark O'Meara

Peter Oosterhuis

Francis Ouimet

Jumbo Ozaki

A.H. Padgham

Anne Marie Palli

Name	Sig.	1st. Day	Ball	M. C. S.	Photo
Cindy Rarick	5	20	25		20
Gladys Ravenscroft	95				175
Horace Rawlins	525				1,150
Betsy Rawls	20	35	45	75	35
Edward Ray	150				365
Michele Redman	5	20	25		20
Susie Redman	5	20	25		20
Dai Rees	75				165
Dean Refram	10				35
Victor Regalado	10				35
Mike Reid	5	20	25		25
Steve Reid	5	20	25		20
Wilred Reid	75				195
Bob Reith	5	20	25		20
Jack Renner	5	20	25		20
Johnny Revolta	50	65	75		125
Cathy Reynolds	5	20	25		20
Richard Rhyan	5	20	25		20
Grantland Rice	95				200
Deb Richard	5	20	25		20
Steven Richardson	5	20	25		20
Angie Ridgeway	5	20	25		20
Fred Ridley	5	20	25		20
Skee Riegel	50				95
Polly Riley	35				75
Larry Rinker	5	20	25		20
Alice Ritzman	5	20	25		20
Patti Rizzo	5	20	25		20
James Robb	475				995
Hillman Robbins	10				35
Kelly Robbins	5	20	25		20
Clifford Roberts	125				250
Loren Roberts	5	20	25		20
Belle Robertson	5	20	25		20
Constantino Rocca	5	20	25		20
Phil Rodgers	5	20	25		20
Chi Chi Rodriguez	5	20	25		20
Bill Rogers	5	20	25	20	25
John Rogers	75				165
Barbara Romack	10	25	35		35
Eduardo Romero	5	20	25		20
Bob Rosburg	10	25	35		25
Clarence Rose	5	20	25		20
Jody Rosenthal	5	20	25		20
Alex Ross	995				2,250
Donald Ross	750				1,595
Charles Rowe	75				195
Hugh Royer	10				35

Arnold Palmer

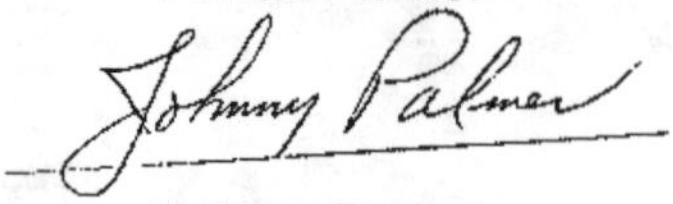

Johnny Palmer

Sandra Palmer

Sam Parks, Jr.

Jesper Parnevik

Craig Parry

Jerry Pate

Billy Joe Patton

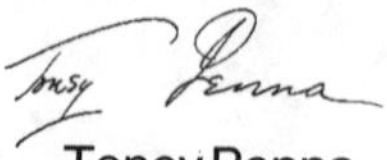

Toney Penna

David Peoples

Alf Perry

Kenny Perry

Peter Persons

Calvin Peete

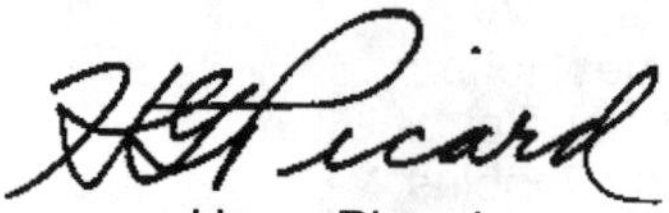

Henry Picard

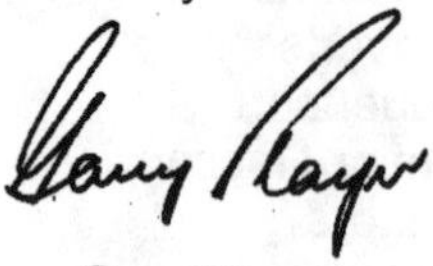

Gary Player

Dan Pohl

Don Pooley

Name	Sig.	1st. Day	Ball	M. C. S.	Photo
Hugh Royer III	5	20	25		20
Mason Rudolph	10	25	35		30
Jack Rule Jr.	10				30
Dave Rummells	5	20	25		20
Paul Runyan	55	65	75	30	125
Charlie Rymer	5	20	25		20
Kim Saiki	5	20	25		20
Harold Sampson	65				195
Anne Quast Sander	5	20	25		20
Bill Sander	5	20	25		20
Doug Sanders	5	20	25		25
Cesar Sanudo	10				30
Gene Sarazen	10	25	35	75	35
George Sargent	195				495
Gene Sauers	5	20	25		20
D. E. Sawyer	50				125
Stephen Scahill	5	20	25		20
Tom Scherrer	5	20	25		20
John Schlee	5	20	25		20
George Schneiter	45				95
George Schoux	45				95
John Schroeder	5	20	25		30
Cindy Schreyer	5	20	25		20
Eddie Schultz	50				125
Ted Schulz	5	20	25		20
Lady Margaret Scott	150				325
Michael Scott	50				125
Nancy Scranton	5	20	25		20
Gib Sellers	10				35
Carol Semple	10	25	30		30
Felix Serafin	35				95
Mrs. G. Henry Setson	95				175
Bob Shave	10				35
Tom Shaw	5	20	25		20
Bob Shearer	5	20	25		20
Patty Sheehan	10	30	35	35	30
Cathy Sherk	5	20	25		20
Denny Shute	150				350
Dick Siderowf	5	20	25		20
Tom Sieckmann	5	20	25		20
Charlie Sifford	5	20	25		20
Jay Sigel	5	20	25		20
Dan Sikes	5	20	25		20
R. H. Sikes	5	20	25		20
Tony Sills	5	20	25		20
Jim Simons	5	20	25		20
George Simpson	50				125
Jack Simpson	625				1,395

Kathy Postlewait

Lee Porter

Sandra Post

Jimmy Powell

Greg Powers

Nick Price

Dillard Pruitt

Ronan Rafferty

Nancy Ramsbottom

Mason Randolph

Sam Randolph

Judy Rankin

Henry Ransom

Cindy Rarick

Betsy Rawls

Edward Ray

Dai Rees

Mike Reid

Name	Sig.	1st. Day	Ball	M. C. S.	Photo
Scott Simpson	5	20	25		20
Tim Simpson	5	20	25		20
Joey Sindelar	5	20	25		20
Vijay Singh	5	20	25		20
Pearl Sinn	5	20	25		20
Val Skinner	5	20	25		20
Jeff Sluman	5	20	25	20	20
Al Smith	45				95
Alex Smith	500				1,295
Ben Smith	5	20	25		20
Bob Smith	10				35
Eric Smith	75				150
Horton Smith	400				950
Macdonald Smith	125				325
Margaret Smith	10	25	35		35
Marilyn Smith	10	25	35		35
Mike Smith	5	20	25		20
Taylor Smith	5	20	25		20
Willie Smith	195				450
J.C. Snead	5	20	25		20
Sam Snead	20	35	65	75	50
Ed Sneed	5	20	25		20
Karsten Solheim	15	30			35
Ross Sommerville	125				295
Carol Sorenson	5	20	25		20
Annika Sorenstam	5	20	25	30	25
Mike Souchak	20	30	35		30
Marley Spearman	5	20	25		20
Muffin Spencer-Devlin	5	20	25		20
Steve Spray	10				30
Mike Springer	5	20	25		5
Sandra Spuzich	5	20	25		25
Hollis Stacy	5	20	25	25	25
Craig Stadler	5	25	35	25	25
Mike Standly	5	20	25		20
Paul Stankowski	5	20	25		20
Bob Stanton	10				30
Alex Stedman	45				95
Jerry Steelsmith	10				35
Sherri Steinhauer	5	20	25		25
Frances Stephens	10				35
Jan Stephenson	5	20	25	25	25
Earl Stewart	20				50
Marlene Stewart	10				35
Payne Stewart	5	25	35	25	30
Ken Still	5	20	25		20
Dave Stockton	5	20	25	30	25

Johnny Revolta

Dick Rhyan

Grantland Rice

Deb Richard

Skee Riegel

Larry Rinker

Alice Ritzman

Patti Rizzo

Clifford Roberts

Loren Roberts

Phil Rodgers

Chi Chi Rodriguez

Bill Rogers

Barbara Romack

Bob Rosburg

Clarence Rose

Jody Rosenthal

Jack Rule, Jr.

Name	Sig.	1st. Day	Ball	M. C. S.	Photo
Dave Stockton Jr.	5	20	25		20
Ralph Stonehouse	50				125
Frank Stranahan	25				75
Curtis Strange	10	30	40	35	30
Andrew Strath	450				950
Ron Strech	5	20	25		20
Steve Stricker	5	20	25		20
Bobby Stroble	5	20	25		20
Herbert Strong	50				100
Louise Suggs	20	35	45	75	35
Mike Sullivan	5	20	25		20
Bruce Summerhays	5	20	25		20
Kevin Sutherland	5	20	25		20
Hal Sutton	5	20	25		30
Robert Sweeny Jr.	75				150
Jess Sweetser	150				325
Nancy Roth Syms	5	20	25		20
Freddie Tait	750				1,995
M. Talman	75				195
Alan Tapie	10				30
Tani Tatum	5				20
Phil Tataurangi	5	20	25		20
J.H. Taylor	400				950
Glenn Teal	10				30
Louis Tellier	75				195
Lance Ten Broeck	5	20	25		20
Brian Tennyson	5	20	25		20
Bob Terney	5	20	25		20
Doug Tewell	5	20	25		20
Jayne Thobois	5	20	25		20
Dave Thomas	5	20	25		20
Bertha Thompson	85				175
Leonard Thompson	5	20	25		20
Martin Thompson	5	20	25		20
Rocky Thompson	5	20	25		20
Hector Thomson	35				85
Jimmy Thomson	45				95
Lena Thomson	75				150
Peter Thomson	20	30	45	75	45
Jill Thornhill	5	20	25		20
Jim Thorpe	5	20	25		20
Albert W. Tillinghast	350				750
Maud Titterton	95				195
Harry Todd	25				75
Tommy Tolles	5	20	25		25
Cyril Tolley	95				195
David Toms	5	20	25		20
Sam Torrance	5	20	25		20

Dave Rummells

Paul Runyan

Doug Sanders

Gene Sarazan (vintage)

Gene Sarazan

George Sargent

Gene Sauers

Ted Schulz

Nancy Scranton

Tom Shaw

Patty Sheehan

Denny Shute

Charlie Sifford

Tony Sills

Scott Simpson

Tom Sieckmann

Val Skinner

Jeff Sluman

Name	Sig.	1st. Day	Ball	M. C. S.	Photo
Bob Toski	5	25	35		30
E.D. Townes	65				125
Jerry Travers	495				995
Jerome Travers	495				995
Walter Travis	495				995
Lee Trevino	15	25	35	35	35
Kirk Triplet	5	20	25		20
W.H. Trovinger	75				150
Ted Tryba	5	20	25		20
Kris Tschetter	5	20	25		20
Chris Tucker	5	20	25		20
Richard Tufts	75				160
Greg Turner	5	20	25		20
Sherri Turner	5	20	25		20
Ted Turner	10				30
Jim Turnesa	50	65			95
Joe Turnesa	45	50			90
Mike Turnesa	35	40			85
Willie Turnesa	50	50			95
Bob Tway	5	20	25	20	25
William Tweedell	95				195
Greg Twiggs	5	20	25		20
Howard Twitty	5	20	25		20
Walt Ulrich	15				45
Ruth Underhill	75				150
Omar Uresti	5	20	25		20
Sam Urzetta	25				75
Stan Utley	5	20	25		20
Angela Uzielli	5	20	25		20
Jessie Valentine	10				35
Tommy Valentine	5	20	25		20
Virginia Van Wie	50				95
Florence Vanderbeck	95				175
Brigitte Varangot	5	20	25		20
Harry Vardon	750				1,750
Ken Venturi	10	25	35	20	30
Scott Verplank	5		20	25	20
Bob Verwey	5	20	25		20
Jim Vickers	5				20
Elsworth Vines	35				75
Donald Vinton	75				195
Mitch Voges	5	20	25		20
George Voigt	75				195
George Von Elm	75				195
Bob Von Hagge	5	20	25		20
Norm Von Nida	20	30	35		35
Ernie Vossler	15				45
Bobby Wadkins	5	20	25		20

Ben Smith

Horton Smith

Marilyn Smith

J.C. Snead

Sam Snead

Karsten Solheim

Mike Souchak

Sandra Spuzich

Hollis Stacy

Craig Stadler

Sherri Steinhauer

Jan Stephenson

Payne Stewart

Dave Stockton

Dave Stockton, Jr.

Frank Stranahan

Curtis Strange

Ron Strech

Louise Suggs

Mike Sullivan

Name	Sig.	1st. Day	Ball	M. C. S.	Photo
Lanny Wadkins	5	20	25	20	25
Grant Waite	5	20	25		20
Duffy Waldorf	5	20	25		20
Colleen Walker	5	20	25	20	25
Cyril Walker	75				195
Michelle Walker	5	20	25		20
Art Wall	5	20	25		20
Frank Walsh	75				150
Lisa Walters	5	20	25		20
Bobby Walzel	10				35
Fred Wampler	10				35
Bud Ward	50				95
Charles Ward	35				75
Harvie Ward Jr.	20	35	45		35
Steve Warga	35				75
Tom Wargo	5	20	25		20
Jo Ann Washam	5	20	25		20
Al Watrous	45				125
Dennis Watson	5	20	25		20
Tom Watson	15	30	45		40
Brian Watts	5	20	25		20
Bert Weaver	5	20	25		25
DeWitt Weaver	5	20	25		20
Karrie Webb	5	20	25		25
Harry Weetman	25				45
D.A. Weibring	5	20	25		20
Tom Weiskopf	10	25	35		25
James West	50				125
Jack Westland	15				45
Joyce Wethered	95				195
Roger Wethered	45				95
J.H. Whigham	125				250
Greg Whisman	5	20	25		20
Charles A. Whitcombe	75				150
Ernest E. Whitcombe	50				95
Reginald A. Whitcombe	50				95
Buck White	35				75
Donna White	5	20	25		25
Jack White	150				350
Orville White	10				35
Barb Whitehead	5	20	25		20
Don Whitt	10				35
Kathy Whitworth	20	35	45	75	35
Mark Wiebe	5	20	25		20
Jim Wiecher	5	20	25		20
Martha Wilkinson	5	20	25		20
Maggie Will	5	20	25		20
Dan Williams	30				70

Hal Sutton

Robert Sweeny

Jess Sweetser

J.H. Taylor

Brian Tennyson

Doug Tewell

Peter Thomson

Leonard Thompson

Rocky Thompson

Jimmy Thomson

Jim Thorpe

Cyril Tolley

David Toms

Bob Toski

Jerome Travers

Jerry Travers

Lee Trevino

Kirk Triplett

Name	Sig.	1st. Day	Ball	M. C. S.	Photo
Eddie Williams	10				30
Henry Williams	10				30
Enid Wilson	50				125
Jim Wilson	50				95
John Wilson	5	20	25		20
Bo Wininger	20				45
Craig Wood	350				700
Norman Wood	5	20	25		20
Willie Wood	5	20	25		20
Jim Woodward	5	20	25		20
Tiger Woods	100	150	300		350
Ian Woosnam	10	25	35	20	30
Lew Worsham Jr.	75				150
J. S. Worthington	65				125
Jo Ann Wosham	10	25	30		30
Robert Wrenn	5	20	25		20
Mickey Wright	20	30	45	75	35
Pamela Wright	5	20	25		20
Jennifer Wyatt	5	20	25		20
Bob Wynn	5	20	25		20
Dudley Wysong	5	20	25		20
Bert Yancey	20	35	45		35
Charles Yates	30				75
Kathy Young	5	20	25		20
Kim Young	5	20	25		20
Bruce Zabriski	5	20	25		20
Babe Didrickson Zaharias	650				1,450
Joe Zarhardt	35				75
Kermit Zarley	5	20	25		20
Walter Zembriski	5	20	25		20
Larry Ziegler	5	20	25		20
Al Zimmerman	60				125
Fuzzy Zoeller	10	25	35	25	30
Richard Zokol	5	20	25		20

Ted Tryba

Kris Tschetter

Richard Tufts

Sherri Turner

Jim Turnesa

Joe Turnesa

Mike Turnesa

Willie Turnesa

Bob Tway

Greg Twiggs

Sam Urzetta

Stan Utley

Virginia Van Wie

Harry Vardon

Ken Venturi

Ellsworth Vines

Jim Vickers

George Von Elm

Norm Von Nida

Bobby Wadkins

Lanny Wadkins

Duffy Waldorf

Colleen Walker

Art Wall

Lisa Walters

Bud Ward

Harvie Ward, Jr.

Tom Wargo

Al Watrous

Tom Watson

Brian Watts

DeWitt Weaver

Harry Weetman

D.A. Weibring

Tom Weiskopf

Joyce Wethered

Roger Wethered

Greg Whisman

C.A. Whitcomb

E.E. Whitcombe

R.A. Whitcomb

Jack White

Kathy Whitworth

Mark Wiebe

Maggie Will

Enid Wilson

Craig Wood

Willie Wood

Tiger Woods (1990)

Tiger Woods (1995)

Tiger Woods (1996)

Jim Woodward

Ian Woosnam

Lew Worsham, Jr.

Jo Ann Wosham

Robert Wrenn

Pamela Wright

Dudley Wysong

Bert Yancey

Charlie Yates

Bruce Zabriski

Babe Zaharias

Kermit Zarley

Walt Zembriski

Larry Ziegler

Fuzzy Zoeller

Richard Zokol

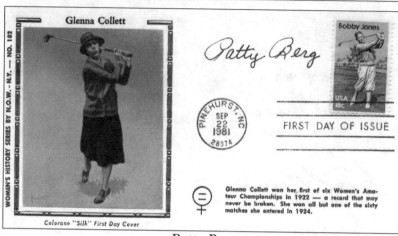

Patty Berg

Billy Casper

Fred Couples

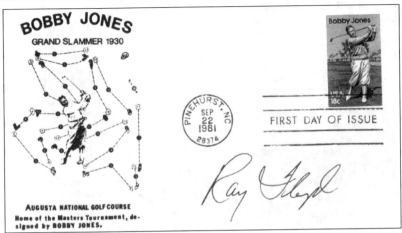

Ray Floyd

Ben Hogan

Hale Irwin

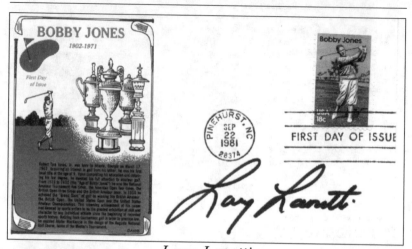

Larry Laoretti

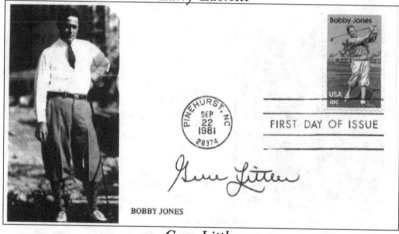

Gene Littler

Cary Middlecoff

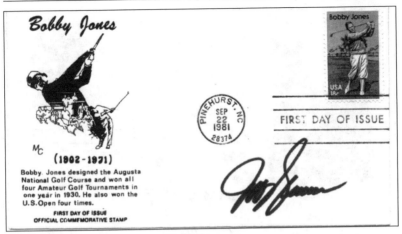

Jeff Sluman

Payne Stewart

Craig Stadler

Gary Player

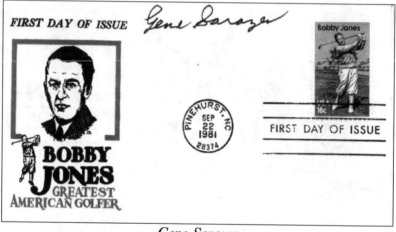

Gene Sarazen

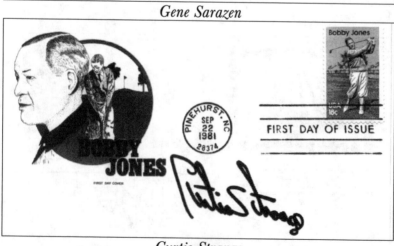

Curtis Strange

Curtis Strange

Ken Venturi

Jack Fleck

Dottie Mochrie

Holis Stacy

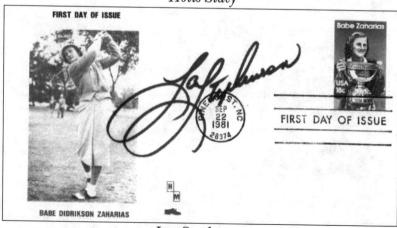

Jan Stephenson

Cindy Rarick

Betsy Rawls

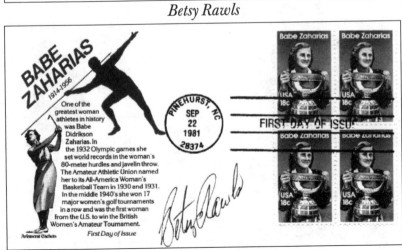

Betsy Rawls

Louise Suggs

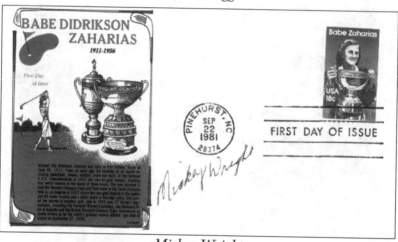

Mickey Wright

Mickey Wright

Kathy Whitworth

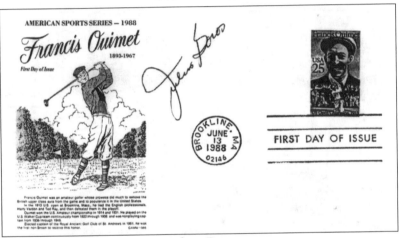

Julius Boros

Craig Stadler

Gene Sarazen

Julius Boros

Tad Moore

Byron Nelson

Gary Player

* BEN HOGAN *

MAJOR TOURNAMENT WINS

(THROUGH 1989)

* MASTERS *
1951, 1953

* U. S. OPEN *
1942 ~1948, 1950, 1951, 1953

* BRITISH *
1953

* PGA CHAMPIONSHIP *
1946, 1948

Ben Hogan

Ben Hogan

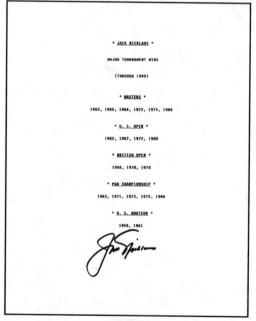

* JACK NICKLAUS *

MAJOR TOURNAMENT WINS

(THROUGH 1989)

* MASTERS *
1963, 1965, 1966, 1972, 1975, 1986

* U. S. OPEN *
1962, 1967, 1972, 1980

* BRITISH OPEN *
1966, 1970, 1978

* PGA CHAMPIONSHIP *
1963, 1971, 1973, 1975, 1980

* U. S. AMATEUR *
1959, 1961

Jack Nicklaus

GENE SARAZEN

Major Tournament Titles

United States Open	1922 . 1932
Masters Tournament	1935
P. G. A. Championship	1922 . 1923 ~ 3 3
P. G. A. Championship	1933
British Open	1932

Gene Sarazen

Gene Sarazen

GARY PLAYER

Major Tournament Titles

United States Open	1965
Masters Tournament	1961 . 1974 . 1978
P. G. A. Championship	1962 . 1972
British Open	1959 . 1968 . 1974

Gary Player

Gary Player

Bibliography

Wood Shafted Golf Club Value Guide
by Pete Georgrady, Arlie Hall Press, 1995.

The Game of Golf and the Printed Word 1566-1985
by Richard E. Donavan and Joseph S.F. Murdoch,
Castalio Press, 1988.

The Golf Club Identification Price Guide
by Golfworks, Ralph Maltby Enterprises Inc., 1993.

Index of Manufacturers

Note:
Books are listed alphabetically by author in chapter six.
Autographs are listed alphabetically by last name in chapter twelve.